THE CONTEMPORARY EDUCATIO IN QUÉBEC

A HANDBOOK FOR POLICY MAKERS
ADMINISTRATORS AND EDUCATORS

William J. Smith

William F. Foster

&

Helen M. Donahue

THEMES AND TRADITIONS IN QUÉBEC EDUCATION

AN APPLIED POLICY RESEARCH SERIES

Research Network on
Education Law and Policy
Faculty of Law, McGill University

Ed-Lex

Groupe de recherche sur
le droit et les politiques en éducation
Faculté de droit, Université McGill

The Contemporary Education Scene in Québec:
A Handbook for Policy Makers, Administrators and Educators

William J. Smith, Ph.D.
William F. Foster, LL.M.
Helen M. Donahue, M.Ed.

Published by:

Ed-Lex   Research Network on Education Law and Policy *
Groupe de recherche sur le droit et les politiques en éducation

Faculty of Law
McGill University
3644 Peel
Montréal, Canada
H3A 1W9

* Formerly, the Office of Research on Educational Policy (OREP).

Printed and bound in Canada.

Canadian Cataloguing in Publication Data:

Smith, William J., 1947-
    The Contemporary Education Scene in Québec: A Handbook for Policy Makers, Administrators and Educators

(Themes and Traditions in Québec Education)
Includes bibliographical references.
ISBN 0-7717-0542-5

    1. Education--Québec (Province) 2. Education and state--Québec (Province) I. Foster, William F. 1943- II. Donahue, Helen M., 1949- III. McGill University. Ed-Lex IV. Title. V. Series

    LA418.Q8S56 1999   379.714   C99-900182-5

Lest we forget ... that the laws, policies, structures and systems that are the subject of this book are supposed to support the teaching and learning that occurs in the classroom, we dedicate this book to the thousands of Québec teachers who, day after day in classrooms and schools across the province, make a difference in the lives of children.

PREAMBLE

As noted on the back cover, this work is part of a series entitled *Themes and Traditions in Québec Education*. *The Contemporary Education Scene in Québec: A Handbook for Policy Makers, Administrators and Educators* is intended for anyone wishing to understand the governance and policy frameworks which guide the Québec education system. It provides a reference guide to policy makers, administrators and educators, notably, school commissioners, school board administrators, members of school governing boards, school administrators and teachers. It comprises five main parts: I - the foundations of the system, the rights of students, including those with special needs, and the policy governance framework; II - the system of governance at the central (provincial), intermediate (school board) and local (school) levels; III - curriculum and school organization of the youth sector of the elementary and secondary system; IV - the management of human and financial resources; V - the recurring policy themes of religion, language and diversity. By virtue of its compact presentation of a considerable amount of material, there is no need to wade through a lot of prose to get to the essence of the subject at hand. A detailed table of contents provides a quick "road map" to every chapter.

Recognizing the need for a shorter more readable text for a wider audience, the series also includes *How Does the Québec Education System Work?: A Primer for School Governing Boards*. This short work is intended primarily for members of school governing boards but is suitable for anyone wanting a short overview of the system. It covers a broad range of topics in a series of short sections (generally 2 pages) that will enable school governors to understand their role in the context of the education system as a whole. Broad coverage and simplicity are the hallmarks of this work; however, each section is keyed to the *Handbook*.

Understanding an education system begins with an understanding of its history and Québec is no exception. The short monograph, *The Historical Roots of Québec Education*, provides an overview of the evolution of the Québec education system in three main chapters: From New France to the Quiet Revolution (historical sketch from the Parent Commission report); The Education System Comes of Age; and, Beyond the Quiet Revolution to the Present.

Finally, as a complement to the *Handbook*, *A Compendium of Source Materials on Québec Education* provides convenient compilation of key primary source materials in English, namely: extracts from the Canadian Constitution and the *Education Act*; complete texts of the *Basic Regulations* and the current MEQ *Directives*; extracts from various other statutes and regulations, as well as MEQ Categories of Disability.

This series builds on an earlier publication that combined the historical roots and contemporary themes, as well as various supplementary materials. This new series could not have been completed without this solid foundation which is due in no small part to the team of people who helped to build it. We wish to thank the following people for their feedback on this latest set of works: Lucie Benoit, Jan Langelier (CÉICI); Keith Fitzpatrick, Shirley Sarna (McGill); Lynn Travers (MEQ); Rosemary Murphy, Joanne Smith (Parents); Nancy Champagne, Ron Hughes, Pierre Webber (QPAT); Barbara Ednie, Jim MacKinnon, Pat Moffa, John Roumeliotis, Thérèse Taylor (School Administrators); Maxine Doherty, Jerry Dunn, Diane Fyfe, Leo LaFrance (School Board Administrators); Margaret Manson, Diane Ratcliffe, Aline Visser (School Commissioners); Stacey Davis, Lindsay Kay (Students); Dennis Manni, Wendy Sturton, Sidney Westlake (Teachers). A special thanks to Rod Elkin, Alan Lombard, and all the people in the OREP team: Andrea Borrelli, Emily Crocco, Aaron Dantowitz, Barbara Pyontka, Greg Smith, and Carolyn Sturge Sparkes, for all their help producing this series.

Every text is a compromise of sorts and this source book is no exception. By virtue of its compact presentation of a considerable amount of material, there is not as much *narrative* as many people might prefer. While there is a definite "story line" to the material presented, there is no doubt that more narrative would help breathe more life into it. For that, the reader will have to consult the many primary and secondary source materials listed in the text.

William J. Smith, William F. Foster, Helen M. Donahue
McGill University
March, 1999

Note to Reader…
Due to the numerous cross-references to different works in this series, we have abbreviated the references as follows:

book title	**referred to as**
The Historical Roots of Québec Education	***Historical Roots***
A Compendium of Source Material on Québec Education	***Compendium***

SUMMARY TABLE OF CONTENTS

ORGANIZATION OF THE HANDBOOK

Overview

The first chapter of this handbook provides an overview of the Québec education system.

Foundations

The next three chapters (2-4) provide an outline of the foundations of the system - the rights of students, including those with special needs, and the policy governance framework. With these rights and framework in mind, the next ten chapters develop various *themes* and *traditions* in Québec education.

Governance

Chapters 5 to 7 describe the system of governance at the central (provincial), intermediate (school board) and local (school) levels.

Curriculum and School Organization

Chapter 8 presents the curriculum and school organization of the youth sector of the elementary and secondary system.

Human and Financial Resources

Chapters 9 to 11 deal with the management of human and financial resources.

Religion, Language and Diversity

Chapters 12 to 14 focus on three recurring policy themes: religion, language and diversity.

Conclusion

The final chapter (15) provides a conclusion and some thoughts about the future.

DETAILED TABLE OF CONTENTS

GLOSSARY OF TERMS AND ABBREVIATIONS

AAESQ	Association of Administrators of English Schools of Québec (formerly QASA & QACSA)
Admission of Exceptional Cases Regulation	*Regulation Respecting Exceptional Cases for Admission to Preschool and Elementary School Education*
Adult Dir	*General Education for Adults: 1998-99 Directives*
Adult General Regulation [Adult Gen Reg]	*Basic School Regulation Respecting Education Services for Adults in General Education*
Adult Vocational Regulation [Adult Voc Reg]	*Basic School Regulation Respecting Education Services for Adults in Vocational Education*
ADM	Assistant Deputy Minister
Affirmative Action Program Regulation	*Regulation Respecting Affirmative Action Programs*
Authority	The right, conferred by law, to make decisions about a particular matter in the education system
Basic Regs	*Basic Regulations* covering both the Youth and Adult sectors
B & B Report	Report of the Royal Commission on Bilingualism and Biculturalism
Bill 22 (1974)	*The Official Language Act*
Bill 63 (1969)	*Act to Promote the French Language in Québec*
Bill 101 (1977)	*Charter of the French Language*
Bill 107 (1988)	*Education Act*
Canadian Charter	*Canadian Charter of Rights and Freedoms*
CAPFE	Comité d'agrément des programmes de formation à l'enseignement
Catholic Regulation	*Regulation Respecting the Recognition of Elementary and Secondary Schools of the Public School System as Catholic and their Confessional Character*
CDPQ	Commission des Droits de la Personne et Droit de la Jeunesse du Québec (referred to under the English term as Human Rights Commission)
CEA	Canadian Education Association
CÉCM	Commission des écoles catholiques de Montréal
CEGEP	General and Vocational College (*Collège d'enseignement général et professionnel*)
CEICI	Centre for Intercultural Education and International Understanding
CEQ	Centrale de l'enseignement du Québec
Chancy Report	Report of the Comité sur l'école québécoise et les communautés culturelles
Chauveau	*Québec (Commission des droits de la personne) and Commission scolaire régionale Chauveau (1993)*
CMEC	Council of Ministers of Education, Canada
COPEX Report	Report of the Comité provincial de l'enfance inadaptée
COPFE	Comité d'orientation de la formation du personnel enseignant
Corbo Task Force	Task Force on Elementary and Secondary Learning Profiles
CPNCA	Management Negotiating Committee for English Language School Boards (formerly CPNCP)
CPNCC	Management Negotiating Committee for Catholic School Boards (now CPNCF)
CPNCF	Management Negotiating Committee for French Language School Boards (formerly CPNCC)
CPNCP	Management Negotiating Committee for Protestant School Boards (now CPNCA)

Crown	In Canada and other Commonwealth countries which recognize the Queen as the formal Head of State, the State is commonly referred to as "the Crown."
CSE [Superior Council]	Conseil supérieur de l'éducation
CSE Act	*Act Respecting the Conseil supérieur de l'éducation*
CSN	Confédération des syndicats nationaux
CTF	Canadian Teachers' Federation
Curriculum Council	Commission des programmes d'étude
Delegated Body	An organization or an individual, or types of organizations or individuals, named by law to exercise authority or voice.
DGFE	Direction générale du financement et des équipments
Directives	Ministerial orders referred to under the French term as *instructions*
Discretion	The term discretion, when used in relation to public authorities means, that the latter has the power to decide a given matter. In other words, the official is not obliged to provide a given benefit or take a certain course of action but can make the decision himself or herself according to his or her own judgment or conscience.
DM	Deputy Minister
DPP	Direction des politiques et projets
DSEA	Direction des services éducatifs aux anglophones (now SCA-DPP)
DVS	Diploma of Vocational Studies
Ed Act	*Education Act*
Education Amendment Act	*Act to Amend the Education Act and Various Legislative Provisions*
EEO	Equal Educational Opportunity
Elementary School Regulation [El Reg]	*Basic School Regulation for Preschool and Elementary School Education*
EPC	Education Policies Committee
Eaton	*Eaton* v. *Brant County Board of Education* (1997)
Education in the Youth Sector: 1998-99 [Youth Dir]	*Education in the Youth Sector: Preschool Elementary School and Secondary School: 1998-99 Directives*
Executive Branch	The executive branch of government is responsible for carrying out the laws enacted by the legislative branch and ensuring their observance. In Canada, the executive branch of a provincial government comprises the Monarch, as represented by the Lieutenant Governor, the Premier and the Cabinet or Council of Ministers, as it is called in Québec. In Canada, the term "Lieutenant Governor in Council" is the formal name of this branch of government.
FCPPQ	Fédération des comités de parents de la province de Québec
FCSCQ	Fédération des commissions scolaires Catholiques du Québec (now FCSQ)
FCSQ	Fédération des commissions scolaires du Québec (formerly FCSCQ)
FTQ	Fédération des travailleurs du Québec
General Education for Adults: 1998-99 [Adult Gen Dir]	*General Education for Adults: 1998-99 Directives*
Governance	The formal system which provides for the exercise of authority by the government or a delegated authority, or "voice" by various bodies representing organizational or individual stakeholders.
IEP	Individualized education plan
Island Council	Conseil scolaire de l'Île de Montréal
Judicial Branch	The function of the judicial branch of government is to interpret, apply and enforce the laws of the State. In Canada, the highest court is the Supreme Court of Canada, which is the court of last resort for appeals. Each province has its own court system.

Law	The term "law" is used in an abstract sense in expressions such as "the rule of law," in a general sense to encompass all forms of legally binding rules - "this must be done by law," and in a more narrow sense to refer to a statute, as opposed to a regulation - e.g. the *Education Act* is a law.
Learning Disabilities Exemption Regulation	*Regulation Respecting the Exemption from the Application of the First Paragraph of Section 72 of the Charter of the French Language which may be Granted to Children Having Serious Learning Disabilities*
Legislative Branch	One of the major functions of government is to make laws. This function is performed by the legislative branch of government (e.g. Parliament of Canada, National Assembly of Québec). The legislature is composed of the elected members of Parliament (MP's) or the National Assembly (MNA's), as the case may be.
Linguistic School Boards Act	*Act to Amend the Education Act, the Act Respecting School Elections and Other Legislative Provisions*
Magna Carta [of Education Laws]	Series of education laws adopted in 1960-61 (S.Q. 1960-61, c.25-34, 37)
Martin-Bouchard Commission	Commission d'étude et de consultation sur la révision du régime des négociations collectives dans les secteurs public et parapublic
MCCI	Ministère des Communautés culturelles et de l'Immigration
MEQ [Ministry]	Minstère de l'Éducation
MEQ Act	*Act Respecting the ministère de l'Education*
MRI	Moral and religious instruction
Obligation	An obligation is a duty, something one must do according to law. An obligation is the opposite of discretion.
OLF	Office de la langue française
Operation 55	Creation of regional school boards in 1964
PACT	Provincial Association of Catholic Teachers (now defunct)
Pagé Report	Conseil de restructuration scolaire de l'Ile de Montréal
PAPT	Provincial Association of Protestant Teachers (now QPAT)
PAPT Entente, 1995-98	*Entente Between the CPNCP and the PAPT, 1996*
Parental Consultation Regulation	*Regulation Respecting the Consultation of Parents Concerning an Application for the Recognition or Withdrawal of Recognition of a School as Catholic or Protestant*
PAS	Administration and Salary Policy Applicable to Administrators (*Politique administrative et salariale*)
Parent Report	Report of the Royal Commission of Inquiry on Education in the Province of Québec
PELO	Programme d'enseignement des langues d'origine
PIC	Professional Improvement Committee
PLE	Programme des langues ethniques
Privilege	A privilege is a benefit to which one is not entitled as a matter of right. No claim in law can be made to a privilege, used in this sense.
Protestant Regulation	*Regulation of the Protestant Committee of the Conseil supérieur de l'éducation Regarding Protestant Moral and Religious Education as well as the Recognition of Educational Institutions as Protestant*
Proulx Task Force	Task Force on the Place of Religion in Schools
PSBGM	Protestant School Board of Greater Montreal
Public Sector Bargaining Act	*Act Respecting the Process of Negotiation of the Collective Agreements in the Public and Parapublic Sectors*
QACSA	Québec Association of Catholic School Administrators (now AAESQ)

QAPSB	Québec Association of Protestant School Boards (now QSBA)
QASA	Québec Association of School Administrators (now AAESQ)
QFHAS	Québec Federation of Home and School Associations
QPAT	Québec Provincial Association of Teachers (formerly PAPT)
QSBA	Québec School Boards Association (formerly QAPSB)
Québec *Charter*	Québec *Charter of Human Rights and Freedoms*
Régimes pédagogiques	French term for the *Basic Regulations*, which constitute the primary regulations governing curriculum and school organization
Regulation	The term "regulation" has many levels of meaning. Broadly, it refers to all *delegated* or *subordinate* legislation - i.e. rules that are made under the aegis of a statute. More narrowly, it refers only to certain types of regulations, such as those adopted by the government and published in the *Official Gazette* of the province.
Right	A right is hereby defined as a "legal right," that is, a power, benefit or immunity which the beneficiary enjoys by law; it is therefore a legally enforceable claim. Generally, the right of one person gives rise to an obligation on the part of another. A right is the opposite of a privilege.
SCA-DPP	Services à la communauté anglophone - Direction des politiques et projects
Secondary School Regulations [Sec Reg]	*Basic School Regulation for Secondary School Education*
Saint-Jean	*Québec (Commission des droits de la personne) and Commission scoliare Saint-Jean-sur-Richelieu (1991)*
School Elections Act	*Act Respecting School Elections*
State	A state is defined as a group of people who occupy a certain territory and who are politically organized under a government which exercises sovereign power on their behalf. The term may refer to the body politic of a nation (e.g. Canada) or a subordinate unit of such a nation (e.g. a province - Québec).
SSD	Secondary School Diploma
Teacher Training Policy Committee	Comité d'orientation de la formation du personnel enseignant
Temporary Exemption Regulation	*Regulation Respecting the Exemption from the Application of the First Paragraph of Section 72 of the Charter of the French Language that may be Granted to Children Staying in Québec Temporarily*
VEC	Vocational Education Certificate
Voc Dir	*Vocational Education Directives: 1998-99*
Voice	The right, conferred by law, to take part in the decision-making process respecting a particular matter in the education system, without having the right to vote or to be a party to any final decision.
Youth Dir	General Education in the Youth Sector: 1998-1999
YOA	*Young Offenders Act*
YPA	*Youth Protection Act*

CHAPTER 1
OVERVIEW AND CONTEXT

Introduction

The education system in Québec shares many characteristics with other systems. Like other jurisdictions in Canada, it has evolved from a small, elementary-level system, directed by church and family, to a comprehensive multi-level system, governed by the State. The system is governed by a series of legislative acts, most notably, the *Education Act* and the *Basic Regulations*. Overall responsibility for the system rests with the provincial Minister of Education, but the administration of educational services is decentralized to school boards which operate a network of elementary and secondary schools. Moreover, Québec educators face many of the same issues confronting educators in other jurisdictions. These include, for example, demands for greater public accountability in light of an increasing number of children at risk and an ever decreasing resource base.

In this chapter, we will attempt to provide an introduction to the Québec education system, first by placing it in the wider context of education in Canada and then by looking briefly at the overall structure of the system. We provide only a glimpse into the roots of the present system, a scant three paragraphs. More details on the historical background can be found in the companion volume in this series, *Historical Roots*. The remainder of this chapter is devoted to a brief overview of the contemporary scene in elementary and secondary education in Québec and is sub-divided into the themes which provide the framework of the book.

The Administration of Education in Canada

The Constitutional Framework

The Constitution of Canada frames the administration of education three ways. Canada's federal system of government means that the powers of government are divided between two jurisdictions - the Federal Government and the provincial governments. Section 93 of the *Constitution Act, 1867* assigns to provincial governments "exclusive jurisdiction" over education, subject to the two other framing devices which follow. First, section 93 itself tempers the provincial government's exclusive authority by requiring it to not interfere with the "denominational rights" provided for therein. These rights were meant to guarantee Catholics and Protestants protection in perpetuity of the rights to denominational schooling which they had by law when a particular province joined Confederation. Following the recent constitutional amendments in Newfoundland and Québec, section 93 denominational guarantees now only apply in Alberta, Ontario and Saskatchewan. Second, the Constitution contains the *Canadian Charter of Rights and Freedoms* [*Canadian Charter*] which contains a variety of individual human rights which provincial governments must respect. Among these provisions is section 23: the right to minority language education (English in Québec and French in the rest of the country) which each provincial government must respect in creating and operating its education system. Before turning to the provincial role in education in light of these constitutional provisions, it is important to note that because of other provisions of the Constitution, the Federal Government still has a role to play in education.

Federal Role in Education

Canada, unlike most countries, does not have a national department or office of education. The general absence of the Federal Government from the Canadian educational scene can be explained only partially by the constitutional division of powers, whereby education is essentially stipulated as a matter of provincial jurisdiction. The explanation of this absence must also take into account Canadian political culture, which has been shaped in part by continuing federal-provincial tensions over various jurisdictional matters, including education, labour force development and training.

The Federal Government is responsible for providing elementary-secondary educational services to residents of the Yukon, Northwest and Nunavut Territories. However, in both cases, federal powers have been delegated to the territorial governments which, for all practical purposes, operate fully autonomous educational systems. It is also responsible for providing elementary-secondary educational services to children of Armed Forces personnel (schools on military bases) and to inmates of federal penitentiaries. The Federal Government used to play a more direct role in technical-vocational *training* (based on the putative distinction between "education" and "training;" the latter not a provincial prerogative according to section 93). Due to pressures from the provincial governments, Ottawa now provides block grants to the provinces which assume responsibility for technical-vocational education and training for both youth and adults.

With the one important exception, discussed below, the Federal Government's role in education is more indirect. It supports education in general by various transfer payments, including minority language programs. The Federal Government also supports post-secondary education through various research grant programs, including: the Canada Council, the National Research Council, the Natural Sciences and Engineering Research Council, the Medical Research Council and the Social Sciences and Humanities Research Council. In addition, various federal government departments sponsor programs which provide grants for various education-related activities (e.g. Human Resources Development Canada [then Employment Immigration Canada] "Stay in School" initiative).

First Nations Peoples

The Federal Government's responsibility for providing elementary-secondary educational services for First Nations Peoples arises first from its constitutional jurisdiction "for Indians and lands reserved for Indians" (*Constitution Act, 1867*, s. 91(24)) but also from historical precedent and treaty obligations. In recent years, the traditional direct provision of education in federally operated schools has been supplanted by schools managed by local First Nations communities. Some students attend schools operated by local school boards, with fees being paid to the latter by the Federal Government. The education of the Inuit, Cree and Naskapi in Northern Québec has been turned over to the province as part of the James Bay and Northern Québec Agreement (see Bezeau, 1995 for a brief summary).

Although control of education by First Nations peoples has increased significantly in recent years, the devolution of authority in education is still very much "in progress." The report of the Royal Commission on Aboriginal Peoples (1996) devotes a chapter to education (see Vol. III, chap. 5) which makes the aspirations of First Nations Peoples clear, namely local control of education under the broad assumption of jurisdiction for Aboriginal self-government.

Council of Ministers of Education

The Council of Ministers of Education, Canada [CMEC] is made up of the ministers of education of the ten provinces and (as observers) two territories; it also comprises an advisory council of the deputy ministers of education and some other officials. It has a permanent office in Toronto and facilitates cooperation among the various jurisdictions, as well as undertaking specific projects agreed to by the members. For example, it publishes, in collaboration with Statistics Canada, various educational statistics and has recently sponsored the Student Achievement Indicators Program. The

Federal Government has no representation on this important national body.

Provincial Systems of Education

In each province, the elementary-secondary education system consists of a central education authority (provincial ministry of education) and in all but one province, local education authorities (school boards) which are responsible for the administration of public schools. The exception is New Brunswick. In 1996, that province abolished school boards whose powers reverted to the Minister of Education who now, through the Education Department, directly administers all schools in the province. Since then, the Government has also set up parent advisory committees at the provincial, district and school levels. Some people see the New Brunswick experiment as a harbinger of things to come. However, it should be noted that New Brunswick has a relatively small student population in a relatively compact geographic territory. It is difficult to imagine the direct administration of schools in a province like Alberta or Ontario.

Whatever its merits, the reorganization of the system in New Brunswick may prove to be constitutionally unsound. This possibility is not because school boards enjoy any constitutional protection under either section 93 of the *Constitution Act, 1867* or section 23 of the *Canadian Charter*. Rather, it is possible that the new structures do not provide sufficient "management and control" of minority language education to Francophone parents. This contestation has not yet reached the courts and may be resolved through remedial legislation. In any event, it reflects the principle that government discretion in the administration of education is not absolute and must be exercised in light of individual *Charter* rights, especially section 23.

Although public schooling has been and continues to be the mainstream provider of services at the elementary and secondary level, private, or independent, schools play an important role in each province. They exist throughout Canada, but the degree to which they are publicly funded and controlled varies greatly. In some provinces, a third option – home schooling – has become an important alternative to public schooling. Colleges, universities and other post-secondary educational institutions, both public and private, make up the remainder of the education system. Frequently, responsibility for post-secondary education is vested in the same minister responsible for elementary-secondary education.

The Québec Education System

Formal Schooling: From Kindergarten to University

Formal schooling begins in Québec at the kindergarten level and continues through university. The system is organized into three major levels: (1) preschool, elementary and secondary; (2) collegial, and; (3) university. The organization of education at each of these levels will be briefly described below. Since the first of these levels is the focus of this text, we will return to this level in more detail in the overview themes which follow. By contrast, education at the post-secondary levels will not be directly dealt with in the remainder of this overview, nor in the text itself.

Preschool, Elementary & Secondary Education

Preschool generally consists of five-year old kindergarten but there are four-year old pre-kindergartens for some students with disabilities and for students coming from economically disadvantaged areas. Elementary education* is presently offered in two cycles: grades 1-3 and 4-6.

Note. Generally, when people refer to "elementary education," they include preschool as well; unless the context indicates otherwise, we will follow this convention throughout this book.

Secondary education also comprises two cycles: secondary I, II and III (or grades 7-9) and secondary IV and V (or grades 10-11). Successful completion of high school is recognized in a secondary school diploma. Secondary education also includes a separate division for vocational education programs, intended primarily for students who have completed a general secondary education. Vocational programs target both youth and adult students; moreover, there are also general education programs for the latter. Both vocational and adult education programs are only offered by those school boards so authorized by the Minister of Education.

Elementary and secondary education is provided to a little more than one million students in a network of more than 2700 public schools administered by 60 French and 9 English locally elected school boards. In addition, another 100 000 students are enrolled in private schools, two thirds of which are government subsidized. As will be seen in later chapters, public schools are governed by the *Education Act*, the *Basic Regulations*, and various others laws and regulations. Private schools are dealt with in the *Act Respecting Private Education* and the accompanying regulations. However, private schools are also subject to the same *Basic Regulations* which apply to public schools.

Collegial Education

One of the unique features of the Québec education system is its network of 47 publicly funded general and vocational colleges - or CEGEPs as they are called after their full title in French (collège d'enseignement général et professionnel). The CEGEP system is a product of the Quiet Revolution and was meant to expand access to a coherent system of post-secondary education which was to be reoriented from the existing priorities of elite classical colleges to the new priorities of science, commerce and technology. First introduced in 1967, they were generally created out of an amalgamation of existing classical colleges, normal schools and technical institutes.

Generally, two types of programs are offered in colleges. The first comprises various two-year general education programs, which are designed to lead to admission to university. The second is made up of various three-year vocational programs which are designed to lead directly to entry into the labour market. In addition to this network of CEGEPs, there are 25 private colleges, 10 institutions operated by government departments, as well as one college which comes under a university.

General education programs include science, social sciences, creative arts, music, fine arts, language and literature, and oral communication arts. Vocational programs are offered in biological sciences, physical sciences, social sciences, administrative sciences and fine arts. There are no tuition fees in CEGEPs; however, there is a fee of $50 per course after five failures in a general program and after seven failures in a vocational program. Private colleges charge tuition fees which vary from institution to institution. Successful completion of college education is recognized by the Diploma of College Studies, issued by the Minister of Education upon the recommendation of the college.

CEGEP education is governed by the provisions of the *General and Vocational Colleges Act* and the *College Education Regulations*, adopted under the aegis of this act. Private colleges are dealt with in the *Act Respecting Private Education* and the regulations adopted under this act (*Regulation Respecting the Application of the Act Respecting Private Education*) but they are subject to the same *College Education Regulations* which apply to CEGEPs. Collegial education, like other levels of the system, has been the subject of various reviews and policy papers since it was created approximately thirty years ago.

The original impact of the creation of the CEGEP system on English education was different from that experienced in the majority French system. First, while the new system reduced the number of years of schooling to meet university entrance requirements from 18 to 16 years in the French system, it increased the number of years from 15 to 16 years in the English system. Second, English CEGEPs could not be created from existing institutions, as there were only two pre-existing English colleges - Loyola and Marianopolis. The former merged with Sir George Williams University to become Concordia University and the latter, previously run by the Sisters of the Congrégation Notre Dame, granting degrees through the Université de Montréal, became a private college. Consequently, all English CEGEPs had to be created from scratch.

University Education

The first serious attempt to establish a university in Québec occurred in 1789, when the Commission on Education, chaired by Judge William Smith, sought to establish a university at Québec City. The plan was part of a grand design for a comprehensive school system of elementary and secondary schools for all students, regardless of religion or language. The plan was opposed by the Bishop of Québec and did not bear fruit for some time. McGill University received a Royal Charter in 1821 and opened in June, 1829, becoming the first Québec university.

A little more than twenty years after McGill opened its doors, Laval and Bishops universities were created (1852 and 1853 respectively), followed by the establishment of the École polytechnique de Montréal in 1873 and the École des hautes études commerciales in 1907 (both now affiliated with the Université de Montréal). At present, there are seven universities in Québec.

Universities, like other educational institutions in Québec, have been evolving from private institutions controlled by the Church to public ones controlled by the State. Laval University grew out of the Jesuit seminary in Québec City and Bishops was founded by the Anglican Church. Today these universities, like the others listed above, are non-denominational and receive the vast amount of their funding from the State.

The Université du Québec [UQ] is unique among the foregoing universities and, like the CEGEPs, is a product of the Quiet Revolution. Created by statute in 1968 (*University of Québec Act*), the UQ was intended to extend access to higher education throughout Québec. It has a central administration in Québec City (but no campus) and is presently made up of eleven constituent campuses.

Henchey and Burgess (1987, p. 108) describe UQ's contribution to higher education in Québec in the following terms:

> The University of Quebec is unique among the province's universities in its structure as a university system with constituent institutions, in its social mission to expand university services to the population, especially adults, in the regional leadership of many of its constituents, and in its academic organization based on modules (groups of students and professors following the same program) and departments (organization of professors in a discipline). In their vitality, diversity of character and often unconventional approaches to teaching, service and research, the universities of the UQ system have provided a stimulating complement to other institutions.

Historical Roots

As alluded to above, the education system in Québec shares many of the characteristics of the education systems in other Canadian provinces. However, the Québec education system has different roots and has therefore evolved differently than other jurisdictions (see *Historical Roots*). Many of these differences reflect the changing relationships between Church, State and education in the province. We have tried to capture these distinctive features in this text by examining the themes and traditions of education in Québec from a variety of perspectives.

The Québec education system has roots in the French and British systems of education, both of which were strongly influenced by Christianity: the French by the Roman Catholic Church, the British by various Protestant denominations. These cultural and religious differences also manifested themselves in different languages, leading to the development of a dualistic education system, one Catholic and predominantly French, the other Protestant and predominantly English.

From New France to the Quiet Revolution

During the French Regime (1608-1760), education was under the authority of the Catholic Church, with minimal State intervention. Between 1760 and 1841, the system was characterized by the establishment of a public education system and an increased State role in education. The period from 1841-1867 witnessed the development of the system and the decentralization of educational governance to local authorities. The culminating event of this period was the creation of the Canadian Confederation and the entrenchment of rights to denominational schools in the Constitution.

The evolution of the system between Confederation and the Quiet Revolution of the 1960s can be divided into two periods. In the first (1867-1907), we see the expansion of public and private educational institutions. In the second period (1907-1961), the education system attempted to respond to a changing world and a changing population. However, despite the breadth of these changing conditions, the structure of the school system remained largely unchanged.

The Quiet Revolution

If Québec had been slow in responding to change throughout the first half of the twentieth century, when it did respond, the State moved with incredible speed to thrust Québec into the modern era, with change affecting virtually every aspect of Québec society. Known by the oxymoron, the "Quiet Revolution," Québec's political climate shifted from the "repressive and deeply conservative regime of the Duplessis era" to a new era of "rambunctious activism" (Gagnon & Montcalm, 1990, p. 3). Many of the education reforms were the result of recommendations of the Royal Commission of Inquiry on Education, also known as the Parent Commission, after the name of its chair, Monseigneur Alphonse-Marie Parent, Vice-Rector of Laval University. Recreating a ministry of education, which had not existed in Québec since 1875, the State took charge of the education system and literally transformed it in a few short years, replacing the Church as the driving force in educational governance in this province.

From the Quiet Revolution to the Present

Just over 30 years have elapsed since the completion of the final volume of the Parent report (1966). In the period immediately following this publication, the Government moved to consolidate its control over every major aspect of the education system. Beginning in 1965, a series of laws and regulations were adopted, culminating in 1981 with new regulations known as the *Régimes pédagogiques*, to regulate curriculum and school organization. In 1968, a law was passed to centralize teacher collective bargaining at the provincial level that led to two decades of heightened conflict and deterioration of employer-employee relations in the education sector. Government spending on education, both in absolute terms and in relation to local sources of funding, grew by leaps and bounds. Although the overall governing structure of the system was a continuing preoccupation throughout this period, until 1998 structural change was limited to the creation and then the dissolution of regional boards for secondary education and the overall reduction of the number of school boards from 1600 in the 1960s to 156 in 1997-98 on the eve of the transformation of the system to linguistic school boards.

Contemporary Themes in Québec Education

The balance of this introductory chapter consists of an overview of the elementary-secondary education system in Québec. It is intended primarily for the reader who is not familiar with the Québec system and attempts to provide some context for understanding the chapters which follow. It is organized around the five themes which provide the framework for the remainder of the text:

- foundations of the system;
- governance of elementary-secondary education;
- curriculum and school organization;
- human and financial resources;
- recurring policy themes.

References to the relevant chapters are included.

Foundations

The foundations of the education system can be found in the overall policy and governance framework and in the rights and obligations assigned to students in general and to students with special needs in particular.

Policy & Governance Framework

The policy and governance framework for education in Québec is first established by the Constitution and which, with two exceptions, is the same as that which applies in other jurisdictions in Canada. The first exception relates to the denominational rights included in section 93 referred to above. A recent constitutional amendment stipulates that these provisions do not apply to Québec. Second, the full scope of the minority language education rights found in the *Canadian Charter* does not apply in Québec (chap. 2).

Education Rights of Students

The rights of children and students are first of all provided for in the *Canadian Charter* and the Québec *Charter of Human Rights and Freedoms* [Québec *Charter*]. Both the Canadian and Québec *Charters* provide for fundamental freedoms, such as freedom of religion and equality rights - the prohibition of discrimination on the basis of various listed grounds, such as race, sex and disability. The *Canadian Charter* guarantees minority language rights but makes no general provision for education as a constitutionally protected right. By contrast, the Québec *Charter* includes education as a human right, subject to the scope of services provided for by law.

Many other student rights are found in the *Education Act* and the *Basic Regulations*. There is a universal right to education in Québec, without exception because of a disability, from 5 to 18 years, and to 21 years for students defined as "handicapped" under provincial legislation. Schooling is compulsory from 6 to 15 years but parents may fulfill this obligation through attendance at public or private schools or through approved home schooling. In addition, parents have a right, subject to enrolment criteria, to choose the school within their school board which suits their preferences.

Other important rights regarding children are found in the *Youth Protection Act* [*YPA*], the *Young Offenders Act* [*YOA*], the *Civil Code of Québec,* the *Act Respecting Access to Documents Held by Public Bodies and the Protection of Personal Information,* and the like. The *YPA* defines child abuse and the duty of educators, among others, to report cases of suspected abuse. While the law obliges everyone to report cases of suspected sexual abuse, teachers are specifically required by the Act to report any form of abuse. The *YOA*, currently under review, deals with criminal justice for youth and is meant to hold young persons responsible for their actions, while recognizing that generally speaking, they should be held to the same level of accountability as adults (chap. 3).

Students with Special Needs

Québec policy has long recognized the right of students with special needs to have access to quality education in the most normal setting possible. Some of the goals of government policy remain an expression of intent, while others have been transformed into rights through the enactment of various laws and regulations.

One of the most critical policy issues respecting the education of students with special needs is placement. On the one hand, many educators, parents and advocates for people with disabilities believe that all children with special needs can - and should be - accommodated in the regular class with their age-appropriate peers. On the other hand, there are also many parents and educators who think that these students should be taught in separate special education classes and schools. Québec school law does not mandate integration and opinion is divided as to the extent to which the equality rights provisions of the Canadian and Québec *Charters* prohibit or restrict segregated placements. Recent court cases in Québec and Ontario suggest that this matter will continue to preoccupy policy makers, educators, parents and others (chap. 4).

Governance

Educational governance is all about control and can be thought of in terms of authority and voice - who has the authority to make key decisions in the education system and who is given the formal means to participate in the decision making process.

Central Level

As alluded to above, the Quiet Revolution heralded the decision of the State to become the driving force in the development of Québec society and education was seen as a key means for directing change. As a result, since the creation of the Minstère de l'Éducation [MEQ or Ministry] in 1964, the shape of educational governance in Québec has been centralized.

However, right from the beginning of the Quiet Revolution, the Government sought to assuage fears of total State control of education by, among various means, the creation of the Conseil supérieur de l'éducation [CSE or Superior Council]. The CSE is composed of members of various stakeholder groups in the educational community appointed by the Minister and is balanced on denominational lines. It also comprises two denominational committees, one Catholic and one Protestant and several specialized commissions. The CSE has, since its inception, provided advice to the Minister on significant policy issues, as well as being a forum for debate and reflection. There have been other formal provincial consultative bodies in the past but their functions have been taken over by the Superior Council. However, other forms of provincial consultation exist; of particular interest to English language schools, is the Advisory Board on English Education, created in 1992 (chap. 5).

Intermediate Level

Despite the tradition, since the 1960s, of State control of education, school boards have continued as the locally elected bodies responsible for the administration of public schools. Their continuation does not, however, reflect any consensus about their configuration or powers - issues that have preoccupied the energy and resources of the system for the past thirty years. This battle over school board reform has been fought in terms of the organizing principle of school board structures, namely whether they should be neutral, denominationally based or linguistically based, as they are now (as of July 1, 1998). However, the persistent leitmotif of this struggle has been local versus State and minority versus majority control of education (chap. 6).

Local Level

Issues of governance have also involved other stakeholder groups, notably teachers and parents, each of which has come to play an important role in the governance of the education system. Québec has a long history of formal parental involvement in schooling. Mandated parent advisory bodies were first created in 1971 at both the school board and school levels. In 1997, the Government adopted new legislation creating "school governing boards" which will play a significant role in managing education at the local level. From this point on, the discussion of educational governance will shift from a single focus on school boards versus the State to a multiple focus including schools versus school boards and the role of parents, the principal and teachers within the school (chap. 7).

Curriculum & School Organization

If the first phase of education reform in Québec was concerned with increasing access to schooling, the second can be characterized as focusing on curriculum and school organization.

Youth Education

In the early 1980s, the Government created a detailed regulatory framework governing these matters. At the same time, the MEQ began to develop new courses of study, together with detailed curriculum guides for teachers. The former set forth the terminal objectives for each course and are mandatory. The latter are meant to provide guidelines and suggestions for teaching the course and are not mandatory. However, they have often been presented to teachers as part and parcel of government curriculum requirements, illustrating how policy implementation may differ considerably from the policy enactment.

The regulatory framework for elementary and secondary education is contained in the *Education Act*, the *Basic Regulations*, known popularly by their French name, the *Régimes pédagogigues*, and the annual education directives of the Minister. This framework spells out the duties and powers of school boards, schools, teachers and principals respecting the provision of educational services. It also sets the parameters that establish the boundaries of this delegated authority (chap. 8).

Vocational Education

Vocational, including technical, education has been a major policy issue in Québec education for more than a decade, during which time we have begun to see this field in a different light. Traditionally vocational education has been undervalued and viewed as a track for the "less able" and those who were not "academically inclined." In 1986, the MEQ carried out a major reform of vocational education. The principal aim of the reform was to ensure that vocational graduates had the skills that employers were seeking. That aim encompassed skills in core subjects (language arts and mathematics), as well as technical or trades subjects.

Previous "short vocational" and "long vocational" programs were eliminated and admission standards to vocational education were raised. Two other innovations should be mentioned. First, to rationalize the use of scarce resources, the MEQ set about to "harmonize" vocational programs in the youth and adults sectors and to encourage "mixed classes" composed of students from both these sectors. Second, the MEQ drew up a "map" of vocational programs, that is an enumeration of what programs could be offered by different school boards in the province.

According to Goode (1994), the reform has been successful in some ways but problematic in others. The predicted rise in clientele has not occurred and the desired exit profile comprising an optimal balance of general core knowledge and vocational skills remains elusive.

Adult Education

Adult education has also undergone considerable change in the past decade or so, inspired in no small part by the report of the Commission d'étude sur la formation des adultes [Jean Commission on Adult Education] (1982). The Commission's recommendations led to a new Ministry policy statement on adult education (MEQ, 1984) that emphasized job-oriented or qualifying education in preference to a broader basic education. The adoption of the new *Education Act* [Bill 107] in 1988 elevated adult education from a marginal responsibility of school boards to a principal component of their educational mandate.

Adults are entitled to free educational services to complete their secondary school general education or vocational studies. The *Education Act* recognizes adult and vocational education centres, as it does schools for youth students. The Government has further stimulated support for adult education by passing legislation which requires large employers to invest at least 1% of their payroll in training. Adult education includes a wide spectrum of services including community and popular education, training in industry and so forth.

The recent Estates General on Education emphasized the need for a new policy direction in adult education, one that would foster life-long learning, recognize the necessity of a diversity of service provision and consolidate existing services to better meet the needs of adult learners. The MEQ has responded with a new consultation document, *Toward a Policy of Lifelong Learning* (1998c). It remains to be seen what changes will emanate from this process but one thing is certain, adult education is now firmly established as a mainstream policy issue.

Human & Financial Resources

Employee Relations

Virtually all Québec public school teachers are members of local unions, each of which is affiliated to one of the provincial teacher associations. The negotiation of teacher remuneration and most major working conditions is conducted at a provincial level between an employer bargaining committee (MEQ and school board association) and a provincial teacher association and leads to a provincial "entente" (e.g. *Entente between the Employer Bargaining Committee for Protestant School Boards (CPNCP) and the Provincial Association of Protestant Teachers (PAPT)*, 1996 [*PAPT Entente: 1995-98*]). Bargaining on a number of other issues is conducted at the local level between school boards and local teacher unions. Teachers have the right to strike during provincial contract talks but not over local bargaining matters. Public sector bargaining has had a history of conflict and hostility but there are signs that this process is evolving toward a more constructive problem solving approach.*

* *Note*. Much of the content of the existing teacher *Ententes* are identical. We have chosen the *PAPT Entente* as an example of these three ententes to cite in this text.

Although most provisions governing teachers as employees are found in the collective agreement, their rights and obligations as professionals are spelled out in various laws and regulations, which also stipulate the rights of students (chap. 9).

The Professional Teacher

The core of any education system is teaching and learning, the day-to-day interactions of teachers and students in individual classrooms throughout the system. The essence of these interactions cannot be captured in an overview of system-level policies and issues. However, an examination of the education system can tell us something about the framework governing these interactions. In particular, we can look at the preparation of teachers and their working conditions, as well as the rights and obligations of both teachers and students.

The training of professional educators, always an important theme, has been given renewed emphasis in the current reform of teacher education programs in Québec. At the present time, pre-service teacher education in English is provided at McGill, Concordia and Bishops.

Until the present, teachers were licensed to teach by the Minister after having completed both teacher pre-service training and two year's probation as a teacher. From now on, the previous probation system will be eliminated and teachers will receive a permanent teaching license upon completion of their B.Ed. program (chap. 10).

The Funding of Public & Private Schools

In contrast to a history of local funding for education in Québec, today the Government is the major funder of public education, supplying approximately 85% of total revenues. In addition to controlling the amount of money it will supply for education, the Government also controls the rules of the "funding game." Not only can the Government decide how it distributes funds and how school boards can use them, it can also decide, if it so chooses, what rules apply to the raising of funds by school boards themselves. Over the past twenty years, the rules governing the distribution of provincial grants have changed dramatically from a relatively simple system, with much discretionary funding, to a very complex system where almost all funds are distributed according to predetermined formulae. During this same period, school boards have gained almost total control over the use of provincial grants. However, given successive cut-backs in provincial funding and the amount of money which must be allocated to pay for relatively fixed costs, this discretion is somewhat illusory (chap. 11).

In addition to providing the majority of funds for public schools, the Government provides subsidies to private schools. There is a long tradition of parental choice of schooling in Québec, including the right to choose private or public schools. One of the major ways in which the Government has supported the exercise of this right has been by the granting, to selected private schools, subsidies which are equivalent to approximately 60% of the level of funding provided to public school boards. In addition to respecting the provisions of the *Basic Regulations*, which all private schools must do, subsidized private schools must respect the law governing access to English instruction.

Recurring Policy Themes

In addition to the foregoing perspectives on the Québec education system, one can examine the system through a consideration of various policy themes. Three such themes which have been of ongoing importance in Québec are religion, language and multiculturalism.

Religion

As discussed above, religion has traditionally been the organizing principle for the Québec education system. For more than 100 years, the system has been bifurcated along denominational lines. The new system of linguistic school boards replaces religion with language as the basic organizing principle, but religion has not disappeared as an important element in Québec school life. Schools are still able to seek official recognition as either Catholic or Protestant, according to a process defined by law. However, this right does not extend to people of other faiths. By express provisions in the *Education Act* and other legislation, the Government continues to provide for special status for Catholics and Protestants (chap. 12).

Language

The importance of language in Québec education is not confined to the definition of school board structures. The fundamental issue is language as a medium of instruction. Prior to the late 1960s, language was not a major policy issue. However, in 1968 a quarrel in a school board in St. Leonard over the provision of English language instruction quickly escalated and became a provincial issue of major importance. The Government passed a law to guarantee freedom of choice respecting the language of instruction. Bitterly opposed by Québec nationalists, a subsequently elected government enacted legislation to restrict access to English schools on the basis of language proficiency tests. This move created more problems than it solved and another government replaced this law in 1977 with the *Charter of the French Language* [Bill 101]. With some exceptions, according to Bill 101, access to English instruction is limited to children with at least one parent who received his or her elementary education in English in Canada. While some would argue that we have achieved some measure of linguistic peace in our schools, the language question is far from being a dead issue (chap. 13).

Multiculturalism

We live in an increasingly pluralistic society, especially in urban centres, and the education system must be sensitive to the needs and aspirations of a diverse clientele. Diversity in schools is also seen in the ethnic diversity of our school population, especially in the Metropolitan Montréal area. Multiculturalism is an important policy issue in public education systems across Canada; however, it has particular significance in Québec because of the aforementioned preoccupation in the province with language. Successive Québec governments have rejected multiculturalism in favour of what is called "interculturalism." This approach consists of the acceptance of cultural diversity in the context where the French language is the medium of a "cultural convergence" between mainstream Francophone society and divers cultural communities (chap. 14).

PART I:
FOUNDATIONS

The quality of a society is measured by the way it treats its most disadvantaged members. It is through its educational system, the main force in the socialization of the individual, that society reveals what it is and what it aspires to be. If one argues that the State has the duty to educate all children, it follows that the school must be open to the greatest possible numbers of children and so organized as to be able to cater to the needs of those who require special attention (Superior Council, 1977, p. 291).

If public education provides the foundation for a free and democratic society, then the rights of students form - or ought to form - the foundation of the education system. The above statement by the Superior Council, itself created to be the education conscience of the system, reminds us that these rights should not be reserved for the best or even for most, but for *all* students. In chapter 2 we begin with the overall policy framework that sets the basic parameters of the education system to shape the exercise of these rights. An overview of the general rights and obligations of students is provided in chapter 3, followed by a discussion of rights which target students with special needs in chapter 4.

The key provisions of the following instruments which are referred to in the chapters of this part are reproduced in the *Compendium*:

Chapter 2

Canadian Charter
Constitution Act, 1867
Convention on the Rights of the Child
Education Act
Québec *Charter*
      Affirmative Action Programs Regulation
Universal Declaration of Human Rights

Chapter 3

Act Respecting Access to Documents Held by Public Bodies and the Protection of Personal
      Information
Canadian Charter
Civil Code of Québec
Criminal Code
Education Act
      Admission of Exceptional Cases Regulation
      Elementary School Regulation
      General Education for Adults: 1998-99
      General Education in the Youth Sector: 1998-99
      Secondary School Regulation
Québec *Charter*
YOA
YPA

Chapter 4

Act to Secure the Handicapped in the Exercise of their Rights
Education Act
      Elementary School Regulation
      MEQ Categories of Disability
      Secondary School Regulation

Introduction

A foundation for a system, like a foundation for a house, begins with a vision and a plan. You cannot build the frames for the foundation, let alone pour the concrete, without knowing the size, shape and weight of the house it is meant to support. These elements can only be determined on the basis of the design of the house which in turn will flow from a vision of what it will look like when completed. When the actual construction begins, the builder must respect the applicable *Building Code* which sets certain parameters and standards for house construction.

The foundation for an education system begins with a set of values and beliefs that the system is meant to promote. The next step is to construct a general policy framework to guide the establishment and direction of the system. Such a policy framework is complex and multi-faceted. It must also respect the system "building code" – the Constitution. For our purposes, the general policy framework comprises two general and very intertwined elements: provision for the governance of the system and the establishment of the rights and obligations of the various stakeholders. Governance is concerned with *authority* - who gets to decide how the education system operates, and *voice* - who gets to participate in these policy and decision making processes. The rights and obligations of the various stakeholders, beyond the exercise of authority and voice, are concerned with service delivery - what instructional and other services can students and parents demand and who must provide them. Governance provisions are found in laws and regulations but the latter are made by those with authority to govern, hence their intertwined relationship.

Accordingly, in this chapter, we first deal with some of the key values underpinning the system, followed by a brief presentation of the constitutional framework. This will be followed by a discussion of the two basic elements of the general policy framework: the overall system of governance and the "regulatory framework" of laws and regulations. It thus provides the backdrop for the discussion of rights which follows in chapters 3 and 4, and the description of governance structures which is included in Part II. This chapter introduces a number of terms and expressions which are defined in the Glossary of Terms and Abbreviations at the beginning of the book. Anyone interested in more information on these topics, should refer to the many publications available (e.g. Atkinson, 1993; Gall, 1995).

Guiding Principles

For purposes of setting forth the major guiding principles of the system, we have decided to focus on human rights and the ethos of educational opportunity, policy themes that were central to the Parent Commission report (see e.g., Vol. I, 1964) and have been stated or implicitly echoed in subsequent policy papers for the past thirty years (see e.g. MEQ, 1979a, 1992d, 1997a).

Human Rights

The underlying ethos of human rights is that people are entitled to certain rights and freedoms just because they are human beings. In order to *qualify* as a human right, the right must be one which is possessed by all human beings, and only by human beings; it must be possessed equally by all human beings and cannot, therefore, be linked to a particular status (e.g. citizen, landowner). Human rights are universal because they are not bound by time or space. In other words, a human right applies to every human being, without regard to the century or country in which the person lives.

The word "right" expresses a moral entitlement - what we believe people *ought* to possess. However, moral rights are small comfort to someone who is being oppressed. In order to prevent oppression, the normative values underlying human rights have been translated into *legal* rights. Only legally enshrined rights can be enforced through the courts. At the present time, human rights are found in a variety of international and domestic laws.

Human Rights & Education

There is a symbiotic relationship between human rights and education. First, education figures prominently in various international instruments used to articulate human rights:

Universal Declaration of Human Rights

Everyone has the right to education ....
Education shall be directed to the full development of the human personality and to the strengthening of respect for human rights and fundamental freedoms (art. 26(1), (2)).

Convention on the Rights of the Child

States Parties recognize the right of the child to education, and with a view to achieving this right progressively on the basis of equal opportunity, they shall, in particular:
  (a) make primary education compulsory and available free to all;
  (b) encourage the development of different forms of secondary education, including general and vocational education, make them available and accessible to every child, and take appropriate measures such as the introduction of free education and offering financial assistance in case of need;
  (c) make higher education accessible to all on the basis of capacity by every appropriate means;
  (d) make educational and vocational information and guidance available and accessible to all children;
  (e) take measures to encourage regular attendance at schools and the reduction of drop-out rates (art. 28(1)).

Schools have a special responsibility to foster human rights, as stated by Leduc and DeMassy in their guide to the Québec *Charter, Sharing a Better Life Together Through Human Rights* (1989, p. 14):

Why do we have human rights and freedoms? Because, when they are recognized for each individual, they give all of us equal power to ensure our basic needs, to express ourselves, to take part in society, in short, to develop fully. School is a suitable place to learn about democracy: to learn how to see that everyone's rights and freedoms are respected, to exercise them while respecting those of others, and so to share relations of mutual respect with others, as equals.

Manley-Casimir and Pitsula (1988-89, p. 40) argue that law and education fulfill similar and complementary functions in our society:

Each in different ways is concerned with fundamental values, their transmission and preservation; each must adapt to and accommodate shifts in values and the reflection of these values in policy and practice; each is inherently normative, that is, concerned with individual and collective mores, social ideals and prized beliefs of the culture .... The school is expected to transmit or impart these norms or expectations about behaviour to the young while the law serves to adjudicate conflicts that arise in the living out of these norms or expectations.

One of the key values espoused by our education system is *equal educational opportunity* [EEO].

Equal Educational Opportunity

EEO is based on a fundamental belief that all children, regardless of race, wealth, ability, or other personal characteristics, deserve the benefit of quality educational services. As stated thirty years ago in the Parent report (Vol.1, 1963, pp. 3-4):

> As much for spiritual and humanistic as for practical reasons ... the education system, as such, must have three goals today:
> - • to make available to all, without distinction of creed, racial origin, culture, social environment, age, sex, physical health or mental capacity, an education of good quality satisfying a wide variety of needs;
> - • to allow everyone to continue his studies, in the field which best suits his abilities, his tastes and his interests, up to the most advanced level he has the capacity to reach, and thus have available to him everything which can contribute to his complete fulfilment;
> - • to prepare all young people for life in society, which means earning their living by useful work, intelligently assuming their social responsibilities in a spirit of equality and freedom, as well as to offer adults every opportunity for self-improvement.

EEO involves many dimensions, including equality of *access* - to participate in schooling, equality of *treatment* - to benefit from appropriate programs and services, and equality of *results* - to achieve the desired outcomes from school. Many people question the ability of the school to contribute to EEO and some contend that schools actually perpetuate inequality. Whether one adopts the optimistic or pessimistic view, the increased demands on public schools to deliver more with less creates negative pressures on the EEO agenda of schools. As stated by Lessard (1991, p. 154):

> All those committed to the development and success of equal opportunity should be wary of present socio-economic conditions and governmental educational policies, which seem to enhance inequality instead of significantly reducing or eliminating it. A global approach that stresses not only transformation of the educational system but also of the society - and economy - in which the system operates is still very much needed today. As we now recognize, it is impossible to change society through education alone .... Reforms in educational policy and practice must go together with reforms in other sectors of society if true egalitarianism is to be achieved within our democratic society.

Constitutional Framework

The constitution is the fundamental law of a nation or state. It establishes the organization of government and the relationship between citizens and the State. In a federal country like Canada, the Constitution also provides for the division of powers between the federal and provincial levels of government.

The Constitution of Canada

The constitutional framework for education in Canada is found in a series of constitutional laws, which collectively are regrouped in the *Constitution Acts, 1867-1982*. The Constitution also includes the *Canadian Charter*.

Functions of Government

One of the purposes of a country's constitution is to spell out the main ways in which government will function. The major functions of government can be described as legislative, judicial and administrative. The legislative function is exercised by the Parliament of Canada and the legislative assemblies of each province and territory.* The judicial function is exercised by the courts and other quasi-judicial bodies. Finally, the executive function is exercised by the Federal or provincial Cabinet, or Council of Ministers as it is known in Québec, and the various departments of government (see chap. 5).

*Note. For simplicity's sake, we will not make any further reference to the Territories; generally, they exercise similar powers in education as the provinces do because of a blanket delegation of powers from the Federal Government.

Division of Powers: Section 93

In a federal country like Canada, the Constitution also provides for the division of powers between the federal and provincial levels of government. For education, the key provision of the Constitution is section 93 of the *Constitution Act, 1867* (reproduced below), which, except for specialized domains where the Federal Government has authority (see chap. 1), gives the provinces exclusive jurisdiction in education, subject to the restrictions stipulated therein.

Until recently, a text such as this would contain a relatively lengthy discussion of section 93. However, the simple but profound recent constitutional amendment: "Subsections 93(1) to 93(4) do not apply to Québec" (*Constitutional Amendment, 1997 (Québec)*), makes such a discussion of purely historical interest. A discussion of this important constitutional amendment and its impact on Québec is included in chapter 6.

Constitution Act, 1867

93. In and for each Province the Legislature may exclusively make Laws in relation to Education, subject and according to the following Provisions:-

(1) Nothing in any such Law shall prejudicially affect any Right or Privilege with respect to Denominational Schools which any Class of Persons have by Law in the Province at the Union:

(2) All the Powers, Privileges, and Duties at the Union by Law conferred and imposed in Upper Canada on the Separate Schools and School Trustees of the Queen's Roman Catholic Subjects shall be and the same are hereby extended to the Dissentient Schools of the Queen's Protestant and Roman Catholic Subjects in Quebec:

(3) Where in any Province a System of Separate or Dissentient Schools exists by Law at the Union or is thereafter established by the Legislature of the Province, an Appeal shall lie to the Governor General in Council from any Act or Decision of any Provincial Authority affecting any Right or Privilege of the Protestant or Roman Catholic Minority of the Queen's Subjects in relation to Education:

(4) In case any such Provincial Law as from Time to Time seems to the Governor General in Council requisite for the due Execution of the Provisions of this Section is not made, or in case any Decision of the Governor General in Council on any Appeal under this Section is not duly executed by the proper Provincial Authority in that Behalf, then and in every such Case, and as far only as the Circumstances of each Case require, the Parliament of Canada may make remedial Laws for the due Execution of the Provisions of this Section and of any Decision of the Governor General in Council under this Section.

93A. Paragraphs (1) to (4) of section 93 do not apply to Quebec.

Canadian Charter

Until 1982, constitutional questions in education were largely limited to disputes over the extent of the restrictions provided for in section 93. (Much of this will be discussed in chapter 6 concerning school board reform.) This situation changed dramatically in 1982 when the Canadian Government patriated the Constitution from Great Britain and entrenched the *Canadian Charter* in the Canadian Constitution.

We will be looking at specific provisions of the *Charter* below and in later chapters; suffice it to say for now, that with the advent of constitutionalized rights and freedoms, provincial governments are now faced with new restrictions in deciding, among other matters, the form and substance of the educational system. The general framework for educational governance under the Canadian Constitution is depicted in Figure 2.1.

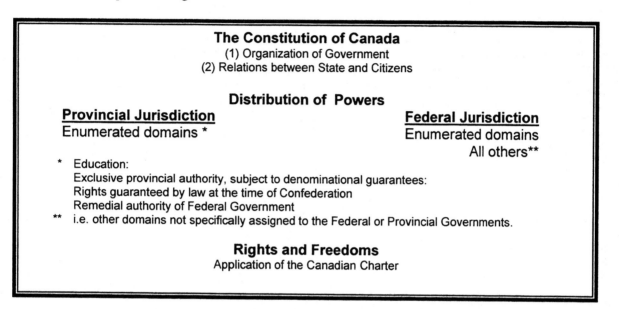

FIGURE 2.1
Constitutional Basis of Educational Governance

Educational Governance

The analysis of school governance in any given jurisdiction begins with an understanding of the construct of governance in the educational milieu. Governance is generally understood to mean the act or manner of governing, or the formal system for controlling the behaviour of others (see Glossary of Terms). In Québec, like other jurisdictions in North America, the system of governance and can be described as a three-tiered framework, with each tier representing a different level of the system, as shown in Figure 2.2.

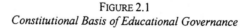

FIGURE 2.2
School Governance Framework

Public bodies can only do what they are authorized to do by law. Some government functions are exercised directly by the National Assembly or indirectly by delegation to the Cabinet or the Minister (of Education). Some functions of the Minister may in turn be delegated to the Deputy Minister of Education. Although civil servants perform many functions on behalf of the MEQ, generally, authority is vested in the Minister or in his or her Deputy.

Central Level

National Assembly

The National Assembly is the only provincial body which can enact *statutes*, often termed acts or *laws*. All elements of the provincial governance framework flow from statutes enacted by the National Assembly. Subject to the constitutional framework discussed above, other policy actors (e.g. school boards) can only exercise the authority or voice which the National Assembly decides to delegate to them.

The Cabinet

The Cabinet, or the Council of Ministers, is sometimes referred to as the Lieutenant Governor in Council, reflecting the constitutional relationship between the Government and the Crown. In Québec law, the Cabinet is referred to as the "Government." Among other functions, the Government is the only body empowered to adopt the *regulations* which are published in the Québec *Official Gazette*. These regulations can only be adopted in accordance with the scope provided for in a statute enacted by the National Assembly.

The Minister

The Minister of Education is an elected member of the National Assembly and a member of the Cabinet. He or she can only exercise the duties and powers assigned by law. Some of these functions are exercised through various ministerial orders. As you will see in chapter 3, the most important ministerial orders are called *directives* or *instructions* (the French term).

The MEQ

Many of the functions of government in education are carried out by civil servants employed in the MEQ. The chief administrative officer of the MEQ is the Deputy Minister who reports directly to the Minister. There is also an Associate Deputy Minister Catholic and an Associate Deputy Minister Protestant, responsible for denominational matters. The Deputy Minister is aided by several assistant deputy ministers who are responsible for various domains of activities. We will examine the role of the Minister and the MEQ in detail in chapter 5.

Intermediate Level

School boards are the key policy actors in educational governance at the intermediate level. School boards, like other public bodies, can only do what they are empowered to do by law. A school board is a public corporation run by a council of commissioners (see definitions of various commissioners in chap. 6). Within the scope of its authority delegated by law (discussed below), the school board takes action through *resolutions* and *by-laws*. A resolution is simply a decision adopted by a vote of the council of commissioners and recorded in the council minutes. A by-law is a special form of resolution which generally can only be adopted following public notice and consultation of school governing boards and the parents committee, as provided for in the *Education Act* (see s. 392-398). We will examine school boards in detail in chapter 6.

Local Level

Schools provide the final - one might say ultimate - tier in educational governance. The school governing board is the body responsible for the governance of the school while the principal is its pedagogical and administrative director. His or her authority is exercised with the collaboration of the school staff.

The school of course is where you find the "front line" in education, where actual teaching and learning occur. Accordingly, many key decisions regarding curriculum and school organization are now made at the level of the school. We will examine them in detail in chapter 7.

The Regulatory Framework

Overview

The Québec regulatory framework refers to the sum of all "rules" - laws, regulations, etc. - governing the education system. It is illustrated below to show how the various sets of rules are *nested* in layers, one inside the other. The rules in one layer must respect those contained in all layers above it, and in turn must be respected by all those in layers below it. It is illustrated below in Figure 2.3.

Constitution
The Constitution is the "supreme law of the land." It includes the *Canadian Charter* which applies to the Federal and provincial governments and protects individuals against State legislation and action (public sector). It guarantees everyone equal benefit and protection of the law without discrimination, together with other fundamental rights.

Québec Charter
The National Assembly may make special laws, for example the Québec *Charter*, which serves to complement the *Canadian Charter*. It provides a wide range of human rights and freedoms and applies to both the public and private sectors in the province.

Education Act
The National Assembly may make ordinary laws, for example the *Education Act,* which is the statute that contains most provisions relating to public education but other statutes are relevant as well.

Regulations
A regulation (e.g. *Basic Elementary Regulation*) is adopted by the Government (Council of Ministers) and generally provides details about matters provided for in the statute under which it is enacted (e.g. *Education Act*).

Ministerial Directives
The Minister of Education may issue directives to provide further details concerning the application of statues and regulations.

School Board Resolutions
School board resolutions are adopted by the council of commissioners and may deal with any matter for which a school board has legal responsibility.

School Policies and Rules
School polices and rules - the final layer - are adopted by the school governing board or the principal, depending on who is given authority by the *Education Act*. By exception to the rule stated above, they need not respect school board policy when the school governing board or the principal is given responsibility to decide a given matter (e.g. number of minutes per subject). In this case, the school can be thought of as being nested in the same layer as the school board.

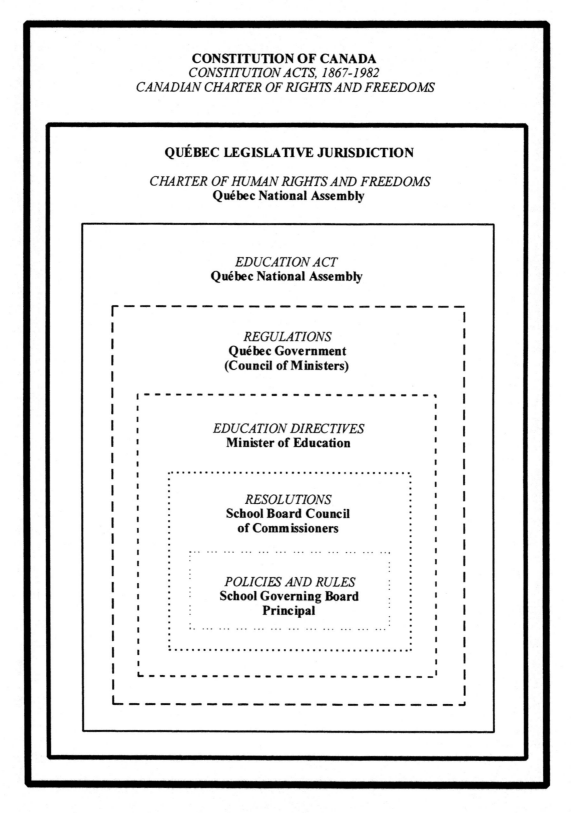

FIGURE 2.3
Regulatory Framework for Québec Education

Canadian Charter

As mentioned above, in 1982, the Government of Canada patriated the Canadian Constitution from Great Britain and in it entrenched the *Canadian Charter*, thereby giving all Canadians constitutionally protected rights and freedoms. The *Charter* applies to both the legislation and government action of the Government of Canada and the provincial governments. It does not, however, apply to matters which do not involve government (e.g. employment in a private sector company). Human rights in such matters are governed by federal and provincial human rights legislation, depending on whether the matter comes under one jurisdiction or another. Thus, for example, commerce comes under provincial jurisdiction, so human rights complaints respecting commercial establishments would have to be dealt with by provincial human rights legislation, as discussed below.

Although education is a provincial matter, the *Canadian Charter* is relevant because public school boards and schools, as well as their officials, operate as "State agents" - that is on behalf of the State - and therefore their actions are subject to the provisions of the *Canadian Charter*. Although private schools and their officials are not regarded as State agents and not subject to *Charter* standards, the legislation governing private schools, like any government legislation, must respect these standards.

The *Canadian Charter* provides for the following categories of human rights and freedoms:

- fundamental freedoms;
- democratic rights;
- mobility rights;
- legal rights;
- equality rights;
- official languages of Canada;
- minority language educational rights.

Canadian Charter of Rights and Freedoms

1. The Canadian Charter of Rights and Freedoms guarantees the rights and freedoms set out in it subject only to such reasonable limits prescribed by law as can be demonstrably justified in a free and democratic society.

2. Everyone has the following fundamental freedoms:
(a) freedom of conscience and religion;
(b) freedom of thought, belief, opinion and expression, including freedom of the press and other media of communication;
(c) freedom of peaceful assembly; and
(d) freedom of association.

15.(1) Every individual is equal before and under the law and has the right to the equal protection and equal benefit of the law without discrimination and, in particular, without discrimination based on race, national or ethnic origin, colour, religion, sex, age or mental or physical disability.

(2) Subsection (1) does not preclude any law, program or activity that has as its object the amelioration of conditions of disadvantaged individuals or groups including those that are disadvantaged because of race, national or ethnic origin, colour, religion, sex, age or mental or physical disability.

The above extract provides you with the fundamental freedoms and equality rights provisions of the *Canadian Charter*, as well as the "limitations clause." The discussion which follows deals with these topics and the "override" clause. For a discussion of freedom of religion, see chapter 12, for a discussion of minority language rights, see chapter 13.

Fundamental Freedoms

Rights are often concerned with providing something to which people would not otherwise be entitled - e.g. right to education. Section 2, by contrast, deals with "fundamental freedoms" which are *liberty rights*, meaning freedom from restraint or interference by the State respecting matters in which they should be able to engage as free human beings. In other words, people have the inherent right, for example, to hold a particular religious belief; as no law is required to grant such right, the purpose of this section is to guarantee that government legislation or action will not infringe upon this right.

As will be discussed below, these fundamental freedoms are not *absolute*; there are limits. For the moment, suffice it to say this section is intended to protect the rights of students, among others, to hold personal beliefs and ideas, to express them, both individually and collectively, and to associate with others. In the school context, this raises the question of school rules which could be seen to limit these rights, for example, school dress codes or staff censorship of a student newspaper. Although there is little Canadian case law on point to provide guidance in this domain, we can expect that some matters will be treated in the same manner as they would outside the school, for example, limiting free speech which is considered to be hate mongering. Other matters will probably recognize the context of the school, for example, a dress code requiring students to wear a uniform.*

*Note. This does not mean that the school can impose *any* dress code (see discussion of religious garb in chap. 12).

Equality Rights

The purpose of section 15 is to grant every individual equal protection and benefit of law. This means that, subject to the limits set forth in the *Canadian Charter* (discussed below), no government in Canada can pass a law or take any action which treats people in a manner which deprives them of their equality rights. In particular, this section guarantees that government shall not discriminate against individuals on the basis of the characteristics listed therein (e.g. race, disability) or any analogous ones. Discrimination does not merely mean treating someone *differently* than others. Sometimes treating people differently is non-discriminatory, just as sometimes treating people the same can be discriminatory. The issue is whether the treatment involves some form of prejudice or disadvantage, whether it results from the same or different treatment accorded to others. Discrimination may be direct - action aimed at an individual who is a member of a target group (e.g. refusing to hire women for a given position) - or it may be indirect - action that is not so aimed but which nonetheless is discriminatory because of the impact the action has with respect to a member of the target group (e.g. requiring all male employees to be clean shaven, which disproportionately affects Sikhs whose religion prevents them from shaving). This latter type of discrimination is often termed *adverse effect discrimination* and is not permitted under the *Charter*.

The second paragraph of section 15 is intended to allow for *affirmative action* programs. Affirmative action programs recognize that some groups have been the object of discrimination over a long period of time and that prohibiting discrimination against them as of some moment in time is not sufficient to remedy past wrongs. Hence, programs are designed to promote the welfare of the target group (e.g. employment equity for women in an industry which has traditionally discriminated against women). Without the inclusion of this second paragraph in section 15, such programs could be challenged as violating the equality principle set forth in the first paragraph (e.g. because they discriminate against men). The second paragraph prevents such a challenge.

Reasonable Limits

As suggested by the above discussion of equality and affirmative action, providing for human rights is almost always a "balancing act," as according rights to some may affect the rights of others. The absence of legally protected human rights means that the government could pass any law it wished;

by contrast, the granting of absolute rights could prevent a government from passing legislation which most people would find reasonable under the circumstances. Perhaps an example will make this point clearer.

Suppose that we wish to enshrine the principle that the government cannot discriminate against persons on the basis of age. On the other hand, most people would agree that children should not be allowed to obtain a driver's license. If there were an absolute prohibition against age-based discrimination, the government would be powerless to prevent a young child from driving a car.

In order to deal with such realities, the *Canadian Charter* contains the "reasonable limits" clause (s. 1, see above). Described by Madame Justice Wilson, in *Operational Dismantle* v. *Canada* (1985), as a "uniquely Canadian mechanism," section 1 provides government with a defence if someone challenges a law or government action as being a violation of some specific *Charter* right. Using the above example, assume a minor challenges a government law which restricts the issuance of a driver's license to persons over 16 years of age. The judge agrees that the law violates section 15 - discrimination on the basis of age. The government can then plead that this restriction is a "reasonable limit in a free and democratic society." If the judge accepts this view, then the case would be dismissed.

The Notwithstanding Clause

There is one more potential limitation on certain *Canadian Charter* rights which deserves a brief explanation - the so called *notwithstanding* clause (s. 33). Section 33 allows the Government of Canada or a provincial government to adopt a law which is contrary to the provisions of one or more of the following *Charter* rights and freedoms:

- fundamental rights (s. 2);
- legal rights (ss. 7-14); and
- equality rights (s. 15).

If a government wishes to invoke section 33, it must declare in the law that it shall operate *notwithstanding* one of these provisions. Such a declaration is valid for five years but may be renewed for an indefinite number of five-year periods. It should be noted that other provisions of the *Canadian Charter* (e.g. minority language rights) cannot be overridden.

Section 33 was included as a political compromise to gain the support of certain provincial premiers for the entrenchment of the *Charter* in the Constitution. Although this override provision appears to be a blatant violation of human rights, it is consistent with our tradition of parliamentary sovereignty and is consistent with the *Canadian Bill of Rights* and provincial human rights codes.

Québec Charter of Human Rights & Freedoms

The Québec *Charter* fulfils some of the same functions as the *Canadian Charter*, as well as others which are not covered by the latter charter. Several provisions of the Québec *Charter* have "primacy" over other Québec legislation (s. 52), which means that other laws and regulations must respect these provisions unless the Québec version of the "notwithstanding" clause is invoked (see below). The provisions which have primacy over other legislation include freedom of conscience and religion and equality rights but not "economic and social rights," such as the right to education.

As a provincial human rights code, the Québec *Charter* applies to matters which come under provincial jurisdiction. Unlike the *Canadian Charter*, the Québec *Charter* applies to various private sector activities that do not involve government (e.g. non-discrimination in employment and goods or services ordinarily offered to the public). The key provisions of the Québec *Charter* concerning education are cited below.

Québec Charter of Human Rights and Freedoms

3. Every person is the possessor of the fundamental freedoms, including freedom of conscience, freedom of religion, freedom of opinion, freedom of expression, freedom of peaceful assembly and freedom of association.

9.1. In exercising his fundamental freedoms and rights [ss. 1-9], a person shall maintain a proper regard for democratic values, public order and the general well-being of the citizens of Québec.

In this respect, the scope of the freedoms and rights, and limits to their exercise, may be fixed by law.

10. Every person has a right to full and equal recognition and exercise of his human rights and freedoms, without distinction, exclusion or preference based on race, colour, sex, pregnancy, sexual orientation, civil status, age except as provided by law, religion, political convictions, language, ethnic or national origin, social condition, a handicap or the use of any means to palliate a handicap.

Discrimination exists where such a distinction, exclusion or preference has the effect of nullifying or impairing such right.

10.1 No one may harass a person on the basis of any ground mentioned in section 10.

40. Every person has a right, to the extent and according to the standards provided for by law, to free public education.

41. Parents or the persons acting in their stead have a right to require that, in the public educational establishments, their children receive a religious or moral education in conformity with their convictions, within the framework of the curricula provided for by law.

42. Parents or the persons acting in their stead have a right to choose private educational establishments for their children, provided such establishments comply with the standards prescribed or approved by virtue of the law.

Fundamental Freedoms

As can be seen from section 3 reproduced below, the fundamental freedoms provided for in the Québec *Charter* are very similar to those found in the *Canadian Charter* (see above; see also chap. 12).

Right to Education & Equality Rights

Québec is one of only two provinces in Canada to specify education as a human right (Saskatchewan is the other). However, the wording of the Québec statute (s. 40, see below) makes education a "circular" right rather than a "stand alone" right by defining the right by what is "provided for by law." In other words, if the Government decided to abolish public schooling, you could not claim that this action violated the Québec *Charter* "right to education." However, given that it is highly unlikely that any government would take such an action, it does prevent the Government from adopting a law which discriminated against anyone on the basis of any of the grounds listed in section 10 (e.g. handicap). (For a discussion on the other education rights (ss. 41-42), see chap. 12.)

Affirmative Action & Special Programs

The Québec *Charter* makes express provision for "affirmative action" programs as well as "special programs:"

Québec Charter of Human Rights and Freedoms

20. A distinction, exclusion or preference based on the aptitudes or qualifications required for an employment, or justified by the charitable, philanthropic, religious, political or educational nature of a non-profit institution or an institution devoted exclusively to the well-being of an ethnic group, is deemed non-discriminatory.

86. The object of an affirmative action program is to remedy the situation of persons belonging to groups discriminated against in employment, or in the sector of education or of health services and other services generally available to the public.
An affirmative action program is deemed non-discriminatory if it is established in conformity with the Charter.

Affirmative Action

Affirmative action programs are limited to those which are intended to ameliorate the conditions of *disadvantaged* groups (e.g. students with disabilities). The Human Rights Commission may propose that a school board, for example, implement an affirmative action program and if its proposal is not accepted, it may apply to the Human Rights Tribunal to order the establishment and implementation of such a program which is then subject to the approval of the Tribunal. It is worthy of note that the *Regulation Respecting Affirmative Action Programs* [Affirmative Action Programs Regulation] has been adopted under the aegis of the Québec *Charter* which provides for affirmative action programs in education; making Québec the only jurisdiction in Canada to have such a regulation. To the best of our knowledge, such an affirmative action program in education has only been contemplated in one case (see chap. 4), but never actually implemented anywhere.

Special Programs

"Special programs" provide preferential treatment to *designated* groups. Because they do not seek to ameliorate the conditions of *disadvantaged* groups, they do not qualify as "affirmative action" under the Canadian or Québec *Charters*. For example, a private school for Catholics would be permitted under section 20 as a special program but would not qualify as an affirmative action program because Catholics are not a disadvantaged group in Québec (see chap. 12 for further details).

Reasonable Limits

The Québec *Charter* does contain a "reasonable limits" clause (s. 9.1) but it applies only to the fundamental rights and freedoms included in that section and not to any equality rights. Although some people would argue that this means that equality rights (s. 10) are absolute, a review of the case law suggests that the courts interpret equality rights in light of some standard of "reasonableness."

Override

The Québec *Charter* also includes an override, or *notwithstanding*, clause (s. 52). The Government can invoke this clause if it wishes to override any right or freedom contained in the Québec *Charter*. Unlike the override provision of the Canadian Charter, there is no time limit on the effect of the override.

The human rights and freedoms found in the *Canadian Charter* and in the Québec *Charter* provide a backdrop for the various statutory rights to education which are contained in the *Education Act* and other legislative acts.

Whether one views it [education] from an economic, social cultural or civic point of view, the education of the young is critically important in our society.... No proof is required to show the importance of education in our society or its significance to government. The legitimate, indeed compelling, interest of the State in the education of the young is known and understood by all informed citizens (*R.* v. *Jones*, 1986, pp. 592, 594).

Introduction

In the previous chapter, we set forth a general policy framework for the direction of the education system, including a brief discussion of how the law is articulated in a series of "nested layers." This chapter is devoted to the inner layers of this framework, namely the statutory rights of children and youth in general and as students in particular. The latter also includes the rights of adult students and of both age groups respecting vocational education. The purpose of this focus is to emphasize the central place which students occupy - or ought to occupy - in the school system. More specifically, we will examine various education rights and then some more general rights applicable to children and youth. Most rights are found in the provincial *Education Act*, but there are some which are found in other statutes as well. Although the right to choose the language of instruction is an important element in the framework defining the rights of students, it has been omitted from this chapter as it is dealt with separately as part of the discussion of education and language (see chap. 13). Likewise, we omit any discussion of rights to religion in schools as these are dealt with in chapter 12.

Sources of Rights in Public Schooling

In addition to the declaration of education as a human right found in the Québec *Charter* (s. 40), most of the rights of students to public school education are contained in the *Education Act* and various regulations and directives. These documents are listed below, including in parentheses, the abbreviations that will be used to refer to them throughout the text.

Education Act		
Elementary School Regulation Secondary School Regulation (El Reg & Sec Reg)		Adult General Regulation Adult Vocational Regulation (Adult Gen Reg & Adult Voc Reg)
General Education in the Youth Sector: 1998-99 (Youth Dir)	Vocational Education Directives: 1998-99 (Voc Dir)	General Education for Adults: 1998-99 (Adult Dir)

FIGURE 3.1
Core of Education Rights

Students also enjoy other rights, some of which are of importance in an educational context.

Examples are rights which are conferred by certain provisions of the *YPA*, the *YOA*, the Quebec *Charter*, the *Act Respecting Access to Documents Held by Public Bodies and the Protection of Personal Information* and the *Civil Code of Quebec*. These rights are discussed in the last section of this chapter.

The Education Act

Some provisions of the Act apply to both "youth" and "adults" but more often the rights of these groups are treated separately. The Act makes specific provision for "vocational education" as a separate sector whose clientele includes both youth and adults.

The Regulations

There are separate regulations for youth at the elementary and secondary levels, and the latter includes provisions governing vocational education for youth. There are two regulations governing adults, one respecting general education, the other, vocational education.

The Directives

There are three sets of annual directives (typically called *Instructions* by their French name); in this case, one respecting general education for youth, one respecting general education for adults and the third respecting vocational education, encompassing both youth and adults.

"Youth" and "adults" are not defined as such in the Act or the regulations but various provisions can be used to arrive at the following definitions:

- A youth is a person from the age of admission (5 years for kindergarten; 6 years for elementary school) to 18 years of age (21 years in the case of a "handicapped person").

- An adult is a person no longer subject to compulsory school attendance (end of school year in which his or her 16th birthday occurs or he or she obtains a diploma, whichever occurs first).

As you can see, these definitions overlap for "young adults" - those between 16 and 18 (or 21) years of age who can therefore choose to continue their education in the youth sector or transfer to the adult sector.

Whose Rights?

Historically the expression "students' rights," at least in so far as it related to students who were children, would have been considered an oxymoron; rights were attained upon reaching the "age of majority" – until then children were viewed as little more than "property" over whom the father had complete authority. Over time paternal authority over children gave way to parental authority; still parents were considered to have the right to make decisions about children as the parents saw fit. Since then, the situation has changed dramatically; today, parental authority is meant to be exercised, not *over* the child, but *on behalf of* the child. No one would now seriously dispute the fact that children, like adults, are persons entitled to the range of human rights enshrined in international and domestic human rights instruments, notably the *Convention on the Rights of the Child*:

Convention on the Rights of the Child

3(1). In all actions concerning children, whether undertaken by public or private social welfare institutions, courts of law, administrative authorities or legislative bodies, the best interests of the child shall be a primary consideration.

12(1). States Parties shall assure to the child who is capable of forming his or her own views the right to express those views freely in all matters affecting the child, the views of the child being given due weight in accordance with the age and maturity of the child.

Children generally are viewed as persons with diminished autonomy. They are presumed to be incapable of making informed choices and therefore incapable of exercising their rights in an effective and meaningful manner. They need a proxy to exercise their rights on their behalf and in their interests; invariably, the parent* is a child's proxy.

Note: For the purposes of the *Education Act*, "parent" means "the person having parental authority or, unless that person objects, the person having custody *de facto* of the student" (s. 13(2)).

However, it is accepted that the presumption of incapacity of children is a rebuttable presumption; that as children mature they can acquire the capacity to exercise their rights for themselves. It is therefore helpful to view the "modern function of parental rights [as being] ... to prepare children and adolescents for maturity, and as minors come to achieve maturity and to exercise autonomy, this may be seen not as a limitation or defeat of parental control, but as a successful discharge of parental responsibility" (Dickens, 1981, p. 485). Until that responsibility is discharged, the *Québec Civil Code* directs in article 33, that the parents (and others) must always act in the best interests of children:

Civil Code of Québec

33. Every decision concerning a child shall be taken in the light of the child's best interests and the respect for his rights.

Consideration is given, in addition to the moral, intellectual, emotional and material needs of the child, to the child's age, health, personality and family environment, and to the other aspects of the situation.

Thus in the following discussion it is important to keep in mind that, while students are the ultimate beneficiaries of the education rights discussed here and elsewhere in the *Handbook* (see chaps 12 & 13), some rights are vested in students (of various ages), others are vested in the parents of students on behalf of their children and yet others are vested in parents in their own right.

A Range of Rights in Public Schooling

Together, the *Education Act* and the various regulations include provisions dealing with:

- the right to attend school and compulsory attendance;
- instructional and student services (see also chap. 8);
- school choice;
- school transportation;
- discipline and expulsion; and

• appeal procedures.

The following provides a summary of these rights, distinguishing between youth and adults as required, but it is not an exhaustive list of rights which students can claim. For details on these and other rights, see the *Education Act*, and the regulations and directives governing youth, vocational and adult education. This discussion does not include those rights pertaining only to students with special needs (see chap. 4), or the rights of students or parents to participation in governance (see chaps. 6 & 7).

Right to Schooling & Duty to Attend

Youth
Attendance at school is both a right and a duty for youth. However, the upper and lower age limits of the entitlement and obligation differ as shown below (Ed Act, ss. 1, 14-18, 241.1, 457.1; El Reg, ss. 32, 41; Sec Reg, s. 79; Youth Dir, s. 4.5.4; *Regulation Respecting Exceptional Cases for Admission to Preschool and Elementary School Education* [*Admission of Exceptional Cases Regulation*]).

Exceptions to Compulsory Attendance
The obligation to attend a public school is not absolute. Four principal exceptions to this obligation are recognized, namely, non-attendance because of: illness or required medical treatment or care excused by the school board; an officially accepted physical or mental handicap that prevents attendance; expulsion from school after proper procedures have been followed; and attendance in approved home schooling or at a recognized private school (Ed Act, s. 15). That a student is gainfully employed is not an excuse for failure to attend school; in fact, the *Education Act* stipulates that it is an offence for a person to employ a student of compulsory school age during school hours (ss. 16, 486).

Age Limit	Right	Duty
Lower Limit: Kindergarten	5 years*	NA
Elementary	6 years*	6 years
Upper Limit:	18 years**	16 years***

FIGURE 3.2
Age Limits for Schooling

*   The general rule is that a child is eligible if he or she attains the age of admission prior to October 1 of the current school year. However, parents can request an early admission provided that the child will attain the age of admission during the school year and meets the eligibility requirements set by regulation.

**   A student who has reached 18 may stay in school for one more year if it is possible for him or her to satisfy the requirements for a diploma or attestation during that year.

***   A student must stay in school to the last day of the school year in which his or her 16th birthday occurs or until he or she obtains a diploma, whichever occurs first.

Responsibility of Parents and Principals
The Act explicitly states that it is the responsibility of parents to take the measures necessary to ensure that their children attend school (s. 17), and of principals to ascertain, in the manner established by the school board, that students do in fact attend school regularly (s. 18). Where a student is repeatedly absent the principal must try to come to an agreement with the student, his or her parents and the persons providing social services to the school which will remedy the situation. If such intervention is to no avail the principal, after notifying the parents in writing, must bring the matter to the attention of the Director of Youth Protection.

Adult

For adult students attendance at school is only a right, not a duty. The right to schooling is specifically for those no longer subject to compulsory school attendance and who are enrolled in an adult education centre (Ed Act, s. 2; Adult Gen. Ed., s. 1).

Right to Education

If the right to schooling is the right to be in school, then the right to education is the right to have something meaningful happen once you are inside. Every student who is eligible for schooling in accordance with the above provisions is entitled to the following general rights to education.

Youth

Every youth student is entitled, without charge, to the educational services that are provided for in the Act and the regulations - i.e. to preschool education, instructional services, student and special services (Ed Act, s. 1; El Reg, ss. 1-20; Sec Reg, ss. 1-19; see definitions in chap. 8). The school board and schools are thus required to implement these services, adapt and enrich the objectives of instructional programs to meet the needs of students and establish a program for each student service contemplated in the regulations (Ed Act, ss. 222, 222.1, 224). The right to a free education extends only to residents of the province (s. 216).

Adults

Every adult student is entitled to the educational services that are provided for by the regulations (Ed Act, s. 2). They include learning services, student services and popular education services. Their purpose includes, among others, increasing adult autonomy, integration into society and helping an adult to enter, remain in or return to the labour market (Adult Gen Reg, s. 2). Educational services are provided free to residents of Québec (Ed Act, s. 3), but persons 18 years of age or older (21 years for handicapped) are subject to the conditions stipulated in the regulations (see Adult Gen Reg, s. 32; Adult Voc Reg, ss. 30-31).

Textbooks & Materials

Youth

Required textbooks and materials must be supplied free of charge but this right does not include workbooks and school supplies. In addition, students have a right to free access to reference and reading material (Ed Act, ss. 7, 230).

It must be noted that students are required to take "good care" of school property placed at their disposal and to return it when it is no longer required. If a student breaches this obligation the school board is entitled to recover the cost of the property from the student or, if he or she is a minor, from the student's parents (s. 8).

Adult

Required textbooks and materials must be placed at the disposal of adult students (Adult Gen Reg, s. 40; Adult Voc Reg, s. 23) but there is nothing in the Act or regulations that states they must be supplied free of charge.

School Choice

Youth

The *Education Act* gives the student of full age (i.e. 18 years) or the parents of other students, a qualified right to choose the school within their school board which best suits their preference (s. 4).* This right, however, is not untrammelled as noted below.

* *Note*. The school board can determine the educational services to be provided in each of its schools (Ed Act, s. 236). The right to choose a school does not imply the right to choose a specific program or insist that particular services be provided in

the school chosen.

Limits on Student/Parent Choice

The choice of school is restricted to schools within the jurisdiction of the school board to which student belongs. Moreover, it is subordinate to the enrolment criteria established by the school board (see below); and the exercise of the right of choice does not entitle the student to transportation beyond school board norms (Ed Act, s. 4).

General Enrolment Criteria

As a general rule, a school board may only establish enrolment criteria where applications to a school exceed the school's capacity (s. 239). The criteria, adopted after consulting the parents' committee, must first consider:

- the students' residences - priority must be given students within the school board's jurisdiction; and

- the distance of students' homes from the school – priority must, as far as possible, be given to students closest to the school.

General enrolment criteria therefore are only applied if necessary after applying the above priorities regarding residence or distance. Furthermore, except in the special case dealt with below, they cannot reflect the conditions or criteria of the "specific project" of a school.*

* *Note*. Enrolment criteria, where permitted, cannot reflect the denominational status, educational project or specific project of a school that has not been approved by the Minister (see below) with the object of excluding otherwise qualified students. Moreover, enrolment criteria are subject to consultation of the parents committee, and teachers as per collective agreement (Ed Act, ss. 193(6), 239, 244).

Criteria for a Specific Project Approved by Minister

Criteria other than those listed above may only be established by a school board if a specific project, which meets the following conditions, has been approved for a school. These conditions are that: the project is requested by a group of parents; the parents' committee has been consulted; and the Minister's approval has been granted for the specific project (s. 240). However, the Act does not specify which factors can be considered in establishing enrolment criteria in such a case, though it is assumed that they must be related to the specific project (s. 240).

Adult

The right of choice for adults is practically the mirror image of the rights accorded to youth. While youth school choice is limited to the school district in which he or she is resident, the adult may choose to enrol in any school board (Ed Act, s. 204). However, contrary to the youth student, the Act does not provide the adult with any legal choice to centres within the board.

School Transportation

According to the *Education Act*, school boards are allowed, but not required, to provide school transportation to their students (s. 291); moreover, they may opt either to provide transportation or to pay students an amount to cover all or part of their transportation costs (s. 299).

Youth

School boards routinely provide transportation to youth students on the basis of grants from the MEQ; if they do so, the following provisions apply (s. 292):

- student transportation before the beginning and after the end of classes each day is free of charge;

- when public transit is used to provide student transportation, the school board may claim from the student that portion of the cost which exceeds the cost of providing beginning and end of day transportation;

- if a school board provides noon-hour transportation to allow students to go home for lunch, it may recover the cost from the students who choose to use this service;

- whether or not a school board provides such noon-hour transportation, the school board (i) must ensure, in the manner agreed upon with the governing boards, the supervision of students who remain at school and (ii) determine the financial conditions on which the noon-hour supervision is to be provided in a school.

Adult

A school board that provides transportation to adult students may claim the cost thereof from the users of such services (Ed Act, s. 293).

Discipline & Expulsion

Youth

Student rights respecting discipline and expulsion are found primarily in the *Education Act*. However, these rights are affected by the provisions of both the *Canadian Charter* and the Québec *Charter*. In addition, in cases where discipline has to deal with "extraordinary" offences that are criminal in nature, the *YOA* comes into play (see discussion below).

The *Education Act* (ss. 76, 77) charges the school governing board with the responsibility for approving the rules of conduct and safety measures which must be proposed by the principal. These rules and measures must be developed in collaboration with school staff through a procedure established by the persons concerned at a general meeting. Once approved, the rules must be transmitted to each student and his or her parents.

The rules of conduct and safety measures should be developed with the cooperation of the student body and other members of the school community as exemplified in the following passage from a high school's *Charter of Rights and Responsibilities* (Sturge Sparkes & Smith, 1998, p. 142):

> This Charter is an attempt to define the nature of [this school] and to explain what we as a school stand for and believe in .... We believe that all members of our community are equal regardless of background, gender and ability. We believe that everybody in the community has a right to be respected, to get a good education and to learn in a safe, clean and friendly environment .... The rights and responsibilities contained in this Charter are seen as being of equal importance to our community; these rights and responsibilities apply equally to all who enter these halls.

A wide variety of sanctions can be used by a school to enforce its rules of conduct and safety measures from loss of privileges (attending a school function, participating in an outing) through detentions to suspensions from school. Students should be advised of the range of sanctions attached to particular "offences." Two sanctions, however, are unavailable to schools: expulsions and corporal punishment (see below).

Suspensions

Suspension, unlike expulsions and corporal punishment, as a sanction for breaches of rules of conduct and safety measures is not treated in the *Education Act*. Thus suspensions would appear to be a sanction available within schools. A suspension is understood to mean the forced withdrawal of the student from school for a temporary period of time; it may vary in length from a day (or part of a day) to several weeks. However, suspensions cannot be used as an indirect method of expelling a student.

As noted above, while the Act is silent on the issue of suspensions, it would appear reasonable that they only be imposed for sufficient cause, that is, for serious or repeated breaches of school rules. Furthermore, it would seem appropriate that if a suspension is imposed for a significant period of time and/or will be reflected in a student's record, it should only be imposed after the student and his or her parents have been provided with the reasons for its imposition and given the opportunity to address the case against the student. Nevertheless, when immediate action is warranted, a suspension may be imposed before a hearing is held but it should not be entered on the student's record before such a hearing. Whether or not a student and his or her parents are granted a hearing at the level of the school, a suspension may be appealed to the council of commissioners (see below).

Expulsion
On the matter of expulsion the *Education Act* states:

Education Act

242. A school board may, at the request of the principal and for just and sufficient cause, and after giving the student and his parents an opportunity to be heard, enrol him in another school or expel him from its schools; in the latter case, it shall inform the director of youth protection.

The Act does not prevent a school board from expelling a student but does require that such a decision be made only for "just and sufficient cause." It also ensures some measure of procedural fairness - the opportunity to be heard, but no guidelines are provided in either the Act or the regulations. Taken together, this means that a student cannot be expelled for frivolous reasons nor can such a decision be made arbitrarily "behind closed doors."

If a school board does make such a decision, the expelled student is excused from the duty to attend school and by extension loses the right to attend school. There is no time limit to expulsions in the Act, no age restrictions (i.e. they apply to students of any age), and the board is under no obligation to find an alternate placement. The only recourse at this point is for the student to move to another school district. However, where a student is expelled the school board must inform the Director of Youth Protection (*YPA*, ss. 38.1, 39).

Corporal Punishment
The *Education Act* contains no provisions regarding corporal punishment, other than that excluding the matter from the mandate of the school governing board. Although some people would argue that any form of corporal punishment constitutes child abuse, Québec law does not define abuse in that way (see discussion below). Furthermore, the *Civil Code* does not prohibit corporal punishment. The only statute in which corporal punishment is explicitly dealt with is the federal *Criminal Code*:

Criminal Code

43. Every schoolteacher, parent or person standing in the place of a parent is justified in using force by way of correction toward a pupil or child, as the case may be, who is under his care, if the force does not exceed what is reasonable under the circumstances.

It should be noted that the purpose of this provision is to exempt from criminal prosecution an educator who uses *reasonable* force in the exercise of his or her duties. This provision could thus apply to a teacher restraining an "unruly" student or to a principal administering corporal punishment. However, this provision does not speak to the issue as to whether a member of the school staff can administer corporal punishment, as that is a matter of provincial jurisdiction. Because of the general silence of the *Education Act*, it is possible that a school board's general duty to maintain discipline would allow it to permit corporal punishment in its schools. However, this same silence probably means that the school board would have to explicitly include such a provision in a local policy before a school official would be entitled to administer corporal punishment.

Adult

The *Education Act* is silent on the establishment of rules governing the conduct of adult students. The only oblique reference to establishing a code of conduct is the authority of the governing board of an adult centre to approve "the operating rules of the centre" (s. 110.2).

Appeal Procedures (Youth & Adult)

The *Education Act* (ss. 9-12) provides for an "in-house" appeal mechanism for any decision taken by the council of commissioners, the executive committee, a governing board or an officer or employee of the school board (see chaps. 6 & 7 for discussion of these groups). A student or parent of a student adversely affected by a decision may make a complaint in writing to the secretary general of the school board briefly explaining the problem and requesting the council of commissioners to reconsider the decision. The council of commissioners may dispose of the matter itself or submit the complaint to a person or committee to investigate and make recommendations. All interested parties must be given an opportunity to present their positions. If the complaint is well founded the council of commissioners may overturn, in whole or in part, the decision and substitute its own. The complainant and the person who made the contested decision must be informed of the council of commissioner's decision and the reasons therefor.

The Act does not specify the grounds upon which a person dissatisfied with a decision may request its reconsideration, nor does it specify the reasons for which a decision may be overturned in whole or in part. However, one can imagine that a simple framework such as the following could be applied. In terms of whether a complaint should be considered, it would seem reasonable to consider any complaint that is made in good faith and within some reasonable time after the original decision was made. Complaints could be considered on the basis of jurisdictional, procedural or substantive grounds. Thus, a decision might be overturned because the body or person did not have jurisdiction to make it. Procedural grounds might involve a serious breach - as opposed to some technical fault - of established rules or procedures. Alternatively, even in the absence of any set procedures, it could be found that the process that was followed was manifestly unfair or unreasonable. Finally, a substantive ground might involve a violation of an existing law, regulation or policy. Alternatively, as in the case of a procedural complaint, it could be found that the substance of the decision was manifestly unfair or unreasonable.

Finally, it may be asked whether subjecting the decisions made by a school or centre governing board to this procedure is antithetical to the thrust of the "new regime" enacted by the *Act to Amend the Education Act and Various Legislative Provisions* [*Education Amendment Act*] (1997) (see chap. 7)? To do so appears to empower the school board to overrule a decision of the governing board. As no parameters are stipulated in the relevant sections of the Act as to the matters which may be appealed, this would also appear to include decisions about those matters over which authority has just been removed from the school board and assigned to the governing board.

Other Student Rights

Right of Youth to Protection

This section deals with child welfare or "youth protection" issues, principally with reference to the *YPA*.

A Societal Problem

In recent years, there has been an increase in the number of cases of child abuse. Whether this trend reflects an increase in the actual number of cases or a greater willingness to report is debatable. Child abuse is not confined to family violence or the very young. As Foster (1993, p. 5) states:

- child abuse is not an isolated problem peculiar to the family or equivalent unit, or to a particular social, cultural, religious or economic group in society;

- the potential victims of child abuse are all children and not merely infants and pre-adolescents; and
- the perpetrators of child abuse may be third parties responsible for a child's welfare or even strangers or children.

Québec, like other provinces, has adopted legislation dealing with child abuse. The *YPA* defines child abuse - a child being any person under 18 years of age (s. 1(c)) - as well as the duty to report different types of abuse. There is specific mention of educators, recognizing the key role of the school in detecting and dealing with suspected cases of abuse.

Child Abuse Defined
The *YPA* defines an abused child as one whose "security or development ... is considered to be in danger." The *YPA* (s. 38) lists eight situations that can constitute abuse. These can be summarized as follows:

- parental abandonment or neglect;
- mental or affective development threatened by lack of care;
- physical health threatened by lack of care, isolation or prolonged emotional rejection by parents;
- deprivation of material conditions of life;
- in the custody of someone whose lifestyle creates risk for the child;
- the child is forced to engage in work which is unacceptable for his or her age;
- sexual abuse or physical ill treatment;
- a child has serious behavioural problems which are not attended to nor corrected by parents.

The *YPA* (s. 38.1) then adds the three conditions in which the security or development of a child is also to be considered to be in danger: first, where a child runs away from home; second, where a child of school age does not attend school or is frequently absent without reason; and third, where a child's parents do not provide the child with care, maintenance and education or do not exercise stable supervision over him or her while the child has been in care (social service agency or foster home).

Duty to Report
The *YPA* distinguishes between the duty to report sexual and physical abuse and that to report other forms of abuse. These different reporting obligations are briefly summarized below.

Sexual & Physical Abuse
The *YPA* requires that *every person* (other than a lawyer in the exercise of his or her profession) who has reasonable cause to believe that a child is the victim of sexual or physical abuse report it to the Director of Youth Protection, without delay (s. 39).

Other Forms of Abuse
The duty to report other forms of abuse is more limited in its application. It is imposed on professionals (other than lawyers in the exercise of their profession) who provide care or assistance to children, employees in public health care or social service institutions, *teachers* and policemen who, in the course of their duties, have reasonable cause to believe that a child is the victim of such abuse. Again the report must be made to the Director of Youth Protection, without delay (s. 39).

Any other person (say, a parent volunteer in a school) who has reasonable cause to believe that a child is the victim of abuse (other than sexual or physical abuse) may report to the Director of Youth Protection (s. 39).

Other Provisions
The *YPA* (ss. 42-44) also includes some other provisions of relevance that must be noted. First, it

requires that adults must provide the necessary assistance to any child who wishes to inform the authorities of a situation that endangers his or her security or development, that of his brothers and sisters or that of any other child (s. 42).

Second, it seeks to protect those who do report child abuse by providing that no one can be prosecuted for reporting suspected abuse or aiding a child, if done in good faith, and no one else shall reveal his or her name without consent (ss. 43, 44).

Third, a failure to comply with the duty to report constitutes an offence punishable by a fine (s. 134).

Rights of Young Offenders

This section deals with "young offenders," that is, the rights and obligations of young persons in the criminal justice system.

Background

In Canada, criminal law comes under federal jurisdiction and the general statute governing "crime and punishment" is the *Criminal Code*. However since 1908, we have had separate legislation to deal with young offenders, namely the *Juvenile Delinquents Act*. This Act placed an emphasis on the treatment of delinquents who were considered in need of guidance and assistance as opposed to being considered criminals.

Forces of Change

In the 1960s and 70s public opinion shifted. As Roher (1997) puts it: "Over time, two significant changes in social attitudes occurred: (i) children were seen as autonomous individuals; and (ii) society became more concerned with protecting itself from a rising level of violent crime and holding criminals, whatever their age, responsible for their actions" (p. 51). In 1982, in response to these pressures for change and the provisions of the newly entrenched *Canadian Charter* (see chap. 2), the Federal Government enacted the *YOA*.

Basic Principles

The *YOA* spells out a number of principles that attempt to balance the need to deal with criminal activity by young persons and the special situation that applies to the latter because of their age. As Bala (1988) says, the *YOA* is not a "Kiddies' Criminal Code" (p. 13). The *YOA* is important to educators where student conduct is criminal in nature. Referring to the aforementioned principles, Roher (1997, p. 52) states:

> What this pot-pourri of principles means for educators is that the students under their care must be recognized as individuals, who may be held accountable for their actions, resulting in significant punishment for acts of violence .... This can mean that educators dealing with acts of violence take on the obligation to ensure that ... [a student's] rights are protected .... Educators can become partners with individuals in the justice system to ensure that students who face criminal charges for violent acts are dealt with in a manner which properly considers what would be the best solution for both the child and society.

Age Limitations

A youth, for the purposes of the *YOA*, is a person between the ages of 12 through 17 (s. 2(1)). However, in some cases, a young person over the age of 14 may be treated as an adult and have their case tried in adult court rather than youth court.

Criminal Investigation & Individual Rights

A youth charged with a criminal offence is entitled to a series of rights emanating from the *YOA* and the *Canadian Charter*. These rights include:

- the right to retain and instruct counsel;

- the right to be notified of one's rights before being questioned by a person in authority;
- the right to be heard and to participate in any processes which take place that lead to decisions which will affect him or her;
- the right to appeal dispositions involving custody, and to appeal any conviction;
- all applicable rights under the *Canadian Charter*, such as the right to be secure from unreasonable search and seizure.

Statements

Normally, school officials are free to question students in the course of investigating an incident of student misconduct. But, if there is a reason to believe that the event may constitute a criminal offence and the offender is between the ages of 12 and 17, the school official is bound by section 56 of the *YOA*. This section states that no statement made by a youth to a peace officer or a "person in authority" will be admissible against the youth unless:

- the statement was voluntary;
- it was clearly explained to the youth, in a fashion easily understood by him or her, that:
    - the youth is under no obligation to give a statement;
    - any statement given can be used against the youth;
    - the youth may consult with both counsel and a parent, relative or other appropriate adult; and
    - the statement is required to be made in the presence of the person consulted;
- the youth was given a reasonable opportunity to consult with counsel and the parent or adult authority;
- the youth was able to give a statement in the presence of the person consulted.

Notwithstanding the foregoing, a statement will be admissible if: (1) a youth chooses to waive the right to consult and to make the statement in the presence of the person consulted; (2) it was given spontaneously before the youth was advised of his or her rights.

For school officials, section 56 is important for two reasons. First, should the police visit a school and demand to question one of the students on a criminal matter, the student could select a teacher or school official as an "appropriate adult" to consult before making a statement. Second, if the person interrogating the student is a school official instead of a police officer, the school official may in certain circumstances be considered a "person in authority." Therefore, the statement of the student would be inadmissible unless he/she was advised of his or her rights and given an opportunity to consult with counsel and an appropriate adult other than the school official doing the questioning. The primary role of school officials in investigating criminal matters and when the police are involved is to provide care for their students during school hours, to safeguard the health and comfort of students as well as to maintain order.

If an educator should act as a counsellor, such a person under the Act would not be considered a person in authority. Therefore, any statement given by the student to a school official acting as a counsellor may be used against the student in court. In other words, the information obtained by a counsellor from a student cannot be considered as privileged information.

The *Canadian Charter* and the *YOA* only require that a youth be informed of his or her rights in light of possible disciplinary action when the latter could lead to criminal charges. Furthermore, it is the court that will determine if the school official was in fact acting as a "person in authority" before the student at the time of their statement. This test is subjective in so far as it attempts to answer the question: "How does the youth perceive the person receiving the statement" (Brown, 1991, p. 107).

Right to Counsel

Section 11 of the *YOA* deals with the youth's right to counsel (a right also found in the *Canadian*

Charter). It states that a youth has the right to retain and instruct counsel "without delay" at any stage in the proceedings against him or her, or before the court considers whether to place the youth in a "diversion" program rather than deal with the youth in court (Roher, 1997, p. 56). More importantly for educators is section 11(2) of the Act requiring that the arresting officer or the officer in charge inform the youth of his or her right to be represented by counsel and given the opportunity to obtain such representation. In other words, a school official who detains a youth for reasons which may lead to criminal proceedings should inform the person in question of his or her rights to counsel and also advise him or her that he or she may wait until counsel arrives before answering any questions.

Arrest & Detention

A school official is able to detain a student for an offence until the police arrive (by informing the student).

Similarly, a school official may arrest a student. However, it is important to note that a school official has no greater powers of arrest than does an ordinary citizen; and a citizen may only arrest a person without a warrant if he "finds the person committing an indictable offence" (*Criminal Code*, s. 494(1)(a)). Thus, a school official may arrest a student who is, for example, drug trafficking or in possession of a prohibited weapon. However, the school official must clearly inform the student that he or she has been arrested and is being detained until the police arrive; and the arrest must otherwise comply with the provisions of the *YOA* respecting the rights of youth.

Sentenced to School

Sentenced to School is the name of an Information Note published by the Canadian Education Association [CEA] (1990). It refers to the fact that Youth Court judges sometimes include attendance at school as part of a youth's sentence. According to a survey conducted by CEA, the school is often not informed of the conditions surrounding the "school sentence" and may not even know that it was ordered. Be that as it may, the *YOA* (s. 38.1) does allow the police to share information with a school where necessary to ensure the safety of the school community or to ensure compliance with bail conditions. However, such information must be kept separate from other information concerning the student and others should only have access to the information on a need to know basis.

In addition to communication problems, many school districts reported conflict between the sentencing provisions of the *YOA* and provincial education legislation, notably around issues of attendance, truancy and expulsion. As one district stated: "the courts have 'sentenced to school' people the school board had only a week before expelled" (see CEA, 1990, pp. 17-18). Similarly, what is the authority of the school board to refuse a student who is no longer of compulsory school age when sentenced to school by the courts? The answer to this and many other questions about the *YOA* are still pending and may well remain unsettled until either the courts provide answers or the Act is amended and clarified.

More Changes to Come

Violence in school is a pressing issue in many school districts in Canada and mirrors, to some extent, a like concern with violence in society at large. Violent crime, and violent youth crime in particular, attracts a good deal of attention, especially from critics who feel that the law is too soft on criminals. Just before this book went to press, the federal Minister of Justice tabled Bill C-68, *Youth Criminal Justice Act*, in the House of Commons. When this bill becomes law it will replace the *YOA*. According to the *Backgrounder* announcing the bill on the Internet (Department of Justice Canada, 1999). Bill C-68 is based on an accountability framework that promotes consequences for crime that are commensurate with the seriousness of the crime. More serious offenders could receive adult sentences, while less serous offenders could be dealt with outside the court process. The new Act to be also offers provinces flexibility in choosing options in certain areas to meet the needs and problems of each jurisdiction. This bill forms part of a wider "Youth Justice Strategy" announced by the Minister in May 1998 that includes prevention, alternatives to the courts and rehabilitation.

Right to Confidentiality & Privacy

The Québec *Charter* recognizes two rights of particular relevance to students in a school context: the right to confidentiality of personal information and the right to privacy. This latter right, for present purposes, may also be seen as embracing the right to freedom from unreasonable search and seizure that is also recognized in both the Québec *Charter* and the *Canadian Charter*.

Right to Confidentiality

Unlike the education legislation of some other provinces the Québec *Education Act* is silent on the matter of access to and confidentiality of student records. However, the Québec *Charter* declares that "everyone has a right to non-disclosure of confidential information" (s. 9) and the *Act Respecting Access to Documents Held by Public Bodies and the Protection of Personal Information* puts this declaration into affect. This latter statute applies to schools boards and schools as they are "public bodies" within the meaning of the Act. Thus, while the Act makes no specific reference to student records, by implication, it provides for the confidentiality of student records, for access to such records by students (if of full age) and parents and for the correction of records which contain erroneous information (ss. 1, 3, 6, 53-58, 83).

Freedom from Unreasonable Search

As noted above, both the Québec *Charter* (s. 24.1) and the *Canadian Charter* (s. 8) recognize the right of persons to be free from unreasonable search and seizure. Provisions such as these are seen to create a right to privacy; a right to be left alone (*Hunter* v. *Southam*, 1984). But this right, like all others, is not absolute.

Personal Searches

What then, it may be asked, is the scope of a student's right to privacy while under the jurisdiction of the school if, for example, he or she is suspected of being in possession of substances or articles in contravention of school rules.

This question was addressed by the Supreme Court of Canada in the recent case of *R.* v. *M.(M.R.)* (1998), in which a high school vice-principal searched a student suspected of being in possession of drugs at a school function. The Court acknowledged that students are entitled to an expectation of privacy, "at least with respect to their body." However, while at school, students' expectations are certainly less than they would be in other circumstances since they (p. 278):

> [K]now that their teachers and other school authorities are responsible for providing a safe school environment and maintaining order and discipline in the school. They must know that this may sometimes require searches of students and their personal effects and the seizure of prohibited items. It would not be reasonable for a student to expect to be free from such searches. A student's reasonable expectation of privacy in the school environment is therefore significantly diminished.

The Court further observed (p. 279):

> Without an orderly environment learning will be difficult if not impossible. In recent years, problems which threaten the safety of students and the fundamentally important task of teaching have increased in their numbers and gravity. The possession of illicit drugs and dangerous weapons in the schools has increased to the extent that they challenge the ability of school officials to fulfil their responsibility to maintain a safe and orderly environment. Current conditions make it necessary to provide teaches and school administrators with the flexibility to deal with discipline problems in schools. They must be able to act quickly and effectively to ensure the safety of students and to prevent serious violations of school rules.

The Court then formulated some general principles applicable to the right of school officials to search students (p. 284):

> (1) A [search] warrant is not essential in order to conduct a search of a student by a school authority.

(2) The school authority must have reasonable grounds to believe that there has been a breach of school regulations or discipline and that a search of a student would reveal evidence of that breach.

(3) School authorities will be in the best position to assess information given to them and relate it to the situation existing in their school. Courts should recognize the preferred position of school authorities to determine if reasonable grounds existed for the search.

(4) The following may constitute reasonable grounds in this context: information received from one student is considered to be credible; information received from more than one student; a teacher's or principal's own observations, or any combination of these pieces of information which the relevant authority considers to be credible. The compelling nature of the information and the credibility of these other sources must be assessed by the school authority in the context of the circumstances existing at the particular school.

Moreover, the Court provided a summary of the consideration pertinent to determining whether a search, though warranted in the circumstances, is reasonable (p. 286):

(1) The first step is to determine whether it can be inferred from the provisions of the relevant *Education Act* that the teachers and principals are authorized to conduct searches of their students in the appropriate circumstances. In the school environment such a statutory authority would be reasonable.

(2) The search itself must be carried out in a reasonable manner. It should be conducted in a sensitive manner and be minimally intrusive.

(3) In order to determine whether a search was reasonable, all the surrounding circumstances will have to be considered.

These principles, which modify the standards that normally govern searches without a warrant, apply to school authorities provided they are not acting as agents of the police at the time (pp. 286-287). However, the mere presence of a police officer at the time a search is conducted by a school official is not, of itself, sufficient to compel the conclusion that the police officer is in fact the authority conducting the search and that the school official is acting as an agent (p. 288).

Locker Searches
It should also be noted that school lockers create an expectation of privacy amongst students. However, these lockers, like students' persons, are not immune from warrantless searches by school officials if the latter have reasonable grounds, as defined above, to conduct such a search.

Dragnet Searches
These searches involve searching a large group of students or lockers in order to discover one or two students who are violating school rules. These searches may be justified in highly unusual circumstances, as where there is reasonable cause to believe that the safety of students is threatened, but not where, for example, one is merely trying to identify the perpetrator of a property offence.

Random searches of students' persons, "just to keep them honest," cannot be justified; such searches of students' lockers, provided they are pursuant to a well publicized school policy, may be justified.

Rights with Respect to Medical Issues

It is increasingly common to find amongst the student population of schools youth who require medication or other health-related services during the school day. This situation raises a number of issues relevant to the rights of students (and, conversely to the obligations of school staff – see chap. 10) which cannot be explored fully here. (For an exploration of these issues see Foster, 1996.) Nevertheless, mention should be made of two matters.

Age of Consent to Medical Treatment
In Québec minors who have attained the age of fourteen years are deemed to be competent to consent to medical treatment (*Civil Code of Quebec*, art. 14); conversely, minors who have not attained that

age are deemed incompetent to consent to medical treatment (art. 18). Thus, as a general rule, parental consent is neither a necessary nor a sufficient condition to the medical treatment of minors over fourteen years, but it is a necessary and sufficient condition to the medical treatment of minors below that age.

The law does not prescribe the form that a valid consent must take; it may be communicated orally or in writing or, indeed, may be inferred from conduct and other circumstances. However, where a student's or parent's consent is needed it is always wise for it to be provided in writing to avoid the risk of subsequent conflicts over to what, in fact, consent was given.

In addition to the requirement that a consent be given by the person (student or parent) who is legally competent to provide it, a consent must meet two further conditions. First, it must be voluntarily given, that is it must be free of coercion and undue influence. Second, it must be informed. An informed consent exists when the person consenting understands the nature and the consequences of the activities to be undertaken by the student or in which the student is to be involved, including any risks inherent in the undertakings or activities which would not be obvious to the student.

Moreover, coupled with the right to consent to medical treatment is the right to privacy and confidentiality with respect to medical matters; a right that exists even as against the minor's parents.

Emergency Medical Treatment

In Québec, every one whose life is in danger is entitled to assistance. This right is conferred by the Québec *Charter* (art. 2):

Québec Charter of Rights and Freedoms

2. Every human being whose life is in peril has a right to assistance.

Every person must come to the aid of anyone whose life is in peril, either personally or calling for aid, by giving him the necessary and immediate physical assistance, unless it involves danger to himself or a third person, or he has another valid reason.

This obligation is owed only to persons whose lives are in peril. However, the law also imposes on persons in special relationships to others (such as teachers with respect to students) a duty to render assistance whatever the nature or severity of the emergency with which they are confronted. This is true whether the emergency takes the form of:

- a "true accident" (e.g. a broken limb in a gym class) in which the nature of the accident, the identity of the victim and the nature and scope of the assistance which is required is not known to school personnel ahead of time; or

- a "foreseen emergency" (e.g. the onslaught of an allergy) in which school personnel have prior knowledge of the identity of the potential victim, the nature of the event which will trigger the emergency and the specific form of assistance required; the only unknown being whether the event will take place which will trigger the need for that assistance.

Members of the school staff who render assistance to others in an emergency must conduct themselves in a competent manner (see chap. 10); whether they have so conducted themselves will be determined in light of all of the circumstances of a particular incident. Teachers and others with no medical or para-medical training will not be expected to react as would a person with such training. However, if a teacher is aware of the appropriate response to a particular emergency (e.g. to the onslaught of an allergy in a student) he or she must act in an appropriate manner.

CHAPTER 4
STUDENTS WITH SPECIAL NEEDS

Introduction

The education of students with special needs has long been a major issue on the Québec policy agenda.* The question of placement occupies a central place in this debate. Parents of children with disabilities have a right to expect that their children will be treated with dignity and receive equal educational opportunities. Their lives depend as much on education as do those of any other students. However, a simple assertion of a basic right does not mean that the provision of such opportunities is simple. If educators are expected to provide appropriate services to children with a wide range of abilities and aptitudes, then they are entitled to expect appropriate support. In a climate of scarce resources, this means making better use of what we do have and developing new paradigms for service delivery. This challenge of dealing with diversity of ability and aptitude is analogous to dealing with the diversity of plurality, the subject of chapter 14.

Note. This chapter does not apply to adult students. There are no specific rights in Québec education law for adult students with special needs.

As in other jurisdictions, government policy on the education of students with special needs has evolved from one whose focus was access to the education system to one focusing on placement and service delivery (for more details see *Historical Roots*, chap. 4). In this chapter, we will look briefly at the evolution of provincial government policy respecting the education of students with special needs. This will be followed by a discussion of the legislative action taken by the government to transform these policy goals into legal rights and obligations. We will reflect on the current state of this policy issue through recent human rights cases. Finally, we will examine a recent policy statement of the MEQ.

Background

The subject of a comprehensive section of the Parent Commission report (1964, Vol. II, ch. 10), the development of special education policy received considerable impetus from the early provincial negotiations with teachers. The decreed agreement which was promulgated in 1972 created the Provincial Committee for Handicapped Children which became known as the COPEX Committee after its original French name - Comité provincial de l'enfance exceptionnnelle (inadaptée). Its influential report (COPEX, 1976) examined the entire spectrum of the provision, administration and financing of special education services and made over sixty specific recommendations. Together with various opinion papers of the Superior Council, it formed the basis for the first major statement of government policy on special education.

In 1979 the MEQ issued a major policy paper, one chapter of which was devoted to special education. The three major themes enunciated therein were grounded in the following statement of principle (MEQ, 1979a): "This policy is based on the right of the child with difficulties to receive from the public school a quality education appropriate to his or her specific needs in the most normal context possible" (p. 64). The chapter was expanded upon in a complementary policy paper (MEQ,

1979b). Together, these policy papers guided the development of special education policy into the 1990s and in some ways continue to serve as the policy basis of the current system.

Disability Categories Defined

The disability categories used by the MEQ are shown in Figure 4.1.

Categories & Labelling

As can be seen below in Figure 4.1, the MEQ divides students with special needs into two clusters: students with difficulties and those with handicaps. The former regroups students with mild problems (11.16% of the total student population - relatively high prevalence*). The latter regroups students with more serious problems (1.26% of the total student population)(MEQ, 1999). Although these clusters are consistent with the categories described in the literature, they were formally introduced into the Québec system to differentiate levels of funding for students with special needs.

* *Note*. Prevalence refers to the number of cases of a disability in a given population, usually reported as a percentage of the total population.

Categorization or labelling of students is controversial, as it may lead to stigmatization and to other problems such as placement by "label" and not by individual needs, or teaching to the child's "label" and not to his or her strengths and weaknesses. Thus, a distinction must be made between categorization for administrative and funding purposes and the use of labels for placement and the provision of services. The CSE (1985) noted that while done in good faith, with the intention of providing increased services, the process of categorization may lead to further marginalization of these students and end up compromising the strategies put into place to provide them with the best education possible.

	Disability	
	Mild	Severe

High
 	
P
r
e
v
a
l
e
n
c
e
 	
Low
	A. Students with Difficulties
	1. Learning Difficulties: Mild; Severe
	2. Behavioural Problems:
	      Behavioural Difficulties;
	      Severe Behavioural Difficulties
	      Linked to Psychosocial Disturbances
	3. Mild Mental Handicaps
		B. Handicaps
		1. Mental Handicaps:
		      Moderate to Severe; Profound
		2. Physical Handicaps:
		      Mild; Severe Motor; Organic
		3. Sensory Handicaps:
		      Visual; Hearing
		4. Severe Developmental Disorders:
		      Congenital Aphasia; Autism;
		      Psychopathological Disorders
		5. Multiple Handicaps

FIGURE 4.1
MEQ Categories of Disability

Current Policy: Educational Success for All

As alluded to in the introduction, provincial policy regarding the education of students with special needs has a long history (see *Historical Roots*, chap. 4), the latest policy paper being *Educational Success for All* (MEQ, 1992b), issued as a special education policy update. This statement affirmed the government's commitment to quality education for all students in the most normal setting possible and identified five general orientations.

The Minister created a special committee to provide advice on the implementation of the five broad strategies suggested by the consultation. These strategies included: the development of educational resources to help students with handicaps learn and become integrated into society; support for organizational measures that promote an equitable and more effective means of taking individual differences into account; support for the ongoing evaluation of how the services provided effect the learning and integration into society of students with handicaps or difficulties; the promotion of respectful attitudes towards students with handicaps or difficulties; and lastly, the provision of guidance and support for the professional development of educators that will prepare them to serve a varied clientele.

Policy Goals & Legislative Action

Policy papers are of interest to practitioners, researchers and others because they express the goals of government in a given domain. However, although they may motivate and encourage individuals and institutions to behave in ways consistent with the orientations of the policy statement, they do not possess the capacity to enforce the principles enunciated therein. When a government wishes to seek compliance with its policy goals, it resorts to some form of legislative action.

As we saw in the discussion on educational governance (see chap. 2), legislative action takes the form of statutes, regulations and other forms of delegated legislation. We have also seen examples of such legislative action in the discussion of the rights of children and students (see chap. 3), and we will see others in the discussion of rights in regard to religion and language (chap. 12 & 13).

The rights of students with special needs are included in various legislative instruments, notably, the *Education Act* and the *Basic Regulations*. These legal rights do not ensure that these students will be provided with all the services which they might desire or even require. However, they do set forth some basic entitlements and, as we will see below, provide the basis for court action if these rights are not respected.

Legislative action is usually based on policy goals that have been previously identified as leading to outcomes that are desired by a given society. We will analyse the rights of students with disabilities in Québec in relation to ten principal policy goals, which have been adapted from an earlier study of special education policy in Québec (Smith, 1989, 1992).*

* Note. The rights discussed in this section are additional rights to those provided to any student, as summarized and discussed in chap. 3.

Equality Rights

It should be noted that these rights bring into play the equality provisions of the Québec *Charter*. As we saw in chapter 2, the protection of equality rights in education is limited to the scope of education rights provided for by law. Once an education right is provided it must be provided without discrimination, for example, on the basis of a disability. A clear and expansive provision of education rights forms a solid basis for an equality rights argument before a human rights tribunal. However, as we will see in a later section of this chapter (see discussion of human rights cases), an ambiguous or narrow expression of education rights forms a very shaky basis for equality.

Right to Education

All students with special needs shall be guaranteed the right to attend school.

The *Education Act* guarantees the right to education for all Québec school-age students; there are no exceptions for students with disabilities. This means that Quebec has a policy of "universal access" to schools. As discussed previously (see chap. 3), the Act allows school boards to expel students for just and sufficient cause. Expulsion exceptions can have a significant impact on students with special needs, if their right to enter the front door of the school is circumvented by the right of the school board to usher them out the back door because, for example, of inappropriate behaviour which is related to their disability. There is nothing in the Act that tempers the board's discretion regarding expulsion in relation to disability-related causes.

The Act also clarifies previously ambiguous wording relating to the board's right to discharge its responsibilities by concluding agreements with other boards and private schools. Parents do not have any right to veto such a decision; similarly, they can request, but cannot require, that such an agreement be concluded. Once again, these provisions are especially important to students with special needs because placement is typically a much more crucial issue for them (as further discussed below).

Finally, as dealt with in chapter 13, Bill 101 extends eligibility for English instruction to otherwise non-qualified children having serious learning problems, as well as to their brothers and sisters. Although this measure is often helpful in meeting the needs of students with learning problems, the requirements of the regulation dealing with identification and assessment are such that there can be long delays before the exemption is granted.

Extended Schooling

Handicapped students shall benefit from 4 year old kindergarten and schooling beyond the normal school leaving age.

The expression "extended schooling" refers to providing additional years of schooling for students with special needs. Québec provides for extended schooling at the preschool (4 year old kindergarten) and high school leaving levels. The *Basic Regulation* (El Reg, s. 33) states that only handicapped students as defined in the regulation are eligible for 4-year old kindergarten, which shall only be offered in schools and according to conditions determined by the Minister.

Of all the definitions of a handicapped student found in various documents, this one has the most restrictive wording, suggesting that this service is only for severe cases. Since the definition is only used for admission to 4 year old kindergarten, it appears that some students would be excluded from this additional year of schooling but would become eligible for special services upon entering 5 year old kindergarten.

The provisions of the Act regarding education beyond normal school leaving age simply extend the right to education to 21 years for a student who is handicapped in the meaning of the *Act to Secure the Handicapped in the Exercise of their Rights*. This Act provides the following definition (s. 1(g)):

Act to Secure the Handicapped in the Exercise of Their Rights

"handicapped person," or "the handicapped" in the plural, means a person limited in the performance of normal activities who is suffering, significantly and permanently, from a physical or mental deficiency, or who regularly uses a prosthesis or an orthopedic device or any other means of palliating his handicap.

Accessibility of Facilities

New schools shall provide barrier-free access and barriers in existing buildings shall progressively be eliminated.

For certain handicapped persons, the right to education becomes moot, if school facilities are not accessible. While accessibility includes the right to school transportation to "get to the school house door," it usually focuses on the right to get "through the school house door" and into all necessary facilities. The movement to normalize the environment for handicapped persons, which is closely associated with the mainstreaming movement discussed below, requires the physical adaptation of transportation and educational facilities for the handicapped.

However, the question of accessibility raises the issue of reasonable limits. In Québec, for example, there are approximately 4 000 public schools; how many should be barrier-free? What level of adaptation is required within school buildings so that programmes, not merely buildings, are accessible to the handicapped?

School Transportation

In Québec, although all school boards provide free transportation to students, there is no right to such services, let alone the right to adapted transportation for students with disabilities. If the school board decides to provide service then it must be free but if it decides not to, for example if grants were reduced and it felt it could no longer afford to, then the school board could simply eliminate the service.

Barrier-Free Access

In terms of facilities, all new construction and renovations in Québec are subject to the *National Building Code of Canada, 1990* (National Research Council of Canada, 1990) which provides for barrier-free access for persons with physical or sensorial disabilities. However, school buildings built before 1976, the year in which provincial regulations first required similar compliance, remain unaffected as regulations foreseen by the legislation have never been adopted.

Improvements to existing buildings are left to administrative discretion and are dependent on available funds. This does not mean that no progress towards the removal of architectural barriers has been made. However, where such access is denied, the absence of any statutory guarantees limits the basis of any claim by parents to general equality rights, such as those found in the Québec *Charter*.

Availability of Services

Various special services shall be decentralized to a regional level.

The availability of services determines the extent to which the right to these services becomes a reality. It is little consolation to the parent of a handicapped child to have a right to specialized services, if the only facility available is several hundred kilometres from home.

The question of availability also raises the issue of reasonable limits. In other words, should the State ensure that highly specialized services are offered in every school, in every school district, or within a given geographic area? It is generally assumed that some limits are reasonable but there is less consensus as to the form these limits should take.

Québec special education policy includes the goal of regional centres. The *Education Act* authorizes the Minister to establish a school as a specialized regional or provincial centre, under the jurisdiction of one or more school boards, pursuant to an agreement with each of the school boards concerned (s. 468). Several specialized schools do exist in the province, many of which are operated in collaboration with local social affairs agencies. However, the absence of any legal provision beyond the authority of the Minister to create them means that there is no legal entitlement to such centres.

Prevention

The prevention of learning problems shall be addressed by early identification of children with learning problems and compensatory education programmes in disadvantaged areas.

This goal illustrates the close relationship between special and compensatory education. For example, in the funding rules, the normalized grant for special education takes into account an index of disadvantage for each school board.

In Québec, entitlement to 4 year old kindergarten for students from disadvantaged areas remains the only legislated decision concerning prevention. The provisions governing this right are similar to those described above for 4 year old handicapped students. The *Basic Regulation* (El Reg, s. 33) states that students living in economically disadvantaged areas as defined in the regulation are eligible for 4 year old kindergarten, which shall only be offered in schools and according to conditions determined by the Minister.

Assessment

Improved assessment procedures shall be provided, beginning with more suitable definitions of disability categories and the introduction of an individualized educational plan [IEP] for students with special needs.

Assessment usually involves the right to the determination of whether or not a student has a disability and if so, a systematic investigation of his or her educational needs. Assessment policy has generally accorded a great deal of attention to the elimination of discrimination or bias, especially by the use of I.Q. tests normed on the majority population. The mandatory use of an IEP is usually seen as a way of ensuring that educational services meet the needs of individual students.

Both specific components of this goal (definitions and IEP) have been addressed by the *Education Act* and various regulations but rights to assessment per se are all but non-existent.

Definitions

The Act includes an expression to denote two groups of students with special needs: handicapped students and students with social maladjustments or learning disabilities [students with difficulties] (see Figure 4.1 at the beginning of this chapter).*

* *Note*. Although the term learning disabilities is used in the English version of the Act, the term learning difficulties would be a more accurate translation of the French "en difficulté d'adaptation ou d'apprentissage."

The distinction between students with problems and those designated handicapped can be traced to changes in the provincial system for funding special education, aimed at limiting grants for students with mild handicaps (Donahue & Smith, 1986). The specific definitions for the different categories of students with special needs are now contained in an administrative document, *Interpretation of the Definitions Used to Classify Students with Handicaps or Adjustment Difficulties* (MEQ, Direction de la coordination des réseaux, 1992).

Until recently, these definitions were included in the annual MEQ Directives (*Instructions*) and thus had the force of law. The interpretation document appears to exist only as a "working document" in English and does not appear to have the same legal status as the Directives. The specific definitions of disability categories are still found in the teachers' *Ententes* (e.g. *PAPT Entente: 1995-98*, App. XXII). While the latter create rights and obligations for teachers and school boards, they do not do the same for students and parents. Thus the legal status of the MEQ definitions is unclear from a rights perspective. School boards must use these definitions for administrative purposes and are obliged to indicate on the student's registration form, which is transmitted to the MEQ, his or her disability category and placement.

Assessing Special Needs

As discussed below (Integration), the *Education Act* (s. 235) requires each school board to adopt a policy on special education services which must include provisions dealing with procedures for evaluating students with special needs; the Act further stipulates that students and parents must be involved in this process (see Participation below). However, neither the Act nor the regulations set forth any entitlement to assessment. The only references as to what triggers an assessment are found in the teachers' *Ententes*. Specifically, a teacher who believes a student has special needs shall refer such student for an assessment via a school level *ad hoc* committee (*PAPT Entente: 1995-1998*, ss. 8.9-04 - 8.9-05).

A subsidiary assessment issue is consent - does the law require student/parental consent before a school board or school can assess a student's special needs.* Québec education legislation is silent on consent. Although many school boards do not assess students without parental consent they do so by virtue of local policy, not provincial law.

Note. The types of assessment contemplated here are those which go beyond traditional testing and evaluation of student achievement, such as intelligence and personality testing and psycho-social evaluation. However, they do not include medical examinations which are assumed to require consent according to health services legislation.

The IEP

The *Education Act* provides for a mandatory IEP (s. 96.14) for all students with special needs. The school principal, with the assistance of the parents, the student and the staff, is legally responsible for the preparation, implementation and periodic evaluation of an IEP for every student with special needs in his or her school. There is no legal requirement for parents to "sign off" on an IEP.

A previous requirement, that the IEP "comply with the norms prescribed by by-law of the school board," has been replaced with a new provision that requires that the IEP "be consistent with a school board's policy on the organization of services" for students with special needs. More importantly, there is now a provision which requires that the IEP must be "in keeping with the ability and needs of the student as evaluated by the school board before the student's placement and enrolment at the school."* This new provision must be read in conjunction with the amendment of the section of the Act dealing with the board's policy on integration (see Integration below).

Note. Placement usually denotes a physical setting, for example the regular class or an enclosed special education class, etc. The French text of this section of the Act speaks of "classement," which would normally refer to a classification in a disability category.

Integration

Special needs students shall be integrated into the "most normal setting possible."

Integration is probably the most widely debated special education policy issue. Government policy must arbitrate between the opposing views of integration advocates, on the one hand, and those who feel that wholesale mainstreaming is detrimental to the education of regular students on the other. A recent brief by the CSE (1996b) on the integration of students with special needs concluded that it is necessary to have a wide range of educational options available for these students and that every school must attempt to find the best educational programs for each student based on his or her disabilities and needs. They stated that regular class placement should be seen as a means of meeting an individual student's academic needs, not as an end in itself and that the integration of students with special needs in regular classes should not be at the cost of the quality of education for all students (see discussion below on draft special education policy statement).

There is no integration requirement in Québec education law; likewise, there is no right to special placement inside or outside the school board. There is no legal requirement to obtain parental consent for any educational placement.*

Note. Such placements would not include any placement in an institution or other setting deemed to constitute placement in care according to health and social services legislation where consent would be required.

From By-Law to Policy

In Québec, section 235 of the *Education Act* has just been amended to require school boards to adopt, after consultation with the special education advisory committee, a policy (as opposed to a by-law) concerning the organization of educational services for students with special needs. A by-law has certain procedural requirements that do not apply to ordinary resolutions. The adoption of a by-law requires the school board to give a 30 day notice of the object of the by-law and send a draft copy to each governing board and to the parents' committee (s. 392). By-laws must be recorded in a registry kept at the school board office (s. 396). Furthermore, a copy of the by-law must be sent to each governing board and to the parents' committee (s. 395), and be posted within certain time limits in each school and centre and published in at least one newspaper that is in circulation in school board territory (ss. 397-398). Such procedures are not required for ordinary resolutions. A by-law is thus more likely to be in wider circulation and its purpose and content known by a wider audience.

However, regardless of form, the board is still given broad discretionary powers to determine its special education policy, in this case, on mainstreaming.

Purpose & Scope

The amended section (s. 235) has replaced the wording describing the aim of this policy - "in order to facilitate their learning and social integration" with the following:

Education Act

235. Every school board shall adopt, after consultation with the advisory committee on services for handicapped students and students with social maladjustments or learning disabilities, a policy concerning the organization of educational services for such students to ensure the harmonious integration of each such student into a regular class or group and into school activities if it has been established on the basis of the evaluation of the student's abilities and needs that such integration would facilitate the student's learning and social integration and would not impose an excessive constraint or significantly undermine the rights of the other students....

The Act still states that the policy shall deal with:

- procedures for evaluating students;
- methods for integrating these students (including support services required for their integration, and, if need be, the weighting of class size norms);
- terms and conditions for segregating those students in special classes or schools;
- methods for preparing and evaluating IEPs.

However, a note has been added to specify that placement in a segregated special school does not constitute the creation of a school with a "specific project" requiring ministerial approval (see discussion of school choice in chap. 3).

Significance of the Changes

There are at least four major points to be noted regarding these changes. First, the change from a by-law to a policy downgrades the formality of the board's statement, as the adoption of a by-law is subject to various procedural rules that are not applicable to ordinary resolutions. Second, the requirement of a school board assessment prior to classification in a category and enrolment in a school seems to place these children in limbo until this process is completed. Furthermore, it does not speak to situations where an assessment is required for students already enrolled in a school. Third, integration is now subject to several conditions. It is meant to be harmonious and is subject to the same prior evaluation referred to above that must demonstrate that integration will both facilitate the student's learning and social integration and will not impose an excessive constraint or significantly undermine the rights of other students. Last, although a school board wishing to create a school for advanced students must seek ministerial permission, it is not required do so if it wants to open a segregated school for students with disabilities.

These changes could have a significant impact on services for students with special needs. It appears that the "burden of proof" respecting integration is now being reversed. In the past, it was assumed that integration was the "normal" state of affairs and the school board had the burden to prove that integration was not workable in a given case. Now, segregation seems to be presumed the "normal" state of affairs, and the parent has the burden to prove not only that integration is good for the individual child but is also not injurious to others - a claim that is frequently made by those opposed to the integration of students with special needs. There may also be a tendency to create more segregated schools and classes for those whose successful integration requires significant additional support services.

Despite the prominence of integration as a major theme of government policy, there is no other specific mention of integration in the Act, nor is it mentioned in any of the regulations or directives.

Appropriate Education

A continuum of services, including educational, remedial and rehabilitative measures, which are appropriate to the needs of each student with special needs, shall be provided.

All of the preceding themes, from access to placement, are intended to support the ultimate goal of the policy - to provide the student with appropriate educational services. As expected, there is considerable divergence of opinion as to what constitutes "appropriate" education, both in general and for a particular child. It is not surprising, therefore, that legislators have been reluctant to spell out such rights in law or that the courts have been cautious in directing school boards in such matters.

According to the *Education Act* (s. 224), every school board must establish a program for each student service and each special education service contemplated by the *Basic Regulations*. These include psychological, psychoeducational, speech therapy, health and social services, instructional services in the home or hospital (for students unable to attend school) and remedial teaching services for students with learning difficulties. The right to appropriate education is also supported by the obligation to establish an IEP for each student with special needs (see Assessment above).

Adaptation of Services

In addition, every school board is required, subject to the *Basic Regulations*, to adapt the educational services provided to students with disabilities, according to their needs. However, the recent amendment of the *Education Act* now stipulates that these needs are determined by the evaluation referred to in section 235 (see Integration above). By this provision, Québec students are now guaranteed access to free and appropriate education.

The particular needs of students can also be met by provisions which allow for exceptions to general rules. The Minister has the general authority to grant exemptions with respect to any provision of the *Basic Regulations* for humanitarian reasons or to avoid a serious prejudice to a student (Ed Act, s. 460; El Reg, s. 56; Sec Reg, s. 78). In addition, a school board may, according to conditions determined by the Minister, exempt certain categories of students from the time prescribed by the student timetable for 4 year old kindergarten or from taking one or more compulsory subjects listed in the regulations (El Reg, s. 55; Sec Reg, s. 77).

Consultation

Parents shall have the right to be consulted on the means for implementing integration.

Provision for transparency in decision making and the consultation of various groups are important elements in the development of any social policy. In the context of special education, the involvement of parents is critical to the success of the efforts of educational professionals on behalf of the child.

The *Education Act* (ss. 185-187) provides for a board level advisory committee on services for students with special needs, composed of representatives of: the parents of such students; teachers and other personnel who work with these students; designated bodies which provide services to these students; and one school principal. The committee advises the board on both the standards for the organization of educational services and the allocation of financial resources to these students.

The committee may also advise the school board on the implementation of an individual student's IEP. It must be consulted before the board adopts the special education policy provided for in the Act (see Integration above) but there is no other specific matter on which the board is obliged to consult the committee. This committee does provide a forum for parents to insist on public debate of board policy before it is adopted but does not have any powers to require any particular action. Finally, according to the recent amendment of the Act, a representative of this committee sits on the board level parent committee (s. 189). The parents' committee has been given a new advisory function which includes informing the school board of the needs of parents of students with special needs identified by the aforementioned representative.

Participation

Parents shall have the right to be associated with the assessment and placement of their child.

Participation constitutes an extension of parental involvement in a consultative role and potentially involves two aspects: involvement in decision making and some form of "due process." The first involves the collaboration of the parents and the professionals, while the second provides for some form of redress if the parents believe that their child's rights have not been respected.

The only specific parental rights with regard to assessment or placement provided for by the Act or the regulations are:

- the right to participate in the development of their child's IEP; subsequently, there is no right to participate in the implementation and evaluation of the plan, merely to receive periodic information on these matters (s. 96.14);
- the right to participate in the evaluation of their child (s. 235);
- in addition to the reporting procedures provided for regular students, parents of a student with special needs are entitled to receive information each month about their child's progress.

As noted above, parental consent to assessment or placement is not required.

Recent Court Cases

As alluded to above, the importance of legal rights, as opposed to moral rights, is that they can be enforced by some means of legal redress. There have been recent cases in Québec and Ontario where parents have had to go to court in order to try and secure what they believed their children were entitled to under respective provincial education and human rights legislation. The use of the latter reflects the view that the battle for the rights of students with disabilities is as much a battle for equality rights as it is a battle for education rights.

Québec: St. Jean-sur-Richelieu & Chaveau Cases

In Québec, like other jurisdictions, the courts have been reluctant, subject to specific statutory direction, to interfere with school board discretion respecting the placement of students with disabilities. Two cases have challenged this judicial status quo: *Québec (Commission des droits de la personne) and Commission scolaire Saint-Jean-sur-Richelieu* (1991) [*St-Jean*] and *Québec (Commission des droits de la personne) and Commission scolaire régionale Chauveau* (1993) [*Chauveau*]. The complaint in each case was upheld by the Québec Human Rights Tribunal and both of these decisions were appealed. The Court of Appeal affirmed the first decision but reversed the second. The Commission des droits de la personne et des droits de la jeunesse [Human Rights Commission] sought leave to appeal the latter to the Supreme Court of Canada but this request was denied.

Human Rights Tribunal Rulings

In *Saint-Jean*, the parents of David Marcil contested the school board's refusal to integrate their son, a nine year old boy with autistic characteristics and psycho-motor and communication difficulties.

The Québec Human Rights Tribunal, per Rivet, J., recognized that integration should be approached on the basis of the child's individual development but also noted that neither law nor provincial policy required integration in every case. She held that the board's refusal to provide the promised partial integration was discriminatory because the decision was based strictly on David's handicap and not on a global evaluation of his strengths and weaknesses and that an integration aide was a means to palliate his handicap, in the meaning of the Québec *Charter*. The Tribunal ordered the board to integrate David, at least on a part-time basis and awarded both material and moral damages.

In *Chauveau*, Danny Rouette, a secondary student with William's syndrome, was refused an integrated placement. In a lengthy decision, Rivet, J., emphasized that decisions about placement and programs should be based on the needs of students, not on preconceived notions based on categories of disability or pre-existing modes of service delivery. While noting that special classes were not per se discriminatory, she emphasized that the regular class constituted the equality norm, against which all decisions should be judged. The Tribunal agreed that Danny had been discriminated against and denied his right to education with appropriate support services. Accordingly, the board was ordered to integrate Danny into a regular class and to pay material and moral damages. The Tribunal further held that the board's general mode of service delivery constituted systemic discrimination and ordered the board to devise and implement an affirmative action program within the next five months.

Court of Appeal Decisions

In *Saint-Jean*, the Court of Appeal held that integration may be a goal of MEQ policy but it is not a legal norm. Stressing the requirement to adapt services, it was held, however, that a board which offered no measure of integration would not be respecting the law. On the question of discrimination, the adaptation of services - be they in regular or segregated settings as set forth in the Cascade model,* was retained as the equality norm. However, it was held that the board did not make reasonable accommodation for David and its actions were therefore judged to be discriminatory.

*Note. The Cascade model refers to a hierarchical series of placements for students with special needs from the most to the least restrictive environment. It is usually shown diagrammatically as an inverted pyramid. Although still widely accepted, it is increasingly criticized as being detrimental to the policy of integration it was supposed to foster.

In *Chauveau*, the Court of Appeal dealt more with the policies and practices of the board, namely, were they discriminatory in general or toward Danny in particular. It was held that the board's offer to place Danny in an occupational class, a life and work skills program with an individualized learning plan was reasonable and non-discriminatory. It was also held that it was proper to base placement decisions in part on his intellectual functioning as it related to his ability to meet the academic standards of the regular program. The claim of systemic discrimination was summarily rejected, but the court noted the problems associated with integration at the secondary level throughout Québec.

Implications

The rulings of the Human Rights Tribunal have been rightly viewed as precedent setting cases, in that they held that a regular class placement constituted the equality norm and that the denial of such placement must be justified in each case. In the wake of the Court of Appeal decisions, what placement rights do students with disabilities really have?

The Court of Appeal seems to have interpreted the equal right to education restrictively, stating that the equality rights provided for in the Québec *Charter* are only modalities in securing those education rights explicitly set forth in law. The Court thus distinguished this type of equality from that found in the *Canadian Charter*, "which recognizes the right to equality in general." This seems to imply that the Québec *Charter* can only be used to challenge the application of an education right found in law. In other words, if the right to regular class placement exists in law, then this right must be provided in accordance with the equality provisions of the Québec *Charter*; however, if regular class placement is not provided for in law, then you cannot claim such a right on the basis of the Québec *Charter*.

The Court of Appeal decisions conclude that the obligation in the *Education Act* to adapt educational services can be met in both regular and segregated settings, contrasting sharply with the interpretation that the adaptation provision of the Act implies accommodation in regular settings, as opposed to placement in segregated settings. Finally, the decisions imply that the courts will apply a different standard at the secondary level, where academic prerequisites seem to be accepted as a *bona fide* requirement for admission to the regular stream.

The foregoing implies that if the denial of regular class placement constitutes, at least in certain cases, discrimination, as generally understood in Canadian law, then the only recourse which remains is a challenge based on the *Canadian Charter*. If the provisions of the *Education Act* and the Québec *Charter* do not provide students with disabilities with equal protection and benefit of law, then they could be held to be of no force and effect. However, the recent ruling of the Supreme Court of Canada in a prominent integration case may have put such a prospect on ice.

Ontario: The Eaton Case

Eaton v. *Brant County Board of Education* (1997) began when a Special Education Tribunal was asked to adjudicate a special education dispute in which the parents of Emily Eaton, a student with multiple disabilities, sought a regular class placement for their daughter. The Tribunal rejected the claim, a decision that was upheld by the Divisional Court, but overturned by the Ontario Court of Appeal.

In brief, the Court of Appeal held that the non-consensual placement of Emily Eaton in a segregated setting was discriminatory and a violation of her rights under the *Canadian Charter*. Reversing the lower court ruling and the original decision of the Special Education Tribunal, the Court of Appeal created a new judicial standard for the placement of students with disabilities, one which had implications not only for Ontario education law but for any jurisdiction in Canada which does not meet the *Charter* standards set forth in this case. This ruling was described as a "landmark decision" and a "turning point in the disabled community's battle for integration." This euphoria was short-lived however.

In February 1997, the Supreme Court of Canada handed down its long awaited reasons in this case in support of its decision rendered the previous October to overturn the Court of Appeal decision and reinstate the original Tribunal ruling. In affirming the latter, the Court found that the Tribunal had "balanced the various educational interests of Emily Eaton, taking into account her special needs, and concluded that the best possible placement was in the special class"(p. 277). The Supreme Court went on to say that "It seems incongruous that a decision reached after such an approach could be considered a burden or a disadvantage imposed on a child" (p. 277).

The final issue dealt with, albeit briefly, by the Supreme Court was the exercise of the child's rights on her behalf by her parents and the decision of the Court of Appeal to the effect that a segregated placement was presumed to be discriminatory, unless agreed to by the parents. The Court noted that the parents' view of their child's best interest was an inadequate approach; what mattered was the child's best interest as determined by "the appropriate accommodation for an exceptional child ... from a subjective child-centred perspective, one which attempts to make equality meaningful from the child's point of view as opposed to that of the adults in his or her life" (pp. 277-278). The test of best interest should not therefore be encumbered by a presumption in favour of integration.

Draft Policy Statement on Special Education

Adapting Our Schools

At the end of March 1999, the Minister tabled a draft policy statement on special education entitled *Adapting Our Schools to the Needs of All Students* (MEQ, 1999). The recent reform of education is offered as the rationale for this paper, namely that the core challenge of the new reform - student success - is especially critical for students with special needs.

The Current Scene

The current scene is presented in terms of various sources of quantitative data on students with special needs and then in light of two recent reports (CSE, 1996b; Commission of the Estates General, 1996a). The data reveal little new in terms of the prevalence of students reported in various categories or the percentage that are integrated into regular settings. However, it is interesting to note that (1) the percentage of male versus female students with special needs is almost two-to-one in both of the "at-risk" and handicapped groupings (66%-34%) and (2) that although the percentage of handicapped students in French and English schools is all but identical, the percentage of at risk students in English schools is higher than in French schools (15.5% versus 12.1%).

In order to provide some insight into graduation rates for students with special needs, the MEQ established a cohort of 100 students and followed them until 21 years. The results were compared with those obtained from a cohort of regular students. In contrast to the latter, whose overall success rate was 83.1%, the following results were obtained:

- visual impairments   44.4%;
- hearing impairments   42.9%;
- mild learning disabilities   37.6%;
- behavioural difficulties   14.9%;
- severe learning disabilities 12.7%.

As mentioned above, these data were complemented by information from two other sources.

The CSE (1996b) deals at some length with ongoing problems associated with integration, mainly in relation to support for teachers. In addition (MEQ, 1999, p. 7):

> The Conseil speaks of unresolved issues that nobody has dared to broach: the lack of precision of the typology used to identify students (some people feel it should be reduced to two categories -students with handicaps and those with social maladjustments or learning disabilities - while others favour a typology based on needs rather than problems); the ambiguity of practices related to grade repetition; the limits of research in education, especially regarding services for students with special needs; and complex questions of an ethical nature (the gap between the specific needs of individual students and the capacity of the school system to meet them) that arise with respect to the education of these students.

Similarly, the Estates General raises a number of concerns about integration; in their own words (Commission of the Estates General, 1996a, pp. 31-32):

> These students [with special needs], their parents and organizations devoted to defending their interests drew **a fairly gloomy picture of current measures** for this clientele. **They were especially critical of integration efforts** and deplored the exclusion of students with special needs, despite their growing number.... It would appear that schools marginalize these students. Few school boards fully integrate them. Too often, they are still confined to special classes or educational institutions rather than integrated into regular classes in their local school.
>
> .... Teachers for their part, denounced **the totally unplanned integration of students**, declaring that such measures are often carried out in haste, without appropriate support.
>
> **Participants were rarely opposed to the integration of students with handicaps or learning or adjustment difficulties** into regular classes or schools. However, while some were in favour of unconditional integration and therefor demanded that special schools be abolished, most participants, from all sectors, agreed that the **integration of these students should meet a fairly wide range of conditions**.

The Context of the Current Reform

The MEQ states that the objective of the curriculum reform is the creation of an entirely new educational environment. The context arising from school-based reform (*Education Amendment Act*,

1997) is presented in terms of (1) the school mission and openness to the community; (2) school autonomy, and (3) transparency and accountability. In terms of special education itself, the paper summarizes the relevant sections of the *Education Act*, as presented above in this chapter. Finally, the paper makes reference to the global context, especially the current climate of constraint (MEQ, 1999, p. 12):

> The world of education is not alone in undergoing profound changes. The entire society of Québec and the structure of its services are in the process of changing. The difficult economic context combined with the complex and varied needs of the population, as well as the desire to reduce the provincial deficit, have led the government to review all the services provided. Cutbacks in education in the past few years may have had an impact on the services for students with special needs, even though budgets for these students have not been directly targeted by these cutbacks.

The need for *prevention* of learning problems is recognized as a priority in this economic context, as is the need to give all students, but those with special needs in particular, qualifications and skills that prepare them for the job market. Other contextual features, such as the need for partnerships, the use of technology, research and training are also mentioned.

Proposed Orientations

The policy orientations presented are quite general in nature and no specific legislation action is proposed. The thrust of the policy proposal is defined as follows (MEQ, 1999, p. 15):

> To help students with handicaps and those with social maladjustments or learning disabilities succeed in terms of knowledge, social development and qualifications, by accepting that success has different meanings for different students, and by adopting methods that favour their success.

Six "lines of action" are delineated:

- Recognizing the importance of prevention and the need to devote additional effort to this task;
- Making the adaptation of educational services a priority for all those working with students with special needs;
- Placing the school organization at the service of the students by evaluating their needs on an individual basis, by ensuring that evaluation is carried out in the environment where they are most comfortable, as close as possible to their place of residence, and by favouring their integration into regular classes;
- Creating a true educational community around the child, starting with the parents and continuing with outside partners and community organizations working with young people, in order to provide more consistent intervention efforts and better-coordinated services;
- Devoting particular attention to students with social maladjustments or learning disabilities;
- Acquiring the means to evaluate the students' progress, improve the quality of services and account for results.

In each case, the paper explains the action to be taken, describes various "favourable factors" and then outlines a number of "suggested strategies" to be taken forward. These include, among others: developing closer cooperation between schools and their daycare service providers; encouraging governing boards to include actions, such as preventive measures, in their educational projects; helping parents who need assistance in developing their parenting skills; facilitating access to vocational education; fostering cooperation with partners outside the school to facilitate school-workplace transition; developing a range of specialized services; and, ensuring that school boards distribute resources for students with special needs fairly and that there is transparency in the allocation and use to these funds.

PART II:
GOVERNANCE

One of the main levers in the process of ensuring that as many students as possible achieve success is the capacity of individual schools to adapt their services to the needs and characteristics of the populations they serve. If each institution is truly to be able to exercise its responsibilities, it must be able to make and act on pedagogical, administrative and budgetary decisions. This calls for a new division of responsibilities between schools, school boards and the MEQ. The Education Act will be amended accordingly (MEQ, 1997a, p. 14).

We began Part I with a description of the overall policy framework respecting the governance of the system and the regulatory framework which sets the system parameters. In Part II, we further develop our exploration of the major policy theme of governance. In another text in this series (*Historical Roots*), we discussed the evolution of the school system from the Quiet Revolution to the present. In terms of governance, we observed three phenomena: the rise of centralized power in the MEQ, failed attempts at school reform and *talk* about the decentralization of power. When the Minister issued the policy statement quoted above, the cynical reaction was *more talk*. However, this time, the talk was followed by legislative action - *Education Amendment Act* (1997). Designed to provide for a "new division of responsibilities between the school, the school board and the government," the heart of the Act is the complete re-writing of chapters III and IV of the Act concerning the role and powers of schools, and vocational and adult education centres. Combined with the impact of the 1997 *Act to Amend the Education Act, the Act Respecting School Elections and Other Legislative Provisions* [*Linguistic School Boards Act*] which provides for the restructuring of the system from denominational to linguistic school boards, the entire system of governance is in a state of major change, the most significant degree of change since the aftermath of the Quiet Revolution. In Part II, we will examine the changes in the exercise of governance at the three principal levels of the system: central (MEQ), intermediate (school board) and local (school).

The key provisions of the following instruments which are referred to in the chapters of this part are reproduced in the *Compendium*:

Chapter 5

Constitution Act, 1867
CSE Act
Education Act
MEQ Act

Chapter 6

Canadian Charter
Constitution Act, 1867
Constitution Amendment, 1997 (Quebec)
Education Act
    Elementary School Regulation
    Secondary School Regulation
School Elections Act

Chapter 7

Education Act
Education Amendment Act

CHAPTER 5
GOVERNANCE AT THE CENTRAL LEVEL

Introduction

The first tier of governing authority in Québec is found at the central, or provincial level. In this chapter, we will provide an overview of governance at this level, notably of the role of the Minister and the MEQ, as well as the role of the CSE and other provincial consultative bodies. One of the distinguishing features of the Québec education system is the formal mechanisms for the participation of different stakeholders in the education system. One of the key reforms of the Quiet Revolution was the establishment of the Superior Council and its denominational committees - one Catholic and one Protestant (see *Historical Roots,* chap. 3, for more details). The Superior Council and other consultative bodies are examples of the formal *voice* in the system of educational governance which was introduced in chapter 2. This chapter will also deal with the "recent edition" of the Estates General on Education and various other provincial level advisory committees.

Government Actors

The National Assembly

As shown in Figure 2.3 in chapter 2, all authority in education is vested in and emanates from the provincial legislature, the National Assembly of Québec. As a general rule, the National Assembly, like any legislative body, *speaks* through statutes adopted by the Assembly. A statute begins as a "bill," (e.g. Bill 107, *Education Act*, 1988) usually introduced by the Minister responsible for the domain covered by the bill (e.g. education). The bill then goes through three "readings:" (1) adoption in principle; (2) clause by clause analysis; and (3) final adoption. The bill is then given royal assent by the Lieutenant Governor and it becomes law. At this point, the bill becomes an "Act." All acts adopted during the year are published individually in the *Official Gazette* and assigned a chapter number for publication in the annual volume of statutes (e.g. *Education Act*, S.Q. 1988, c. 84).

At this point the act has become law. However, although most laws come into force upon their publication in the *Official Gazette*, some laws, or some provisions of a given law, may only come into force at a later date decided by the Government. Acts are then incorporated into a multi-volume consolidation of statutes (*Revised Statutes of Québec*) and assigned a chapter reference number in this consolidation (e.g. *Education Act*, R.S.Q., c. I-13.3). Sometimes laws continue to be spoken of by their pre-passage name (e.g. Bill 107), even though technically this term is no longer appropriate.

The Government

The role of the Government in educational governance is a regulatory one. The *Education Act* (ss. 447-458.) empowers the Government to adopt various regulations, all of which have the force of law. The principal regulations are:

Regulations for Youth Education

The *Basic Regulations* for elementary and secondary (El Reg; Sec Reg) set forth the parameters governing curriculum and school organization at these levels; the secondary regulation includes provisions relating to vocational education for youth. They are discussed in detail in chapter 8.

Regulations for Adult Education

The *Basic Regulations* for adult education set forth respectively the parameters governing general and vocational education for adults (Adult Gen Reg; Adult Voc Reg).

Other Regulations

The *Education Act* also empowers the Government to adopt various other regulations including: the classification of "non-unionizable" positions (i.e. those not covered by the *Labour Code* - see chap. 9) such as school board administrators, school principals, as well as their remuneration and working conditions; the norms, conditions and procedures relating to the construction, renovation or disposal of immovables (school buildings and property); the awarding of contracts for student transportation, and the composition and *modus operandi* of the school board advisory committee on student transportation (see chap. 3); and, the rules for computing the "maximum tax yield" – the amount used in determining the ceiling on local taxation which a school board is entitled to impose (see chap. 11).

The Minister

The *Education Act* assigns the Minister of Education various regulatory powers, as well as a multitude of functions and other powers.

Regulatory Power

The Minister has the following regulatory powers and duties (Ed Act, ss. 456-458): he or she

- may establish a classification of teaching licenses and the standards for the formal training of teachers (s. 456; and see chap. 9);
- shall establish the conditions and procedures for consulting parents concerning the recognition of the denominational status of a school (s. 457; and see chap. 12);
- may determine the cases, procedures and other matters related thereto, in which a school board may admit children who have not attained the age of admission (s. 457.1);
- may determine the cases in which a child may be retained in kindergarten (i.e. not promoted to grade 1) and elementary school (i.e. not promoted to secondary school) (s. 457.1).

General Functions & Powers

The *Education Act* assigns the Minister of Education various general functions and powers (ss. 459-479), including the following:

- to ensure the quality of educational services provided by school boards and set the parameters governing the implementation of the *Basic Regulations* and other related matters - these powers are presented in detail below;
- to establish, after consultation with school boards and subject to the approval of the Conseil du trésor, the annual budgetary rules applicable to school boards. These rules include provisions relating to operating and capital expenditures, as well as to equalization grants, short-term borrowing and debt servicing (see chap. 11).

The Act also gives the Minister some extraordinary powers, namely the power to appoint someone to investigate "any matter respecting the quality of the educational services as well as the management, organization and operation of a school board" (s. 478).

The Government (not the Minister) may also suspend some or all of the powers of a school board during or following such an investigation and appoint a trustee in its place for a period of up to six months (extendable for a further six months) (s. 479).

Educational Services

According to the *Education Act*, the Minister may, by regulation, determine the cases eligible for early admission to preschool or grade 1, as well as various matters related thereto (s. 457.1). However, the vast majority of ministerial functions and powers relating to curriculum and school organization are set forth in a separate division of the Act. The key roles of the Minister respecting educational matters (as opposed to administrative and financial matters), as stipulated in the *Education Act* (ss. 456-471), may be summarized as follows: he or she

- shall ensure quality in the educational services provided by school boards (s. 459);

- may establish the terms and conditions for the implementation of the *Basic Regulations* (s. 459);

- may exempt any category of students from rules governing certification or prior learning (s. 460);

- shall establish the courses of study (compulsory and elective subjects) (s. 461);

- may draw up a list of approved textbooks and instructional material or classes of instructional material (s. 462);

- may establish the credits for each subject and those for which ministerial examinations will be required (s. 463);

- may establish the conditions of admission to vocational education (s. 465);

- may revise, if necessary, the results obtained in ministerial examinations and weight school board marks in such subjects (s. 470);

- shall award diplomas, certificates and other official attestations, as well as transcripts of marks (s. 471).

It would obviously be impossible for the Minister alone to exercise all the responsibilities with which he or she is charged, hence the role of the MEQ.

MEQ

The establishment and operation of the MEQ is governed by a separate statute, the *Act Respecting the Ministère de l'Éducation* [*MEQ Act*]. The scope of the mandate of the MEQ has varied since its inception in 1964. At present, it is responsible for education at all levels of the system: elementary-secondary, collegial and university. Information about the ministry, including current publications, is available on the MEQ Web site (http://www.MEQ.gouv.qc.ca), which includes an English sub-page (/Gr-PUB/m.englis.htm).

Minister

The Minister - an elected member of the National Assembly and a member of the Cabinet - is responsible for the direction and administration of the MEQ (*MEQ Act*, s. 1).

Deputy Minister

According to the *MEQ Act*, the Government shall appoint a Deputy Minister who is responsible for the day-to-day management of the MEQ and its officers and employees (s. 7).

Associate Deputy Ministers

The *MEQ Act* also provides for the appointment of two Associate Deputy Ministers, one Catholic and one Protestant. They are responsible for ensuring that the denominational status of schools recognized as Catholic or Protestant is respected and for securing the exercise of denominational rights in other schools (ss. 7, 8).

Assistant Deputy Ministers

Line authority in the MEQ flows from the Minister to the Deputy Minister to various Assistant Deputy Ministers [ADMs] who are responsible for various units within the MEQ. At present, there are six ADMs each responsible for one of the following areas: elementary and secondary education; the *réseaux* (public school boards/schools, private schools); technical and vocational training; higher education; administrative services; and, the Anglophone community.

Regional Directorates

The central offices of the MEQ are located in Québec City but there are regional offices in each administrative region throughout Québec. Most of the day-to-day contact between school boards and the MEQ occurs through the eleven regional offices.

Conseil scolaire de l'Île de Montréal

In addition to the Montréal regional directorate of the MEQ, school boards in Montréal must deal with another intermediate body, the Conseil scolaire de l'Île de Montréal [Island Council]. Created by the *Education Act* (ss. 399-446), it exercises a variety of duties on behalf of the school boards on the Island, primarily in relation to taxation and borrowing.

The Island Council is composed of representatives of the school boards on the Island of Montréal, the number of which is determined by a formula set out in the Act, plus three persons designated by the Government, after consultation with the parents' committees of the Island school boards At the present time, there are 16 members, 13 representing the 5 school boards (3 French language & 2 English language) and 3 nominated by the Government. The composition of the present Council has provoked a fair amount of controversy in its first year, as it was constantly deadlocked at 8-8, with one side representing the Commission scolaire de Montréal plus the Government nominees, the other side representing the other four school boards.

The principal function of the Council is to levy taxes on behalf of its constituent school boards (s. 434.1). The rate of the school tax cannot exceed the ceiling imposed by law for school boards considered individually. In brief, each of the five school boards determines its own needs from school tax revenue up to the limit allowed by law (see chap. 11). The Council sets a tax rate which will enable it to collect the sum of these needs for all five boards. It may also levy a tax for its own purposes or to support education in economically disadvantaged areas of the boards, which constitutes a special mandate of the Council (s. 434). However, it appears that such expenditures, especially the Council's own expenses, are met by revenues from interest and surplus monies from the regular tax levy.*

* *Note.* These occur due to changes in property evaluation between the time the tax rate is set and the time when it is collected, as well as from retroactive adjustments on evaluation.

If any school board wishes to raise tax revenues which exceed the limits set by law, it must obtain the approval if its electors by referendum (s. 440; see chap. 11) and collect the tax on its own. If the Council decides to raise a separate amount for disadvantaged areas (s. 434) and the amount exceeds the difference between the aggregate amount to be raised for the regular school board levy (s. 434.1) and the aggregate limit set by law, then the Council must gain the approval of all electors on the Island by means of a referendum (s. 444; see also ss. 345-353).

Monies raised by the Council are apportioned among its member boards by rules set forth in the Act. First, each school board receives the amount it requested under the regular tax levy. Second, monies for disadvantaged areas are apportioned according to a formula set by the Council. If a school board wishes to dispute this formula, it may appeal the matter to the Minister (s. 439).

The foregoing summarizes the governing structures at the central level which exercise *authority* in the education system. The remainder of this chapter is devoted to the principal provincial bodies which have formally recognized *voice* in the system.

Advisory Bodies

Superior Council

The Superior Council was created by virtue of the *Act Respecting the Conseil supérieur de l'éducation* [*CSE Act*]. The following is a summary of its composition, duties, powers and organization, based on the provisions of this Act.

Composition

The Superior Council consists of 24 members, of whom at least 16 must be Catholics; at least 4 must be Protestants and there must be at least 1 other (s. 2). The chairs of the two denominational committees (see discussion below) are, *ex officio* (i.e. by virtue of his or her office) members of the Council; the other 22 voting members are appointed by the Government (ss. 4, 6). The Deputy Minister and the two Associate Deputy Ministers are, *ex officio* members of the Council but they are not entitled to vote (s. 7). The Government appoints a president and a vice-president from among the members, one a Catholic, the other a Protestant (s. 8).

Organization

The Superior Council comprises two denominational committees (ss. 15-17; described below) and five commissions (s. 24): elementary education; secondary education; college education; university-level education and research; and adult education. Each of these commissions consists of 9 to 15 members and is empowered to make suggestions to the Council respecting its domain.

Duties

The duties of the Superior Council are to give its opinion to the Minister on the regulations or draft regulations that the Minister must submit to it, as well as on any matter he or she may choose to refer to it, and to submit to the Minister an annual report on the "state and needs of education" (s. 9; discussed below).

Powers

The Superior Council also has certain powers (s. 10). It can receive input from the public concerning education; make recommendations to the Minister on matters within its competence; conduct research; and, make rules governing its internal management.

State & Needs of Education

As noted above, the CSE is required to produce an annual report of the "state and needs of education" in Québec, as illustrated by four recent reports:

- *Éduquer à la citoyenneté* (CSE, 1998b) — The Council's stated aim in this report is to consider the specific contribution the educational system can make to a "new" citizenship, which it states has become more demanding, more comprehensive and richer in potential as a result of the complexity of modern democratic societies.

- *L'Insertion sociale et professionnelle, une responsabilité à partager* (CSE, 1997a) — The subject of this report is the transition from student to active citizen and worker, the role and responsibility of education in helping students make this transition and integrate into society and the work force.

- *Pour un nouveau partage des pouvoirs et responsabilités en éducation* (CSE, 1996a) — This report examines power-sharing among various stakeholders in the education system and urges the government and labour unions to unravel the "Gordian knot" of standardized regulations that hinder the exercise of powers and responsibilities at the grass-roots level.

- *Vers la maîtrise du changement en éducation* (CSE, 1995) — Reviewing what we have learned about change as a process not an event, this report stresses the implications of this lesson, namely that the ability to manage change is at least as important as the decision to change.

Advice To The Minister

As alluded to above, in addition to the annual reports, the CSE has produced a series of briefs, or policy papers for consideration by the Minister and other members of the educational community. They provide policy makers, practitioners, researchers and others interested in Québec education with a wealth of information and reflection on key policy issues, as illustrated by the titles of several recent papers: *L'École, une communauté éducative. Voies de renouvellement pour le secondaire* (CSE, 1998a); *L'autorisation d'enseigner: Le projet d'un règlement refondu* (CSE, 1997b); *L'intégration scolaire des élèves handicapés et en difficulté* (CSE, 1996b). Unfortunately, for many members of the Anglophone educational community, almost none of these papers is available in English. The CSE did publish summaries of the papers in a periodical entitled *Educouncil*, but this publication has been discontinued. However, English summaries of many documents are available on its Web site (General address: http://www.cse.gouv.qc.ca; English sub page: http://www.cse.gouv.qc.ca/index.~GE.htm) and a new French and English publication, *Panorama*, publishes short articles on CSE work.

Denominational Committees

There are two denominational committees, one Catholic and one Protestant. Each consists of 15 members, plus the associate deputy minister, *ex officio*.

Duties

The duties and powers of the two committees, summarized below, are focussed on the denominational aspects of schools and schooling (*CSE Act*, ss. 22, 23). They are to:

- make regulations respecting Catholic or Protestant moral and religious instruction [MRI], pastoral care and guidance;*

- make regulations respecting teacher qualifications for Catholic or Protestant MRI, pastoral care and guidance;*

- approve curricula, guides, textbooks and teaching materials for Catholic or Protestant MRI;

- approve handbooks of objectives and teacher guides for Catholic or Protestant pastoral care and guidance;

- make regulations to recognize educational institutions as Catholic or Protestant and to ensure the confessional character of educational institutions so recognized, as well as those of confessional or dissentient school boards;

- recognize educational institutions as Catholic or Protestant and to withdraw such recognition when such an institution no longer fulfils the necessary conditions;

- make recommendations to the Superior Council or the Minister on matters within its competence.

* *Note.* The principal regulations are: *Regulation of the Protestant Committee of the Conseil supérieur de l'éducation Regarding Protestant Moral and Religious Instruction as well as the Recognition of Educational Institutions as Protestant* [*Protestant Regulation*]; *Regulation Respecting the Recognition of Elementary and Secondary Schools of the Public School System as Catholic and their Confessional Character* [*Catholic Regulation*]; see also *Regulation Respecting the Qualification of Teachers Having Charge of Catholic Religious Instruction in Public and Private and Elementary and Secondary Schools not Recognized as Catholic*; *Regulation Respecting the Recognition of Private Educational Institutions as Catholic and their Confessional Character.*

Powers

Each of the denominational committees also has the power to give opinions, from the point of view of religion and morals, to the Minister respecting other curricula, guides, textbooks and teaching materials. They may receive input from the public concerning matters within its competence, conduct research and make rules governing its internal management.

Advisory Board on English Education

The Advisory Board on English Education was formed in 1993 (MEQ, 1992c) in order to give advice to the Minister on questions affecting the educational services offered in elementary and secondary English schools and to respond to requests for advice by the Minister. At present, the Board is chaired by Gretta Chambers and includes various representatives from the Anglophone educational community, as well as, *ex officio*, the Assistant Deputy Minister for the Anglophone Community (see Web site: http://www.gouv.qc.ca/cela/anglais.htm). Since its inception, the Advisory Board has issued four reports:

- *The Reorganization of School Boards Along Linguistic Lines* (1994).
- *Language Learning in the English Schools of Québec* (1995).
- *The Integration of New Information and Communication Technologies in the English Schools of Québec* (1996).
- *Evaluation of Learning in the English Schools of Québec* (1997).

Provincial Federation of Parent Committees

In contrast to the extensive statutory provisions for parental participation at the school board and school levels (see chaps. 6 & 7), there is no statutory body at the provincial level for parental voice. However, there is a provincial federation of parent committees (FCPPQ - Fédération des comités de parents de la province de Québec).

Quebec Federation of Home & School Associations

The Quebec Federation of Home and School Associations [QFHSA] is a provincial organization that has representation from its various member organizations in local schools. It acts as an independent voice of parents in education and maintains links with school board associations, teacher unions, the CSE and the MEQ (QFHSA, n.d.).

Other Consultative Committees

In 1997, the Government created four new consultative committees.

Curriculum Council
The Curriculum Council [Commission des programmes d'étude] consists of eleven members, of whom a minimum of two must come from the English sector of the education system, all named by the Minister (Ed. Act, ss. 477.2 - 477.7). Its mission is to advise the Minister on all questions relating to the programs of studies established pursuant to the *Education Act* (s. 461).

Committee for the Evaluation of Instructional Resources
The Committee for the Evaluation of Instructional Resources [Comité d'évaluation des ressources didactiques] consists of thirteen members, all named by the Minister (Ed. Act, ss. 477.8 - 477.12). Its mission is to advise the Minister on all questions relating to textbooks and instructional materials.

Teacher Training Program Accreditation Committee
The Teacher Training Program Accreditation Committee [CAPFE - Comité d'agrément des programmes de formation à l'enseignement] consists of nine members, of whom a minimum of two must come from the English sector of the education system, all named by the Minister (Ed. Act, ss. 477.13 - 477.15). Its mission is to examine and approve teacher training programs (see chap. 9 for more details; see also *Historical Roots*, chap. 3).

Teacher Training Policy Committee

The Teacher Training Policy Committee [COPFE - Comité d'orientation de la formation du personnel enseignant] consists of sixteen members, all named by the Minister (Ed. Act, ss. 477.16 - 477.18). Its mission is to advise the Minister on all questions relating to teacher training policy (see chap. 9 for more details; see also *Historical Roots*, chap. 3).

In addition to these standing bodies which provide input on an ongoing basis to the Minister, other bodies are created on an *ad hoc* basis, such as the periodic convocation of the "Estates General" on education (see *Historical Roots*, chap. 4).

Estates General on Education: 1995-96

In 1995, the Government decided that the time was ripe for the convocation of a new Estates General on education. The objectives for this exercise were (Commission for the Estates General on Education, 1996a, p. 131):

- to express the needs and expectations of the general public with respect to education, and at the same time to mount a major initiative to hear the needs and expectations expressed and the contributions required to satisfy them;
- to provide a forum for collective reflection and discussion of the different interpretations of the current and future situation;
- to define objectives for the school in its broadest sense, both now and in the future;
- to establish the broadest possible social consensus with a view to action.

However, contrary to the previous experience, the decision was made to name members of the Commission for the Estates General and send them "on the road" to hold hearings throughout the province. After this consultation process was completed, the Government added a new mandate, namely to prepare a final report, "in which it will set out the trends and priorities as well as any deadlocks and consensuses which emerged at this sitting" (Commission for the Estates General on Education, 1996b, p. 84).

Ten Priority Actions

The Commission set forth ten priority actions for the renewal of the education system, listed below, together with examples of the measures recommended under each action:

- re-establish the principle of equal opportunity - gradually eliminate State support for private schools; provide special support for the most disadvantaged areas; maintain both the principle of integrating students with special needs into regular classes and the range of approaches used for this purpose;
- extend and improve early childhood services - offer non-compulsory full-time kindergarten for five-year-olds; offer half-time kindergarten or day care to four-year-olds (full-time for children from underprivileged backgrounds and cultural communities and children with handicaps);
- restructure elementary and secondary curricula to increase their cultural content - establish "learning profiles" to define the learning students should acquire in elementary and secondary school and "exit profiles" to define the level of educational skills that should be acquired at the end of each level of schooling; embark on comprehensive curricular reform (see chap. 8);
- consolidate vocational and technical education - reinstate a vocational education program which is accessible after secondary III and which leads to a secondary school diploma; maintain "individualized paths for learning" for students who are unable to meet the requirements for entry into vocational programs; undertake a variety of measures to improve service delivery in this area;

- carry out the necessary reorganization to meet the demand for mass higher education - maintain the current CEGEP system, while continuing the implementation of the current reforms at this level; undertake a variety of reforms at the university level and provide the State with the *leverage mechanisms* that will allow it to participate in planning, policy-making and coordination of activities at this level;

- establish a real continuing education system - undertake a variety of reforms including the drafting of a policy on lifelong learning;

- support the main players to support educational success - clarify the responsibilities of educational institutions with respect to student support and supervision; improve pre-service and in-service training of teachers; ensure better cooperation between schools and universities with respect to teacher training and educational research; support teacher, labour, student and parent associations wishing to be involved in school reform; provide Anglophones with greater access to instructional materials in their own language;

- redistribute powers to increase local decision-making capacity and openness to the community - maintain the State's overall responsibility to guide the education system; maintain school boards, in reduced numbers, as an intermediate level of education management; provide for greater community involvement in management at the school level; re-examine the organization of work in schools (see chap. 7);

- continue moving toward a non-denominational system - transform denominational school boards into linguistics boards; repeal section 93 of the *Constitution Act, 1867*; encourage the view that the pursuit of religious goals take place outside the school environment;

- guarantee funding to achieve our educational goals - maintain current level of funding for education (8.5% of GDP); reinforce equalization measures based on socio-economic differences; reduce public funding to private education.

Introduction

School board reform is not a new topic in Québec. It can be linked to the broader constitutional debate between Québec and the federal government over the division of federal and provincial powers, indeed to the very continuation of the country, as presently configured. The debate over school reform can be traced through a series of legislative acts, leading to a recent amendment of the present *Education Act*, through a series of court battles which culminated in a Supreme Court of Canada decision in 1993 (*Reference re Education Act of Québec*) and a constitutional amendment. In this chapter, we will discuss the evolution of this reform, the Supreme Court decision, the constitutional amendment and the new school board structures that were implemented in 1998-99.

Background

Much of the focus on school boards has been on the ongoing saga of school board reform and no attempt will be made here to summarize all that material (see *Historical Roots* for a review). However, in a nutshell, section 93 of the *Constitution Act, 1867* guaranteed that Catholic and Protestant denominational rights in education could not be legislated away by the Provincial Government. After Confederation a dual denominational system of Catholic and Protestant school boards was firmly established and not seriously questioned until the Quiet Revolution of the 1960s. Despite strong recommendations from the Parent Commission to reform the system (see *Historical Roots*, chap. 3), all such attempts had failed when the Government adopted Bill 107 in 1988.

The massive structural reform envisaged by the Parent Report did not take place. Early attempts to substitute unified school boards for denominational boards failed and the hope of reform focussed on linguistic school boards. The first serious attempt in this regard came with Bill 40 in 1983 that was replaced by the *Act Respecting Public Elementary and Secondary Education* in 1984. When this legislation was declared unconstitutional (*Québec Association of Protestant School Boards* v. *Québec* (A.G.), 1985), reform was put on hold until Bill 107 was adopted in 1988. However, even when Bill 107 was declared constitutionally valid by the Supreme Court in 1993 (see above), no action was taken and the transitional regime instituted by Bill 107 remained in effect until the current reform spearheaded by the constitutional amendment of section 93 and the *Linguistic School Boards Act*, discussed below.

Contemporary School Board Reform

Transitional Regime (to June, 1998)

The transitional regime instituted by Bill 107 (1988) was only meant to last a short time - just until the linguistic boards foreseen by that Act were implemented. However, given subsequent developments summarized above (see *Historical Roots* for details), the transitional regime lasted nine years (1989-90 to 1997-98).

The structure of school boards in the transitional regime reflected the changes introduced in the early 1970s by the *Act Respecting the Regrouping and Management of School Boards* (1971), for boards off the Island of Montréal, and the *Act to Promote School Development on the Island of Montreal* (1972), for boards on the Island. There were three types of boards in this system: common, dissentient and confessional. By this time, almost all of these boards were integrated boards (i.e. offered instruction at both the elementary and secondary levels); some provided instruction in both French and English, others in only one language.

Common Boards

With the exception of the dissentient and confessional boards described below, all school boards in Québec were "common," so called because they did not have an *exclusive* vocation relating to one denomination and because they were not constitutionally protected, having been created after 1867. The non-exclusive nature of these boards was subtly indicated by their formal designation as school boards *for Catholics* and school boards *for Protestants*, rather than as Catholic or Protestant school boards. School boards for Catholics were open to Catholics, those for Protestants were open to Protestants,* but both were open to "others" (Ed Act, s. 502). The reference to others included all persons who professed neither Catholic nor Protestant religious affiliation. Boards could offer instruction in French or English, admissibility being determined by Bill 101 (see chap. 13).

* *Note.* The exclusion of Catholics from admission to Protestant boards and of Protestants to Catholic boards may seem ambiguous from a reading of the English version of section 502; however, the French version is clear on this point and seems a more accurate reflection of the intent of the legislator.

Dissentient Boards

There were five dissentient boards in Québec - formed by those who exercised their constitutionally protected right to dissent from joining the regional boards formed in the 1970s. When Bill 107 was adopted there were two Catholic and three Protestant dissentient boards; one of the latter had no students and the others were quite small. Catholic dissentient school boards were open to Catholics and "others;" those for Protestants were open to Protestants and "others" - unless the dissentient board decided otherwise (Ed Act, ss. 498, 504). Boards could offer instruction in French or English, admissibility being determined by Bill 101 (see chap. 13).

Confessional Boards

There were four "confessional" boards - one Catholic and one Protestant board in Montréal and one Catholic and one Protestant board in Québec City. Catholic confessional boards were open to Catholics and "others;" Protestant confessional boards were open to Protestants and "others" (Ed Act, s. 503).* Boards could offer instruction in French or English, admissibility being determined by Bill 101 (see chap. 13). It was assumed that these four school boards were constitutionally protected. However, it was the denominational rights of Catholics and Protestants in these two cities that were protected, not the school boards themselves.

* *Note.* The above comment regarding section 502 applies to section 503 as well.

The Estates General & the Renewed Call for Reform

As discussed in chapter 5, in 1995, the Government established the Commission for the Estates General on Education, whose mandate was to consult the general public with a view to producing the "broadest possible social consensus" on the future direction of education in Québec. According to the interim report of the Commission, there were sharp divisions among stakeholders regarding all denominational aspects of the school system, with as many partisans for the status quo as those for change. However, this divergence of opinion did not deter the Commission from clearly articulating the recommended course of action for the Government to take (1996b, p. 49):

Confessionality must be unlocked at all levels of the system, so that all students can be taught the shared values that we as a society wish to embrace.

First, we must **continue moving towards a non-confessional education system** - in other words we must continue the separation of Church and State. There is now no reason, other than historical impediment, for confessional privilege to restrict the public education system. A fairly general consensus exists regarding the **transformation of confessional school boards into linguistic school boards**.

The Commission went on to recommend that the constitutional impediment to reform be settled once and for all by either amending or repealing section 93.

The Constitutional Amendment

Following the publication of the Estates General reports, the Minister announced that the Government intended to proceed with the implementation of linguistic boards and, to that end, would seek a bilateral constitutional amendment, that is one requiring only the consent of Ottawa and the province concerned. Ottawa indicated quickly that it would respond favourably to the Québec request, if there were a consensus in Québec in support of the proposed change.

The National Assembly unanimously adopted a resolution in support of the Constitutional amendment, unanimity having been secured by including the following declaration in the preamble to the resolution (cited in *Report of the Special Joint Committee*, 1997, p. 23):

WHEREAS ... the National Assembly of Québec reaffirms the established rights of the English-speaking community of Québec. More specifically, whereas Quebeckers whose children are admissible in accordance with Chapter VIII of the Charter of the French Language have the right to have them receive their instruction in English language educational facilities under the management and control of this community, as provided by law, and which are financed through public funds;

However, consensus in the National Assembly did not mean consensus in the community.

Opposition to the Amendment

The proposed constitutional amendment was criticized by many because of the refusal of the Government to hold hearings or otherwise engage in public debate about the proposal. Several Anglophone groups stated that their long standing support for linguistic boards (at the time of the adoption of Bill 107) had always been predicated on the replacement of the denominational guarantees in section 93 by linguistic ones.* This pronouncement was coupled with the assertion that the minority language education rights provided for in section 23 of the *Canadian Charter* were insufficient and did not match those found in section 93. Moreover, some groups saw the constitutional amendment as unnecessary for the implementation of linguistic boards and viewed it as a move toward the abolition of denominational schools and religious instruction (Boudreau, 1999). Thus, the opposition, at least in some cases, co-mingled constitutional rights with statutory rights, that is those granted by Bill 107 which were not protected by section 93 (see chap. 12). However, although these rights were legally quite separate issues, it was not unrealistic of these critics to suppose that once constitutional rights were abrogated that the others would be next.

Note. It should be noted that Bill 107 did not include any constitutional guarantees based on language, merely a preservation of those based on denomination, which would not apply to the new linguistic school boards.

An Alternative Perspective

In response to these critics, the Office of Research on Educational Policy at McGill circulated a discussion paper which suggested that if school board reform was now inextricably linked to the proposed constitutional amendment, then the critical issue was whether the gain of linguistic boards warranted the loss of the guarantees provided by section 93: a good deal of the debate seemed to turn on whether or not section 23 constituted an adequate substitute for section 93 (Smith, 1997). At a forum for leaders of the English community sponsored by the Faculties of Law and Education at

McGill University, Professor Pierre Foucher provided his answer to this question (1997, p. 16):

> From a linguistic point of view, I have no hesitation whatsoever in recommending that the English community in Québec go ahead with section 23 ....
>
> Constitutions are national documents that embody common values and shared goals. With regard to minority language rights, they were part and parcel of the very foundation of the country. Linguistic duality is one of the operating principles of the federation and minority language education rights are one of the means to accomplish that purpose. Even if it is not perfect, it is the best one that we can have so far and it has proved to be quite useful. Let us not hesitate to exploit all of its potential.

Although a consensus appeared to be emerging in support of this analysis, it was neither unanimous nor solid, as attention turned toward Ottawa to see how the Federal Government would respond.

The Special Joint Committee

Despite the misgivings of some, the Federal Government introduced a bill into Parliament in the spring of 1997 to accede to the Québec request for a constitutional amendment. The bill died on the order paper because of the calling of a Federal election but was re-introduced when Parliament resumed sitting in the fall. The proposed amendment was the subject of public hearings by the Special Joint Committee of the House of Commons and Senate. There were those who supported the amendment and those who opposed it. Most of the opposition was based on a desire to maintain denominational rights in addition to linguistic rights. In addition, there were those who sought a *quid pro quo* from the Québec Government over section 23 of the *Canadian Charter* for supporting the abolition of section 93 rights.*

* Note. Essentially, the "deal" being sought was that the Government would authorize the coming into force of section 23(1)(a) of the *Canadian Charter* which provided for admissibility to English schooling on the basis of language first learned and still understood (see Foster & Smith, 1997a).

The following gives some flavour of the range of opinions expressed at the hearings:

> It is not up to the state, the politicians, the religious leaders, nor even the teachers to judge for parents and their children whether or not the latter should be granted a denominational school system and Catholic instruction in the schools. One will hear the following types of comments from the proponents of a secularized school system: "the children can't even make the sign of the cross when they start school" or "the children make their First Communion and then are never again seen at Mass" or "the parents neither know nor practice [*sic*] their faith". Whether or not the above is true, is irrelevant. As long as the parents continue to choose denominational schools, no one has a right to deprive them of it (Citizens for the Constitutional Right to Denominational Schools, 1997, p. 13/3).

> Remove the constraints of section 93 is to follow up on the large consensus expressed throughout Québec on the modernization of the school system.
>
> Remove the constraints of section 93 is to express our attachment to freedom of conscience and religion as well as the principle of equality among people that transcends the legitimate diversity of their religious options.
>
> We believe that the support for freedom of conscience and religion is a fundamental basis of our democracy. Freedom of religion would not mean much however if it did not imply equality rights for everyone, whether they profess a religious belief or not and whatever their particular religious belief may be. This implies that there cannot be an official religion and that the State must not favour any religious group.
>
> The structure of the school system on the basis of two privileged denominations contravenes this value.... In a democratic system based on the respect of fundamental freedoms, it is unacceptable that persons who are neither Catholic nor Protestant must choose between these two privileged denominations in order to exercise their right to schooling (Centrale de l'enseignement du Québec, 1997, p. 11/9 [free translation]).

For the past 130 years, Canadians have promoted their unique social and religious values. However, our society has also become pluralistic, outward-looking and respectful of people's right to choose.

These values which are the envy of other nations should not, however, be seen as a reason for maintaining a complex, inappropriate and inequitable school board structure given that the confessional guarantee is not one that applies to the Québec population as a whole....

From the moment the initial components of the reform plan were announced, parent committees from Montreal and Québec City school boards lost no time letting us know that they disagreed with the large number and overlapping of school boards in Montreal and Québec City.

The FCPPQ supports reform based on linguistic considerations, provided services that meet the religious and cultural need of Catholic and Protestant groups continue to [be] offered (Fédération des comités de parents de la province de Québec, 1997, p. 27/2).

Upon the termination the hearings, the Joint Committee concluded that "overall, it appears that, although some witnesses expressed their concerns with respect to the proposed amendment, there is a consensus in Quebec society supporting this change" (*Report of the Special Joint Committee*, 1997, p. 6). It therefore recommended passage of the amendment which was subsequently approved by the Commons and Senate, receiving Royal assent in December 1997. Simply put, the amendment abrogates the denominational rights found in the Constitution, by inserting the following at the end of section 93: "Subsections 93(1) to 93(4) do not apply to Québec" (*Constitutional Amendment, 1997 (Québec)*).

Defining a consensus is never an easy task. It is not meant to signify unanimity, nor is it a simple majority of 50% plus one. It may signify agreement among key stakeholder groups - formally recognized associations - or it may signify convergence of opinion at the grass roots. Time will tell perhaps whether the consensus which the Special Joint Committee concluded existed was real or imagined and, if real, whether it was predicated on a continuance of denominational rights within the new linguistic school boards. Prior to the beginning of the hearings, in its letter to the Federal Government, the Assembly of Quebec Bishops stated: "Our approval for changing the status of school boards has always been accompanied by one condition: that the denominational guarantees established by Bill 107 be maintained. The rights clearly recognized under that legislation are at the heart of our historic heritage" (cited in *Report of the Special Joint Committee*, 1997, p. 32).

By contrast, the Québec Minister of Education made it clear to the Committee in her presentation that no such guarantees were implicit in the proposed amendment: "There is a linguistic minority in Quebec. With Bill 109 [*Linguistic School Boards Act*] we are ensuring the right of this minority to administer its own school system. It is now up to Quebec to determine the place of religion in the school to take into account the pluralism of Quebec society" (cited in *Report of the Special Joint Committee*, 1997, p. 37). As will be seen later in this text (see chap. 12), the debate on this issue has barely begun.

Linguistic School Boards Act (1997)

Even before the constitutional amendment was tabled in the House of Commons in Ottawa for consideration, the Government of Québec had adopted the *Linguistic School Boards Act* to provide for the implementation of linguistic boards.

Denominational School Board Structures Eliminated

The *Linguistic School Boards Act* eliminated denominational school board structures as follows. First, it replaced the existing network of common boards for Catholics and common boards for Protestants with a new network of French language and English language school boards. Second, it eliminated the four confessional boards in Montreal and Québec City. Third, it eliminated existing dissentient school boards. However, it included interim provisions, pending the amendment of section 93, for the establishment of "confessional councils" as structures within the new linguistic school boards in Montréal and Québec City and for the creation of dissentient boards elsewhere. Given that the amendment of section 93 was given Royal assent before January 1, 1998, this provisional regime never came into force.*

* *Note.* Section 68 of the *Linguistic School Boards Act* provided for the elimination of confessional councils and dissentient boards if section 93 was given Royal assent before this date.

A New Transition Process
The *Linguistic School Boards Act* (1997) provided for the implementation of the new system as of July 1, 1998, just one year after it came into force (June 19, 1997). In the interim period, provision was made for the establishment of provisional councils and the transfer and accreditation of staff (Ed Act, ss. 111-112, 509-540).

New School Board Territories
In August 1997, the official "Territorial Division Order" was published. It created two new networks of 60 French language school boards and 9 English language boards. The latter are listed below (geographic territory indicated in parenthesis):

- Central Québec School Board ("Greater Québec," St. Maurice, Saguenay);
- Eastern Shores School Board (North Shore, Lower St. Lawrence, Gaspesia);
- Eastern Townships School Board (Bedford, Eastern Townships);
- English-Montréal School Board (Montréal [except West Island]);
- Lester-B.-Pearson School Board (West Island of Montréal);
- New Frontiers School Board (Châteauguay Valley);
- Riverside School Board (South Shore);
- Sir-Wilfred-Laurier School Board (Laval-Laurentian);
- Western Québec School Board (Outaouais, Abitibi).

Provisional Councils
Provisional councils were mandated to undertake all tasks related to the formation of the new linguistic school boards, including the transfer of personnel (see chap. 9), division of assets, admission of new students, etc. Formed in September 1997, each council was composed of elected and parent commissioners from the existing school boards in its territory which offered instruction on the September 30, 1997, to at least 100 students in the language of instruction of the new linguistic board. The elected commissioners on a council had to be eligible to be electors in the linguistic board in question. The number of elected commissioners from each existing board was prorated according to the percentage of students originating from its schools: from 1 commissioner if the ratio was less than 10% to 12 if the ratio was 90% or higher. Two non-voting parent commissioners were chosen, at a general meeting called for that purpose, by and from all parent commissioners from the existing boards concerned who had children in the territory of the linguistic board in question (Ed Act, ss. 510-523).

School Board Structure

A school board is a "legal person" established in the public interest (Ed Act s. 113). As school boards are created by statute, their powers are restricted to those that are expressly conferred on them by legislation (that is, the *Education Act* and other relevant statutes), and those, which while not expressly conferred, are necessary to the effective exercise of their express powers. Similarly, as creatures of statute, school boards can only act through their council of commissioners, director general and other officers.

All school boards are structured in accordance with the main elements shown in the following chart; however, the details of the board administration structure do vary somewhat from board to board.

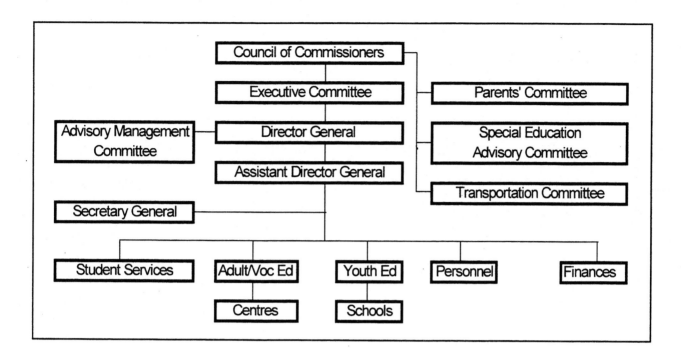

FIGURE 6.1
School Board Organization

Council of Commissioners

The council of commissioners is the governing body of the school board, composed of elected school commissioners and parent commissioners.

Elected Commissioners

An elected commissioner is elected by voters in a given school district in accordance with the *Act Respecting School Elections* [*School Elections Act*]. Normally school board elections are held every four years on the third Sunday in November; however, the election of the first commissioners of the new linguistic school boards was set for mid-June, 1998 (*Act Respecting the Election of the First Commissioners*, 1997). The *School Elections Act* (s. 6) provides for the division of the school district into electoral wards, from 1 ward if there are fewer than 2 000 students to 21 wards if there are 25 000 students or more. The Government may authorize exceptions to these norms.

The S*chool Elections Act* specifies a number of events, including failure to attend seven consecutive meetings, on the occurrence of which a vacancy can arise in the council of commissioners (ss. 191-194). Should a vacancy arise when there is 12 months or less left in the term of the departed commissioner the vacancy is filled by the council of commissioners after consulting the parents' committee (s. 199). If, on the other hand, there remains more than 12 months in the term of the departed commissioner an election must be held in the ward in which the vacancy has arisen (s. 200).

Qualified Electors: The Proposal

The version of the *Linguistic School Boards Act* (1997) introduced upon first reading proposed two standards for electors: one to apply in the case of French language boards, the other to English language boards. Specifically, the latter group was to be restricted to persons who were qualified for admission to English schooling under Bill 101 or whose children so qualified. The Government defended these provisions as being consistent with the *Canadian Charter* (i.e. that electoral qualifications followed entitlement to minority language instruction).

The proposal was strongly denounced by the Anglophone community. It saw the proposal as "evidence of the intention of the Government to further reduce the viability of the English school system and as a harbinger of other restrictions to come in other fields such as health care and access to government services" (Smith & Foster, 1997b, p. 7). Francophone nationalists by contrast saw the Anglophone demand to open up the electoral list as a backdoor attempt to enlarge the admission criteria to English schooling. Such a reaction stemmed in part from the continuing demands from Anglophone groups during the hearings on the *Linguistic School Boards Act* for the application of section 23(1)(a) of the *Canadian Charter* to Québec (see chap. 13).

Qualified Electors: The Result
The final version of the *Linguistic School Boards Act* removed the Bill 101 criterion, but the need to assure Francophone nationalists that Bill 101 was not affected led to the inclusion of a statement in the *School Elections Act* to that effect (see chap. 13). However, even after all that the law did not leave the two school systems on an equal footing as the following summary of the key provision of the Act governing the entitlement to vote shows (s. 15):

- Any elector who has a child enrolled in a school may vote in an election of that school board.
- Every other elector can vote in the French language school board "unless he has chosen to vote" for the English language school board.

The difference in wording in the second clause cited above is subtle but important, especially when combined with another section of the Act regarding the practical application of the law (s. 40). In brief, the starting point for drawing up an electoral list is the list of all electors (for the school district) prepared by the Chief Electoral Officer of Québec. Those persons with children in the English language board of that territory and others who have sent in a written notice that they wish to be on the English language board list are removed and put on a list of electors for the latter. Thus, the original list becomes the base list for the French language board but anyone, other than a parent, who wishes to vote for the English language board must get himself or herself inscribed on the list.

Parent Commissioners

A parent commissioner is elected annually by the parents' committee (see section on Advisory Committees below) to represent them; there is one such commissioner for the elementary level and one for the secondary level (Ed. Act, s. 143). Parent commissioners are not entitled to vote; nor can they be appointed chairperson or vice-chairperson of the board (s. 148).

The term of office of parent commissioners is one year (s. 145); and they may serve their full term whether or not their child continues to attend a school within the school board (s. 147). However, should the office of parent commissioner become vacant, the parents' committee shall elect a replacement (s. 147).

Operation of the Council

The *Education Act* treats in some detail a range of matters relating to the operation of the council of commissioners (ss. 154-178).

The director general of the school board must convene the first meeting of the council of commissioners, which must be held within 15 days of the general election of the commissioners (s. 154).

Chairperson and Substitute
The commissioners appoint a chairperson and a vice-chairperson from among their members whose

term of office is co-extensive with their terms as commissioners unless they are earlier removed (Ed Act, s. 155). Until the chairperson is appointed the meetings of the council of commissioners are presided over by one of their members selected by the commissioners (s. 156). A vacancy in the office of chairperson or vice-chairperson has to be filled within 30 days (s. 157).

The function of the chairperson is to preside over meetings of the council of commissioners and to "maintain order" at the meetings (s. 159).

Meetings

The council of commissioners must, by by-law, fix the day, time and place of its regular meetings and it must hold at least four regular meetings every school year (Ed. Act, s. 162). Provision is also made for the calling of special meetings by two commissioners (ss. 163-165), and, in some cases, for the participation of commissioners in meetings by telephone (s. 169). However, according to Bill 101 (s. 19), the notice must be given in French as well as in English.

Meetings of the council of commissioners are open to the public; but they may be held *in camera* (i.e. closed to the public) for the purpose of dealing with any matters liable to be prejudicial to a person (s. 167). Although meetings are open to the public, only commissioners may take part in the deliberations of the council. However, the council of commissioners must provide for a question period at public meetings to allow other persons present to put oral questions to the commissioners (s. 168). According to Bill 101 (s. 19), the agenda must be provided in French as well as in English.

The quorum for meetings is a majority of the members of the council who are entitled to vote (s. 160). The decisions are taken by a majority of the votes cast by the members present and entitled to vote with the chairperson having a casting vote in the case the vote is equally divided (s. 161).

Minutes must be kept of each meeting in a register, known as the "Minutes of Proceedings," which, after their approval, must be signed by the person presiding at the meeting and the secretary general (s. 170). The minutes, once duly approved, are open to inspection by the public (s. 172). According to Bill 101 (s. 19), a French version of the minutes must also be kept.

When the council of commissioners amends, repeals or replaces an existing by-law or resolution, this has to be clearly recorded in the "Book of By-laws" or the "Minutes of Proceedings" in the manner specified (s. 171).

Remuneration

The *Education Act* authorizes the council of commissioners to determine whether its members should be remunerated and to fix the level of their remuneration (subject to such maximum amounts established by the government) for the services they provide to the school board. They also are entitled to establish allowances to defray expenses incurred in the performance of their functions (s. 175).

Code of Conduct

The council of commissioners must, by by-law, establish a code of ethics and professional conduct (Ed Act, ss. 175.1-175.4). The code must, among other things, set out the duties and obligations of the commissioners, rules for the disclosure of personal interests and the identification of conflicts of interest and enforcement mechanisms. It permits the code to establish standards of conduct that vary according to the various classes of commissioners or which apply only to certain classes of commissioners.

The *Education Act* also specifically prohibits a commissioner who has a direct or indirect interest in any matter which may give rise to a conflict between the commissioner's interests and those of the school board from influencing or participating in a decision dealing with that matter (s. 175.4). Should a commissioner derive a benefit in violation of these provisions he or she is liable to the State for the value of the benefit so derived (s. 175.3).

Moreover, commissioners must: act within the scope of their functions and powers; exercise the care, prudence and diligence that a reasonable person would exercise in similar circumstances; and act with honesty and loyalty and in the interests of the school board and its population (s. 177.1).

Members of the council of commissioners may not be prosecuted for acts performed in good faith in the discharge of their functions (s. 177). However, if a commissioner is prosecuted for an act done in the exercise of his or her functions, then, subject to certain limitations, the school board is obliged to assume his or her defence (s. 177.2). Moreover, a school board is empowered to take out liability insurance for the benefit of commissioners and other employees (s. 178).

Executive Committee

Each school board must establish an executive committee composed of 5-7 voting members of the board including the chair of the board and a commissioner representing the parents' committee. The director general takes part in committee meetings but cannot vote. The executive committee exercises the functions and powers delegated to it by the council of commissioners (Ed Act, ss. 179-182).

School Board Administration

Just as the business of the MEQ is conducted by a variety of officials under the direction of the Deputy Minister, the business of a school board is conducted by a variety of persons under the leadership of the director general.

Director General

The director general is the most senior administrator of the school board and is answerable to the council of commissioners and assists it in the exercise of its duties (Ed Act. s. 144). He or she takes part in the meetings of the council but does not have a right to vote. The director general is responsible for the day-to-day management of the activities and resources of the school board and for the overall supervision of all board employees. There are specific conflict of interest provisions which apply to the director general (ss. 198-203).

Advisory Committee on Management

Every school board must establish an Advisory Committee on Management, under the direction of the director general, composed of school principals, principals of adult education centres and members of the executive staff of the school board. Principals must constitute a majority of the committee (Ed Act, ss. 183-184).

Jurisdiction

The jurisdiction of the school board covers youth students resident in the school district and those placed under the board's jurisdiction pursuant to the *YPA*, the *YOA* or the *Act Respecting Health and Social Services*. In addition, any persons who wish to be enrolled in vocational or adult education come under the jurisdiction of the school board whether or not such persons reside within the jurisdiction of the board (Ed Act, s. 204).

However, the jurisdiction of English language boards extends to those persons who, according to Bill 101, are entitled to receive instruction in English and who elect to come under the jurisdiction of the English language board (Ed Act. ss. 205, 207).

Thus, all persons are presumed to come under the jurisdiction of the French language board unless they are entitled to come under the jurisdiction of the English language board and choose to do so.

School Board Duties & Powers

Like any public body a school board can only do what it is empowered, expressly or by necessary implication, to do by law. Its "duties" include those things a board *must* do while its "powers" include those that it *may* do at its discretion (Ed Act, ss. 204-301).

Authority to Delegate

The *Education Act* expressly provides that a school board may, by by-law, delegate some of its functions and powers to the director general, an assistant director general, a school or centre principal or any other member of the executive staff of the board (s. 174). Where such a delegation is made the person to whom the function or power is delegated must perform them under the direction of the director general (s. 174).

Transitional Measures

The *Education Amendment Act* (1997, s. 198) requires every school board, after consulting with the governing boards of schools and adult and vocational centres, to establish the approach to be taken for 1998-99 and 1999-2000 for the gradual implementation of certain powers now vested in governing boards. These transitional measures apply to: the powers of school governing boards over educational services (Ed Act, ss. 84-89); most of the powers of school principals (ss. 96.15, 96.16); the powers of centre governing boards over educational services (s. 110.2); most of the powers of centre principals (s. 110.12); and the corresponding former powers exercised by school boards over youth (ss. 222-224, 229-231, 233, 237, 244) and adults (ss. 246, 248-249).*

The transitional measures are meant to accommodate two realities: (i) the fact that the new distribution of powers came into force after many decisions affecting the 1998-99 school year had already been made; and, (ii) the different states of readiness of individual schools and centres to assume these new responsibilities. (For a discussion of these powers see chap. 7.) The "approach" to be adopted by each school board therefore permits a different implementation plan for different matters and for different schools or centres. It should be noted that school/centre governing boards must be consulted on the approach envisaged and that regardless of the details of same, the full implementation of the new distribution of powers must be effected by July 1, 2000.

*   In each case we have shaded the text and included a note to this effect to remind the reader of these transitional measures.

More Transition - Reconciling Existing Policies

When the new linguistic school boards were formed they became successors to the previous denominational school boards from which they were formed. As such, they inherited the "rights and obligations" of the previous boards (Ed Act, s. 218), that is the assets and liabilities of the previous boards, and other like financial and contractual rights and obligations. However, the new school board did not inherit the existing policies of the previous boards; they ceased to exist on June 30, 1999. Accordingly, one of the first tasks of the provisional councils, and then the new linguistic school boards, was to identify such policies and adopt new ones, especially when the previous policies of the former boards were contradictory. Given the time that such a process could take, a new linguistic school board might have opted to adopt interim policies as a transitional measure, in particular for those matters that the law requires the school board to have a policy in force or which are particularly pressing. Until such new policies, be they interim or permanent, are adopted, there are no policies as the previous ones are of no force or effect.

General Powers

The key general function of the school board is to "ensure that the persons who come under its jurisdiction are provided the educational services to which they are entitled under this Act" (Ed Act, s. 208). Until now, the board has had an unfettered discretion to discharge this responsibility either directly or by agreement with another school board or body. The *Education Act* now stipulates that it may only contract out its responsibility for providing "educational services" (instructional, student and special services as defined in the *Basic Regulations*) if it "can establish that its resources are insufficient" or if it agrees to a parent's request. Furthermore, the board must make sure that "the services are provided as near the students' [*sic*] place of residence as possible" (s. 209). Subject to the foregoing, a school board may enter into an agreement with another school board, or private educational institution for the provision of a range of services to students coming under its jurisdiction but it must first have consulted the students, if of full age, and the parents of other students who are likely to be affected by such arrangements (s. 213). In addition, and subject to certain parameters, a school board may enter into an agreement with a foreign government or international organisation for the provision of educational services provided they have been judged by the Minister to be equivalent to those provided for in the *Basic Regulations* (s. 214). Similarly, with the authority of the Minister, a school board may enter into an agreement of association with a private educational institution or a general or vocational college (s. 215.1).

School boards do not have the power to determine the language in which its educational services are to be provided in schools. The *Education Act* states that French language boards must provide educational services in French, and English language boards must provide those services in English (s. 210). However, the vocational training and adult education services provided by school boards may be in French or English although admissibility to such services may be limited by law (s. 210).

Establishment of Schools & Centres

A principal function of school boards is the establishment of schools and centres within their territories. (This matter is dealt with in some detail in chap. 7.)

Educational Services for Youth

The principal functions of the school board respecting general educational services for youth are summarized below (Ed Act, ss. 221-244). In keeping with the shift of authority to the schools (see chap. 7), the Act now recasts many school board responsibilities from "shall do x" to "shall ensure that x is done." However, it is important to note that the Act does not assign the school board any role in directing *how* these responsibilities should be exercised. In other words, the school board does not have the authority to establish guidelines or parameters which the school must follow.

Thus, under the new scheme of things, the *Education Act* requires that the school board shall ensure that schools: implement the *Basic Regulations*, though school boards may grant exemptions for individual students or a special school project (s. 222);[1]* implement the compulsory and elective subjects, including exemptions for individual students (s. 222.1);[1]* provide approved free textbooks and instructional materials (s. 230);* and evaluate student achievement and administer MEQ exams (s. 231).*

The school board shall also ensure that schools provide Catholic and Protestant MRI, and other related matters (ss. 225-228, 241; see chapter 12).

However, the Act requires that the school board shall: establish a program for student services (s. 224);[1]* and, after consultation of the parents' committee, shall establish rules for promotion of students from elementary to secondary school and from secondary cycle I to II (s. 233).[1]*

The Act likewise requires that the school board shall: recognize in accordance with ministerial criteria or conditions, students' learning not covered by the *Basic Regulations* (s. 232); provide for adaptation of services for students with special needs (s. 234; see chap. 4);[1] adopt policy on various matters respecting students with special needs (s. 235; see chap. 4);[1] determine the educational services to be provided by each of its schools (s. 236; see discussion below);[1] establish the school calendar (s. 238);[1] establish the enrolment criteria for schools (s. 239; see chap. 3);[1] and take part in periodic evaluation by the Minster on various specified matters (s. 243).[1]

In addition, the *Education Act* confers certain discretionary powers on school boards in providing that they may: develop local programs leading to an occupation or profession and award attestation of such qualification (s. 223);[1]* and impose board exams at the end of each elementary cycle and secondary cycle I (s. 231).[1]*

Similarly, the school board may establish a school with a specific project (s. 240; see chap. 3);[1] provide derogations for admission to preschool or elementary school for children who do not qualify for admission under the standard rules but who meet the age requirements for such a derogation (s. 241.1); and expel students "for just and sufficient cause," after giving students and parents an "opportunity to be heard" (s. 242; see chap. 3).

Finally, it may be noted that school boards no longer have any role in adopting criteria for new methods of instruction, selection of textbooks and instructional material (s. 229);[1]* or in determining the time allotted to each subject, that compulsory objectives of MEQ programs are achieved, that the minimum time prescribed by Catholic or Protestant regulations is respected, and that rules on certification of studies are respected (s. 237). These provisions have been repealed.*

* *Note*. Provisions subject to "Transitional Measures" - see above.

[1] It is pertinent to note that the *Education Act* (s. 244) requires school boards to consult with teachers in accordance with provisions of the collective agreement on the above matters coming within ss. 222-224, 231, 233-240 and 243.

Educational Services Provided by Schools

A mentioned above, one of the powers of a school board is to "determine the educational services to be provided by each of its schools" (Ed Act, s. 236). This provision is not new but takes on a new significance in the light of the other changes enacted by the *Education Amendment Act* (1997). In other words, what latitude does the school board have in deciding on the educational offering of a given school versus that accorded to the schools themselves? Since section 236 is very general in nature, it must be interpreted in light of other provisions of the Act and the regulations, especially those which deal with specific aspects of educational services.

"Educational services" are defined in the regulations as comprising three types of services: instructional services (developmental services for preschool), student services and special services. Instructional services are not specifically defined but they can be inferred to refer to classroom teaching, that is, the subjects provided for each level of instruction (El Reg, s. 44; Sec Reg, s. 35). Student services are defined by a non-exhaustive list, including guidance, psychological and health services (see El Reg, s. 5; Sec Reg, s. 4). Special services are likewise defined by a non-exhaustive list: additional French instruction (i.e. classes d'accueil), home bound or hospital instruction and remedial teaching (see El Reg, s. 17; Sec Reg, s. 16).

Accordingly, a school board can decide which of these services will be offered in various schools. This power must be read in conjunction with the school board's power to determine, by means of the deed of establishment, the levels of instruction to be offered in each school. On the other hand, the subject offerings for a given grade level are determined by the regulations. The approach to the implementation of the *Basic Regulations*, the adaptation and enrichment of ministry programs, the approval of local programs and the minutes of instruction for a given subject are all now determined at the school level (see chap. 7). Therefore, it is not clear what discretion section 236 actually gives the school board respecting instructional services. Since the locus of authority for the "micro-management" of instruction has clearly shifted to the school, it would be reasonable to construe section 236 as permitting the school board to make macro-level decisions about instruction - a power which would be consistent with the right to assign levels of instruction.

One such macro decision might be the designation of a school as a segregated school for students with disabilities or special learning problems, a power that would appear to be supported by section 235 (special education policy). By contrast, the designation of a school for other specific purposes would appear to be a school prerogative to initiate, either by virtue of its educational project, which cannot entail any special enrolment criteria, or as a "specific project" which, if approved by the Minister, can have school board approved enrolment criteria (see ss. 239-240). Some people have suggested that French immersion programs might constitute a macro decision under the umbrella of section 236. If this is so, school board power is probably limited to deciding *if* a school will offer French immersion and if so at what levels.*

* It should also be noted that French immersion can only be provided to students whose parents have so elected: "The school board may, for students eligible to receive instruction in English and with the parents' authorization, use French as the language of instruction for subjects other than French as a Second Language, in accordance with the procedures established by the Minister (El Reg, s. 46; see also Sec Reg, s. 35).

In terms of student and special services, it would appear that the school board has some discretion to determine which of them will be offered by individual schools. Thus one school may be mandated to provide guidance services, another may not. However, such discretion could not be used to effectively deprive students of services to which they are entitled. For example, according to the Act, Catholic and Protestant MRI, as well as moral instruction must be available in any school where it is requested (ss. 5, 225). By contrast, it is unclear whether related pastoral services have to be offered in every school (ss. 6, 226), and instruction in another religious faith (i.e. not Catholic or Protestant) is only offered in a school when the school board approves a request of the governing board.

Vocational Training & Adult Education

The principal functions of the school board respecting vocational training and adult educational services are summarized below (Ed Act, ss. 245-254).

Under the new scheme of things, the *Education Act* requires that the school board shall ensure that vocational training and adult education centres implement the *Basic Regulations* (though school boards may grant certain exemptions to these regulations) (s. 246),[1]* evaluate student achievement and administer MEQ exams (though school boards may impose board exams in subjects in which there is no MEQ exam and in which one is required in order to obtain a secondary or vocational diploma) (s. 249).[1]*

However, the Act requires that the school board shall itself establish a program for student services and popular education services (s. 247)[1] and take part in periodic evaluation by the Minister on various specified matters (s. 253).

Similarly, the school board shall itself provide reception and referral services for both vocational and adult education (s. 250),[1]* determine the educational services to be provided by each of its centres (s. 251),[1]* and establish the school calendar (s. 252).[1]*

In addition, the *Education Act* confers certain discretionary powers on school boards in providing that they may develop local programs leading to an occupation or profession and award attestation of such qualification (s. 246.1).[1]*

Finally, it may be noted that school boards no longer have any role in adopting criteria for new methods of instruction, selection of textbooks and instructional material (s. 248).[1]*

---

* *Note.* Provisions subject to "Transitional Measures" - see above.

[1]   The *Education Act* (s. 244) requires school boards to consult with teachers in accordance with provisions of the collective agreement on the above matters.

Community Services

The principal functions of school boards respecting community services are summarized below (Ed Act, ss. 255-258).

On the one hand, the *Education Act* confers certain discretionary powers and duties on school boards in this field. They may through manpower training and so forth contribute to technological and regional development and provide cultural, social, sports scientific or community services (s. 255); and, provide meals and lodging to students (s. 257). On the other hand, school boards must, at the request of the governing board of a school, provide child care for preschool and elementary school students in the manner agreed to with the governing board, on the school premises or, if the school does not have suitable premises, on other premises (s. 256).

School boards may require the payment of user fees for any of the above services (s. 258).

Human Resources

The *Education Act* (ss. 259-265) assigns the majority of powers respecting human resources to the school board. It is the employer of all school board, school and centre personnel. School board personnel (including principals) perform their functions under the authority of the director general, whereas school and centre personnel perform their functions under the authority of the principal. In assigning staff to schools and centres, school boards must take into account the staffing requirements submitted by principals (see chap. 7) and ensure that teachers are legally qualified and that other norms are respected.

In addition, although each school board may decide on its own organization chart, it must appoint someone to be responsible for Catholic and Protestant services (see chap. 12), adult services (if applicable) and services for students with special needs.

Financial Resources & Other Services

The principal functions of the school board respecting financial resources and other services (Ed Act, ss. 266-301) are summarized in the next two sub-sections.

Financial Resources

Every school board, after deducting an amount for its own needs and those of its committees, shall allocate amongst its schools (and other institutions), "in an equitable manner and in *consideration* of social and economic disparities and of the needs expressed by its schools," the operating grants allocated by the Minister, school tax proceeds and investment income (s. 275). School boards shall also make public the objectives and principles governing the allocation of grants, taxation proceeds and other revenues among its institutions, the criteria pertaining thereto, as well as the aims, principles and criteria which serve to determine the amount which the board retains for its own uses (s. 275).

School board budgets are required to: indicate the financial resources allocated to committees and to services for students with special needs; treat school and centre budgets as separate appropriations; limit expenditures to the level of revenues, unless otherwise approved by the Minister; include as a revenue any accumulated or anticipated surplus and as an expenditure any accumulated or anticipated deficit; and be transmitted to the Minister (but they are not subject to the approval of the latter).

School boards are responsible for approving the budgets of schools and centres but cannot amend the budgets submitted for their approval by school and centre governing boards (s. 276; for further details, see chap. 11).

Transportation Services

School boards may, with the authorization of the Minister, provide transportation for all or some of its students either itself or by contracting out (Ed Act, ss. 291-301). As previously discussed (see chap. 3), whether or not the school board provides noon hour transportation, it must ensure noon-hour supervision for students who stay at school. Such supervision must be provided according to the terms and conditions agreed to with the school governing boards; but it is the school board that determines the financial conditions under which supervision is to be provided (s. 292). The wording of the provision that treats the matter of noon-hour supervision clearly assigns primary responsibility for this matter to school boards.

Accountability

A number of provisions of the *Education Act* deal with the matter of accountability.

Accountability to School Board

The Act provides for the accountability of schools and centres to the school board. Thus, a school board may require from its educational institutions such information and documents the school board considers necessary for the performance of its functions and powers (s. 218.1). Moreover, if a school or centre does not comply with the provisions of the Act to which it is subjected, the school board, after giving reasonable notice, may take appropriate action such as substituting its decisions for those of the institution (s. 218.2).

Accountability of School Board

Conversely, the Act provides for the accountability of school boards to others. Thus, it is the obligation of the school board to provide to the Minister of Education such information and documents as he or she may request (s. 219) as well as an annual report (s. 220). In addition, school boards must inform the population in its territory of the educational and cultural services it provides, and give it an account of the quality of these services and of the use of its resources (s. 220).

It must also be noted that school boards, to whom management of funds raised through the activities of individual schools or centres is assigned by the Act, must, at the request of the school or centre governing board, give the governing board access to the records of the funds and provide it with any account, report or other information relating to the fund (s. 94).

School Board Advisory Committees

The *Education Act* provides for the establishment of a number of school board advisory committees and expressly states that the school board must consult these committees (and school and centre governing boards) on the matters on which they must be consulted (s. 217).

Parents' Committee

The principal advisory committee for parents at the board level is called the parents' committee. When the Act provided for school committees, the parents' committee was a logical extension of parental participation from the school to the school board level. Despite the creation of school governing boards, this board level committee has not changed its essential composition or vocation. This raises the question as to whether there is a need to provide a board level voice to the school governing boards, how such a committee should be structured, and so forth.

The composition, duties and powers of the parents' committee are set forth in the *Education Act* (ss. 189-197). A parents' committee, which must be established in each school board, consists of one representative from each school elected by the general assembly of parents (see chap. 7) and a representative from the special education advisory committee.

If school boards divide their territory into administrative regions they may replace the parents' committee with a regional parents' committee for each region. Such school boards must still maintain a parents' committee, known as a central parents' committee, composed of delegates from the regional parents' committee and a representative of the special education advisory committee.

The parents' committee fulfills a number of functions and must be consulted by the school board on a number of matters, as summarized below.

Functions of the Parents' Committee
The functions of the parents' committee as specified in the *Education Act* (s. 192) are to: promote parental participation in the activities of the school board; give advice on any matter to facilitate the efficient running of the school board; inform the school board of the needs of parents identified by its representatives from the schools and the special education advisory committee; and give its opinion to the school board on any matter on which it must be consulted (which are listed below).

Matters for Mandatory Consultation
The *Education Act* (s. 193) provides that the parents' committee of a school board must be consulted by the board on a range of matters, namely: changes in the territory of the board; the board's three-year plan for the allocation of its immovables; the list of schools and deeds of establishment; the board's policy regarding school closures (s. 212); the distribution of educational services among the schools; criteria for school enrolment of students (s. 239); the dedication of a school to a specific project and the criteria for school enrolment of students in that school (s. 240); the school calendar; the rules governing promotion of students from the elementary to the secondary level and from the first to the second cycle of secondary school (s. 233); the objectives, principles and criteria governing (i) the allocation of financial resources among the schools and (ii) the amount to be withheld by the board for its needs and those of its committees; and the learning activities established by the school board for parents.

Special Education Advisory Committee

Each school board must establish a special education advisory committee on services for students with special needs (for details, see chap. 4).

Transportation Committee

There is one other board level parent advisory committee provided for in the *Education Act*: the advisory committee on school transportation (s. 188).

The School Board Consultative Process

Matter to be Consulted On	Who Must be Consulted
Amendment or revocation of deed of establishment (ss. 40, 79, 101, 110.1)	School/Centre Governing Board
Selection criteria for the appointment of the principal (ss. 79, 110.1)	School/Centre Governing Board
Appointment of vice-principal (ss. 96.9, 110.6)	Principal
Confessional status of the school (ss. 79, 218)	School Governing Board Parents of the school
Division of powers & functions between school governing boards & the coordinating committee (s. 211)	School/Centre Governing Board
*Rules for the promotion of students from elementary to secondary & from secondary cycle I to II (ss. 193.8, 233)	Teachers Parents' Committee
*Establishment of a program of student services & popular education services (ss. 224, 247)	Teachers
Adaptation of services for students with special needs (s. 234)	Teachers
Distribution of educational services to be provided by each of the schools or centres of the board (ss. 193(5), 236, 251)	Teachers Parents' Committee
School calendar (ss. 193(7), 238, 252)	Teachers Parents' Committee
Enrolment criteria for schools (ss. 193(6), 239)	Teachers Parents' Committee
Periodic evaluation by Minister on specific measures (ss. 243, 253)	Teachers
*Development of local programs leading to an occupation or profession & awarding of attestation (s. 223)	Teachers
*Setting of board exams at the end of each elementary cycle & secondary cycle I (s. 231)	Teachers
Establishment of a school with a specific project & enrolment criteria for same (ss. 193(6.1), 240)	Teachers Parents' Committee
*Criteria for new methods of instruction & for selection of textbooks & instructional materials (s. 229)	Teachers
*Implementation of Basic Regulations (ss. 222, 246)	Teachers
*Implementation of compulsory and elective subjects (s. 222(1))	Teachers
*Evaluation of student achievement & administration of school board exams (s. 249)	Teachers
Provision of reception & referral services for vocational & adult education (s. 250)	Teachers

Matter to be Consulted On	Who Must be Consulted
Changes in the territory of the school board (s. 193(1))	Parents' Committee
3-year plan for the allocation of immovables, the list of schools & the deeds of establishment (s. 193(2))	Parents' Committee
Policy regarding school closure (ss. 193(3), 212)	Parents' Committee
Objectives, principles & criteria governing the allocation of financial services among schools & the amount to be withheld for board's own needs & committees (s. 193(9))	Parents' Committee
The learning activities established by the school board for parents (s. 193.10)	Parents' Committee
Adoption of the special education policy (s. 235)	Teachers Special Education Advisory Committee
Approach to be taken for the implementation of transitional measures (s. 198)	School/Centre Governing Boards

* *Note.* Denotes a transitional measure.

CHAPTER 7
GOVERNANCE AT THE LOCAL LEVEL

Introduction

This chapter deals with the third and arguably the most vital level of educational governance - the school, and the equivalent unit in adult education - the centre. As is noted below in the Background section, traditionally the school has been accorded little legislative space and its powers have been granted more by administrative delegation by school boards than legislative delegation by the Government. With the adoption of the *Education Amendment Act* in 1997, this situation has changed radically and the school has now received a greater recognition in keeping with its role as the primary unit in the school system. One can truly say that now the *talk* on decentralization has passed to *action*.

Background

In 1978, the MEQ made the following statement in a green paper on education reform: "It is clear that there is a greater and greater demand for decentralization of the school system. The Government, for its part, has announced unequivocally that it intends to proceed with decentralization" (p. 114). The plan of action which followed (MEQ, 1979a) did not contain any proposal concerning governance; these were deferred until further consultations with school boards and other stakeholders, many of whom were very wary of the Government's intentions, were undertaken.

In 1982, the MEQ proposed taking forward the notion of school autonomy in a policy paper entitled, *The Quebec School: A Responsible Force in the Community*. This paper advocated making the school "the pivot of the school system" (p. 51) and granting it both critical powers regarding educational matters and the administrative and financial means to exercise these powers. The proposed reform was destined for a "rough ride" and survived only in a diluted form in Bill 40 (1983) which never became law (Milner, 1986). The reform, which was viewed as creating a network of schools with the autonomy of private schools, was opposed both by school boards who saw it as diluting - if not utterly eliminating - their role, and by unions who did not relish the prospect of negotiating collective agreements with 4 000 schools and losing the job security/mobility that the current system provided their members. The controversy over *school* reform was also inextricably bound up in the more long standing debate over *school board* reform which dominated the policy talk of the next decade, namely the restructuring of boards along linguistic, rather than denominational lines (Smith & Foster, 1998). Despite the dominance of school board structures in the educational reform debate, the policy thrust of placing schools at the core of the system never really abated, as will be seen below.

Focus on the School & Centre

Bill 107 (1988)

When Bill 107 was adopted in 1988, its principal aim was the introduction of linguistic school boards; however, it was also designed "to make the school legally more independent of the school board, while preserving its organizational links with the board and the other schools connected with the board. It [the Bill] gives both the school and persons acting for the school a larger say in the decisions of the school board" (Bill 107, Explanatory Note, p. i).

Further Impetus for Change

Subsequent policy papers continued the policy talk about schools as the key to education reform but were cautious in terms of making concrete changes in governing powers (e.g. MEQ, 1993), while the Superior Council (1993b) also advocated the need for a new management model. The momentum for change was given further impetus by the calling of the Estates General on Education. One of the ten priority actions recommended by the Commission for the Estates General (see chap. 5) was a redistribution of powers to increase local decision making capacity and openness to the community. This policy direction was echoed by the Superior Council (1996a) and was followed by a ministerial policy paper, one of the key policy thrusts of which was to provide greater autonomy to schools (MEQ, 1997a, p. 14):

> One of the main levers in the process of ensuring that as many students as possible achieve success is the capacity of individual schools to adapt their services to the needs and characteristics of the populations they serve. If each institution is truly to be able to exercise its responsibilities, it must be able to make and act on pedagogical, administrative and budgetary decisions. This calls for a new division of responsibilities between schools, school boards and the MEQ. The Education Act will be amended accordingly.

The Education Amendment Act

The promised legislation was not long in coming - but first a brief reminder about the legal context of these changes. As we saw in chapter 6, the Government was proceeding with the amendment of the Constitution and the implementation of linguistic school boards, when it decided to table a draft bill on the redistribution of powers among different stakeholders in the education system. Public hearings were held on the draft bill that was subsequently introduced as a legislative bill (Bill 180) and then adopted as law (the *Education Amendment Act*) in December 1997.

This Act radically changes the role of schools inside these new linguistic school board structures, as it provides for a new division of responsibilities between the school, the school board and the Government. The heart of the Act is the complete re-writing of the *Education Act* concerning the role and powers of schools, vocational centres and adult education centres.

A: SCHOOLS

Overview

The *Education Amendment Act* (1997) replaced the previous chapter III of the *Education Act* dealing with the school; the new version is divided into five divisions: Establishment; Governing Board; Parent Participation Organization; Student Committee; and the Principal.

Establishment

The "establishment" of schools is concerned with the basic parameters defining the role of the school, including its creation and closure.

Deed of Establishment

A school is established by a school board by a "deed of establishment" issued annually in accordance with the school board's three year plan. It specifies the school's name and address, the premises at its disposal and the level of instruction it provides. A school's deed of establishment may be amended or revoked by the school board in accordance with the school board's three-year plan (Ed Act, ss. 39-41).

Despite the standard image of a school as an educational institution in a building by itself in one location, three configurations of schools can be inferred from the Act:

- one school in one building;
- one school in two or more buildings (which could be situated in different municipalities);
- two or more schools in one building.

It is also implicit in the Act that there must be a principal for every school and every school has its own governing board. In the first case noted above, the matter is straightforward. However, in other cases, the school board decision as to whether, for example, two buildings should be considered as one school or two schools determines *a priori* whether there will be one governing board or two.

Special mention is made of the situation where two schools* share the same building. In such case, the school board must, at the request of the two governing boards, establish a coordinating committee. This committee is composed of representatives of both governing boards. The school board establishes the distribution of powers and functions between the governing boards and the coordinating committee, as well as the latter's administrative and operational rules (s. 211).

* *Note.* The actual term used in the Act is "institution" which encompasses a school and a vocation or adult centre.

There is no mention in the Act of "institutional schools," a phrase commonly used to denote a grouping of two or more individual schools under the common leadership of one principal. There would appear to be no impediment in the Act to a school board appointing a person to be principal of more than one school. Accordingly, for example, a school board could decide to group three buildings in three communities and establish them as one school under the leadership of one principal. Alternatively, it could decide to establish them as three separate schools and appoint the same person as principal in all three. In the first case there would be one governing board, in the second there would be three. However, once the decision is made to define a school in one way or the other, there is no latitude concerning the establishment of the governing boards. Each school must have a principal and a governing board; it may share its principal with another school but one governing board cannot oversee two schools.

In contrast to the foregoing, the establishment of the school does not settle the question of the parent participation organization. The initial meeting of parents must involve the parents of the school, however, defined by the school board. Accordingly, if the school is defined as three buildings in three communities, one initial meeting would be called for the parents from all three locations. At that time, the parents may decide to form a separate parent participation organization for each building or one for the entire school (s. 96.1; for other details, see below at the end of section A).

The role of the school governing board respecting the amendment or revocation of a deed of establishment is dealt with below.

Annual Three-Year Plan

The *Education Act* states that each year a school board shall establish a three-year plan of allocation and destination of its immovables (s. 211). This provision seems to be a classic oxymoron, with the second and third years of each plan being subject to revision annually, not triennially. The three-year plan must be sent to each regional county, municipality or community whose territory coincides wholly or partly with the territory of the school board.

School Closure

A school board, after consulting the parents' committee, is now required to adopt a policy concerning the maintenance and closure of its schools which must comply with any guidelines that may be established by the Minister (s. 212). The closure of a particular school is subject to consultation with its governing board inasmuch as closure presumably implies a revocation of its deed of establishment (ss. 40, 79(1)).

Purpose

The *Education Act* now defines the purpose of a school as follows:

Education Act

36. A school is an educational institution whose object is to provide to the persons entitled thereto under section 1 the educational services provided for by this Act and prescribed by the basic school regulation established by the Government under section 447 and to contribute to the social and cultural development of the community.

In keeping with the principle of equality of opportunity, the mission of a school is to impart knowledge to students, foster their social development and give them qualifications, while enabling them to undertake and achieve success in a course of study.

A school shall pursue its mission within the framework of an educational project defined, implemented and periodically evaluated in collaboration with the students, the parents, the principal, the teachers and other school staff, representatives of the community and the school board.

Denominational Status

Despite the implementation of denominationally neutral linguistic school boards, the *Education Act* still provides for the recognition of schools as Catholic or Protestant – a matter dealt with in greater depth later in this text (see chap. 12).

Specific Project

The *Education Act* also makes reference to establishing a school for the purposes of a "specific project" but does not define this term nor distinguish it from a school's educational project:

Education Act

240. By way of exception, at the request of a group of parents and after consultation with the parents committee, a school board may, with the Minister's approval, establish a school for the purposes of a specific project, subject to the conditions and for the period determined by the Minister.

The school board may determine the enrollment criteria for the enrollment of the students in that school.

This is a new provision and the discourse surrounding its adoption suggests that it is directed toward the establishment of *elite schools* or *academies* which set admission standards, impose dress codes and undertake other measures to set themselves apart from "ordinary" public schools. Some people see these schools as an appropriate policy response to consumer choice, while offering competition to private schools. Others see them as "public schools in the private interest"* that are antithetical to the concept of the common public school. Whatever one's view on such schools, the scope of section 240 is so broad that it encompasses any *alternative* school.

* Note. This expression is a parody of one used to define private schools eligible for public funding: "a private school in the public interest."

So-called alternative schools include a wide variety of schools from the *academies* mentioned above to *international* schools, *outreach* schools (for dropouts) and others with a specialized curriculum focus (e.g. fine arts). Such schools have proliferated in recent years, especially in Montréal, to the point that at the elementary level if French immersion schools are included in their number, so-called *regular* schools are now in the minority.

To date, the Minister has issued no general guidelines for the acceptance of specific project schools; nor does the Act require that this be done. However, as discussed in chapter 4, the final version of the *Education Amendment Act* (1997) added the note to section 235 of the *Education Act* that specifies that placement in a segregated special school does not constitute the creation of a school with a specific project in the meaning of section 240.

Student Enrolment

The Act stipulates the criteria that a school board - not the school - may establish for student enrolment in its schools; these provisions are examined in detail in chapter 3.

Educational Project

> The educational project gives the school an identity and an image. Above and beyond management methods, participation structures and analytical or evaluation techniques, the educational project is a matter of attitudes. As a joint initiative, the educational project calls for individuals and groups to adopt and develop attitudes along the way that will ensure the success of this initiative (MEQ, 1980b, pp. 16, 85).

The notion of a school "educational project" is not new (see *Historical Roots*, chap. 4), having been first articulated in the Green Paper (MEQ, 1978) and then introduced in the *Education Act* in 1979. A subsequent policy document (MEQ, 1980b) was entirely devoted to explaining the meaning of the educational project but ironically it does not contain a single clear definition of the construct. It does state that "the educational project is ... an initiative by which a school ... adopts a plan of action ... with the participation of the partners concerned" (pp. 13-15). However, the document points out that the project and the plan of action are not one and the same and sums up the discussion of the meaning of the educational project as something that "gives the school an identity and an image" (p. 16).

The newly revised *Education Act* does not add any significant illumination to our understanding about the nature and scope of the educational project merely providing:

Education Act

37. A school's educational project shall set out the specific aims and objectives of the school, and the means by which the educational project is to be implemented and evaluated.

The aims and objectives of the project, and the means by which it is to be implemented, shall be designed to ensure that the provincial educational policy defined by law, the basic school regulation and the programs of studies established by the Minister are implemented, adapted and enriched to reflect the needs of the students and the priorities of the school.

Role of the School Governing Board

As will be outlined later in this chapter, the responsibility for developing a school's educational project rests with the new school governing board. Given the lack of a definition, a paucity of information and the absence of guidelines, how can the governing board best understand and approach the task, in light of the new role of the school in educational governance?

The concept of a school "educational project" was viewed with considerable suspicion and scepticism when it was first introduced. Henchey (1983, pp. 154-55) referred to it as "an anomaly wrapped in illusions" and as "a piece that does not quite fit." The reasons for this view are best understood in light of the overall government policy agenda of that period. As explained in Henchey and Burgess (1987, pp. 93-94):

> The major thrust of the proposals in the Green Paper, the Orange Paper and the régimes pédagogiques had been in the direction of the scientific and technological management of education. This view was the educational philosophy which valued the standardization of timetables, terminal behavioural objectives, detailed curriculum guidelines and systematic and objective evaluation. It was a world-view based on rationality, coherence, consistency, and systems; it was an orientation not peculiar to Quebec, but one which reflected a general trend of back-to-basics, of increased accountability and of competency-based approaches to learning. ... Why, then, would the Ministry promoting such a philosophy, simultaneously be also promoting the notion of decentralization, individualization, and the education project? To some, it was merely a paradox; illogical, inconsistent, and unworkable. ...

Times have changed somewhat; the paradox can now be partially resolved by the allocation of significant power to the school level. At the time of writing, however, it remains to be seen if the central power will devolve some of its regulatory powers to other levels of governance. The concept that each school pursue its individual mission through an educational project that is developed, implemented and evaluated by the school and its community is in keeping with the new role of the school in educational governance.

The educational project can be viewed as that which gives a school a distinctive identity, character or ethos. The goals and objectives set forth in the educational project must enable the school to fulfill its mission, namely to: provide equal opportunity for all; facilitate the full development of students; and ensure success for as many as possible. This is to be accomplished through imparting knowledge to students, developing in them the social skills needed to become productive citizens, and providing them with the necessary qualifications for employment (Ed Act, s. 36). Particular school policies concerning programs, options, subject time, student conduct and other areas, must accord with the goals set forth in the educational project. Furthermore, the educational project must respect the *Education Act*, the *Basic Regulations* and the *Catholic Regulation* (in schools recognized as Catholic) and all other relevant provincial laws, regulations or policies, as well as any particular school orientations as recognized by the minister as a "specific project."

Constraints

First, we have seen in the previous chapter that the school board has the authority to decide what educational services will be offered in each of its schools, for example special education, French immersion, remedial teaching or guidance. Second, at the beginning of this chapter, it was noted that the school board issues a deed of establishment for each of its schools which includes an assignation of the levels of instruction and the premises that it will occupy. Third, as noted above, a school may inherit a denominational status from the previous denominational system of school boards. The school governing board by its own decision cannot revoke this status, but rather must ask the school board to request the appropriate denominational committee of the CSE to do so, following consultation of parents. Fourth, the *Education Act* confers on parents in a school, not the school governing board, the right to request that the school have a specific project. Last, as a general rule, enrolment criteria deal only with capacity and are established by the school board. One can then ask, what control does a school have over its mission, as expressed through its educational project, in light of the foregoing constraints. In many cases, these constraints will not inhibit the development of an educational project and the school will have considerable latitude in developing its plan. For example, where a school board creates a K to 6 school with neutral status and determines that the school itself will provide all educational services for this level. However, the combination of the constraints mentioned above could create serious problems for other schools, such as one that wishes to offer inclusive education to students with various special needs, but has not been assigned any special education services by the school board.

Implementation of the Educational Project

The educational project is implemented by means of a plan of action that is developed in collaboration with all stakeholders. According to Anderson and Rahming (1983) both the process and the product, or plan of action, are important elements of the educational project. In their view, the necessary conditions for success in this endeavour are that:

- the action be initiated from within;
- it be consensus-based;
- it provide for the development of participants both individually and as a group;
- it be adaptable and reflect the diversity that exists within the school community; and
- it allow for "transparency" or visibility, in that the school philosophy and orientation are made explicit and understood by all the stakeholders and the school community.

Both the educational project and the plan of action must be evaluated regularly to ensure that the goals envisaged are being achieved and continue to meet the needs of the students and the school community. When indicated, both the project and the plan will have to be adapted to meet changing needs and conditions, which have been identified during periods of evaluation.

Annual General Meeting of Parents

The tradition of holding an annual general meeting of the parents of a school is continued in the new *Education Act*. In September of each year the chair of the school governing board or the principal must call a meeting of parents (s. 47). This initial meeting of parents must involve the parents of the school, however defined by the school board (see above). Accordingly, if the school is defined as three buildings in three communities, one initial meeting would be called for the parents from all three locations.

The purpose of the annual meeting is to: elect the parent representatives of the school governing board; and elect, from among those already chosen for the school governing board, the parent representative and substitute to the parents' committee (s. 47; see chap. 6).

Parents at this meeting may also determine whether they wish to establish a parent participation organization (s. 96). Where the school occupies more than one building or provides instruction at both the elementary and secondary levels, the parents may decide to form a parent participation organization for each building or for each level (s. 96.1). The parents also decide its name, composition and operating rules (s.96).

The Act does not appear to provide any flexibility that would allow the school to hold the annual meeting after September 30; if no meeting is held or if no decisions are made, then, for the remainder of the school year in progress, there can be no school governing board, no parent participation organization.

School Governing Boards

In this section we present an overview of the election, composition, operation and functions of the newly created school governing boards. These boards replace the former orientation committees.

Election, Term of Office & Vacancies

All elected members must be elected by their peers at elections held by each group during the month of September in each school year (Ed Act, ss. 47-51). Elections held at any other time are without effect except to fill a vacancy.

The members of a governing board assume office as soon as all the voting members of the board (identified below) are elected (s. 53). Elections must be held no later than 30 September of each school year (ss. 47-51). The term of office of parents representatives is two years; that of the representatives of all other groups is one year (s. 54). However, the term for half the parent representatives in the first year of existence of a governing board is one year.

Vacancies are filled for the unexpired portion of the term remaining. Parent vacancies are filled by a decision of the parent representatives on the school governing board; others are filled in the same manner in which the members were elected (s. 55).

Composition

The governing board is composed of a maximum of 20 members consisting of the following (s. 42):*

Voting Members

[1] at least four parents of students, who are not members of the staff of the school, elected by their peers;

[2] four or more staff of the school, including at least two teachers and, if the persons concerned so decide, at least one non-teaching staff member, elected by their peers;

[3] in the case of a school that provides daycare services for children at preschool or elementary school level, a member of the staff assigned to the provision of such services, elected by his or her peers;

Non-Voting Members

[4] in the case of a school providing education to students in the second cycle of the secondary level, two students in that cycle either elected by students enrolled at the secondary level or, as the case may be, appointed by the students' committee or the association representing those students;

[5] two representatives of the community who are not members of the school staff, appointed by the members elected under [1], [2] and [3] above.

* *Note*. The categories of members have been reordered to group voting and non-voting members together

The school board determines the number of representatives of parents and staff on the governing board after consulting with each group concerned. Where there are fewer than 60 students in the school, the school board may, after consulting parents and staff, vary the number of school staff on the governing board. However, in all cases the number of parents [1] and staff representatives [2]+[3] must remain equal (ss. 42-44).

The student and community representatives on the governing board are not entitled to vote (s. 42). The principal must take part in meetings of the governing board but is not entitled to vote (s. 46).

School commissioners can not be members of a governing board of a school within their school board. In addition, they may only attend meetings if authorized by the governing board, and are not entitled to vote (s. 45).

Finally, it should be noted that if fewer than the designated number of parent representatives are elected there can be no governing board and the principal then performs functions and exercises powers of the governing board (s. 52). However, the fact that the number of representatives of any other group (including teachers and school staff) falls short of the required number (either initially or at a later date) will not prevent the formation or functioning of a governing board (ss. 52, 61).

A range of possible combinations of representation on the governing board of an elementary and secondary school are shown below.*

Elementary School

Groups		Number of Representatives				
[1]	Parents	9	8	7	6	5
[2]	Staff	8	7	6	5	4
[3]	Daycare	1	1	1	1	1
Sub-total		18	16	14	12	10
[4]	Students					
[5]	Community	2	2	2	2	2
Total		20	18	16	14	12
Quorum	Parents	5	4	4	3	3
	Total	11	10	8	8	7

Secondary School

Groups		Number of Representatives				
[1]	Parents	8	7	6	5	4
[2]	Staff	8	7	6	5	4
[3]	Daycare					
Sub-total		16	14	12	10	8
[4]	Students	2	2	2	2	2
[5]	Community	2	2	2	2	2
Total		20	18	16	14	12
Quorum	Parents	4	4	3	3	2
	Total	11	10	8	8	7

* Note. The following parameters must be respected by the school board in determining the number of representatives of each group:

[1]=4+ parents and =[2]+[3] (staff & daycare);
[2]=4+ staff, including at least 2 teachers;
[3] if applicable=1 daycare worker;
Sub-Total ([1]..[3])=number of voting members;
[4] if applicable=2 students (secondary, cycle II only-non-voting);
[5]=2 community reps - non-voting;
Total = all members (max = 20);

Quorum = quorum of parents & total number (voting & non-voting).

Operation

Although the *Education Act* enables governing boards to establish their own internal rules of procedure (s. 67), it explicitly deals with a range of procedural issues as outlined below. The procedures reflect a greater transparency in the conduct of business by governing boards than was the case under pre-existing structures. Moreover, the Act stipulates that "every decision of the governing board must be made in the best interests of the students" (s. 64).

Chairperson & Substitute

The chairperson must be selected from the parent representatives and may not be a school board employee (s. 56). The principal presides over the governing board until the chairperson is elected (s. 57).

According to the Act, the chairperson presides over the meetings of the school governing board and signs off on the minutes of previous meetings (ss. 59, 69), but other duties are not specified. Generally, one would expect the chairperson to provide leadership to the school governing board and be the primary liaison between the school governing board and the principal. The chairperson would typically set the agenda for each meeting and ensure that school governing board business, both at and between meetings, is conducted properly and efficiently.

Other Officers

The chairperson of the school governing board (and substitute) is the only officer specifically mentioned in the *Education Act*. However, given the responsibilities of the school governing board, it would seem reasonable to have at least two other officers, such as a secretary and a treasurer, but this decision is up to each school governing board. It could create the position of vice-chairperson; it could combine the roles of secretary and treasurer into one.

The secretary of the school governing board might be expected to circulate the agenda and all relevant materials to members prior to the meeting, record or supervise the recording of the minutes of meetings, and other like duties. The secretary would only be responsible for keeping the register of minutes if the principal so decides, as the Act confers that responsibility on the principal (s. 69).

Given the responsibility of the school governing board respecting the school budget, it would seem appropriate to name someone as a treasurer. That person could be made responsible for the school governing board's own budget or given other duties respecting school finance but could not be expected to administer the school budget; that is the role of the principal (s. 96.24).

Meetings

A school governing board must fix the number of regular meetings which must, according to the *Education Act*, number at least 5 per school year. The rules should provide for special meetings as well (s. 67).

The Act states that the meetings of a school governing board may take place at the school but it could also meet elsewhere (s. 65). If the school governing board wishes to provide for the possibility of telephone meetings, it should do so in its operating rules.

The Act is silent on what is required in order to call a meeting. The school governing board can specify the length and form of any notice of meeting, for example 48 hours written notice, and whether the *draft* agenda or other materials must be included. However, according to Bill 101 (s. 19), the notice must be given in French as well as in English.

It is accepted practice to have a formal agenda for each meeting. The agenda lists the items to be discussed and can have an open item for other points to be added. According to Bill 101 (s. 19), the agenda must be provided in French as well as in English.

The Act states that school governing board meetings, as a general rule, are open to the public; but they may be held *in camera* (i.e. closed to the public) in exceptional cases (s. 68). However, the right to attend does not mean the right to participate. Normally, public participation is limited to a set question period.

A quorum is the number of members who must be present for a meeting to be held. The Act states that a quorum is made up of a majority of the members (voting and non-voting) who are in office, including at least half of the parent representatives (s. 61).

Decisions are taken by majority vote of the voting members present on a motion made; the chairperson having a casting vote. Thus, the chairperson is entitled to a second vote if the initial vote results in a tie (s. 63).

Minutes

The *Education Act* requires that minutes of meetings must be kept in a public register (s. 69). According to Bill 101 (s. 19), a French version of the minutes must also be kept. Copies of these minutes must be kept in a register kept by the principal or a person designated by him or her, and made available to anyone on payment of a reasonable fee. The minutes must be signed by the chairperson or his or her substitute, and the principle or the keeper of the register.

The school governing board decides who shall take the minutes (s. 69). It could be a member of the school governing board or a support staff person from the school, depending on the arrangements made with the principal (s. 65).

Remuneration

While the *Education Act* expressly treats the matter of the remuneration of members of the council of commissioners (see chap. 6), it is silent both as to the remuneration of members of school governing boards and their right to reimbursement with respect to expenses incurred by them in the performance of their functions. Thus, members of school governing boards are not entitled to remuneration for their efforts. However, it would seem reasonable that provision may be made in the governing board's budget for an amount to defray authorized expenses of members incurred in the performance of their functions.

Code of Conduct & Immunity

In recognition of the nature and role of the school governing board in comparison to its predecessor orientation committee, the *Education Act* now includes provisions regarding the conduct and immunity of members of the board (ss. 70-73).

Thus, every member (whether voting or non-voting) of a governing board who has a direct or indirect interest in an enterprise that places the member's personal interest in conflict with the interest of the school must disclose same in writing to the principal. In addition, such member must abstain from voting on, influencing or being present during the discussion of any matter where such conflict is at issue (s. 70).

Moreover, members of the governing board must act within the scope of the functions assigned to them by law. They also must "exercise the care, prudence and diligence that a reasonable person would exercise in similar circumstances," and "act with honesty and loyalty and in the interest of the school, the students, the parents, the school staff and the community" (s. 71).

Subject to certain limitations, the school board is obliged to assume the defence of a member of the governing board who is prosecuted by a third party for an act done in the exercise of his or her duties (ss. 72-73). Moreover, a school board is empowered to take out liability insurance for the benefit of the members of school governing boards (s. 178) (see Girard & Blanchard, 1999).

Functions & Powers

The following provides an overview of the general functions of the governing board, followed by those related to educational services and other specific domains (the headings are the same as those used to describe other school board functions in chapter 6).

As indicated by the notes in the discussion of the powers which follow (e.g. [1], [2], [3], etc.), most decisions are made upon the proposal of the principal, others follow consultation with teachers and so forth. In brief, the *Education Act* provides for three modes of decision making for school governing boards:

- governing board "adopts" but the school board "approves" (e.g. budget);
- governing board approves following proposal by the principal (e.g. student rules);
- governing board approves without the need of a proposal by the principal (e.g. cultural & sports activities).

The second mode, which arguably warrants the most comment, normally requires a proposal from the principal to trigger a decision. Such a proposal must be made within 15 days after a request by the governing board, failing which the governing board may act without such proposal (s. 96.13). Contrary to the provision dealing with the principal's authority to reject teacher proposals, which requires the principal to provide reasons for such rejection (s. 96.15), the Act does not stipulate what discretion the governing board has when dealing with a proposal submitted by the principal. In our view, the governing board *may* approve the principal's proposal but if it does not choose to approve such a proposal, the board must return it to him or her for further consideration. The absence of the qualifier, "with or without amendments" in the relevant provision (a phrase found in the former Orientation Committee provisions), means that the governing board cannot itself amend the principal's proposal prior to giving it its approval.* Presumably this process, returning unapproved proposals to the principal, continues until a satisfactory resolution is reached. This process exemplifies the "balancing act" introduced by the *Education Amendment Act* (1997) regarding the powers of principals versus those of the school governing board. (For the special case regarding budget, see chap. 11).

Transitional Measures

As noted in chapter 6, the *Education Amendment Act* (s. 198) requires every school board, after consulting with the governing boards of its schools to establish the approach to be taken for 1998-99 and 1999-2000 for the gradual implementation of certain powers now vested in governing boards. These transitional measures apply to the powers of school governing boards over educational services (Ed Act, ss. 84-89). In each case we have shaded the text and included a note to this effect to remind the reader of these transitional measures.

The transitional measures are meant to accommodate two realities: (i) the fact that the new distribution of powers came into force after many decisions affecting the 1998-99 school year had already been made; and, (ii) the different states of readiness of individual schools to assume these new responsibilities. The "approach" to be adopted by each school board therefore permits a different implementation plan for different matters and for different schools. It should be noted that school governing boards must be consulted on the approach envisaged and that regardless of the details of same, the full implementation of the new distribution of powers must be effected by July 1, 2000.

General Functions

The *Education Act* assigns certain general functions to school governing boards. Thus, a governing board is required to adopt and oversee the implementation and evaluation of the educational project and to promote communication and coordination among the school's stakeholders (s. 74).

A governing board may advise the school board on any matter the latter is required to submit to it. Such matters are: the amendment or revocation of a school's deed of establishment; the selection criteria for the appointment of the school's principal; the recognition of the denominational status of the school (s. 79); and the division of powers and functions between governing boards and a coordinating committee when one is established (s. 211 – see above). Furthermore, a governing board may advise the school board on any matters that are likely to facilitate the operation of the school or improve the organization of the services provided by the school (s. 78).

Governing boards are also responsible for approving student supervision policies (s. 75)[1] and rules of conduct and safety measures for students (other than those dealing with expulsion and corporal punishment; see chap. 3) (s. 76).[1]

The *Education Act* permits governing boards to pool goods and services and to hold joint activities with other schools or centres of the school board (s. 80).

In conclusion, it may be observed that governing boards are required to furnish school boards both with any information that the latter request that is necessary for school boards to fulfil their functions, and an annual activity report (ss. 81, 82, 218.1). A school governing board must also inform the community served by the school of the services provided and the quality of such services (s. 83). According to Bill 101, the annual reports to the school board and any written report to the community must be in French (s. 23).

[1] Proposed by the principal & developed in collaboration with the school staff (s. 77).

Educational Services

A number of educational powers, previously exercised by school boards, are now exercised by school governing boards. While school boards remain responsible for some educational decisions within their territories (see chap. 6), governing boards now decide on much of the programming details within their schools. (For presentation of all matters relating to educational services, see chap. 8.)

Thus, governing boards have the responsibility of approving the "approach" to the implementation of the *Basic Regulations* (s. 84);[1]* the "overall approach" to the enrichment or adaptation of programs of study to meet the specific needs of students (s. 85)[2]* and to the development of local programs (s. 85).[2]* The school governing board is responsible for approving the time allocation for each subject, while ensuring that the compulsory objectives and the content of the programs of study mandated by the Minister are achieved, MRI course times are respected and that the rules governing the certification of studies are complied with (s. 86).[2]*

Similarly, governing boards are required to approve programming which entails changes to the regular schedule or taking students off school premises (s. 87)[1]* and the approach to programs of student services and special education services (s. 88).[1]*

*Note. Provision subject to "Transitional Measures" - see above
[1] Proposed by the principal & developed in collaboration with the school staff;
[2] Proposed by the principal & developed in collaboration with the teachers.

Community Services

School governing boards are granted two specific powers with respect to what may be termed "community services": first, to organize educational services other than those prescribed by the *Basic Regulations*, including those provided outside regular teaching periods (s. 90); and second, to organize social, cultural or sports activities (s. 90).

Human Resources

Little voice and no authority are granted school governing boards with respect to the staffing of schools, including the appointment of principals, despite the fact that a governing board have to work closely with the latter. In fact, the only role a governing board has in such matters is in giving advice to the school board on the selection criteria for the appointment of the principal to the school (s. 79(2)).

Financial Resources & Other Services

Of particular interest under the new scheme of school governance is the authority conferred on school governing boards with respect to the financial resources of schools.

Thus, governing boards are given the authority to adopt and oversee their own operating budgets (s. 66) and to adopt the school budget proposed by the principal (which budgets must be submitted to the school board for approval) (s. 95).

In addition, governing boards are granted a considerable degree of control over school premises. They may approve the use of school premises and enter into agreements regarding their use (although school board approval is required for agreements of more than one year) (s. 93), including the use of school premises for various activities (cultural, social, sports, etc.) organized by the school board (s. 93).

Governing boards may also in the name of the school board, and subject to the approval of the latter, contract with persons or organizations for the provision of goods and services related to community services (see above) and require a financial contribution from users of those goods and services (s. 91).

Finally the *Education Act* expressly confers on school governing boards the power to solicit donations and contributions for the school, although this must be done in the name of the school board and comply with certain rules (s. 94).

Both the revenues from user fees and donations must be credited to the school account kept at the school board on its behalf (s. 92).

School Administration

The school administration comprises the principal and any vice-principals assigned to the school (ss. 96.8-96.10). Prior to the adoption of the *Education Amendment Act* (1997), the *Education Act* stated that every school was established by a school board "under the authority of a principal" (former s. 38). This phrase was omitted from the amended version (s. 39). The omission reflects perhaps the ambivalence of the new distribution of authority between the school board and the school and among the principal stakeholders of the school - the students, the parents, the staff and the school administration.

Principal

The principal is appointed by the school board in accordance with the criteria established after consulting the governing board (ss. 79(2), 96.8). It may be noted that where two schools share the same premises, the school board may appoint a single principal with one or more vice-principals. If this is done, the school board, after consulting the governing boards concerned, determines the distribution of powers and functions between the principal and the vice-principals (s. 211).

An overview of the general functions of principals is provided below, followed by their functions with respect to educational services and other specific domains (the headings are the same as those used above to describe the functions of the governing board).

As noted, much of the principal's authority is subject to proposals made by teachers or the school staff, as the case may be, according to procedures determined by them at general meetings called for that purpose or failing that by the principal. Proposals must be made by the teachers or school staff within 15 days of a request by the principal. If a proposals is not made within this time frame the principal may act without one. However, if the teachers or the school staff make proposals as requested and the principal does not accept them, he or she must given written reasons for his or her decision (s. 96.15).

Conflicts of Interest

The *Education Act* contains provisions regulating conflicts of interest that may affect school principals (s. 96.11). Briefly put, a principal of a school is prohibited from having a direct or indirect interest in any enterprise that places his or her interests in conflict with the interests of the school.

Functions & Powers

Transitional Measures

The *Education Amendment Act* (1997, s. 198) requires every school board, after consulting with the governing boards of schools, to establish the approach to be taken for 1998-99 and 1999-2000 for the gradual implementation of certain powers now vested in school governing boards. These transitional measures also apply to the powers of school principals arising from sections 96.15 and 96.16 of the *Education Act*. In each case we have shaded the text and included a note to this effect to remind the reader of these transitional measures.

The transitional measures are meant to accommodate two realities: (i) the fact that the new distribution of powers came into force after many decisions affecting the 1998-99 school year had already been made; and, (ii) the different states of readiness of individual schools to assume these new responsibilities. The "approach" to be adopted by each school board therefore permits a different implementation plan for different matters and for different schools. It should be noted that school governing boards must be consulted on the approach envisaged and that regardless of the details of same, the full implementation of the new distribution of powers must be effected by July 1, 2000.

General Functions

The general functions assigned to principals of schools are: providing academic and administrative leadership (s. 96.12); ensuring, under the authority of the director general, the educational services provided by their schools meet the proper standards of quality (s. 96.12); seeing to the implementation of the governing board's decisions (s. 96.12); assisting governing boards in the exercise of their functions (s. 96.13); and ensuring the attendance of students of compulsory school age (see chap. 3).

Educational Services

A principal's functions in the domain of educational services focus on three interrelated matters: students, programs and pedagogy.

A principal must approve the standards and procedures for the evaluation of student achievement (s. 96.15)[3]* and approve the rules for placement of students and their promotion from one cycle to another in elementary school (s. 96.15).[5]*

With respect to students, a principal is also required to develop, together with students, parents, and school staff, IEPs for students with special needs (s. 96.14 - see chap. 4 for details). Finally, upon a request by a student's parents and for good reason, a principal may approve the retention in preschool or elementary school of a student who has not achieved the prescribed objectives at that level. (A principal must report annually to the school board on the number of retentions approved.) (ss. 96.17-96.19).

The programmatic functions of a principal are to approve, in accordance with policies approved by the governing board, local programs of study (s. 96.15);[3]* and, with the authorization of the Minister, the allocation of a greater number of credits to local programs of studies than those prescribed by the *Basic Regulations* (s. 96.16).*

With respect to pedagogical matters it is the principal who approves both the criteria for the implementation of new instructional methods (s. 96.15)[3]* and, subject to the school budget, the textbooks and instructional materials to be used (s. 96.15).[4]*

* *Note.* Provision subject to "Transitional Measures" - see above
[3] Proposed by the teachers;
[4] Proposed by teachers after consulting governing board;
[5] Proposed by school staff (ss. 96.13, 96.15)

Community Services

Principals are assigned no functions that are directly related to community services.

Human Resources

A school principal is charged with the responsibility of informing the school board of the school's needs in terms of human resources and the professional development of staff after consultation with the school staff (s. 96.20). In addition, a principal is responsible for managing the school staff and determines their duties and responsibilities (ss. 96.21, 260), and for the organization of professional development activities as agreed to with staff in accordance with applicable collective agreements (s. 96.21).

Financial Resources & Other Services

It is the principal's responsibility to prepare the school budget and submit it to the school governing board for adoption (s. 96.24). Once the budget receives the approval of the school board, it becomes the principal's responsibility to administer it and to render account to the governing board (s. 96.24).

The principal is also charged with the obligations of informing the school board of the school's needs in terms of material resources, services and physical plant (s. 96.22), and managing the physical resources of the school and rendering account therefore to the school board in accordance with standards and decisions of the latter (s. 96.23).

Miscellaneous

A principal must also participate in the definition of school board policies and by-laws by means of the advisory committee on management (s. 96.25 - see chap. 6) and exercise such other functions as may be requested of him or her by the school board (s. 96.26).

School Advisory Committees

There are now two school level advisory committees, one for parents that replaces the former school committee, and a new one for students.

Parent Participation Organization

As mentioned above, the *Education Act* provides that if the parents of a school (as defined by the school board)* so decide they may establish a "parent participation organization" – unlike the governing board, there is no requirement that a parent participation organization be formed. However, the decision must be made no later than September 30 of each school year at the general meeting called to elect the parent representatives of the school governing board (ss. 47, 96; see discussion of annual general meeting of parents above).

* *Note*. For a definition of "school," see discussion of deed of establishment above.

The parents, however cannot determine the functions of the organization; they are specified in the Act as follows: to promote the collaboration of parents in developing, implementing and periodically evaluating the educational project (s. 96.2); and in participating in their child's schooling and fostering their academic success (s. 96.2). In addition, a parent participation organization may advise the parent representatives on the governing board on any matter on which the latter seek advice (s. 96.3) and on matters of concern to parents of the school (s. 96.3). Consequently, it would appear that an officially constituted parent participation organization cannot undertake fundraising. Finally, the Act provides that a parent participation organization can hold its meetings on school premises and can use, free of charge, the school's administrative services, as agreed to with the principal after consultation of the governing board (s. 96.4).

Student Committee

The principal of a school providing education to students in the second cycle of the secondary level, in accordance with the *Education Act*, shall see to the formation of a student committee during September of each school year (s. 96.5).

It is the students who determine the name, composition and operating rules and elect the members of the committee (s. 96.5). They may decide not to form a student committee or to entrust its function to an association representing them (s. 96.5).

The purpose of a student committee is threefold: first, to encourage the collaboration of students in developing, implementing and, periodically evaluating the school's educational project; second to encourage their participation in fostering academic success and in-school activities; and third, to make suggestions likely to facilitate the proper operation of the school to the student representatives on the governing board and to the principal (s. 96.6).

The student committee can meet on the school premises (s. 96.7).

B: VOCATIONAL TRAINING CENTRES & ADULT EDUCATION CENTRES

Overview

The *Education Amendment Act* (1997) replaces the previous chapter IV of the *Education Act* dealing with centres; the new version is divided into three divisions: Establishment; Governing Board; and the Principal. By and large, the provisions in this section apply equally to vocational and adult centres. However, it should be remembered that the clientele of vocational centres may comprise youth and adult students whose rights differ significantly, as dealt with in other chapters in this text (e.g. see chap. 3).

Establishment

The "establishment" of centres is concerned with the basic parameters defining the role of a centre, including its creation and closure.

Deed of Establishment

A centre is established by a school board by a deed of establishment which shall state the name and address of the centre and indicate the premises or immovables placed at its disposal. The deed must also specify whether the centre is a vocational training centre or an adult education centre (Ed Act, s. 100). A centre's deed of establishment may be amended by the school board in accordance with the school board's three-year plan (s. 101). Unlike the analogous provision for schools (s. 40), this text does not include any mention of the revocation of a centre's deed of establishment. (The role of the centre governing board respecting the amendment or revocation of a deed of establishment is dealt with below.)

Annual Three-Year Plan

As noted with respect to schools (see above) the *Education Act* states that each year a school board shall establish a three-year plan of allocation and destination of its immovables (s. 211) which includes those assigned to centres.

Coordinating Committee

Where two centres share the same premises, the school board must, at the request of the governing boards, establish a coordinating committee. This committee is composed of representatives of both governing boards. The school board establishes the distribution of powers and functions between the governing boards and the coordinating committee, as well as the latter's administrative and operational rules (s.211).

Centre Closure

There is no requirement that school boards adopt a policy concerning the maintenance and closure of its centres; this is only required of school boards with respect to schools (s. 212). The closure of a particular centre is subject to consultation with its governing board inasmuch as closure presumably implies a revocation of its deed of establishment (s. 110.1(1)).

Purpose

Vocational training centres and adult education centres are institutions with a mission to provide persons with the educational services prescribed by the *Basic Regulations* governing vocational training and adult general education (s. 97). If requested by a school board, an adult education or vocational centre shall provide a general education program to students in vocational training programs (s. 98).

Student Enrolment

The *Education Act* (s. 2) states that every person no longer subject to compulsory school attendance is entitled to the educational services prescribed by the *Basic School Regulation for Adult Education* within the scope of the programs offered by the school board pursuant to this Act.

Centre Governing Boards

In this section we present an overview of the election, composition, operation and functions of the newly created centre governing boards.

Election

No date is stipulated by which the elections must be held, nor is there any definition of the annual term of office. It may be assumed that the members of a governing board assume office as soon as the members of the board (identified below) are elected.

Composition

The governing board of a centre consists of a maximum of 20 members who are either appointed or elected for a maximum term of two years (s. 102):

[1] students attending the centre, elected by their peers according to the procedure determined by the principal after consulting with the students or the students' association, if any;

[2] at least four member of the staff of the centre, including at least two teachers and, if the persons concerned so decide, at least one non-teaching professional staff member and at least one support staff member, elected by their peers according to a procedure set out in their respective collective agreements or failing that, according to the procedure determined by the principal after consulting with the persons concerned;

[3] at least two persons appointed by the school board after consulting with the socio-economic and community groups in the territory principally served by the centre;

[4] in the case of a vocational training centre, at least two parents of students attending the centre who are not members of the staff of the centre, elected by their peers according to the procedure determined by the principal;

[5] at least two persons appointed by the school board from within the enterprises of the region which, in the case of a vocational training centre, operate in economic sectors corresponding to the vocational education programs offered by the centre.

The school board determines the number of representatives of each group on the governing board after consulting with each group concerned. However, in all cases the number of staff representatives cannot exceed the total number of representatives of the other groups (s. 103). All representatives have the right to vote.

The principal of a centre must take part in meetings of the governing board but is not entitled to vote (s. 104). A school commissioner, if authorized by the governing board, may take part in its meetings but is not entitled to vote (s. 105).

The mere fact that the representatives of a group fall short of the required number does not prevent the formation of a centre governing board (s. 106).

Operation

Although the *Education Act* enables governing boards of centres to establish their own internal rules of procedure, it explicitly deals with a range of procedural issues by reference to the rules stipulated for school governing boards in sections 57 to 73 (s. 108), as summarized below. It is worth reiterating that a number of procedural rules reflect a greater transparency in the conduct of business by centre governing boards than was the case under pre-existing structures. Moreover, the Act stipulates that "every decision of the governing board must be made in the best interests of the students" (s. 64).

The chairperson, who may not be a school board employee, is selected from the representatives on the governing board other than those of the students and centre staff (s. 107). The quorum is established as a majority of the members who are in office (s. 61). Decisions are to be taken by majority vote of the voting members present, the chairperson having a casting vote (s. 63). Thus, the chairperson is entitled to a second vote if the initial vote results in a tie.

Meetings of governing boards are public (but may be held *in camera* in certain cases) (s. 68), and minutes must be kept in a public register (s. 69). Copies of the governing board's minutes must be made available to anyone on payment of a reasonable fee (s. 69).

A governing board must meet at least 5 times per school year (s. 67). If it should lack a quorum for 3 consecutive meetings, the school board may order that the governing board's powers and functions be suspended; in this event the locus of power becomes the centre principal (s. 62).

Remuneration

While the *Education Act* expressly treats the matter of the remuneration of members of the council of commissioners (see chap. 6), it is silent both as to the remuneration of members of centre governing boards and their right to reimbursement with respect to expenses incurred by them in the performance of their functions. Thus, members of centre governing boards are not entitled to remuneration for their efforts. However, it would seem reasonable that provision may be made in the governing board's budget for an amount to defray authorized expenses of members incurred in the performance of their functions.

Code of Conduct & Immunity

In recognition of the nature and role of the centre governing board in comparison to its predecessor orientation committee, the *Education Act* now includes provisions regarding the conduct and immunity of members of the board (ss. 70-73).

Thus, every member of a governing board who has a direct or indirect interest in an enterprise that places the member's personal interest in conflict with the interest of the centre must disclose same in writing to the principal. In addition, such member must abstain from voting on, influencing or being present during the discussion of any matter where such conflict is at issue (s. 70).

Moreover, members of the governing board must act within the scope of the functions assigned to them by law. They also must "exercise the care, prudence and diligence that a reasonable person would exercise in similar circumstances," and "act with honesty and loyalty and in the interest of the [centre], the students, the parents, the [centre] staff and the community" (s. 71).

Subject to certain limitations, the school board is obliged to assume the defence of a member of the governing board who is prosecuted by a third party for an act done in the exercise of his or her duties (ss. 72-73). Moreover, a school board is empowered to take out liability insurance for the benefit of the members of centre governing boards (s. 178).

Functions & Powers

The following provides an overview of the general functions of the centre's governing board, followed by those related to educational services and other specific domains (the headings are the same as those used to describe school board functions in chap. 6).

As noted below, much of the centre governing board's authority is subject to proposals made by the principal with the collaboration of teachers or centre staff according to procedures determined by them at general meetings called for that purpose or, failing that, by the principal. Many decisions of the governing board are made following proposals made by the principal (see below). The *Education Act* stipulates that the governing board is free to act if the principal fails to produce a requested proposal within 15 days (s. 110.10).

Transitional Measures

As noted in chap. 6, the *Education Amendment Act* (1997, s. 198) requires every school board, after consulting with the governing boards of centres to establish the approach to be taken for 1998-99 and 1999-2000 for the gradual implementation of certain powers now vested in governing boards. These transitional measures apply to the powers of centre governing boards arising from section 110.2 of the *Education Act*. In each case we have shaded the text and included a note to this effect to remind the reader of these transitional measures.

The transitional measures are meant to accommodate two realities: (i) the fact that the new distribution of powers came into force after many decisions affecting the 1998-99 school year had already been made; and, (ii) the different states of readiness of individual centres to assume these new responsibilities. The "approach" to be adopted by each school board therefore permits a different implementation plan for different matters and for different centres. It should be noted that centre governing boards must be consulted on the approach envisaged and that regardless of the details of same, the full implementation of the new distribution of powers must be effected by July 1, 2000.

General Functions

The *Education Act* assigns certain general functions to centre governing boards. Thus, they are required to oversee the implementation of and periodically evaluate the policies and action plan of the centre and seek the collaboration of the centre's stakeholders in the process. Governing boards must also "encourage communication of information, dialogue and concerted action" between these parties (s. 109).

A governing board must advise the school board on any matter the latter is required to submit to it. Such matters are: the revocation or amendment of a centre's deed of establishment (s. 110.1(1)); the selection criteria for the appointment of the centre's principal (s.110.1(2)); and the division of powers and functions between governing boards and a coordinating committee when one is established (s. 211 – see above).

Furthermore, a governing board may advise the school board of any matters that are likely to facilitate the operation of the centre or improve the organization of the services provided by the centre (s. 110).

The *Education Act* permits governing boards to pool goods and services and to hold joint activities with other centres or schools of the school board (s. 80).

In conclusion, it may be observed that governing boards are required to furnish school boards both with any information that the latter request that is necessary for school boards to fulfil their functions, and an annual activity report. Governing boards must also inform the community served by the centre of the services provided and the quality of such services (ss. 81-83).

Educational Services

The responsibilities of centre governing boards include: approving the "approach" to: the implementation of basic regulations;[1]* the implementation of programs of studies;[2]* and the implementation of programs relating to student services and popular education prescribed by the *Basic Regulations* which are determined by the school board or provided for in an agreement made by the school board[1]* (s. 110.2(1)-(3)). The governing board must also approve the operating rules of the centre[1]* (s. 110.2(4)).

* *Note*. Provision subject to transitional measures - see above.
[1] Proposed by the principal & developed in collaboration with the school staff.
[2] Proposed by the principal & developed in collaboration with the teachers (s. 110.2).

Community Services

Centre governing boards have the power to organize social, cultural or sports activities (s. 110.3).

Human Resources

The only role a centre governing board, like a school governing board, has in the matter of human resources is in giving advice to the school board on the selection criteria for the appointment of the principal to the centre (s. 110.1(2)).

Financial Resources & Other Services

A centre governing board is also given authority over financial services by reference to those stipulated for school governing boards in sections 93 to 95 (s. 110.4).Thus, centre governing boards are given the authority to adopt and oversee their own operating budget (s. 66) and to adopt the centre budget proposed by the principal (which budgets must be submitted to the school board for approval) (s. 95).

In addition, governing boards are granted a considerable degree of control of centre premises. They may approve use of the premises and enter into agreements regarding their use (although school board approval is required for agreements of more than one year), including the use of centre premises for various activities (cultural, social, sports, etc.) organized by the school board (s. 93).

Governing boards may also in the name of the school board, and subject to the approval of the latter, contract with persons or organizations for provision of goods and services related to community services (see above) and require a financial contribution from users of those goods and services (s. 110.3).

Finally the *Education Act* expressly confers on centre governing boards the power to solicit donations and contributions for the centre, although this must be done in the name of the school board and comply with certain rules (s. 94).

Both the revenues from user fees and donations must be credited to the centre account kept at the school board on its behalf.

Centre Administration

The centre administration comprises the principal and any vice-principals assigned to the centre (ss. 110.5-110.7). Prior to the adoption of the *Education Amendment Act* (1997), the *Education Act* stated that every centre was established by a school board "under the authority of a principal" (former s. 98). This phrase was omitted from the amended version (s. 100). The omission reflects perhaps the ambivalence of the new distribution of authority between the school board and the centre and among the principal stakeholders of the centre - the students, the parents, the staff and the centre administration.

Principal

The principal is appointed by the school board in accordance with the criteria established after consulting the governing board (s. 110.5). It may be noted that where two centres share the same premises, the school board may appoint a single principal with one or more vice-principals for each location. If this is done, the school board, after consulting the governing boards concerned, determines the distribution of powers and functions between the principal and the vice-principals (s. 211).

Conflicts of Interest
The *Education Act* contains provisions regulating conflicts of interest that may affect centre principals (s. 110.8). Briefly put, a principal of a centre is prohibited from having a direct or indirect interest in any enterprise that places his or her interests in conflict with the interests of the centre.

Functions & Powers

An overview of the general functions of principals, followed by their functions with respect to educational services and other specific domains (the headings are the same as those used above to describe the functions of the governing board) is provided below.

As will be noted below, some of the principal's authority is subject to proposals made by teachers or the centre staff, as the case may be, according to procedures determined by them at general meetings called for that purpose. Proposals must be made by the teachers or centre staff within 15 days of a request by the principal. If a proposal is not made within this time frame the principal may act alone (s. 110.12).

Transitional Measures
The *Education Amendment Act* (1997, s. 198) requires every school board, after consulting with the governing boards of centres, to establish the approach to be taken for 1998-99 and 1999-2000 for the gradual implementation of certain powers of a centre principal arising from section 110.12 of the *Education Act*. In each case we have shaded the text and included a note to this effect to remind the reader of these transitional measures.

The transitional measures are meant to accommodate two realities: (i) the fact that the new distribution of powers came into force after many decisions affecting the 1998-99 school year had already been made; and, (ii) the different states of readiness of individual centres to assume these new responsibilities. The "approach" to be adopted by each school board therefore permits a different implementation plan for different matters and for different centres. It should be noted that centre governing boards must be consulted on the approach envisaged and that regardless of the details of same, the full implementation of the new distribution of powers must be effected by July 1, 2000.

General Functions

The general functions assigned centre principals, in addition to providing academic and administrative leadership (s. 110.9), are: ensuring, under the authority of the director general, the educational services provided by their centres meet the proper standards of quality (s. 110.9); seeing to the implementation of the governing board's decisions (s. 110.9); and assisting governing boards in the exercise of their functions and seeing to the implementation of their decisions (s. 110.10).

Furthermore, the centre principal is charged with ensuring that proposals to the governing board are submitted within 15 days of a request by the latter. If this does not occur, then the centre governing board may act on its own (s. 110.10).

Educational Services

A centre principal's functions in the domain of educational services focus on two matters: students and pedagogy.

With respect to students with special needs, a principal of a vocational centre is required to develop, together with the student, the student's parents, and centre staff, IEPs for students with special needs and to see to the implementation and periodic evaluation of the plans (s. 110.11).*

Note. It is assumed that this provision refers only to youth students given the general lack of special education provisions for adults in the *Education Act*.

More generally, the principal is also responsible for approving the standards and procedures for the evaluation of student achievement in keeping with the *Basic Regulations* and subject to any ministerial or school board examinations (s. 110.12(3));[3]*

In pedagogical matters, it is the principal who approves both the criteria for the implementation of new instructional methods (s. 110.12(1))[3]* and, subject to the centre budget, the textbooks and instructional materials to be used (s. 110.12(2)).[3]*

Note. Provision subject to "Transitional Measures" – see above
[3] Proposed by the teachers (s. 110.12).

Community Services

A centre principal has no functions with respect to community services.

Human Resources

The principal of a centre is given the same authority over human resources as a school principal (s. 110.13). Thus, a centre principal is charged with the responsibility of informing the school board of the centre's needs in terms of human resources and the professional development of staff after consultation with the centre staff (s. 96.20). In addition, a principal is responsible for managing the centre staff and determines their duties and responsibilities (ss. 96.21, 260), and for the organization of professional development activities as agreed to with staff in accordance with applicable collective agreements (s. 96.21).

Financial Resources & Other Services

Likewise a centre principal is given functions identical to those of a school principal with respect to financial and other services (s. 110.13).

It is a centre principal's responsibility to prepare the centre budget and submit it to the governing board for adoption (s. 96.24); once the budget receives the approval of the school board, it becomes the principal's responsibility to administer it and to render account to the governing board (s. 96.24).

The principal is also charged with the obligations of informing the school board of the centre's needs in terms of material resources, services and physical plant (s. 96.22), and managing the physical resources of the centre and rendering account therefore to the school board in accordance with standards and decisions of the latter (s. 96.23).

Miscellaneous
A principal must also participate in the definition of school board policies and by-laws (s. 96.25) by means of the Advisory Committee on Management (see chap. 6), and exercise such other functions as may be requested of him or her by the school board (s. 96.26).

PART III:
CURRICULUM AND SCHOOL ORGANIZATION

More than ever, daily life now requires that all members of society have the intellectual skills needed to use technology and various media and to deal with organizations.

The economic vitality and prosperity of a country are no longer contingent on whether or not it possesses raw materials. With the advent of international competition, knowledge, along with scientific and technological expertise, has become the key to wealth and power.

The exponential growth in knowledge, the speed at which knowledge is renewed and the explosive rate of technological innovation have led to the emergence of the "knowledge based society." To feel at ease in this society, every individual needs to master more knowledge and to be able to assimilate new knowledge on an ongoing basis (Inchauspé Task Force, 1997, pp. 13-14).

Part III of this source book deals with what is arguably the core of educational policy - curriculum and school organization. It comprises only one chapter dealing with youth education.

The key provisions of the following instruments which are referred to in the chapters of this part are reproduced in the *Compendium*:

CSE Act
 Catholic Regulation
 Protestant Regulation
Education Act
 Elementary School Regulation
 Secondary School Regulation

Introduction

Provincial policy governing curriculum and school organization in the youth sector is undergoing major change. Since December 1996, we have seen the publication of the report of the Estates General (1996b), the report of the Task Force on curriculum (1997) and a ministerial policy paper (1997c). In the past, the framework governing curriculum and school organization has been highly centralized, with the MEQ directing all major elements of the system. At the time of writing, much of the regulatory framework remains the same, but this is expected to change in the near future, with a devolution of more authority to those directly involved. The first step in this process has already begun, in that the new distribution of powers introduced into the *Education Act* by the *Education Amendment Act* (1997) provides schools with increased responsibilities in this area (see chap. 7). In this chapter we will describe and discuss these changes which constitute the most significant revisions to curriculum and school organization in more than a decade.

Note. Language of instruction is an important element in the framework used to determine "what gets taught;" it has been omitted from this chapter as it is dealt with separately as part of the discussion of education and language (see chap. 13).

The expression "curriculum and school organization" tries to capture an eclectic set of elements which, when taken together, constitute what is taught and how educational and other related services are delivered in schools. The chapter begins with an examination of current provincial policy and then proceeds to outline the critical elements of the regulatory framework governing curriculum and school organization in the youth sector.

Background

In 1978, the MEQ engaged in extensive consultation with the educational community on a number of educational issues. The consultative document - or the "green paper" as it was commonly called, was meant to take the educational reforms begun in the Quiet Revolution into a new phase (MEQ, 1978, p. 10):

> With the passing of time it has become clear that the original reform [of the Quiet Revolution] was, of necessity, concerned primarily with the physical problems of the school, the problems of "brick and mortar." As a consequence, the educational aspects did not receive all the attention they required during this period.

In 1979, the MEQ published *The Schools of Québec: Policy Statement and Plan of Action* (MEQ, 1979a), a document which was portrayed as a compendium of government decisions aimed at translating into action the ideas, experiences and aspirations of those involved in the day-to-day operation of schools. This paper and others published around the same time (MEQ, 1979b, 1980a) were to set the policy agenda in education for the next decade. If there is one unifying theme in all of these actions, it is the focus on the MEQ as the agent of change. It was at this time that the

Government adopted the first comprehensive education regulations and the expression *Régimes pédagogiques* entered the vocabulary of the system.

In 1992, the Minister published a new plan of action, *Joining Forces* (MEQ, 1992d), a document quite different in tone and focus from the earlier Plan (MEQ, 1979a). The 1992 paper recognizes that "we must motivate students [and] ... have faith in teachers ... [that] we cannot expect to achieve our goal without the special support that parents can offer ... [and] school boards must make a firm commitment to educational success ..." (pp. 3-4). Rather than seeing itself as the central driving change agent, the MEQ was recast in the role of facilitator. The following year, the MEQ advanced the general debate on educational reform in a paper entitled *Moving Ahead* (MEQ, 1993). This paper proposed, among other initiatives, increasing flexibility for schools and school boards, with the State focussing on setting goals and evaluating the performance of the education system as a whole. Arguably, this paper was the successor to an earlier paper, *The Québec School: A Responsible Force in the Community* (MEQ, 1982). Although this paper dealt with various educational issues, it was primarily concerned with the restructuring of the educational system to provide for a greater role of parents in a revitalized school which was to have greater autonomy and responsibility. Too radical for its time and too entangled with the debate over school board reform, this paper faded from view. However, its decentralizing policy orientation resurfaced in the early 90s policy papers (MEQ, 1992d, 1993) and can be directly linked to the current reform (MEQ, 1997a).

Provincial Policy

As suggested in *Joining Forces* and *Moving Ahead* (MEQ, 1992d, 1993 - see *Historical Roots*, chap. 4), as well as in various reports and opinion papers of the Superior Council (CSE, 1993a, 1993b, 1993c, 1994a, 1994b, 1994c), there is a growing preoccupation with the ability of the school system to "deliver the goods." These various documents also reflect a shift in emphasis in the role of the MEQ and other stakeholders in the system. The MEQ is now portrayed as a facilitator of the actions of others - those closest to the student, while concentrating itself on accountability and evaluation. This avowed orientation is coupled with a focus on the results or outcomes of the education system.

Advice from the Superior Council

As discussed earlier (see chap. 5), one of the key roles of the CSE is to provide advice to the Minister of Education upon request. As part of the ongoing dialogue on educational reform (see chap. 6), the CSE (1993b, 1993c) has suggested that the time has come for a new model of educational management; in other words, a major revision of the framework governing curriculum and school organization.

Prevailing Bureaucratic Model

The CSE noted that in modernizing the education system 25 years ago, the State opted for a centralized approach in order to achieve uniform standards of quality and equity. Since then, the CSE claimed that collective agreements and budget cuts have undermined much of the intended progress, the former by introducing rigid employee relations structures and the latter by relegating education to a lower social and political priority. In particular, the budget cuts "widened the gap between society's demands and schools' ability to meet them; and tightened controls and restricted the actions of those within the organization" (1993c, p. 1).

Toward a New Model

The CSE advocated the implementation of a new management model that aims at bringing educational administration closer to the school and the classroom, where teaching and learning takes place. In its own words (1993c, p. 2):

> In the Council's opinion, this new management model should be based on a dynamic which is essentially educational, with student-teacher interaction being the priority. Consequently, its aim

should be streamlined administrative structures and reduce the number of hierarchical levels in favour of increased support for education.

The CSE recognized that such a major shift in the management of the system will take time: "The cogs in a massive mechanism such as education, which have been turning in one direction for a quarter of a century, cannot suddenly change direction without something giving way" (1993c, p. 3). While recognizing that the new model may seem somewhat utopic, it believed, nonetheless, that educators and administrators will have both the will and the means at their disposal to effect the necessary changes.

Preparing Our Youth for the 21st Century

In March 1994, the Minister of Education created the Task Force on Elementary and Secondary Learning Profiles [Corbo Task Force], chaired by Claude Corbo, the rector of the Université du Québec à Montréal. The mandate of the task force was "to define the learning profile students finishing elementary or secondary school are expected to have, i.e., *the integrated core of skills and attitudes each student should have mastered by the end of the two main stages of basic instruction*" (Corbo Task Force, 1994, p. 43).

Although one might conceive of this mandate as a very daunting task, requiring many months of research and reflection, the Minister had a different perspective in mind. He stipulated that the task force report be "a concise, short text ... that will be accessible to the general public and contain statements that are clearly worded and easy to find" (p. 43) and delivered in two months time.

The resultant report, *Preparing Our Youth for the 21st. Century* (Corbo Task Force, 1994), was delivered on time and published in June, 1994. The report identified six major areas of learning, which form the basis for the discussion which follows: These six areas include: methodology (learning skills); language; mathematics; life in society; science and technology; and, physical education and the arts. The remainder of the report lists the various skills and knowledge relating to each of these areas which it believes students should have at the completion of elementary and secondary schooling.

Even though the tabling of the Corbo report was followed by a change in government and consequently a new Minister of Education, the thrust of the report was not lost, as will be seen below in both the reflections of the Estates General, and the curriculum policy reform that followed.

Estates General

The interim report of the Commission for the Estates General (1996a) identified proficiency in French as the number one priority, followed by proficiency in English second-language, with "honourable mention" given to third language acquisition. The report also reflected an emphasis on culture, in particular history and the humanities.

The final report (Commission for the Estates General, 1996b) proposed a restructuring of the curriculum, using the Corbo report as a starting point. It recommended that "learning profiles" be developed to define the fundamental learning that students should acquire in elementary and secondary school and that efforts be made to ensure that the "exit profiles" for a given level of education coincide with the entry profile for the following one. Furthermore, the report stressed that steps must be taken to ensure that students attain the established profiles before proceeding to the next level. The revision of the curriculum was to be based on four principles: respect the mission of each level of education by providing the necessary continuity between them; encompass the three education goals and four types of knowledge ("learning to learn, to be, to do and to live together"); extend common-core general education to the end of Secondary III and provide for diversification from Secondary IV on; and ensure balance between the various subjects. In order to achieve the restructuring proposed, the Estates General report recommended that a multi-sector task force be established with a view to implementing reform by the year 2000.

A New Direction for Success

Following the Estates General report, the Minister of Education published the main guidelines for the reform of the education system. The main goal of the reform is to ensure that as many students as possible succeed. Specifically, the objectives are that 85% of students of a given generation will obtain a secondary school diploma before the age of 20, 60% a college diploma and 30% an undergraduate degree by the year 2010. Seven "lines of action" are proposed as a means of achieving these objectives. The seven "lines of actions" identified are discussed below.

Seven "Lines of Action"

Provide Services for Young Children

The MEQ recognizes that early childhood services are vital to student success and persistence in school. It therefore advocates that the range of services available at this level be broadened to meet the needs of a diversified student population, including the provision of special support to parents and children in certain communities where children are more at risk of failure. Furthermore, it believes that the effectiveness of government intervention can be increased by better coordinating the actions of the various ministries, organizations and agencies involved.

Teach the Essential Subjects

In order to ensure student success, a consensus must be reached as to the content of the core curriculum and on the degree of diversification that is desired or necessary. Decisions must be made as to what subjects will be taught and the program content must be both updated and enriched.

Give More Autonomy to Schools

The MEQ maintains that individual schools must be given more autonomy in a reformed system. This can be achieved by increasing the responsibility and scope of action of individual schools and by creating more decentralized patterns of work. Furthermore, if schools are to become more autonomous, the pedagogical leadership of school principals must be strengthened and the expertise of teachers must be recognized and given better support. Lastly, the MEQ recognizes that there is a need to strengthen the links between schools, school boards and local communities and to clarify the degree and scope of accountability that each level has.

Support Montréal Schools

The guidelines recognize that Montréal public schools, facing the dual challenge of poverty and the integration of newly arrived immigrant students, require special support measures if their students are to achieve the desired levels of success. In addition to the support provided by the government and the public education system, it is recommended that other avenues, such as partnerships between schools and local communities, be developed and that Montréal's intellectual, financial and community resources be used more effectively to promote student success

Intensify the Reform of Vocational & Technical Education

One of the ten priority actions set forth in the report of the Commission for the Estates General (1996b) was the urgency for intensive reforms in technical and vocational education and the MEQ guidelines addressed this need. The new programs developed are to provide students with qualifications that will allow them to either join the work force or continue their studies. The general education component of vocational and technical programs must be re-evaluated, a variety of training approaches should be used to respond to the different aptitudes and interests of students who should be able to follow different paths leading to certification. Furthermore, every effort must be made to ensure that vocational and technical education programs meet labour market requirements and students are to be encouraged to go on to more advanced programs by building bridges between the different levels of education. Vocational education centres must be given increased responsibilities in the above areas. Lastly, students, parents and the business community must be made more aware of vocational and technical education as valid options. The goal is to quadruple, over the next five years, the number of vocational education diplomas awarded to students under 20 years age.

Consolidate & Rationalize Post-secondary Education

The MEQ guidelines also address the need for reforms in post-secondary education. At the college level they recommend that the academic responsibilities of the colleges and their autonomy as to how work is organized be increased. Concerted action and partnerships between institutions are to be encouraged. Finally, any new measures that are implemented must be given time to have an effect. At the university level, the guidelines call for a rationalization of the supply of university programs, a review of the current funding rules and the development of a true social contract between Québec society and Québec universities.

Provide Better Access to Continuing Education

The last of the seven "lines of action" proposed in the MEQ guidelines deal with the need to provide better access to continuing education. Education is in reality a lifelong process and consequently there is a need to ensure that this concept is taken into account throughout the education system. Therefore, the continuing education services provided must reflect the diversity of adults' needs. In particular, there is a pressing need to introduce effective strategies to combat illiteracy. Lastly, the role and the responsibilities of the various players in the continuing education field must be clarified.

Montréal Schools

As a follow-up to the new plan of action, the MEQ published a supplementary brochure to address the significant disparities in student success rates in different areas of greater Montréal (MEQ, 1997b). Students in disadvantaged areas, and those from cultural communities in particular, appear to experience greater difficulties in school in comparison with other students, and many more of them seem to lag behind their peers in academic achievement. The brochure outlines special measures in nine areas to be implemented for Montréal schools: early childhood services; elementary school and the first cycle of secondary school; students from immigrant families; immediate preparation for employment; vocational education; cooperation between schools and communities; complementary efforts by the education and health and social services networks; access to cultural resources; and, increased professional support for the school team.

Inchauspé Report

The mandate of the Task Force on Curriculum Reform, chaired by Paul Inchauspé [Inchauspé Report] (1997) was mandated to make recommendations "concerning the changes to be made to the elementary and secondary curricula in order to satisfy the demands of the 21st century." Its mandate specified the areas on which proposals for change were expected. The Task Force thus continued the process of curriculum reform begun by the Estates General on Education. Its report defined the issues more clearly and presented the rationale for proposed changes. The aim was to mobilize and energize the individuals who would be responsible for implementing change on a daily basis in schools and classrooms.

The results to be achieved through the proposed curriculum reform are categorized as follows:

- mission of instruction;
- mission of socialization;
- mission of providing qualifications;
- the use of time;
- the use of leeway and autonomy;
- evaluation and certification.

We have not included any details of this important report because its major strands have been carried forward in government policy, which is described in detail in the following section.

Québec Schools On Course

This policy statement outlining the new direction to be taken by Québec schools was made public in 1997 (MEQ, 1997c). It reflects the proposed shift in the role of the MEQ and the new focus on the results and outcomes of the education system. The new policy states that the goal of improving the quality of the education students receive must begin with changes in the educational environment. It identifies four areas of curriculum reform and three corresponding "necessary adjustments." The four areas where changes are needed are the educational environment, the content of the curriculum, the organization of teaching and the programs of study. In order to implement changes in these four areas, a number of adjustments are deemed necessary with respect to procedures for evaluation and certification, teaching materials, and pre-service and in-service teacher training and development. The curriculum changes and adjustments advocated are briefly summarized below.

The Desired Educational Environment

Changes to the content and organization of the education offered in the schools must be based on principles, aim to promote the success of all students and satisfy the six conditions discussed below.

Focus on Essential Learning

The success of students is based on the mastery of the language of instruction and of the second language, mastery of the fundamentals of mathematics, knowledge of their own history, basic knowledge of the principal means of artistic expression, knowledge of the fundamentals of science and the development of effective work methods. Personal development and social skills should be taught either as a part of a specific program of study or across the curriculum, as well as in day-to-day school life.

Improve the Cultural Content of the Programs of Study

In the future, there will be more emphasis on the subjects traditionally associated with culture, such as languages, arts education, and history. These subjects will be taught from a cultural perspective, which means, for example, that language learning will include the study of literature and of literary history. Furthermore, to ensure that the teaching of cultural content is not left solely to teachers, it will be set out explicitly in the revised programs of study.

Introduce More Rigorous Standards in School

The high standards expected by schools must be understood and accepted by students, teachers and parents, and attained by an ever greater number of students. To achieve this goal, each school must therefore provide for the weaker, slower students and for those who learn differently by offering learning strategies adapted to their needs and appropriate assistance and support measures.

The standards referred to above must be reflected in the main components of the standard curriculum, as well as in all schoolwork, homework and individual study.

Subject-time allocation. Students must understand the intent of the courses and activities they are asked to engage in, and realize that what they are expected to learn is both useful and meaningful.

Programs of study. Objectives must be clear and standards explicit, as well as the progression from one grade or cycle to the next and the connections between a given subject and others in the curriculum. In order to promote coherent, integrated learning and to avoid redundancy, in the new curriculum appropriate sequences for learning content and skills will be established in all subject areas to show the progression of the learning content across grade levels.

Evaluation methods. Schools must regularly evaluate students' progress; both the means used to carry out this evaluation (assignments, examinations, tests) and the communication of results (progress reports, report cards, statements of marks) must be fair, accurate and easy to understand for students and parents.

Teaching materials. Textbooks and other materials that are made available to students must be authoritative and suggest learning activities that stimulate students' curiosity and love of learning.

Give Individual Attention to Students

Schools must do all they can to prevent failure and must provide all students with the best education possible throughout their school years. Accordingly, schools will offer students with difficulties or handicaps every opportunity to develop their talents and abilities to the fullest extent possible. School staff must share the conviction that all children can learn, if they are given the necessary means, and believe that they are capable of acquiring much more complex knowledge than we often give them credit for.

Prepare Students for Lifelong Learning

A school's long term objective must be to engage students from an early age in a process of lifelong learning, while giving them the motivation to do so. The reform of the curriculum must therefore be guided by a desire to: promote intellectual development that requires an active engagement on the part of the student in its discovery and construction; arouse the intellectual curiosity of students by having them ask questions and compare ideas with their peers and their teachers; and focus attention on the integration of knowledge, i.e., the ability to make connections between fields of knowledge and to reorganize them.

Placing Schools at the Service of Students

The various components of the curriculum must be structured in such a way as to give teachers full scope for independent action and allow them to make pedagogical decisions on the basis of students' interests. Therefore, the format and content of the programs of study and of the methods of evaluation, the rules and practices relating to the certification of studies and report cards, and professional development activities must allow teachers the leeway they need to act as professionals and use their judgment. Furthermore, the structure of the students' timetables and the use of school time must be based on the learning to be achieved by students, not on standard norms.

Curriculum Content

Essential learning is intended to ensure that all students master basic knowledge and skills. It relates to both fields of study and cross-curricular learning.

Fields of Study

There are five fields of study: languages; technology, science and mathematics; social sciences; arts education; and personal development.

Languages: Students must master their first language (or the language of instruction). Emphasis will also be placed on the acquisition of a second language and a third language given the linguistic context of North America and the globalization of economic activity and communications.

Technology, Science and Mathematics: Technology refers to the range of means used by humankind to produce what it needs for survival and comfort. In order to understand the world in which they live, students must be introduced to it at an early age. They must be familiar with the work methods that are specific to science: investigation, methodical observation, experimentation, verification and the construction of models. Students must also acquire and be able to use methods of calculation, since mathematics is an integral part of everyday life.

Social Sciences: The rapid evolution of society during this last half century has resulted in increasingly complex forms of social organization with increasingly complex ways of functioning. History, citizenship education, geography and economics must allow students to understand institutions, to be aware of and understand humans as social beings, and to trace the roots of present-day society. Students must have a thorough knowledge of the main events of our own and of world history and of the main space-time reference points. This means committing them to memory. Their knowledge of these events must be evaluated periodically. The policy states that in this province, the teaching of history is of particular significance, given the need for Quebec society to open itself up to other cultures and to confront various interpretations of the past.

Art Education: Students open their minds to other dimensions of reality through contact with the world of artistic expression and works of art in all of their various forms. An effective arts education must therefore introduce students to the various languages and theories that will help them develop their creativity and give them the knowledge they need to apply what they learn, as well as the opportunity to do so. It must also bring students into contact with, and help them to understand works of art from their own artistic and cultural environment by providing opportunities to visit cultural venues and meet with artists. Lastly, students must be exposed to works of art that are part of the cultural heritage of humanity and of their own country, and give them the knowledge they need to interpret and understand these works.

Art education must cover all forms of artistic expression. However, the basic common core should generally consist of the visual arts and music, which should be studied primarily as universal languages, but also as means of creating.

Personal Development: Although all the activities in which students participate in school contribute to their personal development, values are explicitly explored in moral education and religious education. Moral education includes the study of religion as a permanent phenomenon so that students who do not take religious education will have some knowledge of one of the major aspects of human civilization. This does not mean, however, that value-related issues are developed only in these subject; they must also be incorporated in other subjects and be a part of cross-curricular learning.

Physical education and health education are also included in the realm of personal development. Students will increase their chances of keeping fit throughout their lives if they integrate personal hygiene, sports, knowledge of human physiology, healthy eating habits and a balance between work and leisure into their lifestyle at an early age.

Cross-Curricular Learning

In addition to the curriculum content, schools must also encourage the development of skills and attitudes that do not fall exclusively within an individual subject area. The policy identifies four categories of cross-curricular learning:

Intellectual skills. Schools must better equip students to carry out intellectual work. This can be achieved by having them develop their memory, undertake projects and follow them through to completion, develop their critical sense and learn to communicate.

Methodological skills. All teachers must ensure that students learn to organize their work and to collaborate with others. All students must develop their capacity to use appropriate methods to process information, especially those methods offered by new information and communications technologies.

Attitudes and behaviours. The schools must teach students how to live in society by providing intercultural education (with emphasis on respect for differences), entrepreneurship education, environmental education, media education and health education.

Language skills. Mastery of language skills must be a concern in all subjects and for all teachers.

The policy states that cross-curricular learning will be introduced into the curriculum in two ways. First, since some cross-curricular learning relates to specific subjects, it will be addressed in the appropriate programs of study. Other cross-curricular learning, however, relates to all of the subjects in the curriculum. It will therefore be outlined in separate booklets for each of the elementary and secondary levels. Each booklet, called the "program of programs," will be designed for teachers and other school professionals with student-related responsibilities.

The Organization of Teaching

Compulsory schooling comprises two distinct stages: *common-core basic education*, from the first year of elementary school to the end of the first cycle of secondary school followed by *diversification* in the second cycle of secondary school. These two stages are reflected in the standard curriculum.

Common-Core Basic Education

Common-core basic education extends from the first year of elementary school to the end of the first cycle of secondary school, namely, secondary III. It now also includes preschool education, or kindergarten, which is offered on a full-day basis to all five-year-olds to promote the overall development of young students and to help ensure that they all start elementary school with the same chances for success.

Elementary school must allow students to acquire the basic knowledge and skills that will help them to develop their ability to think for themselves and to assimilate the content they will cover in secondary school. While acquiring essential basic knowledge, students must also begin formally learning the work/study methods required for higher levels of study. They also need to familiarize themselves with other learning content, the main characteristics of society and the values to be promoted within society. In the future, the elementary level will be reorganized into three two-year cycles in order to: redistribute content into multiyear stages that are more compatible with the psychological profile and stages in development of elementary school children. This will make it possible for new concepts to be introduced in the first year and consolidated in the second. It will also facilitate earlier end-of-cycle evaluation in order to increase the effectiveness of remedial measures designed to keep students from repeating a grade and develop alternatives to grade repetition, a practice which induces a feeling of failure without addressing the underlying problem. Finally, the new organization of cycles will promote and encourage the creation of small teams of teachers who will be able to follow the same students throughout a two-year period, or at least team teach the two years together.

The relative importance of certain subjects in the overall curriculum will be modified in order to emphasize specific learning content. In the first cycle of elementary school, greater emphasis will be placed on the *language of instruction* (particularly reading and writing) and *mathematics*. *French as a second language* will continue to be taught as of grade 1. Schools will be encouraged to continue to use the immersion approach which many of them have already adopted. A French immersion program will be developed and provided for in the *Elementary Regulation*, which will be amended accordingly. Students will start taking *English as a second language* sooner, more specifically, in grade 3. The Minister and the school communities are invited to explore different types of organization approaches for the teaching of English as a second language and to adopt innovative teaching methods so that courses better meet public expectation.

From grade 3 onwards, new emphasis will be placed on the teaching of *history*, which will include *citizenship education*. *Art education* will continue to be a compulsory subject as of grade 1 and courses will focus mainly on music and the visual arts. This decision is not intended to prevent schools with an established tradition of teaching dance or drama from continuing to do so if they so desire. All schools are strongly encouraged to offer extracurricular activities in all of the artistic disciplines.

The programs of study will be updated so as to clearly identify essential content and will include enrichment content. Schools that choose to teach enrichment content in a subject area will have the flexibility to increase the time allotted for that particular subject area.

The first cycle secondary (secondary I to III), will be same for all students since they will be completing the common-core basic education. This period of in-depth study will provide more formal learning in the various subject areas in order to gradually prepare students for the second cycle. Major changes will be made with respect to the subject-time allocation and the emphasis given to certain subjects.

More time will be devoted to *French as the language of instruction*. French teachers will consequently have fewer students and will therefore be able to provide a greater number of writing activities and to supervise students' work more closely. The number of credits allotted for *French as a second language* will increase from four to six at each grade level of the first cycle. The number of credits allotted for mathematics in secondary III will increase from four to six.

Greater emphasis will be place on *history*, which will be taught at each grade level and will include citizenship education. A new series of *science* courses will be introduced for the three grade levels of the first cycle. These courses will include technology-related content. A *third language* will be formally introduced as an optional subject starting in secondary III. However, students who satisfy the certification requirements for the second language earlier than is required will be allowed to take a third language course as of secondary I or II. The number of credits allotted for optional subjects in secondary III will increase from four to six. Students may choose their optional courses in no more than two of the following categories: arts education, technology, modern languages or a locally developed program.

Diversification: The Second Cycle of Secondary School

The second cycle of secondary school extends over two years, secondary IV and V. The two years of the second cycle are aimed at consolidating students' basic education through a common core of learning in the basic subjects, notably languages and mathematics, but also history and citizenship education, understanding the contemporary world and science. The second cycle will also allow for some diversification in students' basic education and give those who wish to do so the opportunity to earn a first vocational qualification. Experimental diversification programs currently under way in a number of schools should be continued in order to determine the parameters according to which they might be implemented in all schools. The second cycle of secondary school will allow for some diversification in both general and vocational education.

The number of credits allotted for optional subjects will increase from 16 to 24. At each grade level, students will choose their optional subjects from no more than two of the following fields of study: languages; social sciences; science, mathematics and technology; arts education; personal development; and vocational education. As is currently the case in mathematics and science, programs at two levels of difficulty will be offered in both French and English as the language of instruction and as a second language. The higher number of credits for the advanced program will be taken from the credits allotted for optional subjects.

In secondary IV, the number of credits allotted for the basic mathematics program will be reduced from six to four in order to balance the secondary-level mathematics courses. A middle-stream program will be introduced in secondary IV and V, and the prerequisites for certain college programs may be adjusted accordingly. In secondary V, a new course entitled Understanding the Contemporary World will replace the current economics course. The purpose of this new course, which will include essential content in the field of economics, will be to correct the weaknesses often noted among secondary school graduates with respect to knowledge of geography and particularly of contemporary world history.

The *Basic School Regulation for Vocational Education* will specify the conditions under which students will be allowed to take general education and vocational education courses concurrently, the requirements for obtaining a diploma and, where applicable, the requirements for admission to college-level programs.

The Canvas of Programs

The program of study for each subject and the "program of programs" which identifies cross-curricular learning form the very core of the curriculum. They are the product of democratic choices as to what should be taught to all students in Québec but must nonetheless allow teachers greater flexibility in the classroom. Greater transparency needs to be introduced into the program development process since programs must reconcile the standard curriculum, professional autonomy and collaboration with partners. The policy paper makes the following suggestions for introducing more transparency.

The Programs of Study

Most of the elementary and secondary school programs will be revised over the next few years, either to provide enrichment or to adjust them following changes to the subject-time allocation. As regards *design*, the programs for both elementary school and the first cycle of secondary school will be reorganized to include the cultural aspect of a given subject, so as to incorporate new information and communications technologies. The concern for adapting content to the needs of students with handicaps or learning difficulties will be clear from the very start of the design process.

To provide for professional autonomy, the choice of teaching methods, strategies and approaches will be left to teachers' discretion. Furthermore, programs will be designed to cover about 75 percent of the allotted time to give teachers the flexibility to enrich or adapt content according to students' needs. The programs will include a limited number of learning objectives, and the knowledge and skills to be acquired will be clearly set out Simple, straightforward language, free of any technical jargon will be used in the drafting of the programs.

Furthermore, programs will be developed from two perspectives: a "vertical" perspective, to provide a grade-by-grade description of all the courses in a given subject and to show the progression in their content; and a "horizontal" perspective, to describe all of the learning content covered in a given year or cycle in order to make explicit the connections and coherence between the various subjects. Finally, a simplified version of each program will be published for students, parents and the general public.

The "Program of Programs"

Cross-curricular learning will be described in a separate document intended for all school staff with student-related responsibilities. All educators, depending on their roles or the subject they teach, are responsible for helping students to develop the skills or attitudes identified in the "program of programs." Essentially, the "program of programs" will outline the attitudes and skills to be acquired by students with respect to intellectual work and knowledge in general. It will also specify what students must learn with respect to: work/study methods; attitudes and behaviours in private life; social skills; and language skills.

A Provincial Curriculum Board

The *Education Act* will be amended to create a Provincial Curriculum Board, whose mandate will be to establish the general framework for the development and revision of the programs of study on the basis of the orientations announced in the policy statement, and to coordinate the program development and revision process. The board will advise the Minister and make recommendations on the general design of the curriculum. It opinions and recommendations will be published. The Minister will continue to be responsible for approving the general orientations and content of each program, within the framework of a curriculum which will remain standard for all students in Québec. The provincial curriculum board will make recommendations on the development and revision of all programs, and on any issue related to curriculum content. It will also examine the curriculum on an ongoing basis. The board will include experts in each of the curriculum areas, but many seats will be reserved for school personnel, particularly teachers.

Recent Advice from the Superior Council

Early in this chapter, we mentioned that advice from the Superior Council in the early 90s (CSE, 1993a, 1993b) formed part of the impetus for curricular change. The Council has of course stayed in tune with recent developments and provided further input in annual reports and several briefs (e.g. CSE, 1998a, 1998c, 1998d).

Programs of Study & the Regulations

In its most recent brief, *Les enjeux majeurs des programmes d'études et des régimes pédagogiques* (CSE, 1999), the Superior Council makes a number of recommendations on curriculum reform at the elementary and secondary levels. Generally supportive of the current reform as set forth in recent policy papers (MEQ, 1997a, 1997c), the CSE focussed its brief on seven key issues.

Cycles & Cross-Curricular Learning

The CSE supports the new system of organizing elementary education into three two-year cycles and secondary education into two cycles; it also recommends that a certificate be issued after the first cycle of secondary education. The CSE also acknowledges the considerable value of cross-curricular learning, those skills which can be acquired in several subject areas.

Secondary School Diploma

The CSE approves of increasing the number of credits required for a Secondary School Diploma [SSD] from 54 to 60 but does not support the addition of the following required courses: mathematics, English and second language in secondary V; science and technology in secondary IV. The CSE feels that this requirement is inconsistent with the notion of a second cycle which encourages students to choose more demanding courses in order to better prepare themselves for college. Instead, it encourages them to choose less difficult courses in compulsory subjects.

Concurrent General & Vocational Education

While encouraging the largest possible number of students to complete an SSD, the CSE welcomes the new conditions for studying for the Diploma of Vocational Studies [DVS] or the Vocational Education Certificate [VEC] before the age of 18.

Time Allotted to French Language of Instruction

The CSE has reservations concerning the allocation of 24 credits rather than the current 18 to French language of instruction in the first cycle of secondary education, particularly since this increase eliminates the leeway allowing various optional courses to be offered. Increasing the time allotted does not guarantee ultimate student mastery of French.

Diversification

Currently, secondary school offers a considerable number of paths that allow for adaptation and remediation (upgrading, change to the vocational stream) and enrichment (international education, art-study and sport-study programs). In the CSE's opinion, it is far from certain that this differentiation remains essential if educators work increasingly according to cycles, with much more adaptable programs of study and ongoing support. The new *Basic Regulation* should make a clear distinction between responsibilities with respect to differentiated curricula and describe the paths encouraged by the MEQ.

Elementary School

The CSE recommends that the number of hours of classroom time at the elementary level be increased to 25 from the current 23.5. It also reiterates its view that it would be extremely unfortunate if an introduction to science, history and geography were removed from the first cycle of elementary education and replaced by mathematics and language of instruction.

Other Conditions Underlying the Reform's Success

The Council is concerned that the schedule and means for implementing the revised programs leave insufficient room for informing and mobilizing schools.

Regulatory Framework

The three principal sources of authority for curriculum and school organization are the *Education Act*, the *Basic Regulations* and the annual education directives (*Youth Dir*). As was seen in earlier chapters, the *Education Amendment Act* (1997) made considerable changes to the division of powers in the *Education Act* regarding educational services, differences that one would expect to cause similar changes in the regulations. Although such changes are anticipated, at the time of writing, they remain to be adopted.

Scope of Educational Services

According to the regulations, educational services consist of developmental and cognitive learning services (kindergarten), instructional services (elementary and secondary), student and special services.

Educational Services
The purpose of educational services is to promote the students' overall development and integration into society (El Reg, s. 1; Sec Reg, s. 1).

Developmental & Cognitive Services
Developmental and cognitive learning services are intended to enable preschool students to integrate gradually into society beyond their family (El Reg, s. 2; Sec Reg, s. 2).

Instructional Services
Instructional services are intended to enable students to acquire the basic learning necessary for their overall development and integration into society (elementary) and continue their overall development and facilitate their personal and social orientation (secondary) (El Reg, s. 3; Sec Reg, s. 3).

Student Services
Student services are intended to help students by providing support for learning, contributing to their individual growth and sense of belonging to the community, helping them overcome particular difficulties and ensuring their emotional and physical well being. The regulations list ten specific student services (El Reg, s. 4; Sec Reg, s. 4).

Special Services
Special services are designed to help students benefit fully from other educational services by gaining prerequisite skills, providing support in the language of instruction, second language and mathematics and adapting instruction or the organizational framework for instruction. The regulations list three specific special services (El Reg, s. 5; Sec Reg, s. 5).

Courses of Study

Courses of study comprise provincial and local courses.

Provincial Courses of Study
The Minister of Education is responsible for establishing the courses of study at the elementary and secondary levels. The elementary subject grid includes a *suggested* number of hours per week for each subject. The secondary subject grid does not contain any specific hours but it does include the number of credits associated with each subject and the statement that each credit is equivalent to 25 hours of instruction (Ed Act, s. 463; see El Reg, s. 44; Sec Reg, ss. 34-35). However, the Catholic and Protestant regulations do stipulate the minimum time that must be devoted to MRI, namely in elementary school 60 hours per year for Catholic MRI and 100 minutes per week for Protestant MRI, and in secondary school, 50 hours per year for each (*Catholic Regulation*, ss. 10, 11; *Protestant Regulation*, s. 6).

Subject to the above, it is the school governing board that is now responsible for approving the allotment of time for each compulsory and elective subject, as developed with the collaboration of the teachers and proposed by the principal, while ensuring that the compulsory objectives and the content of the courses of study mandated by the Minister are achieved and that the rules governing the certification of studies prescribed by the *Basic Regulations* are complied with (s. 86).*

* *Note.* Provision subject to "Transitional Measures" - see chap. 7.

French Immersion

The above subject grids make no provision for immersion (e.g. instruction in French of subjects other then French as a second language) but the regulations state that the school board may approve such programs for students "eligible to receive instruction in English" and whose parents so authorize (El Reg, s. 46, Sec Reg, s. 35).

Local Courses of Study

The school governing board is now responsible for approving the "overall approach" to the development of local programs; however, the programs themselves are approved by the principal, upon the proposal of teachers (Ed Act, ss. 85, 96.15).*

* *Note.* Provision subject to "Transitional Measures" - see chap. 7.

Enrichment & Adaptation of Programs

The school governing board is responsible for approving the "overall approach" to enrichment and adaptation of programs of study (Ed Act, s. 85).*

* *Note.* Provision subject to Transitional Measures" - see chap. 7.

Organization of Educational Services

Overall Implementation

The school governing board is responsible for approving the approach proposed by the principal for the implementation of the *Basic Regulations* (Ed Act, s. 84)*, the implementation of programs of student and special education services (s. 88)* and any programming which entails changes to the regular schedule or which entails taking students off school premises (s. 87).*

* *Note.* Provision subject to Transitional Measures" - see chap. 7.

Setting the Parameters

The school year is defined by the *Education Act* as July 1 to June 30 (s. 13). Every school board shall establish the school calendar and weekly or cyclical instructional timetable of its schools, taking into account the provisions of the various parameters, notably: compulsory and elective subjects (described above); prescribed time for students' class size; and teaching time (see below).

Number of Days of School

The *Basic Regulation*s require that every school shall be open for a maximum of 200 days, at least 180 of which must be teaching days (El Reg, s. 30; Sec Reg, s. 31). The balance of days in the year are "pedagogical days" and are devoted to planning and professional development for school staff.

Establishing the School Calendar

The school board, after consultation with the parents' committee and any local negotiations with teachers, establishes the "school calendar" for each of its schools, that is, which days will be teaching days, planning days or holidays.

The Student Timetable

The *Basic Regulations* state that the weekly instructional timetable is 23 hours and 30 minutes for kindergarten and elementary students and 25 hours at the secondary level (El Reg, s. 43.; Sec Reg, s. 33). The latter is typically set forth in a grid of so many periods of instruction per day - for example, six 50-minute periods per day.

Daily Starting & Ending Times

Since school boards are given authority over the calendar and the weekly instructional timetable of their schools, as well as over transportation, it can be inferred that they also have responsibility over daily starting and ending times (subject to any local negotiations with teachers), although there is nothing in the Act or the regulations which clarifies this role.

Class Size

The regulations and directives are silent with respect to class size norms; the *PAPT Entente, 1995-98* however, stipulates the "average" (across the school board) and "maximum" (individual) class sizes. The latter, which may be exceeded upon request with payment of compensation, are summarized below (class averages are 2, sometimes 3 lower than maximum; for other details, see *PAPT Entente, 1995-98*; 8-2.00).

Categories	Maximum Class Size		
	Kd	El	Sec
Regular	22	29[a]	32[b]
Classes d'accueil[c]	18	19	19
Special Ed - Mild		17	20
Special Ed - Severe	6-10[d]	6-12[d]	6-14[d]

[a] Grade 1=25; Grade 2/3=27;

[b] IPL course = 20; tech exploration/ITT = 23;

[c] French schools only;

[d] Range only shown; varies by disability category.

Teacher Workload

"Teacher workload" - the time assigned to teachers for classroom instruction (teaching time), supervision and other specified duties - is stipulated in the *PAPT Entente, 1995-98*; the principal provisions are summarized below (for other details, see *PAPT Entente, 1995-98*; 8-5.00).

Categories	Teacher Worload		
	Kd	El	Sec
Individual teacher workkload	23 hrs	23 hrs	20 hrs
Average teaching time		20 hrs, 30 min	17 hrs, 5 min

Instructional Methods, Textbooks & Materials

In accordance with the *Education Act*, the Minister draws up a list of approved textbooks and instructional material or classes of instructional material. Where applicable, textbooks and materials must also be approved by the Catholic and Protestant committees (s. 462).

However, upon the proposal of the teachers, the principal is now responsible for approving the criteria regarding the implementation of new instructional methods and, after consulting with the governing board, for approving the textbooks and instructional material required for the teaching of the programs of studies (s. 96.15(2)(3)).*

* *Note.* Provision subject to "Transitional Measures" - see chap. 7.

Evaluation of Learning

Evaluation is the process that consists in the gathering, analyzing and interpreting of information relating to the achievement of the learning objectives determined by the programs of studies and to the students' overall development (El Reg, ss. 38, 50; Sec Reg, s. 42).

Role of the Teacher

Every teacher is responsible for evaluating the performance of students in his or her charge and reporting according to the system in effect in the school.

Role of the Principal

Upon the proposal of the teachers, the principal establishes the standards and procedures for the evaluation of student achievement that are consistent with those prescribed by the *Basic Regulations*, subject to the examinations that may be imposed by the Minister or the school board (Ed Act, s. 96.15(4)).*

* *Note.* Provision subject to "Transitional Measures" - see chap. 7.

The Role of the School Board

The school board's role is to ensure that schools evaluate students and administer the examinations imposed by the Minister or the school board (Ed Act, s. 231).

The school board may now only impose internal examinations in the subjects it determines at the end of each elementary cycle and of the first cycle of the secondary level (Ed Act, s. 231).*

* *Note.* Provision subject to "Transitional Measures" - see chap. 7.

Role of the MEQ

The Minister may impose examinations in the subjects that he or she determines in both elementary and secondary school (Ed Act, s. 463).

Promotion

Promotion to Elementary School

Normally, promotion from kindergarten to elementary school is automatic. However, if a child has not met the objectives of preschool education, a parent may request that the child be retained for one year and the principal is now responsible for determining if the request should be granted (Ed Act, s. 96.17).

Promotion in Elementary School

Normally, promotion in elementary school from one grade to another is also automatic; however, grade promotion may be denied once during elementary schooling (El Reg, s. 42).

Subject to this proviso, the principal, upon the proposal of the teachers, is now responsible for approving the rules governing the promotion of students from elementary cycle 1 to cycle 2 (Ed Act, s. 96.15(5)).*

* *Note.* Provision subject to "Transitional Measures" - see chap. 7.

Promotion to Secondary School

Normally, promotion from elementary to secondary school occurs after six years but promotion may be accelerated by one year, if the student has acquired sufficient emotional and social maturity, or delayed by one year, if the student has not met the objectives of elementary education. The latter is initiated by a parental request and the principal is now responsible for determining if the request should be granted (Ed Act, s. 96.18; El Reg, s. 42; Sec Reg, s. 29).

Subject to the above, the school board, after consulting the parents' committee, is responsible for approving the rules governing the promotion of students from elementary to secondary school (Ed Act, s. 233).*

Note. Provision subject to "Transitional Measures" - see chap. 7.

Promotion in Secondary School

At the secondary level, promotion is determined on a program-by-program (subject-by-subject) basis, unless there are special pedagogical situations or organizational constraints. Students may enroll in a program only after obtaining the prerequisites, if any, for that program. The school board may, in special situations, exempt a student from that requirement (Sec Reg, s. 37).

Subject to the above, the school board, after consulting the parents' committee, is responsible for approving the rules governing the promotion of students from secondary cycle 1 to cycle 2 (Ed Act, s. 233).*

Note. Provision subject to "Transitional Measures" - see chap. 7.

Secondary Certification

Graduation

According to the *Secondary Regulations* (s. 69), the Minister shall award an SSD to a student who has accumulated 54 credits in secondary IV and V, including the following compulsory credits: 6 credits in secondary V language of instruction; 4 credits in secondary V second language; 4 credits in secondary V mathematics or a secondary IV mathematics program determined by the Minister pursuant to section 461 of the *Education Act* and whose objectives present a comparable level of difficulty; 6 credits in secondary IV physical science; and 4 credits in secondary IV history of Québec and Canada (Sec Reg, s. 69).

However, the current annual directives (Youth Dir, s. 2.2) state that the above is suspended and replaced by the following, namely students must accumulate 54 credits in secondary IV and V, at least 20 of which must be at the secondary V level or in vocational education. Included must be the following: 6 credits in secondary V language of instruction; 4 credits in secondary IV or V second language instruction, for students those language of instruction is French; 4 credits in secondary V second language instruction, for students whose language of instruction is English; and 4 credits in secondary IV History of Québec and Canada.*

Note. In addition to the above, Bill 101 stipulates that no secondary school leaving certificate may be issued to a student who does not have the speaking and writing knowledge required by MEQ courses of study (s. 84).

Admission to a College Program

According to the 1998-99 directives, to be admitted to a college program, a person must have an SSD and have successfully completed secondary IV physical science, secondary V second language, secondary V mathematics or its equivalent secondary IV course.

Reporting

Student report cards are obviously a means of communicating information to parents but they are also an integral part of the evaluation process, which has become the responsibility of the school principal (see above). The *Basic Regulations* have yet to be revised in light of the changes introduced by the *Education Amendment Act* (1997), but it seems reasonable to conclude that report cards are now a school matter, to be decided on by the principal upon the advice of teachers.

The school board must ensure that the parents of each student receive, at least five times a year, a written evaluation report (four of which must be school reports) on the student's academic performance, behaviour and attendance. The minimum information to be supplied in the school report is also specified. Moreover, not less than once a month, information shall be provided to the parents of students: (1) whose performance puts them in danger of failing the current school year; (2) whose behaviour does not comply with the school's rules of conduct; (3) for whom a special education program providing for that information was prepared (El Reg, ss. 39-40, 51-52; Sec Reg, s. 43-44).

PART IV:
HUMAN AND FINANCIAL RESOURCES

The conception of the teaching profession is at a crossroads. There are two dominant contradictory images evident ... teacher as technical actor vs moral actor. The technocrat or bureaucratic image conceives of teachers as giving knowledge and following and applying rules. The moral actor as artisan and craftsperson sees teaching as transforming students. These are ideal types, of course, and it is likely ... that a mixture of the two is required. There is no denying, however, that in the quest for solutions the teaching profession may find itself being led or going down one road or another (Fullan, 1990, p. 142).

Education is a human resource intensive enterprise and human resources absorb a considerable proportion of the financial resources of the education system. Part IV examines the human and financial resource bases of the system. In chapter 9, we begin by exploring the role of teachers as employees, including the current state of the collective bargaining process. Chapter 10 continues with the discussion of teachers as professionals and the renewal of their role in the development of education policy and direction. Chapter 11 provides an introduction to the funding of public education in the province.

The key provisions of the following instruments which are referred to in the chapters of this part are reproduced in the *Compendium*:

Chapter 9

Canadian Charter
Education Act
Québec *Charter*

Chapter 10

Civil Code of Québec
CSE Act
Education Act
    Regulation Respecting Teaching Licences

Chapter 11

Act Respecting Municipal Taxation
Education Act

Introduction

Teachers must be considered in light of their status as employees, as well as their status as professionals. The distinction between professional and employment issues is not clearly demarcated; many issues could be dealt with satisfactorily under either heading. In this chapter, we will focus on teachers as employees. A discussion of employment issues usually considers the two dimensions of personnel policy - process and content. Teachers, like other public and para-public sector employees in Québec, are unionized and engage in collective bargaining at both the provincial and local levels. The bargaining process is a complex one and has resulted in long complex collective agreements, part of the content dimension, which cover a wide range of subjects and determine the working conditions of teachers and other personnel. In addition to the rights and obligations of teachers which arise from these agreements, we will look at other sources of law which are important to teachers, especially the *Canadian Charter* and discuss other aspects of teachers' working life as public school employees, such as their role in policy making. In the next chapter, we will discuss the role of teachers as professionals.

Employee Relations in Québec Education

Sources of Legislative Authority

Québec has arguably the most complex system of employee relations in education in Canada. The system is governed by a series of interlocking statutes. The principal ones are listed below.

Canadian Charter
The *Canadian Charter* provides the legal backdrop to the system; as in other areas such as student rights (see discussion in chap. 3), all Québec laws must respect the rights and freedoms provided for therein, especially, in terms of employee relations, fundamental freedoms (s. 2) and equality rights (s. 15).

Québec Charter
The Québec *Charter*, like the *Canadian Charter*, protects fundamental freedoms and equality rights; in addition, it contains several provisions directly related to human rights in employment.

Education Act
There are some provisions of the *Education Act* which affect teacher working conditions and others which provide the basis for determining the remuneration and working conditions of administrators.

Labour Code
The *Labour Code* has a similar scope to the legislation found in many jurisdictions and covers issues

such as collective bargaining and arbitration; it has specific provisions applicable to the public and para-public sectors, including education.

Public Sector Bargaining Act

In addition to the provisions of the *Labour Code*, collective bargaining is also governed by a separate statute: the *Act Respecting the Process of Negotiation of Collective Agreements in the Public and Parapublic Sectors* [*Public Sector Bargaining Act*].

Other Legislation

There are a variety of other statutes which play a part in regulating the working conditions and work environment of teachers and other education employees (e.g. *Act Respecting Labour Standards*; *Act Respecting Occupational Health and Safety*; *Charter of the French Language*) which we will not be considering in this brief discussion.

Categories of Personnel

The Québec education system comprises unionized, non-unionized and non-unionizable personnel. Unionized personnel include all employees who are members of a bargaining unit formed under the provisions of the *Labour Code*. Non-unionized personnel refers to employees who are entitled to become unionized but who are not unionized. Non-unionizable personnel are employees who are not entitled to become unionized. The various categories of personnel are enumerated in Table 9.1.

TABLE 9.1
Categories of Personnel

Administrative (Non-Unionizable Personnel)
Senior Executive: Directors General* & Full-Time Deputy Directors General

Executive:
     School Board Directors, Coordinators &
     School Principals, Vice-Principals

Managerial: Superintendents* & Foremen
Unionized (& Unionizable) Personnel
Teachers
Non-Teaching Professionals: Education Professionals & Business Professionals
Support Staff: Technical, Para-Technical, Clerical & Trades

* *Note*. Contrary to the vocabulary used elsewhere, in Québec the chief executive officer of the school board is called a director general. The Québec managerial position of "superintendent" is often called a "manager" in other jurisdictions where the term "superintendent" refers to the chief executive officer or to a senior officer in those jurisdictions where the chief executive officer is called the "director of education."

Administrative & Salary Policy for Administrators

The administrative and salary policy applicable to administrators, usually termed the "PAS" after the French term (*la Politique administrative et salariale*), is determined by the Government, after consultation with the different groups of administrators involved. During the past several years, there have been different procedures for developing and publishing the PAS in the Catholic and Protestant sectors. In the former, the PAS took the form of a regulation adopted under the aegis of the *Education Act*; there was one regulation for senior executives, one for board level executives and managers and a third for school level executives. In the Protestant sector, instead of a regulation there were two administrative documents: one for senior executives and a second for all other categories of administrative personnel.

The Government has just adopted a single regulation governing all administrative personnel in the new linguistic school board structures *(Regulation Respecting the Conditions of Employment of Management Staff of School Boards)*. The content of the regulation is decided upon by the Government following consultation with various advisory committees, as listed below:

Committee of Directors General
This committee is composed, on the one hand, of representatives of the MEQ, the QSBA and the FCSQ and, on the other hand, of representatives of the Association des directeurs généraux des commissions scolaires and the Association of Directors General of English School Boards of Quebec.

Advisory Committee of Administrators
This committee is composed, on the one hand, of representatives of the MEQ, the QSBA and the FCSQ and, on the other hand, of representatives of the Association des cadres scolaires du Québec, the Association des cadres de Montréal and the Association of Administrators of English Schools of Quebec [AAESQ].

School Administration Personnel Committee
This committee is composed, on one hand, of the representatives of the MEQ, the QSBA and the FCSQ and, on the other hand, of two representatives of the Fédération québécoise des directeurs et directrices d'etablissement d'enseignement and one representative of each of the following associations: the Association des directions d'école de Montréal, the Assiciation québécoise du personnel de direction des écoles, the AAESQ and the Association des cadres scolaires du Québec.

Centre Administration Personnel Committee
This committee is composed, on the one hand, of representatives of the MEQ, the QSBA and the FCSQ and, on the other hand, of representatives of the Association des cadres scolaires du Québec, the AAESQ, the Fédération québécoise des directeurs et directrices d'établissement d'enseignement, the Association des directions d'école de Montréal and the Association québécoise du personnel de direction des écoles.

Accreditation of Teachers & Other Personnel
In Québec, bargaining certificates are locally held vis-à-vis employer school boards. The general rules provided in the *Labour Code* for the accreditation of unionized personnel apply, with the exception that certain time limits of this process have been adjusted to dovetail with the time line of the bargaining process (see below).

Accreditation & the New Linguistic School Boards
According to the *Linguistic School Boards Act* (1997), unions could file petitions to represent employees in the new linguistic boards (including voluntary certification agreements) by September 30, 1998. Any competing petitions would be decided by secret ballot no later than January 31, 1999. Fifteen days after certification, the collective agreement of the certified union would be the only agreement to apply. In the case where a union was a party to more than one agreement, or where the new union was the result of a voluntary amalgamation, the board and the union could choose the agreement, failing which the agreement of the largest group applied (Ed Act, ss. 530.3 - 530.13).

Collective Bargaining for Teachers & Other Personnel

As stated briefly above, collective bargaining for teachers is governed by a special set of rules which will be presented below.

The Bargaining "Players"

The management side of the bargaining table is composed of representatives of the Government and provincial school board organizations: the FCSQ and the QSBA. The management side forms a joint bargaining committee according to the provisions of the *Public Sector Bargaining Act*. In elementary-secondary education, there are two such committees: the Management Negotiating Committee for French Language School Boards [CPNCF]* and the Management Negotiating Committee for English Language School Boards [CPNCA].*

* *Note*. The acronyms reflect the official French names (Comité patronal de négociation pour les commissions scolaires francophones/anglophones). These replace the former management committees for Catholic [CPNCC] and Protestant school boards [CPNCP].

For many years, teachers have been represented provincially by one of three unions: Centrale de l'enseignement du Québec [CEQ], the Provincial Association of Catholic Teachers [PACT] and the PAPT, all of which have tended to coordinate their positions when dealing with provincial management groups. The CEQ represented all teacher groups in the Francophone sector of Catholic school boards and some groups in the Anglophone sector, while the PACT represented the majority of the latter; the PAPT represented all teachers in Protestant school boards in both the Francophone and Anglophone sectors.

This situation has changed, with the transition to Francophone and Anglophone school boards (see discussion of accreditation and linguistic boards above). The CEQ retains its name and represents all local unions in Francophone school boards. The PAPT has changed its name to the Québec Provincial Association of Teachers [QPAT] and now represents local unions in the Anglophone school boards.

The Bargaining Process

Despite the local accreditation process (see above), all major negotiations are conducted at the provincial level. In order to try and set some parameters for the negotiation of salary, the Government created the Institut de recherche et d'information sur la rémunération, which is responsible for conducting comparative analyses of remuneration in the public and para-public sectors in Québec in relation to any other groups and producing an annual report.

According to the *Public Sector Bargaining Act*, bargaining occurs within mandatory time lines. The union (e.g. QPAT) is supposed to file its demands 150 days prior to the expiry of an agreement and the employer group (e.g. CPNCA) must file its proposals within 60 days. Although these time lines may help start the process in a timely fashion, they do not guarantee that the bargaining process will be accelerated. In fact, to use an old expression, many of the time lines mandated by law are "more honoured in the breach than in the observance." The bargaining process occurs first at the provincial and then at the local levels.

Provincial Level Bargaining

Most of the negotiations occur at what are called *sectorial* bargaining tables for different employer-union groups in the public - i.e. government departments - and para-public - i.e. education, health and social services (e.g. CPNCA-QPAT) sectors. Negotiations begin upon the expiry of the present contract (usually a 3-year term, plus possible extensions). During this phase, unions have the right to strike, subject to *essential services* provisions (generally confined to hospitals and other health care agencies). Salaries and most working conditions are negotiated at individual sectorial tables; however, the presence of representatives of the Government and a given union cartel (e.g. CEQ-QPAT) at different sectorial tables makes the possibility of significant inter-sectorial differences illusory.

In addition to informal inter-sectorial bargaining, negotiations are also conducted with each of the major union federations (*centrales*). Global remuneration parameters and some other matters are negotiated here. Although this forum is not provided for in the legislation, arguably, the most important financial parameters are bargained here. Most recently, the government and the unions have been seeking to institute "win-win" collective bargaining (discussed below) - a very different approach than that followed in the past (see *Historical Roots*, chaps. 3 , 4 & 5).

Local Level Bargaining

Local bargaining takes place between school boards and the local teachers' union. According to the legislation, negotiations are on-going, as there is no fixed term to the local contract which ensues from this process and which contains a limited number of predetermined issues. In practice, local negotiations follow the provincial bargaining cycle. There is no right to strike at this level.

The Saga of Collective Bargaining Continues

In the mid 1960s, collective bargaining was largely uncontrolled by the Government (for more details, see *Historical Roots*, chap. 3). It took place between the employer, a local school board, and the local union. In 1967, in response to a number of labour disputes involving teachers and local school boards, the Government passed a law, the *Act to Ensure for Children the Right to Education and to Institute a New Schooling Collective Agreement Plan,* to order teachers back to work, establish a uniform salary scale for all Québec teachers and centralize teacher collective bargaining at the provincial level. The first round of provincial bargaining for teachers resulted in a collective agreement in 1968, the second in a decreed settlement in 1972. These first two rounds of negotiations were marked by considerable conflict, both between union and management and within the union and management groups. These problems and special legislation continued through five further rounds of negotiations to round 7 (1990), which was the prelude of more change to come. That change was prompted by a period of severe economic constraints, constraints that are still binding on the system today.

Hard Times & a New Approach

In 1993, the Government adopted the *Act Respecting the Conditions of Employment in the Public Sector and the Municipal Sector,* the purpose of which was to prolong existing public sector collective agreements by two years and to freeze wages and premiums during this period. In addition, the Government stipulated that it would obtain a 1% reduction in the total cost arising from the application of the collective agreements. This was to be accomplished by imposing up to three days of unpaid leave or by any other equivalent measure.

In the same year, the Government, its employer partners (FCSQ, QSBA) and the teacher unions (CEQ, PACT and PAPT) signed an umbrella agreement (*accord-cadre*) to guide future negotiations. Described as a "strategic change in direction" (*virage stratégique*) from past practice, the agreement included the following important principles (cited in Lombard, 1995, Appendix):

- that the parties recognize the need to increase efficiency in the present economic and budgetary context;

- that the parties recognize that an in-depth examination of the organization of work may allow for savings, increased productivity and improved quality of working life;

- that the parties agree to work together to achieve these objectives and are ready to examine the collective agreements and other factors which influence the organization of work.

Lombard (1995) reports that management and union representatives have taken part in some joint training and that while success was mixed, the results have been generally positive. In the education sector, the parties have used this new approach to deal with the need for further economies and to reach an agreement to change the timing and frequency of salary payments, resulting in a saving of 10 million dollars. Despite this success, Lombard is not optimistic about the future of the new approach (1995, pp. 12-14):

> Paradoxically it now seems highly unlikely that the present process will continue as per the "accords-cadres". In fact, article 9 of the agreement states that notwithstanding a date of expiry of June 30, 1996 the expiry will occur on June 30, 1995 if there is disagreement on salary policy for 1995-1996. That disagreement appears a certainty, particularly since the subject of remuneration has not been broached in any serious way by the parties.
>
> In the short term then it is inevitable that the new process will come to a halt. It must also be

understood that the early results of bargaining do not seem to contain very much which would encourage a union to continue to support the process. Whatever training the parties have had, and no matter how good or thorough the training may be, it is still a normal reflex to look only for one's own gain in the process.

There is also in union mythology a strong aversion to what is often referred to scornfully as concession bargaining. The unions will therefore probably decide to fall back on the conventional forms of negotiation provided for in the labour code. The decision, in itself, will not, however, necessarily mean the end of the process.

From the point of view of this writer, the choices are really far more limited. Stripped of the surrounding verbiage the real essence of the new form of bargaining is no different than what ought to have always been the case: both parties need to understand profoundly their own positions and those of the other party. And those positions must be merged so that both sides find mutual gain and benefit.

In reality, the far greater challenge for the future lies with the government. It is abundantly clear that, for the process to work, information must be exchanged and understood by the parties. It is precisely that lack of information, particularly in the economic area, which has handicapped the present process.

It is quite impossible for the parties to discuss, at length and over much time, minor issues and then have major cuts announced by decision of one of the parties without any preparation and joint consideration of the question. The process requires, as a minimum, that all parties be prepared to lay on the table the problems to be solved.

If it is difficult for unions to look ahead, it seems to be impossible for governments to do so. At a minimum the government will have to decide what its economic objectives are for at least the next three years. This does not seem likely in the Québec context. When the idea was put forward a senior government official could only shrug and indicate that what he said had a shelf life of three or four months at best.

Next year will be one of decision. It is in the nature of democratic political institutions to procrastinate, yet it seems evident that the referendum will have to be held or cancelled and that the second year of federal cuts will force the Québec government into some budgetary action. Many observers feel that the window of opportunity for fruitful discussion extends only to November or December of 1995. The hard decisions are in the timetable for January and February of 1996 at the latest.

Round Eight: A Holding Pattern

In 1996, the eighth round of provincial bargaining concluded with a new *Entente* in force until 1998 (*PAPT Entente: 1995-98*). The round was characterized by "concession bargaining" to go some way toward government targets for cost reductions. Although several cost-cutting measures were agreed to, many of them were temporary rather than "structural" in nature, that is the measures only applied for a specified period of time. Accordingly, few long-term savings resulted from this process and the matter of economic concessions can be expected to figure in the forthcoming round of negotiations. Perhaps the most significant part of the agreement concerned pension plans where a temporary early retirement scheme allowed almost ten thousand teachers, some as young as fifty, to leave teaching and be replaced by younger personnel.

Round Nine: In Progress ...

At the time of writing, round 9 is in progress and so little can be said about it at this point in time. However, in addition to the matter of economic concessions mentioned above, another major issue has already arisen - salary equity. In general, salary equity aims at eliminating or at least reducing unwarranted differences within and across various employment groups, in relation to redressing lower remuneration patterns for women in the work place. For teachers, salary equity involves two aspects. The first considers the remuneration paid to teachers in comparison to other professional employment categories. The second is more complex and is concerned with the use of years of schooling as a determinant of teacher remuneration.

For thirty years the provincial salary scale for teachers has been a "grid" consisting of several categories each based on successively higher levels of schooling, and a number of steps recognizing experience. At the present time, there are seven categories, the highest of which is reserved for holders of a doctorate, while each category has 15 steps. One moves "up the steps" one at a time, for each year of experience but one only moves "across the grid" as one acquires higher levels of schooling. Thus, two teachers with the same experience doing the same job will receive different salaries if one of them has more years of schooling. This practice violates the Québec *Charter* which stipulates:

Québec Charter of Human Rights and Freedoms

19. Every employer must, without discrimination, grant equal salary or wages to the members of his personnel who perform equivalent work at the same place.

A difference in salary or wages based on experience, seniority, years of service, merit, productivity or overtime is not discriminatory if such criteria are common to all members of the personnel.

The absence of years of schooling as an exception in the second paragraph of this provision means that its use as a salary determinant is prohibited. The problem can be solved by creating a unitary scale with experience steps but no differential categories based on schooling. It remains to be seen, however, how the discourse on salary equity will be reconciled with the discourse on economic restraint, as the implementation of such a change would entail a recurrent cost of hundreds of millions of dollars per year.

The Results

The end of the bargaining process - by whatever route it takes - results in a collective agreement which contains the salary and working conditions applicable to the group of employees in question. The agreement is binding on the parties for the duration stipulated therein (usually three years). During the life of the agreement there is no right to strike. If the parties (either provincial or local) wish to amend the *Entente* or the local agreement, as the case may be, they may do so in writing.

If disagreements arise regarding the interpretation or application of the agreement, then the local union (or school board) may file a grievance. If the grievance cannot be settled locally, then it is referred to arbitration (see discussion below on teacher rights).

The Collective Agreement
The collective agreement constitutes the labour contract between the employer (the school board) and the union (of teachers). Because bargaining is conducted at more than one level, the collective agreement consists of two parts: the *Entente* and the local agreement. The *Entente* includes all matters negotiated at the provincial level (e.g. *PAPT Entente, 1995-98*), including those settled at the central table, while the local agreement contains locally negotiated matters.

Bargaining Subjects
The following is a list of the major subjects contained in the *Entente* and the local agreement:

TABLE 9.2
Bargaining Subjects

A. Provincial Entente
GENERAL
    Release time for union activities
    Seniority
    Security of employment
    Parental rights
    Remuneration
    Class size provisions
    Workload
    Students with special needs
    Regional disparities
    Grievance arbitration procedures
ADULT EDUCATION*
VOCATIONAL EDUCATION*

B. Local Agreement
    Certain union prerogatives
    Consultation and participation
    Regulations governing absences
    Assignment and transfer
    Social leave
    Discipline and dismissal

*The *Entente* contains separate chapters dealing with teachers in adult education (11-0.00) and vocational education (13-0.00). Each of these chapters constitutes an "agreement within the agreement" as they provide a complete set of provisions, some of which simply state that section "x" of the "regular" portion of the *Entente* applies.

Transfer Norms for the New Linguistic School Boards

According to the *Linguistic School Boards Act* (1997), the norms for the transfer of non-unionized staff from the previous denominational school boards to the new linguistic boards were to be determined by regulation, while those applicable to unionized personnel were to be negotiated by November 30, 1997, failing which an arbitrator would decide by January 15, 1998. The CPNCP and the PAPT reached an agreement on November 29, 1997 that remains in force until June 30, 2000. The agreement provides for the rules to be followed in determining which teachers were to be transferred to which new board, and to settle a number of related issues, such as the transfer of monies from the professional improvement fund, establishment of recall lists and so forth.

Each provisional council was responsible for establishing the administrative structure and staffing plan of the new school board and, in co-operation with other councils and after consultation with staff associations, for preparing a staff transfer plan in accordance with the above master agreement. Individual staff members were informed of their new employer by June 30, 1998. Reassignment of unionized staff was to be made in accordance with the new employment conditions effective as of July 1, 1998 (Ed Act, ss. 523.1-523.16).

Teacher Working Conditions & School Organization

The rights and obligations of teachers are not simply determined by the *Education Act*; many important provisions governing the teacher's working life are contained in the *Entente*. The following is a combination of actual extracts and summarized text of the general principles governing teachers' duties and the list of the general duties of teachers, as provided for in the *PAPT Entente, 1995-98*:

PAPT Entente 1995-98

8-1.01 The conditions for exercising the profession of teaching must be such that the pupil may benefit from the quality of education which he or she is entitled to expect and that the board and the teachers have the obligation to provide to him or her.

[**Summary of 8-1.02 to 8-1.07**:

The following matters shall be the subject of consultation with the teachers' consultative committees, as provided for in the collective agreement:

- introduction of new pedagogical methods;
- choice of approved textbooks and teaching materials;
- any change in the report cards used by the board;
- student evaluation policy of the board;
- system for teacher evaluation of students and reporting of same;
- system for monitoring and reporting late arrivals and absences of students;
- instructional timetable.

The MEQ pedagogical guides are only intended as guidelines for teachers.]

8-2.01 The teacher shall provide learning and educational activities to pupils and shall participate in the development of student life in the school.

Within this framework, the teacher's characteristic responsibilities shall be:

- to prepare and present courses within the guidelines of the authorized programs;
- to collaborate with the other teaching and nonteaching professionals of the school in order to take the appropriate measures to meet the individual needs of pupils;
- to organize and supervise student activities;
- to organize and supervise industrial training periods;
- to assume the responsibilities of "encadrement" [*] for a group of pupils;
- to evaluate the performance and progress of pupils for whom he or she is responsible and report on them to the school administration and to parents according to the system in effect ...;
- to supervise the pupils for whom he or she is responsible as well as any other pupils when they are in his or her presence;
- to monitor the late arrivals and the absences of his or her pupils and report them to the school administration according to the system in effect ... ;
- to participate in meetings relating to his or her work;
- to perform other duties which may normally be assigned to teaching personnel.

* *Note.* "Encadrement" is defined in the *Entente* (s. 8-7.01(a)) as: "intervention with a pupil or a group of pupils to promote the pupil's personal and social development and to encourage him or her to assume his or her responsibilities as regards his or her own education."

Legal Rights of Teachers

Today, teachers have many legal rights which protect them both inside and outside the workplace but this was not always so. Consider this extract from a 1915 employment contract:

[The teacher is] not to keep company with men; to be home between the hours of 8:00 p.m. and 6:00

a.m. unless in attendance at a school function; not to loiter downtown in ice cream stores; not to leave town at any time without permission of the chairman of the board, and not to get in a carriage or automobile with any man except her father or brother.

As is seen in the discussion which follows, times have changed somewhat!

Sources of Teacher Rights

The rights of teachers, like those of students, parents and others, are found in law (see overview in chap. 1). Like the regulatory framework governing education in general (see Figure 2.3 in chap. 2), teacher rights are "nested in layers," in that each set of rights is found in a legal instrument (e.g. employment contract, collective agreement) which is subject to enabling legislation (e.g. *Labour Code*), which is subject to the Québec *Charter*, which in turn is subject to the *Canadian Charter*. These layers also reflect a gradation from specific to general, both in terms of the types of rights and the scope of application. Thus, for example:

- the innermost layer, the employment contract deals with the term of engagement of an individual teacher;

- the local collective agreement deals with assignment and applies to teachers in a given school board;

- the *Entente* includes the salary scale and applies to all teachers affiliated with a given provincial teachers' federation;

- labour legislation stipulates rights to join a union and applies to all employers and employees in Québec;

- the Québec *Charter* prohibits sexual harassment and applies throughout Québec to all matters falling under its jurisdiction;

- the *Canadian Charter* guarantees equal protection and benefit of law and applies throughout Canada to all matters falling under its jurisdiction.

In the remainder of this brief section, we will look at the framework of employment rights provided by these layers.

Employment Rights

As outlined above, an individual teacher's rights begin when he or she signs an employment contract with the school board. This contract specifies the employment status of the teacher - full-time, part-time, by-the-lesson - and the duration of the contract. In terms of teacher rights, it merely makes reference to those contained in the collective agreement, which is the core instrument in providing teacher rights in Québec.

As indicated above in Table 9.2, the collective agreement contains many topics, each of which includes a mixture of rights and obligations. For example, the agreement spells out the rights of a teacher respecting discipline and dismissal. As these matters are part of the local agreement, the provisions vary from one board to another. However, in general, they include the grounds for discipline and dismissal and the procedures that must be followed if the board wishes to reprimand, suspend, dismiss or non-reengage* a teacher. If the teacher wishes to contest the measure imposed by the board, he or she can take the matter to the union.

* *Note.* The term "non-reengagement" is used to denote a decision of the board not to renew the teacher's contract at the end of the school year. The term "dismissal" is used to refer to a decision to terminate a teacher's contract during the school year.

Grievance-Arbitration Process

It is up to the union to decide whether there are grounds to file a grievance with the school board; these grounds could be procedural, substantive or both. Procedural grounds arise when the board has not followed all the procedures specifically laid down in the collective agreement or those generally required by applicable principles of law. Substantive grounds - or the merits of the case - refer to the reasons given for the action taken (e.g. dismissal). The union may disagree with the allegation made by the board - e.g. that the teacher's alleged conduct toward the principal was insubordinate - or that the conduct warrants the measure imposed - i.e. the teacher may have conducted himself or herself in an inappropriate manner but the conduct in question did not justify dismissal.

If the matter is not resolved, the union may refer the case to arbitration for adjudication. This means that the case will be argued in front of an arbitrator who has the jurisdiction to settle the dispute. His or her decision is final and binding on the parties and, generally speaking, can only be appealed if there is a manifest error in law in the decision. The costs of this process are borne by the union, the school board and the MEQ. There is no direct cost to a teacher unless he or she decides to retain separate counsel.

Grievance-arbitration procedures only apply to a disagreement over the interpretation or application of the collective agreement. This means that if a teacher believed that his or her rights were being infringed but the rights in question did not arise from the collective agreement, then the grievance-arbitration process could not be used to seek redress. Since other forms of redress can be time consuming and costly, it is to the teacher's advantage to be able to ground rights in the collective agreement.

Introduction

Professionalism is generically defined by several characteristics, including extensive professional training. The standing of teachers in the community varies and recent reforms in teacher education, as well as an increased role for teachers in school level decision making will enhance their image as professionals. Québec teacher education programs have undergone substantial revision and this process provides an opportunity for the renewal of the teaching profession in this province. This renewal process was given further impetus in 1997 with the redistribution of powers under the *Education Amendment Act*, which included the formalization of teacher participation in policy making. These measures confirm the critical role that teachers play in educational policy development

Next to the student, the teacher is the most important person in the education system. Although other educational professionals, such as principals, psychologists and guidance counsellors interact with students, the vast majority of "contact time" between students and the system is through teachers. In this chapter, we will examine the role of the teacher as a professional, what that role means and how it is framed in the Québec education system.

Professions, Professionals & Teaching

If we asked the "average person on the street" to name several professions, we might expect law and medicine to figure high in the number of responses. Opinion might be mixed, however, if respondents were asked whether they thought teaching is a profession and, by extension, if teachers are, or should be considered as, professionals. Before attempting to address this question, we will briefly examine the characteristics of professions and professionals.

Characteristics of a Profession

Several authors have attempted to describe the characteristics of a profession. Most of these definitions include some notion of an occupational group based on specialized knowledge and standards of conduct. Ryan and Cooper (cited in Giles & Proudfoot, 1994, pp. 335-336) provide the following criteria to decide whether a given occupational group constitutes a profession:

- it renders a unique, definite, and essential social service;
- it relies upon intellectual skills in the performance of its service;
- it has a long period of specialized training;
- both individual members and the professional group enjoy an extended degree of autonomy and decision-making powers;
- it requires its members to assume personal responsibility for their actions and decisions;
- it emphasizes the rendering of services more than personal financial rewards;

- its members accept and are governed by a code of ethics;
- it is self-governing and accepts responsibility for controlling the conduct of its members.

A professional can thus be thought of as someone who practices a recognized profession. However, the word "professional" is also used as an adjective to describe individual and organizational behaviour, especially in contrast to "bureaucratic" behaviour.

Bureaucratic versus Professional Frameworks

Kirp (1983) states that "the way a policy problem gets defined says a great deal about how it will be resolved" (p. 74). Among the various policy frameworks described by Kirp are two which are relevant to this discussion: the *bureaucratic* and the *professional* frameworks. Hoy and Miskel (1987, p. 130) compare the two approaches thus:

> Both bureaucrats and professionals are expected to have technical expertise in specialized areas, to maintain an objective perspective, and to act impersonally and impartially. Professionals, however, are expected to act in the best interests of their clients, while bureaucrats are expected to act in the best interests of the organization.

There are several other ways in which the two approaches contrast, as summarized below.

Dimension	Bureaucratic	Professional
Basis of authority	Position	Knowledge
Reference group	Hierarchy	Colleagues
Standards of conduct	Organization-based	Discipline-based
Decision making	Rule-based	Individual judgment

It is not surprising that these contrasting approaches lead to conflict inside organizations where, for example, an individual with a professional orientation works for an organization which expects bureaucratic compliance or, alternatively, where the organization expects its managers to behave as professionals, while they want a set of rules to live by.

Using this discussion as a basis, we can proceed to address our original question regarding teachers as professionals.

Teachers as Professionals

Allowing for some exceptions, especially for people trained many years ago, teachers in Canadian public schools are highly trained, with at least a bachelor's degree, and often with advanced degrees in some specialized field. Some of the argument about teachers as professionals stems from the fact that, unlike lawyers and doctors, for example, you do not choose your teachers in a public school. Teachers are employees of a school board and governed by a complex set of rules and regulations, most of which are not of their own making.

Another factor sometimes considered in assessing teachers as professionals is their involvement in unions. Some people argue that professionalism and unionism are incompatible constructs and that teachers have devalued the teaching profession through union activities. On the other hand, it can be argued just as cogently that teachers are professionals but they are also employees, as opposed to independent professionals, and have a right to protect their interests and rights as employees (see *Historical Roots*, chap. 4).

CTF Policy: The Teaching Profession

Since the regulation of the teaching profession is a provincial matter, there are no regulatory provisions which apply to all teachers across Canada. However, teachers themselves, through the Canadian Teachers' Federation [CTF], have developed a set of national policies regarding the teaching profession (CTF, 1991-92). The CTF, founded in 1920, is a national organization whose membership consists of provincial teacher organizations - not individual teachers. It has adopted a number of policy statements which set forth "goals and beliefs to which its member organizations jointly subscribe, as evidenced by a formal resolution of a General Meeting of the Federation" (p. 81). The following is the statement regarding the Nature of the Teaching Profession (pp. 82-84, section numbering and resolution dates omitted):

- The teacher provides a personal service to each student, based on the specialized application of the teacher's understanding of the learning process and designed to meet the needs of each individual within the individual's society.
- The teaching profession should reflect the general participation rate of women, visible minorities and the disabled in the population.
- It is the responsibility of the teacher:
  a) to review his/her own level of competence and effectiveness, and to seek necessary improvements as part of a continuing process of professional development;
  b) to perform his/her professional duties according to an appropriate code of ethics, and appropriate standard of professional conduct;
  c) to recognize that teaching is a collective activity, and to seek the most effective means of consultation and of collaboration with his/her professional colleagues;
  d) to support, and to participate in, the efforts of his/her professional association to improve the quality of education and the status of the teaching profession;
  e) to assess progress and practices within his/her classroom, school or jurisdiction and to seek improvements.
- It is the right of the teacher:
  a) to be the final authority in the means of implementation of a program in his/her classroom;
  b) to be free from unwarranted interference in the organization of the learning experience in his/her classroom;
  c) to be directly involved in the determination of all professional decisions within a school;
  d) to criticize the educational program within his/her school or school jurisdiction district without reprisals or harassment provided that such criticism occurs ethically within the confines of the teaching profession.
- It is the right and responsibility of the teaching profession:
  a) to participate in defining the goals of education;
  b) to devise appropriate sets of learning programs, and remedies for specific difficulties;
  c) to develop instruments for the evaluation of the educational process and to be involved in the execution of such evaluation;
  d) to be involved in the design and the production of resource materials and to determine their selection for the learning process;
  e) to be involved in the planning and the selection of systems, facilities, organizational patterns, and administrative structures for the educational process.
- It is the responsibility of the teaching profession:
  a) to promote the continuous improvement of professional conduct, and of conditions of learning, and of teaching;
  b) to establish its own code of ethics, and standard of professional conduct, its own criteria for professional qualifications, and its own procedures for the assessment of professional competence;
  c) to strive to attain, for each teacher, a level of status and of economic standing appropriate to the education and responsibilities of the professional teacher;
  d) to protect each teacher from interference in the proper discharge of professional duties.
- It is the responsibility of the teaching profession:
  a) to cooperate with institutions of teacher education to establish entry qualifications and educational programs suitable to such institutions;
  b) to cooperate with institutions of teacher education to provide appropriate practical experience for teachers-in-training;
  c) to cooperate with institutions of teacher education to evaluate potential graduates of such institutions.
- It is the responsibility of organizations of the teaching profession:
  a) to assume, to administer, and to discharge effectively the collective responsibility of the profession;

b) to maintain autonomous status and effective democratic self-government within the organization;

c) to maintain the principles of professional unity and collegial relationship among all certificated teachers within the jurisdiction of the organization;

d) to ensure that professional development activities are offered in French to their members who use French as the language of instruction;

e) to exert pressure on the various ministries and/or departments of education urging them to offer and subsidize professional development courses for Francophone teachers in minority situations;

f) to impress upon teacher education institutions the need to offer professional development and retraining courses that meet the specific needs of Francophone teachers in minority situations;

g) to impress upon teacher education institutions the need to offer professional development and retraining courses that meet the specific needs of teachers of French as a second language in core French and Immersion programs.

Professions in Québec: The Professional Code

There is a law in Québec entitled the *Professional Code*, which defines a number of occupations as professions and recognizes a corresponding number of professional corporations. Among other purposes, this Code serves to define two types of professions - those with protected practice and those with a protected name. Those designated as a protected practice (e.g. law, medicine) exclude from the practice of that profession, anyone who is not a member in good standing of that professional corporation. Those designated as having a protected name (e.g. psychology, social work) exclude from using the name of that profession, anyone who is not a member in good standing of that professional corporation. In other words, no one can practice medicine unless he or she is a member of the Professional Corporation of Physicians; by contrast, anyone can practice psychology, whether a member of the Professional Corporation of Psychologists or not, but cannot call himself or herself a psychologist, unless he or she is a member of the Corporation. Teachers are not mentioned in the *Professional Code*.

Teacher Training in Québec

One of the many recommendations of the Parent Commission in 1964 (see discussion in *Historical Roots*, chap. 3) was to have the universities assume responsibility for pre-service teacher training, a function previously assumed by normal schools (e.g. St. Joseph's Teachers' College) and university affiliated teacher colleges (e.g. McGill University's Macdonald College). In the intervening years, many changes have occurred in the professional preparation of teachers (see Henchey & Burgess, 1987, pp. 158-163, for a brief review).

For the past several years, persons wishing to enter the teaching profession in Québec had two options: the Bachelor of Education program (B.Ed.) and the Diploma in Education program. The B.Ed. program was of three years duration and included both academic and teacher preparation. The diploma program, offered to persons who had already obtained a bachelor's level degree and met certain requirements, comprised only teacher preparation courses. We have recently instituted a new program, which will be discussed below. The new program, unlike the old one, entitles the graduate to obtain a teaching diploma, which is a permanent teaching license, an approach that is quite different from the past (see discussion on Teacher Certification below).

In recent years, there has been much policy talk in the educational milieu about *reform* and *restructuring*. Educational reform has been coming in "waves" for the past several years. The first wave generally took a "top-down" perspective, emphasizing scholastic standards and teaching quality, while the second was more "bottom-up," focusing on new ways of restructuring schools and empowering teachers. Pre-service and in-service education of teachers are important components in this overall reform movement.

Teacher Education Reform in Québec

In 1992, the MEQ published *Joining Forces* (MEQ, 1992d), a general policy paper on educational reform (*Historical Roots*, chap. 4) where it announced that as part of its overall educational reform strategy, it would be re-examining the education of pre-service teachers. Subsequently, the MEQ published a series of papers on teacher education reform. One of the first of these papers dealt with the renewal of the teaching profession.

The Challenge of Teaching

The MEQ began its reflection on the reform of teacher education with a paper that recognized an obvious - but often forgotten - truth: that "because teachers play a crucial role in shaping the success of the children and adolescents they teach, it is essential that we direct our attention and our efforts to the renewal and recognition of the teaching profession" (MEQ, 1992a, p. 1).

Competencies of New Teachers

Much of the thrust of the reform of teacher education in Québec has to do with defining the competencies which new teachers should have upon entering the profession. To date, four teacher training policy papers have dealt with the competencies of teachers in various fields of teaching:

- preschool and elementary education (MEQ, 1994a);
- secondary general education (MEQ, 1992f);
- the arts, physical education and second language education (MEQ, 1997d);
- special education (MEQ, 1996a).

Some common highlights from these four papers are summarized below. Similar papers for vocational and adult education have yet to be published.

General Orientation & Guiding Principles

Each of the four MEQ teacher training policy papers contains a general statement of the new orientation that teacher training ought to take, beginning with the recognition that teacher competence lies essentially in the ability of the teacher to stimulate and guide students through the learning process, through a complex set of interactions. In addition to making ongoing professional judgments and adjusting to the needs of students in light of their own situation and the wider societal environment, the latter two policies add a statement about the importance of teacher/student relationships: "Teaching also involves caring about students and this emotional commitment on the teacher's part is an essential ingredient of effective student/teacher relationships" (MEQ, 1997d, p. 15). Each paper also outlines five guiding principles for teacher training: a broad general education; versatility; teacher's personal development; practical training; and, integrated training. The policy paper on training teachers for special education adds a sixth guiding principle: enriching basic teacher training with training in special education.

Awareness of the Cultural & Social Dimensions

The vital importance of a teacher's knowledge of the broader context in which he or she is teaching is addressed and emphasized in each policy paper. As expressed in the most recent one (MEQ, 1997d, p. 40):

> The role of the school is not only to foster intellectual growth. As a social institution, it has the responsibility to educate all children and youth so that they grow into independent individuals and responsible citizens. The school is also expected to provide students with equal opportunities and the best possible conditions for learning. It is therefore important for future teachers to reflect on the role of the school in society and on issues relevant to knowledge and educational paths and trends

The paper also lists the following knowledge-based competencies that support this professional policy dimension of teaching (p. 40):

- knowledge of the school system, its history and structure, and the ability to understand the school system's influence on Québec society;
- knowledge of the factors which influence the orientations of the school system, more particularly, the confessional or linguistic status of schools, the social roles of women and men in the school system, ethnic and cultural diversity, and the citizen's role in school organization;
- knowledge of the laws, regulations and policies governing the Québec school system (particularly those related to special education);
- knowledge of the history of the profession and the ability to identify with the profession;
- knowledge of the factors which influence student performance in school and the ability to help create conditions conducive to the success of the greatest number of students;
- knowledge of the government policies related to education, particularly cultural policy and policy regarding health and social services;
- knowledge of the social and cultural stakes involved in the increasing use of NCIT [new communication and information technologies] in teaching and learning.

Teacher Training: Program Accreditation & Policy Development

Much of the recent policy talk in Québec education circles, as elsewhere, recognizes the importance of collaboration in achieving meaningful educational reform. Two provincial committees deal with teacher training, one with accreditation of programs, the other with policy development, as briefly summarized below.

CAPFE

This teacher training program accreditation committee, known as "CAPFE," an abbreviation of its official French name (Comité d'agrément des programmes de formation à l'enseignement) (see chap. 5), consists of nine members appointed by the Minister after consultation with interested parties. More particularly, it is composed of (Ed Act, s. 477.14):

- the chairperson who shall be, alternatively, an education sector professional and a person from the university education sector;
- three members chosen from the ranks of elementary/secondary teachers;
- one teaching sector professional;
- three members drawn from the ranks of teachers in the university sector;
- one member drawn from the university education sector who has had experience at the preschool, elementary or secondary school level.

At least two members of the committee must represent the English-language education sector. In addition the Minister may appoint two associate members (who have no right to vote), one to be chosen from the ranks of MEQ employees and the other from the ranks of the managerial staff of school boards.

The committee shall examine and approve the teacher training programs for preschool, primary and secondary teachers (s. 477.15). The committee shall also:

- make recommendations to the Minister concerning teacher training programs required for the issue of teaching licenses; and
- advise the Minister on the determination of the qualifications needed to teach at the elementary and secondary levels.

Although only recognized in law with the adoption of the *Education Amendment Act* in 1997 (Ed Act, ss. 477.13-477-15), it has been in operation since 1992 (see MEQ, 1996b). This committee reflects a "new way of doing business," in which people from the field not only take an active part but actually make up the majority of the committee which decides on the accreditation of teacher education programs.

COFPE

Another provincial committee on the orientation of teacher education programs, known as "COPFE," an abbreviation of its official French name (Comité d'orientation de la formation du personnel enseignant), consists of sixteen members, fifteen of whom are appointed by the Minister. More particularly, it is composed of (Ed Act, s. 477.17):

- a president;
- six members chosen from the ranks of elementary and secondary school teachers;
- three members chosen from among the commissioners and the members of the managerial staff of the school boards, including a principal of an institution;
- three members chosen from the university education sector;
- one member chosen from the ranks of parents, students or business leaders;
- one member chosen from the ranks of MEQ employees.

At least two members of the committee must represent the English language educational sector. The chairperson of the CAPFE is also a member of this committee.

The mission of the committee is to advise the Minister on all questions pertaining to teacher training policy for the elementary and secondary levels (s. 477.18). At the request of the Minister or of its own initiative, it may propose guidelines and make recommendations to the Minister relating to:

- the identification of teacher training priorities;
- draft regulations relating to teacher training;
- teacher training and professional development;
- all aspects of the teaching profession related to the training of teachers.

Although also only recognized in law with the adoption of the *Education Amendment Act* (Ed Act, ss. 477.16-477.18), it has been in operation since 1993 (see MEQ, 1996b).

New Teacher Education Programs

All new programs take the form of a four-year B.Ed. degree. Thus, there will no longer be any diploma programs for students who have completed a first degree. These students may be admitted to the B.Ed. program with advanced standing, but it is presumed that they will have to complete all the practicum experience in the new program (see below), which likely means that someone in this situation will have to spend two years or more beyond their first degree in order to complete the new B.Ed. program, depending on an evaluation of previous course work.

The Practicum

Another policy paper in the series on teacher training, *The Practicum* (MEQ, 1994b) emphasizes the importance of the practicum in the pre-service training of future teachers: "It gives them an opportunity to reflect on different teaching practices and to become familiar with all of the educational duties carried out by a school staff. In so doing, it ensures that their training will be comprehensive, well-rounded and rewarding" (p. 1). The practicum policy consists of four key elements:

- practical training;
- partnership;
- the cooperating teacher; and
- action research.

Practical training in a real classroom setting supervised by the university in collaboration with schools and school boards is the substance of the practicum. It must comprise at least 700 hours spread over the four-year program, but mainly concentrated in the final year.

The partnership consists of three partners: the university, school boards and schools. The university role includes, among others: responsibility for overall coordination; defining the roles of cooperating teachers and selecting and supervising them in collaboration with the school system; and supporting action research in schools. The school board role includes, among others: responsibility for providing administrative and educational support; and participating in university research in the area of teacher training. The school role includes, among others: responsibility for working with the university in selecting and supervising cooperating teachers; and in the designing, organizing, supervising and evaluating practicum activities.

The policy provides for two principal mechanisms for administering the partnership. The first is a regional management committee, chaired by the university that includes representatives from the MEQ and local educational institutions. The second is a protocol, signed by the university and the school boards, a role now recognized in the *Education Act* (s. 261.1).

Cooperating teachers play a "special role" in practicum supervision: "They possess the knowledge and expertise necessary to guide student teachers in the gradual acquisition of teaching skills and in the development of a professional code of ethics" (p. 9). Recognizing that student teachers are being initiated into a very complex profession, the cooperating teachers act as advisors to student teachers, participate in their evaluation and help guide them "as they explore the various facets of the school system and of the professional environment" (p. 9). The policy spells out various criteria for the selection of cooperating teachers, and states that they should receive training in practicum supervision of 30 to 60 hours duration and recommends that their efforts should be recognized in terms of their workload.

Action research is included as a final element in the policy, noting that it can contribute in significant ways to the advancement of teacher training (p. 13):

> One of the results of various research projects aimed at improving the practical training of teachers has been the development of a special type of cooperating school where the coordination and supervision of practicums provides a basis for other joint activities in the areas of experimentation, research and professional development.

In conclusion, this policy paper builds on research into good practice and sets the stage for an enhanced teacher training program and ongoing collaboration between the university and the school system.

Teacher Certification

The requirements for teachers to be legally qualified, the exceptions to this general rule and the conditions governing the revocation of a teacher's license are found in the *Education Act*. For many years, the primary regulation dealing with legal qualification was *Regulation No. 4* (*Regulation Respecting Teaching Permits and Teaching Diplomas*), adopted under the aegis of the *CSE Act* (s. 30). Other regulations adopted under this Act spell out the qualifications of teachers of moral and religious instruction. A new regulation concerning legal qualifications, *Regulation Respecting Teaching Licences*, has been in force since September 1997 (see Laverdière, 1999).

Teaching Licences

The *Education Act* provides for the licensing of teachers (ss. 23-25). The Act used to state simply that except for specific cases, every teacher must possess a valid Québec teaching license. The Act now replaces this expression "every teacher" by the following: "To provide preschool education services or to teach at the elementary or secondary level, a teacher must ..." (s. 23). Similarly, the word "teachers" in section 25 is replaced by the following expression: "preschool education providers or elementary or secondary-level teachers." All such persons still require a teaching license but one has to query the change of wording and whether it is harbinger of a change in the status of teachers at the preschool level. The exceptions to the requirement to be legally qualified remain the same except for the addition of a person providing instruction under the *Private Schools Act*. These exceptions are (s. 23):

- a teacher hired by the lesson or by the hour;
- a person providing instruction in an enterprise under the *Private Schools Act*;
- a casual supply teacher;
- a person providing instruction which does not lead to an official diploma, certificate or attestation;
- a person issued a *tolerance*, a certificate granted by the Minister in exceptional cases.

A Change in Scope

According to the new *Regulation Respecting Teaching Licenses* and a MEQ information document (1997e), a teaching license now defines the right to teach, rather than a qualification in a particular level or field of teaching, as it had in the past. New licenses will stipulate the language of instruction (see below) and authorize the bearer to teach in preschool, elementary or general secondary education programs.

According to the MEQ (1997e), this new approach is meant to increase the mobility of teachers across levels and fields of teaching. It is the responsibility of the school board and school officials to ensure that teachers have the competencies required for their teaching assignments. There are two principal forms of teaching licenses, as defined below.

Transitional Measure

According to the MEQ (1997e), teaching licenses for vocational and adult education will continue to be issued under the former regulation until the revision of the teacher training programs for these sectors has been completed. However, the probationary period requirements of the new regulation (described below) apply.

Language of Instruction

The license to teach is issued for one language of instruction, either French or English, according to the language in which the majority of the individual's training was given. Persons trained in another language must pass a ministry exam, which is also available to someone licensed in French or English who wishes to be qualified to teach in the other language.

Teaching Diploma

In the past, graduates from teacher education programs were issued a teaching permit, following which they had to successfully complete a two-year probation period before obtaining a teaching diploma. This is no longer the case. A teaching diploma is now awarded upon graduation from one of the new teacher education programs,* and enables pre-service teachers to complete the equivalent of probation requirements during their university program (see below).

A teaching diploma may also be issued to an individual who has been issued a teaching permit and has satisfied the following requirements:

- for the graduate of one of the old teacher training programs listed in Schedule II - successfully completed probation;
- for the person with an out-of-province teaching license - successfully completed a course on the Québec education system and successfully completed probation.

---

* *Note*. The new programs are listed in Schedule I of the Regulation and include:

Bishops: B.A. and Diploma in Education; B.Sc. and Diploma in Education;
Concordia: Bachelor of Arts with a Speciality in Preschool and Elementary Education;
McGill: Bachelor of Education, General Secondary Program; Bachelor of Education, Preschool and Elementary Program.

Teaching Permit

A teaching permit is now used in two cases:

- for the graduate of a teacher education program listed in Schedule II of the *Regulation Respecting Teaching Licences*;
- for the person who possesses a legal teaching license from outside Québec* provided that person has also completed a university program which is equivalent to (a) a 90 credit program plus a 30 credit teacher training program given by a Québec university or (b) a 90 credit program including a 30 credit teacher training program given by a Québec university.

* *Note.* The former "Provisional Teaching Authorization" is no longer issued by the Minister.

It is valid for a 5 year period and may be extended by 2 year periods by the Minister if the candidate satisfies the following conditions:

- he or she has taught a minimum of 400 hours during the five years in which the permit has been in force, or if it had already been extended, 200 hours during the previous extension;
- he or she has successfully completed during the five years in which the permit has been in force, a minimum of four three-credit courses in a teacher education program in a Québec university;
- he or she has successfully completed during a previous extension, a minimum of two three-credit courses in a teacher education program in a Québec university.

Moreover, a teaching permit may be renewed, even if the above delays have expired if the candidate successfully completed a minimum of four three-credit courses in a teacher education program in a Québec university in the two years preceding a request for such renewal by the candidate.

Teacher Probation

Previous System

The previous probation system (MEQ, 1992e) was designed to enable newly qualified teachers to prove their professional competence and integrate them into the teaching profession. The primary responsibility for the probation system at the school level rested with principals who were responsible for forming and overseeing the probationary committees which were created for each probationary teacher. These committees included a representative of the school administration and the overseeing teacher. The committee was responsible for evaluating the probationary teacher who was also expected to complete a self-evaluation.

New System

For teachers graduating in the new teacher education programs, the previous probation system has been replaced by the evaluation of student teachers during the practicum. As stated above, new teachers will receive permanent teaching licenses upon graduation. According to the new *Regulation Respecting Teaching Licences*, the probation period is now used for permit holders, that is graduates from the old teacher education programs and persons with an out-of-province teacher license.*

The probation period now consists of 1 200 hours of teaching in a recognized educational establishment, However, the duration of the probationary period may be reduced to 600 hours if during this time the candidate has taught at least 200 hours within a twelve month period for the same school board.

The school principal is responsible for evaluating teacher probation and preparing a report of his or her evaluation. The school board is responsible for issuing an attestation to every person who successfully completes his or her probation period and for informing any individual that he or she has failed the probation period and, in either case, of informing the Minister of the decision. A person who fails a probation period may apply within 60 days for a second probation period. A second failure is final.

* *Note.* This requirement for out-of-province teachers is new; previously, the only requirement in the Regulation was the successful completion of the course on the Québec education system.

Moral & Religious Instruction

Teachers who teach MRI are also subject to the regulations of the Catholic and Protestant Committees of the CSE. Moreover, teachers may refuse to teach MRI for reasons of conscience (see below; see also chap. 12).

Revocation or Suspension of Teaching License

The *Education Act* (ss. 26-35) stipulates the conditions under which a teaching license may be suspended or revoked. The following is a summary of these provisions:

- Any person may, under oath, file a written complaint to the Minister against a teacher for misconduct or immorality or for a serious fault in the performance of his or her duties.

- If the Minister feels that the complaint is frivolous, he or she so notifies the complainant, giving reasons; if he or she considers that the complaint is admissible, he or she transmits a copy to the teacher and the school board and the following procedures apply.

- The Minister convenes an investigative committee of three persons to inquire into the complaint.

- The Minister may, at his or her discretion, order that the teacher be relieved of his or her functions during the investigation.

- The committee sets its own rules of procedure but must give the teacher an opportunity to be heard before rendering its finding.

- If the committee considers that the complaint is not well founded, it may dismiss the complaint, and so inform, giving reasons, the Minister, the complainant, the teacher and the school board.

- If the committee considers that the complaint is well founded, it must transmit its findings, with reasons, to the Minister, together with its recommendation regarding the sanction to be imposed.

- Upon receipt of the committee's findings and recommendation, the Minister may suspend, revoke or attach conditions to the teaching license of the teacher; in the case of an unqualified teacher (engaged by "tolerance") the Minister may prohibit the school board from continuing to employ the teacher. The Minister shall so inform the complainant, the teacher and the school board and shall also provide a copy of the decision of the committee.

Teacher Rights & Obligations

Many rights and obligations of teachers are spelled out in the *Education Act* (ss. 19-21). Other rights and obligations are found in the provincial *Entente* governing teachers (see chap. 9). Other obligations may be imposed by other enactments. No attempt is made here to canvass all the rights and obligations of teachers.

Education Act

19. In accordance with the educational project of the school and subject to the provisions of this Act, the teacher has the right to govern the conduct of each group of students entrusted to his care.

The teacher is entitled, in particular,

(1) to select methods of instruction corresponding to the requirements and objectives fixed for each group or for each student entrusted to his care;

(2) to select the means of evaluating the progress of students so as to examine and assess continually and periodically the needs and achievement of objectives of every student entrusted to his care.

20. Every teacher has a right to refuse to give moral and religious instruction of a religious confession on the grounds of freedom of conscience.

No teacher may be dismissed, suspended or disciplined in any other way for exercising his right under this section.

21. A teacher wishing to exercise the right described in section 20 shall so inform the principal, in writing, within the time and in the manner determined by the school board.

Any refusal to give moral and religious instruction of a religious confession stands until the principal receives notice in writing to the contrary.

22. A teacher shall

(1) contribute to the intellectual and overall personal development of each student entrusted to his care;

(2) take part in instilling into each student entrusted to his care a desire to learn;

(3) take the appropriate means to foster respect for human rights in his students;

(4) act in a just and impartial manner in his dealings with his students;

(5) take the necessary measures to promote the quality of written and spoken language;

(6) take the appropriate measures to attain and maintain a high level of professionalism;

(6.1) collaborate in the training of future teachers and in the mentoring of newly qualified teachers;

(7) comply with the educational project of the school.

Duty to Provide for Health-Related Needs of Students

As noted above (see chap. 3) it is increasingly common to find amongst the student population children who require medication or other health-related services during the school day. This is a cause of serious concern to school personnel whose "job descriptions" do not specifically include attending to the health-related needs of students. While school personnel may, of course, *volunteer* to administer medication to students under their care, the question remains, are they *legally obliged* to do so when so requested by their employer? There exists little legislative or judicial guidance to answer this question.

Emergency Assistance

It appears to be clear that school staff are legally obligated to render assistance to students in an emergency (see chap. 3).

Non-Emergency Assistance

The obligations of school staff in this regard may be expressly treated in the provisions of collective agreements, or the terms of individual contracts of employment where such exist. But what is the position where these instruments are silent on the matter?

Administrators

The answer would appear to be reasonably clear with respect to in-school administrators as school boards can require that they perform this function. In-school administrators are the school board presence in schools and it is the implicit (if not explicit) expectation that they will perform such functions as are required by their positions (Ed Act, s. 96.26). Thus, given that school boards are obliged to ensure that students' health related needs are met while at school, by extension, in-school administrators may be required to bear the ultimate responsibility for ensuring that these needs are met even if that means personally having to administer to them.

School Staff

While legislation sometimes assigns to school staff specific functions and duties (for example, Ed Act, s. 22 - see above), these provisions do not expressly deal with the responsibilities of school staff with respect to the health and welfare of students. However, as was observed in *The Winnipeg Teachers' Association No. 1 of the Manitoba Teachers' Society* v. *The Winnipeg School Division No. 1* (1976, p. 704) the mere fact that no statutory provision or collective agreement expressly deals with this matter does not necessarily mean that they owe students no obligations in this regard. Rather, in such circumstances the position of school staff is to be (p. 705):

> governed by standards of reasonableness in assessing the degree to which an employer ... may call for the performance of duties which are not expressly spelled out. They must be related to the enterprise and seen to be fair to the employee and in furtherance of the principal duties to which he is expressly committed.

Moreover, the mere fact that school staff may be inconvenienced by the duty assigned does not, *per se*, compel the conclusion that it is unreasonable (p. 706).

It should be noted that for the purposes of this discussion, "school staff" refers to all employees who have some at least some responsibility for students, i.e. school secretary, child care worker, teacher, etc. The term would not include employees such as maintenance personnel.

Thus, it would appear that in determining whether teachers, for example, may be under an implied duty to administer medication to pupils, three questions must be answered. First, does the employment relationship of teachers contemplate the assignment to them of duties in relation to matters not expressly dealt with by legislation or contract? The answer to this question, at least with respect to teachers appears to be "yes" - the list of their duties in the *PAPT Entente, 1995-98* (see above, chap. 9) is not exhaustive, it is "open ended". Moreover, in view of the fact that teachers, like other school staff, are subjected to the general obligation to pay due attention to the health, comfort and safety of the students in their charge, it would appear to follow that the proper discharge of this obligation may require that they perform a range of specific duties.

Second, it must be asked, does administering to the health related needs of students relate to a school's "enterprise" and further the principal duties to which teachers, like other school staff, are expressly committed? Again the answer must be "yes" - if it is accepted that, on the one hand, the general purpose of the "enterprise" is to ensure that all children of school age have access to their local school and to both educational and, when required, necessary support services; and, on the other hand, one of the principal duties to which school staff are committed is to attend to the health, comfort and safety of students in their charge.

The third question is, is the assignment to teachers, for example, of the duty to administer to the health related needs of students fair and reasonable in the circumstances? Some would argue that it is never fair nor reasonable to assign this duty to teachers since (Saskatchewan Teachers' Federation, 1989): teachers "have not been trained to provide health care services" (p. 3); their "education generally does not acquaint educators with the effects of medication, possible side effects, or the incompatibilities of drugs" (p. 1); and "the standard of care expected will be higher if a teacher has represented himself or herself as being an expert in medical matters" (p. 4).

However, even if it is accepted that medical professionals are "far more familiar with drugs, their side effects and their dangers than [school staff and that] signs of overdose and other contraindications obvious to a medical professional may mean nothing to a person trained to teach children reading" (Bezeau, 1995, p. 330), these arguments do not support the conclusion that it is never fair or reasonable to require school staff to administer to the health related needs of students. The arguments overlook the facts that: the school staff are not asked to undertake tasks that require medical expertise or special training; school staff, like parents, can be warned of, and instructed in, the "signs of danger" where appropriate. Merely administering to the health related needs of students does not constitute a holding out that one is an expert in medical matters. School staff would not be expected either to have the knowledge and expertise of, or to live up to the standard of care demanded of, medical professionals - they would be expected only to have the knowledge of, and to conduct themselves as would, a reasonable and prudent parent (*Myers* v. *Peel County Board of Education*, 1981).

Therefore, in light of the foregoing, it is suggested that it is not possible to reach the general conclusion that the "job descriptions" of school staff can never include administering to the health related needs of students. Rather, the law on the issue, such as it is, suggests that a more appropriate conclusion is that school staff may legally be obligated to perform such functions when it is fair and reasonable to so do.

Liability of School Staff for Negligence

The *Civil Code of Québec* stipulates that:

Civil Code of Québec

Art. 1457. Every person has a duty to abide by the rules of conduct which lie upon him, according to the circumstances, usages or law, so as not to cause injury to another.

Where he is endowed with reason and fails in this duty, he is responsible for any injury caused to another person and is liable to reparation for the injury whether it be bodily, moral or material in nature.

This provision provides for the liability of all persons, including school staff, whose fault, negligence or want of care in circumstances of a case results in harm to another. The standard by which the minimum level of acceptable conduct of a person is determined by asking, how a "bon père de famille" or a reasonable person in the same position would have acted in the same or similar circumstances. Thus, in essence, negligence or fault on the part of school staff consists in the failure on their part to exercise reasonable care in the performance of their professional obligations to their students - of doing something a "reasonable teacher," for example, would not have done, or failing to do something a reasonable teacher would have done, in a particular situation.

Thus, school staff must exercise reasonable care when supervising students in the classroom, the laboratory, the gymnasium, the school halls and the playground and when on field trips. This obligation may commence before the start of the official school day and may continue after its termination. The obligation to exercise reasonable care also extends to maintaining reasonable order and discipline amongst the students in the care of a member of staff. School staff must also exercise reasonable care when instructing students in all activities that have inherent dangers, such as gym activities, laboratory experiments, technical and vocational activities and sports. They must also exercise reasonable care in responding to emergencies whether or not the emergency is the result of their negligence or that of the student or a third party or of an accident. The same is true when school staff transport students in their own vehicles. These are merely illustrations of activities in which school staff engage, and to which the duty to exercise reasonable care extends; it does not purport to be an exhaustive listing of such activities.

Educational Malpractice

While it has long been accepted that educational institutions and their staffs may incur liability for physical injury suffered by students as a result of negligence (see above), school staff appear to enjoy an immunity from liability for, what is commonly referred to as, "educational malpractice" (the educational equivalent of medical malpractice). Educational malpractice may be defined as institutional or staff incompetence which results in non-physical harm to a student, such as the failure to attain that level of learning he or she would probably have attained if he or she had received a reasonable and competent education. Educational malpractice could also arise if the student was misinformed as to the level of his or her abilities or improperly diagnosed with respect to his or her special educational needs (Foster, 1986).

Some two decades ago it was suggested that, given the growth in the professional accountability movement, "educational malpractice suits loom as a great potential threat for educational institutions and educators alike" (Newell, 1978, p. 4). These predictions have only proved to be partly accurate: some aggrieved students have indeed asked the courts to impose liability on educators and educational institutions for educational malpractice but such cases have been few and have not proved to pose a real threat to educators as none have been successful.

To date, courts, have refused to impose liability on school staff for malpractice. However, no appeal court has yet been asked to determine whether a claim for educational malpractice is sustainable. Moreover, in one case, *Gould* v. *Regina (East) School Division No. 77* (1997), the court, while observing that "it is surely not the function of the courts to establish standards of conduct for teachers in their classrooms, and to supervise the maintenance of such standards," did not dismiss out of hand the possibility of the courts entertaining a malpractice action where "the conduct is sufficiently egregious and offensive to community standards of acceptable fair play ..." (para. 47). This suggests that the door may not be completely closed to all who may wish to pursue an educational malpractice claim and that a court may be prepared to impose malpractice liability on educators or educational institutions in the appropriate circumstances.

Further support for this contention is to be found in two recent English cases (*X (Minors)* v. *Bedfordshire County Council*, 1995, and *Phelps* v. *The Mayor and Burgesses of the London Borough of Hillingdon*, 1997). They both recognize that educators and educational institutions may incur liability for educational malpractice (all be it in a special education setting).

Liability for Student Conduct

The *Civil Code of Québec* provides that:

Civil Code of Québec

1460. A person who, without having parental authority, is entrusted by delegation or otherwise, with the custody, supervision or education of a minor is liable, in the same manner as the person having parental authority, to reparation for injury caused by the act or fault of the minor.

Where he is acting gratuitously or for reward, however, he is not liable unless it is proved he has committed a fault.

This provision creates a rebuttable presumption of fault on the part of the school staff. That is, where harm is inflicted by a student who is under the supervision of a member of staff, the latter is presumed to have failed to adequately supervise the student. To avoid liability, the member of the school staff must establish that he or she had not in fact been negligent in the supervision of the student.

Vicarious Liability and the Personal Liability of School Staff

According to the *Civil Code of Québec* (art. 1463) an employer bears "vicarious liability" for the faults of its employees when committed within the course and scope of their employment. Thus, school boards bear liability for the wrongs committed by school staff which are the cause of harm to their students. But this principle does not relieve school staff from personal liability; all that it does is allow the injured party to seek compensation from both the school board and the member of the school staff in question. If the injured party only brings an action against a school board it can seek indemnification from the employee who inflicted the harm.

However, some school staff may be protected from personal liability by "hold harmless" clauses which may be in their collective agreements, such as the following example from the *Entente Between CPNCP and PAPT* (1980).

Entente Bewteen CPNCP and PAPT (1980)

5-9.01 The school board shall undertake to assume the case of every teacher whose civil responsibility might be at issue by the actual performance of his duties during the working day (or outside the working day when the teacher is carrying out activities expressly authorized by the competent authority) and shall agree to make no claim against the teacher in this connection, except in a case of serious fault or gross negligence on the part of the said teacher when he has been found guilty of such by a court of law.

Such clauses are an undertaking by the employer to provide legal representation for its employees, to pay any judgement which may be rendered against its employees, and not to seek indemnification from its employees. Normally, there are limits to the protection afforded by such clauses in that they do not cover employees guilty of intentional wrongdoing or gross fault.

Consent & Waiver Forms

Consent forms, sometimes called "permission forms," must be distinguished from "waiver" forms or clauses. Permission forms are typically used to obtain parental consent, for example, for student participation in a field trip. A waiver is designed to release the school board and school staff from civil liability for negligence causing harm to a student. In the case, for example, of a field trip that involved potential risks, such as swimming, a waiver may well be included. Such a form signed by parents may preclude them from suing but it will not prevent the student from suing. Indeed, even if the form were also signed by the student it would not be binding on him or her for the student, as a minor, cannot effectively enter into such a contract.

However, as Hoglund (1997) has noted, waiver forms may "be difficult to enforce because courts have tended to interpret such documents very strictly. In particular, courts have held that where, in the context of a school excursion, there is evidence of negligence, carelessness or recklessness on the part of the school board or teacher, [such forms] may not be enforceable" (p. 4).

Involvement of Teachers in Policy Making

As suggested by the statement made by Michael Fullan quoted at the beginning of Part IV, teaching can be seen primarily as a technical occupation or a profession. The latter image, which underlies this chapter, is enhanced by the involvement of teachers in the wider education enterprise and not merely as the "applicators" of the policy decisions of others. In this section, we will examine the various ways that the Québec system provides for the involvement of teachers in this wider policy debate.

Provincial Level

One of the by-products of the evolution of provincial collective bargaining for teachers in the 70s and 80s (see *Historical Roots*, chaps 3 & 4) was the creation of organized, articulate and powerful provincial teacher federations. Since that time, teachers have had a significant policy voice at the provincial level. They have influenced educational policy at the bargaining table directly, by successfully placing a variety of educational matters on the bargaining agenda, and indirectly, by the impact of negotiations on educational policy and school organization. Whether one views this influence as a positive or a negative force, there can be no doubt as to its effectiveness.

In chapter 5 we discussed the composition and role of the Superior Council and its constituent commissions and committees, all of which include significant teacher representation, as does the Advisory Board on English Education. We also noted in that chapter and in others that the Minister has formed a number of advisory committees on curriculum, instructional resources, teacher training programs (CAPFE) and teacher training policy (COPFE); once again, teachers are significant players in all of these advisory bodies.

In addition to their participation in these statutory bodies, teachers take part in *ad hoc* commissions such as the Estates General, both as members of such commissions and as presenters of briefs. They also participate in a variety of other forums that may have a lower public profile but nonetheless contribute significantly to the operation of the system.

School Board Level

As we have seen in chapter 6, teachers are involved in the policy making process at the level of the school board, especially with respect to educational services, by virtue of provisions of the *Education Act* and the *PAPT Entente: 1995-98*.

Education Act
According to the *Education Act* (s. 244), the following functions and powers are exercised after consultation with teachers, as per the procedures provided for in their respective collective agreement (see chap. 6 for details):
* implementation of the *Basic Regulations*;
* the implementation of compulsory and elective subjects;
* local programs leading to an occupation;
* programs for student and special services;
* board exams at end of each elementary cycle and secondary cycle I;
* rules for promotion of students from elementary to secondary school and from secondary cycle I to II;
* adaptation of services for students with special needs;
* policy on various matters respecting students with special needs;
* educational services to be provided by each of its schools;
* the school calendar;
* enrolment criteria for schools;
* school with a specific project;
* periodic evaluation by the Minister.*

* *Note.* Provision subject to "Transitional Measures" - see chap. 7.

PAPT Entente, 1995-98
The *PAPT Entente: 1995-98* provides that the local agreement between a school board and the teachers' union shall include a chapter (4-0.00) on the "method, subjects, procedures or participation of teachers." When translated into "plain speak," this means that school boards and teachers can decide on what matters teachers should be "consulted" or in which decision making processes they should "participate" and the procedures that should apply.* Generally speaking, local agreements have included provisions on a board level consultative committee, a school level consultative committee (dealt with below) and professional improvement.

The board level consultative committee is commonly called the "Educational Policies Committee" [EPC]. Typically, the local agreement lists a number of subjects on which teachers must be consulted and provides that the EPC may express its opinion on relevant educational matters. The Professional Improvement Committee [PIC] is a parity committee formed to administer a PIC fund, presently set at $160 x the number of full-time teachers in the employ of the school board. Its mandate typically consists of determining the scope of professional improvement activities to be financed by the fund, and approving individual applications according to criteria and procedures stipulated in the local agreement.

Note. Whether this chapter should be entitled "Consultation" or "Participation" of teachers was itself a matter for negotiation, as the latter term implied, in the minds of many, a union attempt to *intrude* into the "management prerogatives" of school boards and schools.

School Level

Teachers are involved in the policy-making process at the level of the school, especially with respect to educational services, by virtue of provisions of the *Education Act* as we have seen in chapter 7 and the *PAPT Entente: 1995-98.*

Education Act

Among the many changes brought about in the *Education Act* by the *Education Amendment Act* (1997), was the enhanced role of teachers in school-level decision making. First, teachers figure prominently in the composition of the school governing board. Second, they play a critical role in many of the matters that come to the board for decision and others that are the responsibility of the principal.

The decision-making process contemplated by the revised Act is complex, with some matters "adopted" by the governing board (but "approved" by the school board), others approved by the governing board, and others approved by the principal (see chap. 7). Among the matters that must come before the governing board upon the proposal of the principal, there are several that must first be developed in consultation with the school staff (ss. 84, 87, 88, 110.2):

- student supervision policy (youth sector);
- rules of conduct and safety measures (youth sector);
- approach to the implementation of the *Basic Regulations* (youth, vocational and adult sectors);
- programs of student services (youth, vocational and adult sectors);
- programs of special education services (youth sector);
- programs of popular education services (adult sector);
- programming which entails changes to regular schedule or which entails taking students off school premises (youth sector).

Others must be developed in consultation with teachers (ss. 85, 86):

- overall approach to the enrichment or adaptation of programs of study (youth sector);
- overall approach to the development of local programs (youth sector);
- time allocation for each subject (youth sector).

In terms of those matters falling under the responsibility of the school principal, there are several that must be decided following the proposal of the teachers (ss. 96.15, 110.12):

- local programs of study (youth, vocational and adult sectors);
- criteria for the implementation of new instructional methods (youth, vocational and adult sectors);
- textbooks and instructional materials (youth, vocational and adult sectors);
- standards and procedures for the evaluation of student achievement (youth, vocational and adult sectors).

There is also one matter that must be decided following the proposal of the school staff (s. 96.15): the rules for the placement of students and their promotion from one cycle to another in elementary school (youth sector).

PAPT Entente: 1995-98

As mentioned above, by virtue of the delegated authority provided for in the *PAPT Entente, 1995-98,* local agreements have included provisions on a school level consultative committee. Often called the "school council" or the "staff council," the local agreement typically lists a number of subjects on which teachers must be consulted by the principal and provides that the council may express its opinion on relevant educational matters.

CHAPTER 11
THE FUNDING OF PUBLIC EDUCATION

Introduction

The interaction of social purpose and schooling arrangements prompts the development of financial models perceived to be supportive of the broad social purposes and more specific goals assigned to schooling. Across the western world the increasing diversity of fiscal and governance arrangements for schooling reflects then a similar divergence in perceived social and educational purpose.

The above statement by Paquette (1991, p. 45) serves to introduce the important but often ignored subject of educational finance and its relation to the education system as a whole. Arguably any fundamental discussion of education starts with a consideration of the purpose and goals of education. Such a beginning may lead to many paths of discussion about curriculum, school design and so forth, but sooner or later the question of money comes to the surface. As David Selden, then President of the American Federation of Teachers, once observed (cited in Thomas, 1973, p. 475):

The insidious influence of the law of economics on educational theory and tactics is little understood and seldom acknowledged. Yet this relationship is fundamental to any discussion of the quality of education. Money does not educate children; teachers and other educational workers do. Spending money on education will not in itself guarantee that children will be educated, but it is certain that children cannot be educated without it.

Why then, if finance is so obviously important, does it not figure more prominently in the typical conversation about education, except for the habitual sub-text that there is never enough money? Perhaps the answer lies in the view of educational finance as "an arcane art practiced in the nether regions of bureaucracy" (Anderson & Flemming, cited in Posno, 1986, p. 33) or as "a refuge for the methodologically minded and something to be avoided by those humanists in education who see their emphasis as being on children, instruction, and qualitative aspects of schooling" (Ward, 1987, p. 463). The purpose of this chapter is to demystify this image of educational finance, while providing a clear picture of how public education is funded in this province.

Background

The funding of public education in Québec has gone through several major phases. Prior to the creation of the MEQ in 1964 and the assumption of responsibility by the State for the overall direction and development of education, education funding was primarily a local matter, with the majority of funds coming from local school taxes. Beginning in 1964, the newly formed Ministry began to publish the annual *"Règles budgétaires"* [Budgetary Rules] which set forth the rules governing State support of education.

Throughout the 1970s, the public school system was primarily funded by a combination of revenues from local taxation and provincial grants. In brief, each school board levied a basic property tax based on a provincially set tax rate ("normalized" tax rate); this action qualified the board for budget balancing grants from the MEQ. If it wished additional funds, it increased the local tax rate by the amount required to produce the level of funds desired.

In 1980, the funding system changed radically, with the elimination of a normalized tax rate and the imposition of a ceiling on local taxation. In brief, the Government replaced the revenue that had accrued from the normalized property tax by additional grants. The school board was allowed to tax up to a predetermined ceiling and if it wished to exceed this ceiling it had to obtain the approval of its electors in a referendum. Government grants were supposed to cover 100% of the basic cost of education but this regime only lasted ten years. In 1990, a series of changes were introduced resulting in the current funding system which will be discussed below (for details about the preceding period, see *Historical Roots*).

Goals For Funding Public Education

Education is widely recognized as both a "private good" and a "public good." As a private good, it reflects the desires of individuals and their families for education because of the benefits it can bring them. As a public good, education has value to the public at large and is associated with the economic, political and social well-being of society. The arguments for the public funding of education derive largely from this public dimension. Traditionally, educational finance policy goals have included equity, efficiency, liberty (or choice) and adequacy (see e.g. Guthrie, 1988).

Equity

Equity can be considered in terms of the inequality of resources provided to different groups and the provision of a minimum standard of education. This perspective is expressed as the goal of *horizontal equity* - that the quality of education should not be a function of wealth, other than the wealth of the state as a whole. However, equity is also considered in terms of disparities in need and cost. This perspective recognizes that disadvantaged groups may require additional resources to redress existing inequalities and that certain programs are more costly to run than others. This goal is termed *vertical equity* (Michaud, 1989).

In the past, the Budgetary Rules set forth various goals for the funding system, stating, for example, that: the Rules were intended "to provide for a coherent development of education throughout Québec according to an equitable distribution of the government resources available for education; to bring about, step by step, a long term reform of educational system structures and pedagogical methods; to promote the sound administration of school boards" (MEQ, 1970, p. 6). Fifteen years later, the Budgetary Rules still spoke of an equitable distribution of government resources but other objectives were replaced by the goal of fostering local autonomy (MEQ, Direction générale des ressources matérielles et financières [DGRMF], 1985). However, since that date, the Budgetary Rules have been silent on the goals of the funding system.

The goal of equity can now be inferred from the *Education Act* which stipulates that the budgetary rules must be drafted to provide "an equitable apportionment with regard to the allocation of subsidies applicable to the operating expenses of school boards" (s. 472). Furthermore, the Act states that the Budgetary Rules must provide for "an equalization grant for every school board whose fiscal resources are insufficient for a particular school year" (s. 475). Together, these provisions set both vertical and horizontal equity as funding policy goals.

Efficiency

Educational efficiency, as Bezeau (1993) says, is easy enough to define in the abstract but difficult to come to grips with in reality. Simply put, "an efficient education system produces the maximum possible output at the minimum possible cost. To achieve efficiency, education systems must maximize output per unit of cost" (p. 381). Efficiency is a concept arising from the study of economics, namely "production functions" and the "input- output" model of schooling, as illustrated below:

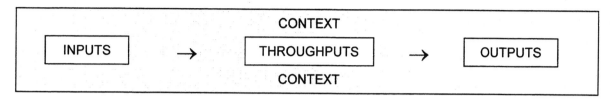

FIGURE 11.1
Input-Output Model of Schooling

According to Richards and Ratsoy (1987): "The basic question associated with the education production function is this: how do the resources used in schools (teachers' time, books, space and furnishing, etc.) combine to produce educational outcomes (skills, knowledge, attitudes, etc.)?" (p. 103). Thus viewed, educational productivity is similar to the theme of *school effectiveness*, although the latter has generally not paid much attention to questions of cost, a theme dealt with almost exclusively in the school finance literature. However, that attitude may be changing. Chapman and Walberg (1992) argue that raising educational quality is no longer adequate as a goal statement: "Not only must educators increase outcomes, they must also raise efficiency - a goal that subsumes quality" (p. 17).

There is nothing explicit in the funding policy that speaks to the goal of efficiency. One can of course argue that efficiency is so obvious as a funding goal that it need not be stated. Nevertheless, if the goal were deemed to be important, one might have expected it to be stated in some fashion, even if only for its symbolic value.

Liberty

The third general goal mentioned above is liberty, or choice – the freedom to choose from among alternatives, the provision for diversity. At a conference sponsored by the Canadian Teachers' Federation, Jane Gaskell (1995) stated that choice had become a key educational policy issue throughout the world. As she says: "Choice" in education has become loaded politically, but its implications are rather unclear. The 'right to choose' is a powerful slogan, defined by its opposites: coercion, submission, monotony, and by its associations: freedom, abundance, self-expression, self-fulfilment" (p. 1).

Educational finance plays its part in promoting liberty by allowing for diversity in the public school system and providing for other options outside the system, namely private and home schooling. Within the public system, the funding policy can allow for decentralized decision making on budget – where revenues should be directed and how public funds should be expended. Perhaps the ultimate form of financial decentralization is the use of the "voucher system." In brief, voucher financing of education consists of giving parents a voucher which they can use to purchase educational services in both public and private schools. "The idea is to establish a free market for education in which schools would succeed or fail according to their popularity with consumers" (Bezeau, 1995, p. 188). In other words, instead of allowing school boards or schools to use funding as a policy lever, this power is given directly to parents.

Québec has never experimented with a voucher system but choice has long been a key element of its policy framework (see chaps. 12 & 14). The goal of liberty is further supported by the decentralization of decision making with respect to budget (discussed below).

Adequacy

The goal of adequacy is perhaps the most important yet most difficult concept to discuss, for it begs the question "How much is enough?" or as Paquette (1989) has phrased it: *The Quality Conundrum: Assessing What We Cannot Agree On.* Without the concept of adequacy, the fact that a given funding policy satisfied various other criteria may be a very moot point. Accordingly, there needs to be an understanding of what the funding system is intending to provide - and on such fundamental objectives there may well be widespread disagreement. The level of funds provided can then be assessed in terms of these objectives, provided they are expressed in measurable terms, to see if they are achieved.

The Québec system provides a good illustration of the conundrum while underscoring the value of the concept. When the Government introduced the "full funding" model in 1980-81 for basic education costs and restricted local taxation (for all practical purposes) to a small amount for "additional" expenditures, everyone understood the concept, even if no one could measure the demarcation between basic and additional. The metaphor used at the time was that the Government would pay for the *stew* and local taxation could be used to add some *spice*. However, as the provincial funding became more global, the reality of the concept began to wane. After all, it is fine to say that one is still paying for the stew, but the product is no longer the same when one can only buy a half pound of mutton instead of the former one pound of lamb – it's still stew but not the same stew.

Sources & Objects of Education Funding

Sources of Revenue

The first issue concerning revenues can be framed in the following manner: "Will education be paid for by the parents of children in school, by the taxpayers in the local school district or all taxpayers in the province?" Second: "Will education be paid for by taxes on income, sales or property, by user fees or by other means?" Property tax is the primary local source of revenue for school boards, while provincial revenues are derived from a combination of taxes on income, goods and services.

In Canada, public education is financed by a "mixed-funding" model, that is, by a combination of provincial and local funds but the "mix" varies considerably from province to province. It is also important to remember that the level of local funding is ultimately determined by provincial governments. Subject to certain constitutional provisions, provincial governments have exclusive jurisdiction over elementary and secondary education. Consequently, the province determines what types of revenues a school board may collect and any relevant conditions which the latter must respect. Provincial control of local revenues, when combined with conditions imposed for the use of provincial grants (discussed below), is therefore a powerful determinant of local autonomy.

In Québec, as alluded to in the Introduction of this chapter, the relative proportion of different sources of revenue for education has varied considerably over the years, as shown below in Table 11.1.

TABLE 11.1
School Board Revenues for 1972/73 to 1996/97

Year	1972/73	1976/77	1980/81	1984/85	1988/89	1992/93	1996/97
Provincial Grants	61.96%	75.92%	92.43%	91.89%	90.77%	85.65%	82.04%
Local Taxation	32.98%	20.74%	4.12%	4.29%	4.67%	9.47%	11.76%
Other	5.06%	3.34%	3.46%	3.81%	4.56%	4.88%	6.20%
Total	100.00%	100.00%	100.00%	100.00%	100.00%	100.00%	100.00%

Source. Statistiques de l'Éducation, published by the MEQ, various years.

As can be readily observed from this table, the vast majority of revenues are accounted for by provincial grants and local taxes. The remaining "other" funds come from a variety of sources, including transfer payments, service fees, and so forth. It should be noted that these revenues do not include any "unofficial" sources of funds, that is, monies that are not accounted for by school boards. Typically, the latter comprise school activity fees, and monies from fundraising that are not transmitted to the school board or accounted for in any formal way. In the future there will be little such money as funds raised by school governing boards have to be deposited in a school board account.

Budgets & Expenditure Categories

The second half of the finance equation consists of the "objects" of the funding system – on what are we spending money? At the point that these decisions are being made, it becomes useful to begin speaking of a "budget." Simply put, a budget is a financial plan, or a program plan showing the revenues and expenditures associated with a given program. Burrup, Brimley and Garfield (1993) provide the following definition of a budget (p. 317):

> A budget may be defined as a specific plan for implementing organizational objectives, policies, and programs for a given period of time. It embodies (1) descriptions of organizational activities and services requisite to attainment of organizational goals, (2) estimates of expenditures and their allocations, and (3) forecasts of fiscal resources available to support the plan.

Although some people speak of the "original" budget and the "revised" or "updated" budget, generally, the budget should be thought of as a *static* document; once approved, it does not change. It is then used as a baseline to track *actual* activities, revenues and expenditures on an ongoing (usually monthly) basis. In Québec, the budget is prepared on an annual basis and contains three major categories: the operating budget; the investment budget; and, the debt service budget (described below). At the end of the year, the final results of the financial year are recorded in the *financial statements* of the school board in a form prescribed by the MEQ.

Operating Budget

The operating budget includes all "current" revenues and expenditures anticipated for the year; current expenditures include all those which are not "capitalized" (see investment budget below). Like any budget, it is compartmentalized along two dimensions, one programmatic, which relates to work to be done or services to be performed (e.g. instruction, administration), the other, economic, which relates to the nature of the revenues (e.g. grants, taxes, fees) or expenditures (e.g. salaries, travel, supplies). On the programmatic side, the operating budget in Québec currently includes the following major categories:

General Educational Activities: Youth
This category includes classroom instruction (teacher salaries and materials), support services, student services, and school principals and vice-principals, and the professional development of personnel involved therein.

General Educational Activities: Adults
This category includes analogous expenditures for the general education services provided to adults.

Vocational Educational Activities: Youth & Adults
This category includes analogous expenditures for the vocational education services provided to youth and adults.

Administration
This category includes the school board's administrative costs, namely executive personnel (excluding principals and vice-principals), administrative and clerical personnel, and other non-salary costs for general administration, data processing, etc.

Maintenance ("Equipment")
This category includes building upkeep and repairs, maintenance, energy and security.

School Transport
This category includes all costs for school transport.

Investment Budget
Formerly called the "Capital Budget," this budget is meant to cover capital investments for moveable property, equipment and machinery for general education, vocational education and daycare, building improvements and renovation, and the development of data processing systems.

Debt Service Budget
This budget covers the cost of long-term borrowing for major capital expenditures e.g., school construction. (Short-term loans to deal with cash flow problems to meet expenses pending the receipt of periodic MEQ grants are included in operating costs.)

Responsibilities for Financial Management

We have seen earlier (Parts I & II) that the governance of education in Québec is shared among different stakeholders operating at different levels of the system. In this section, we will examine the distribution of responsibilities for financial resource management at the three main levels of the system: central (MEQ), intermediate (school boards) and local (schools).

MEQ

The Minister of Education (see chap. 5) is responsible for establishing, after consultation with school boards and subject to the approval of the Conseil du trésor [Treasury Board], the annual Budgetary Rules applicable to school boards (Ed Act, s. 472). The *Education Act* also confers upon the Minister, with some exceptions, the power to suspend or cancel all or part of the grants to be paid to a school board if it refuses or neglects to comply with a provision governing it.

The Budgetary Rules are published each year by the MEQ and include provisions relating to operating and capital expenditures, as well as to equalization grants, short-term borrowing and debt servicing. Funding regulations have never been considered as "light reading" and the Québec Rules are no exception. The current edition (MEQ, Direction générale du financement et des équipments [DGFE], 1998a) runs 120 pages and is accompanied by a complementary information document (MEQ, DGFE, 1998b) which takes another 150 pages to help explain the Rules themselves. However, the information is well presented and the MEQ is always ready to provide any necessary explanation. In addition to this general information on the current rules for determining provincial grants, each school board receives its own *"Paramètres d'allocation"* [funding parameters] which provide a detailed breakdown of the grants for the school board for the year in question. The publication of the draft Budgetary Rules is the trigger for the annual budgetary process of school boards and schools described below.

School Boards

The Budgetary Process
The management of financial and other resources is a cyclical process, as shown below in Table 11.2.

TABLE 11.2:
The School Board Budgetary Process

Date	Step
Feb	MEQ tables draft Budgetary Rules and Parameters for consultation
Mar 1	School notifies teachers of total/partial school closings
	School Board publishes the objectives, principles and criteria regarding: allocations to schools; and, the amount reserved for its own needs and its committees
Apr 1	School Board provides preliminary allocations to schools
	School Board determines provisional teacher staffing needs
	Principal determines provisional teacher staffing needs
	MEQ publishes final Budgetary Rules and Parameters
	School Board provides provisional allocations to schools
	Principal proposes budget to Governing Board
	Governing Board adopts budget (with or without modifications)
	Governing Board submits budget to School Board
	School Board approves school budgets (or rejects – cannot modify)
	School Board adopts its budget
Jun 30	School Board submits its budget to MEQ
Sep 30	Enrolment data for funding purposes certified
	School Board provides definitive allocations to schools

Allocation of Funds to Schools

Until this year, all financial power at the intermediate and local levels was vested in the school board; this is no longer the case. As outlined previously (see chaps. 6 & 7) and discussed below, schools now have an important role to play in financial decision making. These changes affect the school board, which in addition to managing its own financial affairs, has now become both the "banker" for its schools and the "guardian of equity." Hence its first obligation, according to the revised *Education Act* is, after deducting an amount for its own needs and those of its committees, to allocate among its schools, vocational and adult centres, "*in an equitable manner* and *in consideration of social and economic disparities and of the needs expressed* by the institutions," the operating grants allocated by the Minister, including equalization grants, school tax proceeds and any investment income (s. 275, emphasis added).

It should be noted that the operating grants provided by the MEQ include funds for teacher salaries, other educational costs, administration and maintenance, but not monies for capital or debt servicing (see discussion above). The flow-through allocation to schools also includes monies for the operation of governing boards.

In this new role, the school board is acting as a conduit for flow-through grants from the MEQ but with one important nuance. Rather than simply supplying funds to schools as indicated by the Budgetary Rules, the school board is responsible for assuring the equitable distribution of available funds. Given the potential "dark side" of school decentralization – widening the gap between rich and poor schools, this is an important function indeed. Furthermore, the school board acts as a "fund holder" for schools, banking on their behalf, certain revenues received by the school (see discussion below).

In addition, the school board must, following consultation of the parents' committee (s. 193(9)), make public the objectives, principles and criteria respecting: (1) the allocation of grants, taxation proceeds and other revenues among its institutions; and, (2) the amount which the board retains for its own uses and that of its committees (s. 275).

The school board is also responsible for *approving* the budgets *adopted* by schools and centres but cannot amend the budgets submitted.* The Act is silent as to what happens if it does not approve the budget but one can assume that the school then reconsiders and resubmits its budget and this process continues until approval is obtained. During this time, the budget is without effect but the school board can authorize payment of such expenses it determines are appropriate.

* *Note*. The Act used to state that the school board approved school budgets "with or without amendments." This expression has been dropped from the Act.

Adoption of the School Board Budget

The amended *Education Act* (ss. 277, 279, 280) states that every year the school board shall adopt its operating, investment and debt service budgets (see above), which shall then be transmitted to the Minister (but are not subject to the approval of the latter). The school board budget shall:

- indicate the financial resources allocated to committees and to services for students with special needs;
- treat school and centre budgets (including monies for governing boards) as separate appropriations;
- limit expenditures to the level of revenues in the budget, unless approved by the Minister;
- include as a revenue any accumulated or anticipated surplus;
- include as an expenditure any accumulated or anticipated deficit.

According to the combination of the foregoing provisions, the school board is only in direct control of the board level portion of its budget, as illustrated below.

Operating Costs										Invest	Debt
Board	School A	School B	School C	School D	School E	School F	School G	School H	Etc.	Board	Board

FIGURE 11.2
School Board Budget

Schools

The School Budget

With the passage of the *Education Amendment Act* in 1997, the "school budget" takes on a new level of meaning. In the past, the school budget consisted of those items over which the school board delegated spending power to the principal (typically materials and supplies) but which were still accounted for in the school board's financial system. In addition, the school might have had its own "school fund" with its own bank account to deal with locally raised funds from the sale of supplies, fundraising events, etc.

As indicated above, the school budget is now mandated by the *Education Act* and constitutes a separate component of the school board budget. The school board acts as a financial agent on behalf of the school, banking and accounting for this fund, but authority for the budget is vested in the school, more specifically, in its governing board. The school budget includes, on the revenue side, all government grants, local tax revenues, any investment income allocated by the school board (s. 275), revenues raised by the school from the provision of goods and services (ss. 90, 92) and from donations solicited by the governing board in the name of the school board (s. 94). On the expenditure side, the school budget now includes all operating expenditures of the school, that is, the salaries for the principal, teachers, office, custodial and other staff, and all non-salary expenses for teaching materials, office supplies, maintenance, etc. Thus, the only school level expenditures excluded from the school budget are items covered by the school board's investment budget for capital, e.g. major repairs to the school, and its debt service budget for long-term borrowing.

The Budget Process
We saw in chapter 7 that the general mode of decision making in the school is for the governing board to approve, or not, proposals put forward by the principal. Decision making regarding the budget is an exception to this general rule.

Financial responsibility is divided between the principal and the school governing board. The principal initiates the formal budgetary process by preparing the annual budget and submitting it to the governing board. However, given that the majority of the budget will be for teacher salaries, the process begins with the time lines provided for in the teacher *Ententes* regarding assignment, transfer and determination of surplus (see budget process chart above; see also chap. 9). Like the school board budget, the school budget must maintain a balance between revenues, including board allocations and school revenues, and expenditures (s. 96.24).

Adopting & Approving the Budget
According to the *Education Act*, the governing board is responsible for *adopting* the budget proposed by the principal and submitting it to the school board for *approval* (s. 95). This is only one of three places in the Act where the governing board's power is described in terms of adoption, rather than approval, the others being the adoption of the educational project (s. 74) and the governing board's annual report (s. 82), neither of which, unlike the budget, is subject to the prior proposal of the principal. The word "adopt" is also used to describe the process which the school board undergoes to decide on its budget.

Administering the Budget
Following adoption by the governing board and approval by the school board, the principal is charged with *administering* the budget and rendering account to the governing board for same (s. 96.24). The principal is also responsible for *managing* the physical resources of the school; however, in this case, he or she is accountable to the school board, not the governing board (s. 96.23). He or she is likewise responsible for managing the staff of the school in accordance with the applicable collective agreements or regulations (remembering that the school board is the employer of all staff) (s. 96.21). However, one must note that the governing board itself is responsible for overseeing the administration of its annual operating budget (which is part of the school budget) and rendering account to the school board for it (s. 66).

Budget "Ownership"
By this point, the reader would be justified in asking the question: "Whose budget is it – the school governing board's or the principal's?" "Just what authority does the governing board have over budget?" The first question in this regard is the level of discretion which the governing board has with respect to the budget so submitted. Can it make changes to the budget proposed by the principal or must it, like other proposals, be referred back to the principal if the governing board does not wish to adopt it? Second, what are the implications of the answer to this question respecting the other aspects of school administration – educational activities, human and other resources?

Discretion
To answer the first question, one must recognize that the wording of the governing board's authority over budget is not treated in the same manner as its authority over educational matters. In educational matters, the principal is the key decision maker and the governing board has only the authority to approve or not. In this case, the word "approve" is given the meaning usually found in law: "to confirm, ratify, sanction or consent to some act or thing done by another" (*Black's Law Dictionary*, 1990, p. 102). Thus, the principal's decision over, for example, student supervision policy, is subject to ratification by the governing board but the primary ownership of the policy rests with the principal. This approach reflects the balance between the professional role of the principal and the lay role of the governing board.

By contrast, the word "adopt" generally means: "to accept, to appropriate, choose or select. To make that one's own (property or act) which was not so originally" (*Black's Law Dictionary*, 1990, p. 49). Thus, the school budget "belongs" primarily to the governing board, as the school board budget belongs to the school board. In both cases, the elected lay members of the public are responsible for the public funds entrusted to their care. In the case of the school budget, an extra step is added to the process – the approval or ratification of the budget by the school board. However, this process does not detract from the school governing board's ownership of the budget any more than the former requirement that a school board budget be approved by the Minister detracted from the school board's ownership of its own budget. Perhaps in time, the approval of the governing board's budget by the school board, like its supervisory role over the portion of the budget set aside for the operation of the governing board, will be likewise discontinued. Accordingly, we conclude that the governing board can make changes to the budget proposed by the principal and the governing board is the primary decision maker respecting the school budget. The fact, as noted above, that the principal renders account to the governing board for the administration of the school budget is consistent with this view.

Implications

In terms of the implications of this interpretation, it should first be noted that a budget is primarily a set of spending estimates and the adoption/approval of a budget signifies the power to spend. However, the budgetary authority given to one body cannot be used as an indirect means to assume another power which is assigned to a different body.

Given that the vast majority of a school's budget is consumed by personnel costs, largely teacher salaries, the question arises as to the interplay between budget decisions – the responsibility of the governing board – and personnel decisions - the responsibility of the principal, subject of course to the provisions of applicable agreements and regulations. The *Education Act* is perhaps not as clear as it could be in this regard and there will undoubtedly be situations where budgetary decisions will drive personnel decisions and others where the reverse is true. Thus, for example, the Act gives the school board the authority to decide what educational services shall be offered in each of its schools. Within this framework, the principal is responsible for deciding on the staffing needs of the school. The process for determining the number and type of staff to be retained in a school, versus those declared excess or surplus, is set forth in the applicable collective agreement. A governing board could not subvert this decision-making process by adopting a budget that did not provide for the staff resulting from this process. If it did so, this would likely result in the non-approval of its budget by the school board. On the other hand, there well may be other staffing matters that are not subject to such elaborate procedures and would be dependent on available budget.

In the final analysis, the Act attempts to balance a number of competing interests and there are a variety of issues that will require clarification as this new distribution of powers is worked out in practice. Ultimately, the success of the system will not depend on the meaning of a particular clause but on the goodwill and common sense of all participants to make the system work, as required by the Act "in the best interests of the students."

Provincial Grants System

Overview

As mentioned above, the provincial grants for public education are set forth in the annual Budgetary Rules and funding parameters particular to each school board. The following description of the grants' system is based on the Rules for 1998-99 (MEQ, DGFE, 1998a, 1998b) and a simulated set of parameters as they would apply to an individual school board. The following provides an overview of the grants' system but does not attempt to present the details which are necessary for a more "fine grained" understanding of the Rules. In brief, the Rules cover the three major budget categories listed below:

Operating Funds
Investment Funds
Debt Servicing

FIGURE 11.3
Major Budget Categories

Operating Grants

The operating grants account for the vast majority of provincial grants. They are provided in the form of general block grants, termed *"Basic Allocations,"* calculated separately for different expenditure categories, and subsidiary block grants, termed "Supplementary Allocations." Finally, the Rules provide separately for equalization grants, as shown below.*

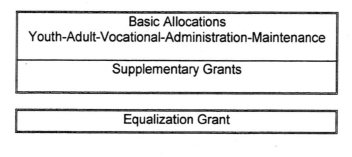

FIGURE 11.4
Major Operating Grants

* *Note.* Grants for school transport have just been transferred from the ministère des transports to the MEQ and are not included in the Budgetary Rules.

The funds received from the basic and supplementary allocations, as well as the equalization grant, are completely *transferable*; that is, the school board, subject to respecting its legal and contractual obligations, can use the funds as it sees fit. In other words, grants provided for teacher salaries may be used to buy textbooks, and vice versa. These grants are made without the condition that all monies be spent within the current fiscal year. If at the end of the year, there is a surplus of funds, it belongs to the school board; similarly, the school board is responsible for any year-end deficit which may occur.

In theory, transferability is a very positive feature of the current grants' system. However, in practice, it is somewhat less so as transferability is only of practical value if after meeting the basic obligations for paying salaries for "x" teachers required to staff classes for "y" students, and other basic costs (heating and lighting), there is enough money left over to create a discretionary spending fund. The following provides a brief description of the basic, supplementary and equalization grants.

Basic Allocation: Youth Educational Activities

Until the change in the Budgetary Rules in 1997-98 (MEQ, DGFE, 1997a, 1997b), this grant was supposed to cover all "base costs" for the Youth Education envelope as defined above. However, since 1997-98, the grants have been reduced by eliminating the portion of the previous grant estimated to cover the salaries of principals and vice-principals. Henceforth, school boards are expected to cover such costs from local taxation revenues.

The calculation of this grant is extremely complex and involves the use of a computer simulation of the number of teaching positions required in each school board in order to calculate the amount "for school organizational problems." The method can be summarized as follows:

Youth Ed. Grant		
	=	Instructional Grant
	+	Non-instructional Grant

Instructional Grant		
	=	Base per capita amounts*
	X	Salary adjustment factor**
	X	No. of students***
	+	amount for school organizational problems****

Non-instructional Grant		
	=	Standard per capita amounts* X No. of students***

Notes:
*   different amounts applied for regular and special needs students;
**   specific to each school board (to cover the variation in average salary costs);
***   enrolled as of September 30, 1998.;
****   specific to each school board (to cover various school organizational problems).

FIGURE 11.5
Youth Education Grant for 1998-99

Basic Allocation: Adult Educational Activities

Until the change in the Budgetary Rules in 1997-98 (MEQ, DGFE, 1997a, 1997b), this grant was supposed to cover all "base costs" for the Adult Education envelope as defined above. However, since 1997-98, the grants have been reduced by eliminating the portion of the previous grant estimated to cover the salaries of principals and vice-principals. Henceforth, school boards are expected to cover such costs from local taxation revenues. The 1998-99 grant for adult education consists of a *closed envelope* and an amount for distance education. The closed envelope makes a distinction between students 18 years of age and under and those over 18. The grant itself is calculated by multiplying specified per capita amounts for human resources [HR], support resources [SR] (specific amounts for each school board) and material resources [MR] (provincial amount) times the full-time equivalent [FTE] number of students considered.

Basic Allocation: Vocational Educational Activities

Until the change in the Budgetary Rules in 1997-98 (MEQ, DGFE, 1997a, 1997b), this grant was supposed to cover all "base costs" for the Vocational Education envelope as defined above. However, since 1997-98, the grants have been reduced by eliminating the portion of the previous grant estimated to cover the salaries of principals and vice-principals. Henceforth, school boards are expected to cover such costs from local taxation revenues. The 1998-99 method used to calculate this grant is a mixture of that described above for youth and adult education. The only students considered for funding purposes are those who complete a course during the school year in question (1998-99); courses taken but completed the following year are counted at that point for financing. Thus, funding is not provided for students who begin a course but never complete it. However, a "drop-out" factor compensates for this lack of HR funding by increasing the base amount by 15% for students under 20 years of age and 10% for other students.

Basic Allocation: Administration

Until the change in the Budgetary Rules in 1996-97 (MEQ, DGFE, 1996a, 1996b), this grant was supposed to cover all "base costs" of the school board administration envelope as defined above. However, since 1996-97, the grants have been all but eliminated, leaving only an amount to take into account particular cost factors, namely school board isolation, dispersion and size. Consequently, only a limited number of school boards now receive this grant. School boards are expected to cover basic administrative costs from local taxation revenues.

The 1998-99 grant is calculated by multiplying per capita amounts for three factors: size, isolation and dispersion and "additional dispersion" (occasioned by new territorial division of linguistic school boards in 1998-99) by the number of students recognized for this grant - the same as the number of students considered for calculating the maximum tax yield (see below), that is a weighted number of the student population in 1997-98.

Basic Allocation: Equipment

Until the change in the Budgetary Rules in 1990-91 (MEQ, Direction générale du financement [DGF], 1990a, 1990b), this grant was supposed to cover all "base costs" of the maintenance envelope as defined above. However, since 1990-91, the grants have been all but eliminated, leaving only an amount to take into account particular cost factors, namely "excess space," and isolation/dispersion. School boards are expected to cover basic maintenance costs from local taxation revenues.

The 1998-99 grant is calculated by multiplying per capita amounts for two factors: isolation/dispersion and "excess space" (amount of total building floor space in the school board which exceeds the norms set by the MEQ – norms that used to be used for funding this envelope) by the number of students recognized for this grant - the same as the number of students considered for funding Administrative costs (see above).

Supplementary Allocations

Supplementary allocations are a collection of additional grants for various objects, as defined in the Budgetary Rules. Some are granted automatically to those school boards which qualify according to the norms stipulated in the Rules; most are granted following the approval of a request for funds. Although they target specified funding objects, they are considered to be block grants because the money does not have to be spent on the object of the grant. Former categorical grants - "specific allocations" – have been eliminated from the operating grants system.

Equalization Grant

The equalization grant is meant to offset the lack of revenues from a relatively low tax base and is thus meant to complement the revenues arising from the latter source, as described below following the discussion of taxation.

Grants for the Capital Investment Fund

Basic Allocation

The basic allocation is meant to pay for the cost of acquiring moveable property, equipment and machinery and major renovations. The unused portion of this grant may be used to pay off a portion of capital indebtedness authorized by the Minister. This allocation is considered a block grant and amounts are transferable within this envelope and with that described below for supplementary allocations.

The grant itself is calculated by the sum of the following: a base amount of $44,464 to each school board; standard per capita amounts for moveable property, equipment and machinery, and for major renovations; and amounts specific to each school board for the development of data processing systems, and for isolation.

Other Capital Grants

The Budgetary Rules provide for supplementary and specific grants. As alluded to above, supplementary grants are transferable within the Investment envelope with basic allocations; by contrast, specific allocations are neither transferable among themselves nor with the other capital grants described above.

Grants for Debt Servicing

This grant is meant to defray the cost of long-term borrowing authorized by the Minister. It comprises two elements: one for the reimbursement of capital and amortization; the other for the payment of interest and other charges.

Property Tax Revenue

Overview

Property taxation is generally considered as a "regressive tax" because, among other reasons, its uniform tax rate creates a heavier burden on lower income tax payers. However, almost by default, property taxation has remained as the mainstay of revenues for local governments, including school boards and municipalities, throughout North America. Québec is no exception to this trend. It is not surprising, therefore, that municipalities have long been concerned with the use of property taxation as a revenue for school boards, as this practice is seen as direct competition for the same tax dollars needed to fund increasingly cash-starved municipalities.

As summarized at the beginning of this chapter, the system of the "full funding" of the basic costs of education by the province was a direct result of pressure by the municipalities to exclude school boards from the property tax field. The compromise of replacing the normalised tax rate by provincial grants and imposing a ceiling on the right of school boards to levy any "supplementary" tax contained the problem. However, when the Government began to reduce provincial grants and increased the school board taxation in 1990, the opposition of the municipalities came back to the surface.

Property taxes are a function of a number of variables, which we will regroup under two headings : the tax base, and the tax rate. Thereafter, we will briefly discuss the particular condition that applies in Québec – the surtax referendum.

The Tax Base – Standardized Assessment

Establishing the tax base relies primarily on municipalities in accordance with the *Act Respecting Municipal Taxation*. For our purposes, property is defined as including land, buildings and improvements ("immoveables"). It is usually classified as residential, industrial, agricultural, commercial or unused (vacant). Establishing the "real value" of property is done by an assessment of the "fair market value" of the property, that is "the price that would prevail if a sale occurred between a buyer and a seller" (Rebore & Rebore, 1993, p. 53). Each municipality develops an evaluation roll on which is inscribed the amount retained as the evaluation of each taxable property. Recognizing that evaluation practices will vary from one municipality to another, the *Act Respecting Municipal Taxation* (s. 264) provides for the application of a comparative factor to create a "standardized assessment" of the value of property across municipalities. Thus, the tax base of the school board consists of the standardized assessment of all property from all the municipalities in its territory.

Individual property owners with children in school pay their taxes to the school board or boards where their children are enrolled. Other individuals may choose the board to which they wish to pay their taxes. Other property owners (e.g. corporations) pay a portion of taxes to each of the school boards having jurisdiction over the territory in which the property is situated, the apportionment being established on the basis of the student population of each school board.

Setting the Basic Tax Rate

Except on the Island of Montréal, each school board in Québec sets, within the parameters set by law, the tax rate it wishes to levy for the coming school year. On the Island of Montréal, this function is performed by the Island Council (see chap. 6). Since the school board exercises no control over the value of the tax base, the tax rate is the only lever it has to increase or decrease revenue from property taxes. In Québec, the tax rate is expressed as so many cents per $100 of standardized assessment, for example, $0.27/$100. Thus, at this tax rate, a property owner whose standardized assessment equals $100,000 would pay $270 in school taxes.

As alluded to above, since 1980-81, school boards have been restricted by a "double ceiling" respecting the setting of the local tax rate. The current ceiling (Ed Act, s. 308) is defined as the lesser of two amounts: (1) the revenue accruing from a tax rate of $0.35/$100; or, (2) the maximum tax yield set by law ("per capita ceiling"). The latter is calculated as follows:

Example: For a school board with 6 500 (weighted) students:

Maximum tax yield	=	
		basic amount (school board with at least 1,000 students)
	+	per capita amount
	x	by the number of recognized students (actual number multiplied by weighting factors)
Maximum tax =	$176,449* + ($588.18* x 6 500) = $3,999,619.	

* **Note**. As per current regulation (Regulation Respecting the Computation of the Maximum Yield of the School Tax for the 1998-99 School Year, 1998).

The use of a double ceiling means that the restriction on local taxation effects rich and poor school boards differently. As shown above, the per capita ceiling is set by a formula that does not take into account the property wealth of the school board. Thus, the school board with a high level of property evaluation can set a low tax rate to raise the amount of money set by the ceiling, while the school board with a low level of property evaluation will have to set a higher tax rate to raise the same amount of money. Consequently, the poorer school boards will be capped by the ceiling of $0.35/$100, while the richer school boards will be capped by the per capita ceiling. Put in other words, the amount the poor school board collects from a tax rate of $0.35/$100 will fall below the amount set on a per capita basis, and hence is capped by $0.35/$100, the lower of the two. By contrast, with a tax rate of $0.35/$100, the rich school board could collect far more money than that set by the per capita ceiling, and hence is capped by the per capita ceiling, the lower of the two.

For 1998-99, the tax rate is calculated as follows:

- Step 1: Determine weighted student population (number of students in different regular and special categories times the weighting factors supplied: see Table 11.3);

- Step 2: Determine the maximum tax yield (apply the formula outlined above, using the amounts set by regulation);

- Step 3: Compare the tax revenue from a tax rate of $0.35/$100 versus the maximum tax yield; the lower of the two constitutes the ceiling.

TABLE 11.3:
The Weighted Student Population: 1998-99

Categories	Factors
Preschool (4 yrs)	1.00
Preschool (5 yrs): Regular	1.80
Preschool (5 yrs): Accueil/Fr	2.25
Elementary: Regular	1.55
Elementary: Accueil/Fr	2.40
Secondary (Youth): Regular	2.40
Secondary (Youth): Accueil/Fr	3.40
Vocational (Youth & Adult)	3.40
Adult General (16-18 yrs)	2.40
Adult General (19 yrs +)	2.40
Handicapped (Youth)	6.40

The Referendum

Normally, this is the end of the process and the school board sets its tax rate at or below the applicable ceiling. If, however, it wishes to exceed the ceiling it must obtain the approval of its electors to do so by means of a referendum (see Ed Act, ss. 308, 345-353). The ballot must specify whether the proposed tax rate exceeds the standard tax rate ($0.35/$100), the maximum tax yield, or both. If the referendum is successful, then the approved rate becomes the ceiling applicable to that school board for that school year and the next three years.

Although the referendum mechanism theoretically provides a door to open up the tax levy, for all practical purposes it provides for a door that is posed so high that no one can reach it to open it. When the school boards originally contested the constitutionality of the referendum (*Québec (A.-G.)* v. *Greater Hull School Board*, 1984), the plaintiff school boards filed evidence that the cost of holding a referendum, combined with the uncertainty of success – Who votes to pay more taxes? – made the referendum illusory as a means to exceed the ceiling. Despite these arguments the mechanism was upheld by the courts and continues in force today.

Equalization Grant

As mentioned above, the equalization grant is meant to offset the lack of revenues from a relatively low tax base and is thus meant to complement the revenues arising from the latter source, as described above. The actual equalization formula is very simple:

Equalization Grant	=
Maximum tax revenue -	Tax revenue from maximum tax rate.

The maximum tax revenue is determined by a formula set by regulation (shown above). The tax revenue from the maximum tax rate is the amount which the school board can raise set by applying the lower of the two ceilings on taxation (shown above). If the tax revenue which would be obtained by charging the maximum tax rate is greater than the maximum tax yield, then no equalization grant is payable. In other words, this formula assures that all school boards will have access to the amount prescribed as the maximum tax yield, either from local taxes or a combination of local taxes and the equalization grant.

Table 11.4 shows an example of two school boards to illustrate the determination of maximum tax revenues and the equalization grant; the two boards are identical except as regards their respective property assessment. Board A has a standardized assessment of 1.5 billion dollars, Board B, 500 million. Each has a weighted student population of 6 500 students; hence, each has the same maximum tax yield of $3,999, 619 ($176, 449 + $588.18 x 6500). Board A would raise $5.25 million with a tax rate of $0.35/$100, while Board B (with only 1/3 the tax base) would only raise $1.75 million. According to the "lesser of the two" rule, Board A's ceiling is fixed at $3.99 million (maximum tax yield), which will give rise to a tax rate of $0.27/$100. By contrast, Board B's ceiling will be set at $0.35/$100, which will generate $1.75 million. In addition, Board B will receive an equalization grant of $2.24 million, while Board A will receive none.

TABLE 11.4
Maximum Tax Revenue and Equalization

Details	Board A	Board B
Assessment	$1,500 Mil	$500 Mil
Students	6,500	6,500
A) Max Tax Yield	$3.99 Mil	$3.99 Mil
B) $0.35/$100	$5.25 Mil	$1.75 Mil
Applicable Ceiling	A: Max yield	B: $0.35/$100
Maximum Tax Rate	$0.27/$100	$1.75 Mil
Maximum Tax Revenue	$3.99 Mil	$0.35/$100
Equalization	$0	$2.24 Mil
Total (tax + equalization)	$3.99 Mil	$3.99 Mil

Changes in the Ceiling on Taxation

It should noted that the amounts for the above formula are published in a regulation each year. Since their first year of publication (*Regulation Respecting the Number of Admissible Students for the Computation of the Maximum Yield of the School Tax,* 1990) they have been increased only minimally; however, the weighting factors for determining the number of recognized students have been increased significantly (see below). This has the effect of raising the per capita ceiling. Because the actual ceiling for any given school board is the lower of the two possible ceilings, raising the per capita ceiling has the effect of increasing the number of boards capped by the ceiling of $0.35/$100, which has not been raised since 1990.

Selected Categories	Factors		
	1990-91[a]	1996-97[b]	1997-98[c]
Elementary: Regular	1.00	1.20	1.55
Secondary (Youth): Regular	1.45	1.75	2.40

a. *Regulation Respecting the Number of Admissible Students for the Computation of the Maximum Yield of the School Tax,* 1990.
b. *Regulation Respecting the Computation of the Maximum Yield of the School Tax for the 1996-97 School Year,* 1996.
c. *Regulation Respecting the Computation of the Maximum Yield of the School Tax for the 1998-99 School Year,* 1998.

The raising of the per capita ceiling was not done to increase school board spending power from local tax revenues. It was done to partially offset the decrease in government grants over the past several years (see discussion of operating grants above). Those school boards which remained capped by the ceiling of $0.35/$100 saw no change in local tax revenue and could not therefore absorb the cut. In their case, the raising of the per capita ceiling meant that they received compensation for the lost grants by way of the new equalization formula (see above). Those school boards capped by the per capita ceiling saw that ceiling rise, with the increased tax revenue being used to offset the loss of the grants. Being capped by the per capita ceiling, they received no equalization payments. Because, as explained above, the richer school boards are capped by the per capita ceiling, the successive raising of this ceiling has had the effect of increasing the tax burden on the ratepayers in school boards with a higher overall tax base. In fact, at the time of writing, the per capita ceiling is now so high that practically every school board in the province is capped by the lower ceiling of $0.35/$100.

The sharp rise in property taxes in recent years has rekindled the opposition of municipalities to the right of school boards to raise property taxes in support of education. As a result of this pressure and a continuing struggle between the municipalities and the Government over the latter's successive moves to download various fiscal burdens on municipalities, the Minister of Municipal Affairs created a commission (Commission nationale sur les finances et la fiscalité locale) to examine local taxation and related matters The Commission report is expected shortly and whatever it proposes, will undoubtedly provoke strong reactions all around as the Government, school boards and municipalities all struggle to meet rising expectations with ever diminishing resource base.

PART V:
RELIGION, LANGUAGE AND DIVERSITY

There is some disturbing evidence from within Canada and beyond that societies establish a pecking order in which they rank incoming groups .... This ranking can be the basis of some powerful self-fulfilling prophecies. School systems often reflect wider societal opinion and thus, perhaps unwittingly, contribute to the perpetuation of both lower and higher expectations as to how individual students are likely to achieve.

What is required to ensure successful integration is a major effort on the part of the school to indicate clearly how much the students, and the cultural and linguistic groups of which they are a part, can contribute to the intellectual and social life of the school (Handscombe, 1989, p. 25).

This final section of the source book can be characterized, to coin an oxymoron, as a "focus on diversity." Seen as a problem by some but as a source of richness by others, schools today comprise an incredibly diverse population, which in turn reflects the nature of contemporary society. We have divided Part VI into three chapters, dealing respectively with religion, language, and multiculturalism/interculturalism and education. This division is convenient for some aspects of the topics considered but we are conscious of the fact that the lines between these issues are blurred. We begin with religion, the dominant cultural symbol in the early stages of our education system. Language, which has gradually supplanted religion as the dominant cultural symbol, is treated next. Finally, in chapter 16, we examine the attempt to reconcile the competing societal forces in a province where the majority is itself a minority.

The key provisions of the following instruments which are referred to in the chapters of this part are reproduced in the *Compendium*:

Chapter 12

Canadian Charter
Constitution Act, 1867
CSE Act
    Catholic Regulation
    Protestant Regulation
Education Act
    Parental Consultation Regulation
MEQ Act
Québec *Charter*

Chapter 13

Bill 101
    Learning Disabilities Exemption Regulation
    Regulation Respecting Requests to Receive Instructions in English
    Temporary Exemption Regulation
Canadian Charter
Education Act
    Elementary School Regulation
    Secondary School Regulation
School Elections Act

Chapter 14

Canadian Charter
Education Act

CHAPTER 12
EDUCATION AND RELIGION

Introduction

This chapter will deal with the role of religion in the Québec education system. In Québec, and in Canada generally, the public school system has been deeply influenced by religion. However, this influence has been exercised strictly by the Christian faith, namely through the Catholic and Protestant denominations. In previous chapters we have seen some examples of how religion has played an important part in the evolution of the Québec education system. Prior to the current implementation of linguistic boards, as provided for in the *Linguistic School Boards Act* (1997), Québec school boards were still divided along denominational lines. However, even with this new non-denominational reorganization, religion has not ceased to be a critical element in the design and operation of the education system.

Freedom of conscience and religion is a fundamental human right recognized in both international and domestic law. It is suggested that the traditional dominance of the Catholic and Protestant denominations must give way to a wider range of religious beliefs if we are to respect the diversity of contemporary Québec society. As stated by Foucher at a symposium on school board reform at McGill (1997, p. 16):

> One has to question, at the end of the 20th century, the maintenance of school privileges for two denominations in a multicultural, pluralistic Québec. My own stand on this issue is that we could find other ways to accommodate the legitimate needs for religious instruction within our school system, but with a spirit of equality and non-discrimination.

In this chapter, we will look at the various provisions governing the place of religion in Québec schools and explore, through some court cases from outside Québec, some critical issues respecting education and religion We will also briefly discuss how a recent task force established by the Minister has examined the questions raised by Professor Foucher in the passage cited above.

Background

The debate over the place of religion in the school system is as old as the system itself. Even the briefest examination of education in New France reveals the critical role of the Catholic Church and the latter's relation to the State. The role of the Church did not change with the arrival of the British in 1763. When Canada became a Dominion, almost one hundred years later, the compromise which resulted from existing tensions over the "management and control" of schools was set forth in section 93 of the *British North America Act, 1867* (now the *Constitution Act, 1867*). In brief, section 93 prohibited legislation that was prejudicial to the denominational rights which Catholics and Protestants had by law in 1867 (see chap. 2). Post-Confederation educational acts put the final denominational stamp on Québec's school system. Subsequent legislation and practice confirmed and deepened the denominational division of the school system. The system did not change in any significant way until the Quiet Revolution of the 1960s.

The massive structural reform envisaged by the Parent Report, namely the secularization of the school system did not take place. For the next thirty years, the debate over religion and the school system focussed on school board reform. As mentioned at the beginning of chapter 6, early attempts to substitute unified school boards for denominational boards failed and the hope of reform turned to linguistic school board reform. The first serious attempt in this regard came with the *Act Respecting Elementary and Secondary Education* in 1984. When this legislation was declared unconstitutional, reform was put on hold until Bill 107 was adopted in 1988. Despite the ongoing legal obstacles to reform, a growing consensus was emerging that the denominational school system had outlived its day. However, even when Bill 107 was declared constitutionally valid by the Supreme Court in 1993 (*Reference re Education Act of Québec*, 1993), no action was taken and the system was put back "on hold" until the current reform spearheaded by the constitutional amendment of section 93 and the *Linguistic School Boards Act* (1997)(see chap. 6). As the question of school reform became settled, other questions about the place of religion re-emerged, and, as with other aspects of the current system reform, the focus was now on the school.

Freedom of Religion

The Canadian Constitution contains two sets of provisions that are relevant to this discussion. The first, contained in section 93 of the *Constitution Act, 1867*, no longer applies to Québec (see chap. 6). The second set is found in the fundamental freedoms included in the *Canadian Charter* (and also the Québec *Charter*), as introduced as part of the "foundations" of our system (see chap. 2).

Canadian Charter of Rights and Freedoms

2. Everyone has the following fundamental freedoms:
(a) freedom of conscience and religion;
(b) freedom of thought, belief, opinion and expression, including freedom of the press and other media of communication;
(c) freedom of peaceful assembly; and
(d) freedom of association.

Québec Charter of Human Rights and Freedoms

3. Every person is the possessor of the fundamental freedoms, including freedom of conscience, freedom of religion, freedom of opinion, freedom of expression, freedom of peaceful assembly and freedom of association.

A Fundamental Human Right

The core of the fundamental freedom of religion was expressed thus by Dickson J. in *R.* v. *Big M Drug Mart* (1985, pp. 353-354), a case challenging Sunday closing laws for stores:

> The essence of the concept of freedom of religion is the right to entertain such religious beliefs as a person chooses, the right to declare religious beliefs openly and without fear of hindrance or reprisal, and the right to manifest religious belief by worship and practice or by teaching and dissemination. But the concept means more than that.
>   Freedom can primarily be characterized by the absence of coercion or constraint. If a person is compelled by the state or the will of the another to a course of action or inaction which he would not otherwise have chosen, he is not acting of his own volition and he cannot be said to be truly free. One of the major purposes of the *Charter* is to protect, within reason, from compulsion or restraint. Coercion includes not only such blatant forms of compulsion as direct commands to act or refrain from acting on pain of sanction; coercion includes indirect forms of control which determine or limit alternative courses of conduct available to others. Freedom in a broad sense embraces both the absence of coercion and constraint, and the right to manifest beliefs and practices. Freedom means that, subject

to such limitations as are necessary to protect public safety, order, health, or morals or the fundamental rights and freedoms of others, no one is to be forced to act in a way contrary to his beliefs or his conscience.

The Supreme Court of Canada states unequivocally that protecting one religion over others is unacceptable in a truly free society, one which accommodates "a wide variety of beliefs, diversity of tastes and pursuits, customs and codes of conduct" (p. 336).

Freedom of Religion & Pluralism

Freedom of religion is an essential component in the structuring of a pluralistic society. In a pluralistic society (see chap. 14), various racial, ethnic and cultural groups co-exist, each with their own characteristics, typically defined by their customs, values, religion and language. One of the critical policy issues in promoting religious pluralism is the role of the State.

In Great Britain, the Church of England is the official state religion, with the reigning monarch being the head of the Church. In the United States, the opposite situation prevails, where the principle of the separation of Church and State is enshrined in the U.S. Constitution. In Canada, as is often the case, we have adopted an approach that lies somewhere in the middle. The preamble to the *Canadian Charter* states that "Canada is founded upon the principles that recognize the supremacy of God and the rule of law." The State does not endorse any one religion over another; however, the constitutional privileges granted to Catholics and Protestants in education have been a significant exception to this general rule.

Religion & Education in Québec

Religion has traditionally played a significant role in education in Québec, albeit in different ways and at different levels. These differences can be considered under five headings: provincial structures, school board structures, the status of individual schools, the teaching of moral and religious instruction [MRI], and State support of private schools.

Provincial Level

At the provincial level, there are denominationally based provisions regarding the Ministry and more particularly, the Superior Council.

Ministry of Education
As elsewhere, the key education structure at the provincial level is the Ministry of Education. Unlike other jurisdictions, however, the MEQ includes the positions of Catholic and Protestant Associate Deputy Minister. Each associate deputy minister is "responsible for ensuring that the denominational status of educational institutions recognized as Catholic or Protestant is respected and for securing the exercise of denominational rights by Catholics and Protestants in other educational institutions" (*MEQ Act*, s. 8).

Superior Council
As dealt with in chapter 5, the composition of the Superior Council is based on the historic division of the school system and its structures between Catholics and Protestants. This division is further reflected in its two denominational committees and the absence of the recognition of any other faith in both its structure and *modus operandi*. The role of the two denominational committees is discussed below in relation to school status (for other details, see chap. 5).

School Board Level

School Board Structures
The structures of school boards in Québec have been dealt with earlier (see chap. 6) and only a brief synopsis will be included here. As of July 1, 1998, the former network of Catholic and Protestant confessional boards, Catholic and Protestant dissentient boards and common boards for Catholics and for Protestants were completely replaced by a non-denominational network of French and English language school boards. At the level of the school board, no denominational structures remain.

Denominational Positions
Although each school board decides on its own organization chart, it must appoint one person to be responsible for administrative support to schools recognized as Catholic and Protestant and for MRI and pastoral or religious care and guidance services provided in its schools. If it prefers, the school board may appoint two persons, one to be responsible for services for each denominational group (Ed Act, ss. 260-263).

School Structures

In an earlier discussion of schools (see chap. 7), we saw that schools are distinct entities in the Québec school system. The ethos of each school is determined by the school's educational project which sets forth the values and objectives of the school.

Recognized Denominational Schools
The *Education Act* provides for the existence of three classes of public common schools: schools with no denominational status, Catholic schools and Protestant schools. According to the *Education Act*, a school board may apply to the Catholic or Protestant Committee of the Superior Council to have one of its schools legally recognized as being Catholic or Protestant, provided that it has consulted the parents of the school and the school governing board. It *may* similarly apply for the withdrawal of such recognition but it *must* do so at the request of the governing board following consultation of parents (ss.79(3), 218). The consultation of parents must take place in accordance with a regulation adopted under the *Education Act* (see below).

As a transitional measure in the implementation of linguistic boards, schools from the former confessional or dissentient boards, and those previously recognized as Catholic or Protestant, remain Catholic or Protestant until either the Catholic or Protestant Committee, of its own initiative, revokes such recognition, or a request for the withdrawal of such recognition is made by a provisional council (prior to June 30, 1998) or a new school board (after July, 1998). In any event, the new school board must consult parents and the governing board before the end of three years on the advisability of maintaining or withdrawing the confessional status of a school (Ed Act, ss. 218, 520).

The recognition of schools as either Catholic or Protestant is also governed by regulations adopted under the aegis of the *CSE Act* (see below).

Regulation Respecting Parental Consultation
Where a school seeks confessional status, the parents of the school must be consulted and a poll conducted (*Parental Consultation Regulation*). More particularly, the regulation requires that, within specified delays, certain information must be provided to parents, namely:

- the purpose and date of poll;
- the relevant provisions of the *Education Act* which define student/parent rights respecting MRI and related services;
- the characteristics of a school once denominational status is conferred; and
- the conditions and procedures for consultation.

The regulation also prescribes the use of a standard ballot form, on which there are three choices: Catholic; Protestant; and neutral.

Regulation of Catholic Committee

The *Catholic Regulation* contains the two following general provisions regarding the recognition of a school as Catholic.

Catholic Regulation

4. A public school recognized as Catholic shall integrate the beliefs and values of the Catholic religion into its educational project, while maintaining respect for freedom of conscience and of religion.

23. The staff of a public school recognized as Catholic, as well as any person working there, the parents and the pupils shall be respectful of both the public and Catholic character of the school.

The principal is responsible for ensuring the implementation of such an educational project and must report at least every five years, via the school board, to the Catholic Committee on the evaluation of the school as a denominational institution. The regulation requires adherence to the programs of Catholic MRI and pastoral animation (discussed below).

Regulation of Protestant Committee

The *Protestant Regulation* contains the two following general provisions regarding the recognition of a school as Protestant.

Protestant Regulation

4. An educational institution recognized as Protestant may organize activities of a religious nature which are intended to create a sense of belonging to the same religious tradition, to provide an opportunity to celebrate important events of a religious nature and to contribute to the development of a sense of personal identity.

No pupil, however, shall be required to participate in such activities if, for reasons of conscience, an exemption is requested in writing from the head of the educational institution by the parent.

A pupil who has reached the secondary three level may make that request.

5. A teacher shall respect the philosophy and confessional character of a recognized educational institution.

In the performance of his duties, a teacher shall respect the pupil's personal religious or ideological point of view.

Every teacher shall have knowledge of the moral development of the child.

A school recognized as Protestant must also follow the prescriptions contained in the regulation governing MRI (see below).

Moral & Religious Instruction

The Québec *Charter* contains the following provision respecting MRI.

Québec Charter of Human Rights and Freedoms

41. Parents or the persons acting in their stead have a right to require that, in the public educational establishments, their children receive a religious or moral education in conformity with their convictions, within the framework of the curricula provided for by law.

Like section 40 of the Charter, which establishes education as a human right (see chap. 2), the right to religious instruction is tempered by reference to the framework provided by law. As we will see below, this framework, effectively limits this right to persons of the Catholic and Protestant faiths. The *Education Act* and the regulations adopted under the aegis of the *CSE Act* provide for various rights and obligations regarding MRI, as well as pastoral/religious care and guidance (see the Ed Act, ss. 5-6, 225-228, 241).

According to the *Education Act*, every student has the right every year to choose between Catholic MRI; Protestant MRI; moral instruction; and, if offered by a school, MRI in another religious denomination. According to the Act, Catholic and Protestant MRI, as well as moral instruction must be available in any school where it is requested. MRI in another religious denomination is only offered in a school when the school board approves a request of the governing board to do so. The exercise of the right to choose is vested: in students of full age (18 years); in students in the last three years (grades 9-11) of secondary school; and in parents of other students (ss. 5, 225, 227, 228).

The school board must ensure that students/parents indicate their choice each year at the time of registration. Failing such indication, if a choice has been made in a prior year, a student/parent will be deemed to have made the same choice; if no prior choice has been made, a student/parent will be deemed to have chosen moral instruction (s. 241).

Catholic and Protestant students also have a right to student services of pastoral care and guidance if Catholic, and religious care and guidance if Protestant, but it is not clear that such services have to be offered in every school (ss. 6, 226).

Protection of Catholic & Protestant Privilege

Many people believe that all of the preferential treatment accorded Catholics and Protestants in the Québec education system is based on section 93 of the *Constitution Act, 1867* and could not be changed by the Government, except by constitutional amendment. In fact, this is only partly true.

Constitutional Provisions

Until December 1997, the authority of the Government of Québec over education was limited by section 93 of the *Constitution Act, 1867* (see *Historical Roots*, chap. 4). This section precluded the making of laws that prejudicially affected denominational rights that existed by law at the time of Confederation. When the *Canadian Charter* was drafted, it was obvious that such constitutional guarantees conflicted with the newly entrenched rights to freedom of religion and conscience in section 2 and equality in section 15. To ensure that no one could argue that the new *Canadian Charter* provisions superseded section 93 rights, the following provision was added to the *Charter*.

> ### *Québec Charter of Human Rights and Freedoms*
>
> **29.** Nothing in this Charter abrogates or derogates from any rights or privileges guaranteed by or under the Constitution of Canada in respect of denominational, separate or dissentient schools.

Although this clause shields from a *Canadian Charter* challenge those provisions of provincial legislation which are maintained because of section 93, it does not shield from review any provisions in the legislation which are not necessary in order to respect section 93. Furthermore, as we saw in the discussion of school board reform (see chap. 6), section 93 guarantees no longer apply in Québec and so this shield is henceforth non-applicable in this province.

Québec Policy

When the Government of Québec adopted Bill 107, it included denominational provisions that went beyond those required by section 93. These include all provisions that deal with the recognition of denominational schools and MRI programs offered in school boards where constitutionally protected denominational rights did not apply. The Government was able to do this by including the following derogations in the *Education Act*.

> ### *Education Act*
>
> **726.** The provisions of this Act which grant rights and privileges to a religious affiliation shall apply despite sections 3 and 10 of the Charter of human rights and freedoms (R.S.Q., chapter C-12).
>
> **727.** The provisions of this Act which grant rights and privileges to a religious confession shall operate notwithstanding the provisions of paragraph *a* of section 2 and section 15 of the Constitution Act, 1982 (Schedule B to the Canada Act, chapter 11 in the 1982 volume of the Acts of Parliament of the United Kingdom).

You will recall from our earlier discussion of human rights and freedoms (see chap. 2) that the inclusion of these provisions is made possible because of the *notwithstanding* provisions of the *Canadian Charter* (s. 33) and the Québec *Charter* (s. 52). Contrary to what one might assume, these provisions were not included to protect section 93 rights from a *Canadian Charter* challenge; as you saw above, section 29 is more than sufficient for that purpose. Sections 726 and 727 of the *Education Act* are there expressly to protect those denominational rights that go beyond those that are constitutionally protected. Québec is the only jurisdiction in Canada to override *Canadian Charter* rights to protect denominational privilege in public schools.

Accordingly, there never was a constitutional imperative that required the Government to provide such additional rights to Catholics and Protestants, to the exclusion of members of other religious faiths. Likewise, there was no reason why other faiths could not have been offered equal protection; in such a case, there would no longer be any need for sections 726 and 727. To date, the accommodation of other religious faiths has been confined to the private school option. However, this situation may be about to change (see Task Force on the Place of Religion, below).

Religion & Freedom of Choice

The right of parents to have alternatives to and funding for "mainstream" public schooling is an important educational policy issue in Canada. There have been several instances of parents challenging the State monopoly on education, as well as continuing demands from various groups for State funding of denominationally-based private schools. Québec has had a long tradition of supporting such demands, as illustrated by the following provisions of the *CSE Act*.

CSE Act

Preamble

Whereas every child is entitled to the advantage of a system of education conducive to the full development of his personality;

Whereas parents have the right to choose the institutions which, according to their convictions, ensure the greatest respect for the rights of their children;

Whereas persons and groups are entitled to establish autonomous educational institutions and, subject to the requirements of the common welfare, to avail themselves of the administrative and financial means necessary for the pursuit of their ends; ...

These provisions date from the original version of the Act adopted in 1964 and are also included in the *MEQ Act*, adopted the same year. They are declarative in nature and do not confer any substantive rights. However, they do reflect the commitment made by the Government to respect such rights as it began to construct a State-run school system during the Quiet Revolution.

Parents in Québec who wish an alternative educational placement for their children on religious grounds have three possibilities: an alternative school in the public system; a private school; and home schooling.

Alternative Public Schools

As discussed with respect to student rights (see chap. 3), parents have a right, within limits, to choose the school in their school board that suits their preferences. Accordingly, parents who wish their children to attend a Catholic or Protestant school can choose a school that has been so recognized by the procedures summarized above. If no such school exists, they can seek to have their neighbourhood school declared Catholic or Protestant, as the case may be.

As also mentioned above, there is no provision in the *Education Act* or the regulations which provides for the recognition of a school in terms of any other religious faith. A school could decide to adopt an educational project that reflects a particular religious denomination. However, such a course of action could run into problems in light of the protection of freedom of religion under the *Canadian Charter* and the Québec *Charter* (see discussion in chap. 2 on *Charter* immunity).

Private Schooling

In addition to the exemption from public schooling for students registered in a recognized private school (Ed Act, s. 15(4)), the following provisions of the Québec *Charter* are relevant to a consideration of the private school option.

Québec Charter of Human Rights and Freedoms

20. A distinction, exclusion or preference ... justified by the charitable, philanthropic, religious, political or educational nature of a non-profit institution or of an institution devoted exclusively to the well-being of an ethnic group, is deemed non-discriminatory.

42. Parents or the persons acting in their stead have a right to choose private educational establishments for their children, provided such establishments comply with the standards prescribed or approved by virtue of the law.

Special Programs

Section 20 of the Québec *Charter* can be considered as a "special program" which permits *prima facie* discriminatory practices in non-profit organizations. For purposes of this discussion, section 20 permits otherwise discriminatory behaviour by private schools – that is, it deems such behaviour to be non-discriminatory - if it can be justified by the nature of the school, but not by factors that are *incidental* to the school's vocation (see *Brossard (Ville)* v. *Commission des droits de la personne du Québec*, 1988).

In a recent case (*Collège Notre-Dame du Scare-Coeur* v. *Commission des droits de la personne du Québec*, 1994), a private Catholic school relied on section 20 to refuse to admit a student with a disability, because her disability prevented her from taking part in the complete physical education program. The trial judge rejected the student's complaint, concluding that the exclusion was based on the educational character of the institution and that it was therefore immune from a charge of discrimination. However, there was no discussion of how the religious nature of the school justified discrimination on the basis of disability. The case has been appealed.*

* *Note.* Based on the reasoning of the Supreme Court of Canada in *Brossard*, it would appear that section 20 covers public denominational schools (i.e. those officially recognized as Catholic or Protestant) but not "ordinary" public schools; however, the trial judge in *Notre-Dame* stated that section 20 only applies to private institutions.

Right of Choice

The right to choose the private school option is limited by the provision that private schools must comply with the standards set by law. It is suggested that the spirit of this restriction is simply to ensure that private schools provide an appropriate level of educational services. However, it is recognized that this restriction could be seen as an unwarranted interference in the right of private denominationally based schools to decide on the appropriate curriculum for their students.

Private School Funding

Contrary to the practice prevailing in most provinces, Québec subsidizes private schools that are accredited by the Minister. At the present time, these subsidies equal approximately 60% of the per capita amount allocated by the government to support students enrolled in public schools.

The effect of this funding is to give the right to private education included in the Québec *Charter* some practical meaning. This contrasts with the situation prevailing in other jurisdictions (e.g. Ontario) where parents who desire private denominationally-based schools must defray all such costs, without the benefit of government subsidies, as recently affirmed by the Supreme Court of Canada in *Adler* v. *Ontario* (1996).

Home Schooling

As alluded to above, school choice is not limited to choosing between public and private schooling. Parents have a right to choose home schooling as an alternative to public schooling, provided that the school board accepts that the child is receiving an *equivalent* educational experience (Ed Act, s. 15(4)). This can be viewed as a reasonable limit or as unreasonable interference, depending on one's point of view.

Until recently, home schooling has been less popular in Quebec than in other jurisdictions in Canada. However, the demand for this alternative seems to be growing. At present, parents cannot demand any support services from school boards, something that is provided for in some provinces. Undoubtedly, there are some school boards and individual schools that do provide support on an *ad hoc* basis. However, as school boards receive no grants for students enrolled in home schooling, it seems likely that boards would want to recover the costs of any services provided. This in turn may prompt parents to seek some kind of voucher support, as has often been sought for private schooling in several other jurisdictions throughout North America (Brown, 1985).

Religious Beliefs, Public Schools & Discrimination

Schools are important social institutions and serve a variety of, sometimes contradictory, purposes. In addition to teaching young people knowledge and skills that will help them develop their individual personalities, they prepare them to take part in the collective life of society. Schools can be structured to preserve and enhance one religious group or to support diversity and pluralism. The following provides highlights from one court case outside Québec that illustrates contemporary issues concerning religion and education, and recent debates inside Québec over religious holidays and the wearing of the hijab in public schools.

Teaching Religion versus Teaching about Religion

A series of court cases in several Canadian provinces have demonstrated that various traditional practices in public schools* relating to Christian religious instruction and exercises violate the constitutionally guaranteed freedom of religion and freedom from religious discrimination. Furthermore, merely excusing students from participating in them is not an adequate response.

*Note. In this context, "public" schools are equivalent to common non-denominational schools in Québec.

The one case we will look at (*Canadian Civil Liberties Association* v. *Ontario*, 1990) concerns a school board in Ontario and the application of provincial regulations regarding religious instruction. In brief, the Ontario *Education Act* and provincial regulations (at that time) mandated the teaching of religious education in schools where the parent so wished and stipulated that no student was required to take part in such instruction. There were similar provisions regarding religious exercises but they were not at issue in this case.*

* Note. The Ontario Court of Appeal had already found that the holding of Christian religious exercises in public schools violated the freedom of religion provisions of the *Canadian Charter* (*Zylberberg* v. *Sudbury Board of Education*, 1988).

The school board in question had developed its own curriculum on religious instruction. This curriculum was at first exclusively Christian, but the board subsequently modified it to incorporate sections about other religions. Parents were given three options with respect to participation in this program: (a) take part; (b) opt for an alternate program taught in clergy-run classes; (c) opt out completely. A group of parents challenged both the provincial regulatory framework and the curriculum of the school board.

The Ontario Divisional Court rejected the petition of the parents but was reversed on appeal. The Court of Appeal framed its consideration of the petition in terms of teaching religion versus teaching about religion (p. 4):

> The crucial issue in this appeal is whether the purpose and the effects of the regulation and the curriculum are to *indoctrinate* school children in Ontario in the Christian faith. If so, the rights to freedom of conscience and religion under s. 2(a) of the *Canadian Charter of Rights and Freedoms* and the equality rights guaranteed under s. 15 of the Charter may be infringed. On the other hand, it is

conceded that education designed to teach about religion and to foster moral values without indoctrination in a particular religious faith would not be a breach of the Charter. It is indoctrination in a particular religious faith that is alleged to be offensive.

After a lengthy analysis, the Court of Appeal found that both the regulatory framework and the curriculum provided for religious indoctrination and that the provisions of the latter concerning other religions did not mitigate this finding. With respect to the exemption provisions, the Court restated its conclusion in *Zylberberg* (see above *note*), namely that: "The exemption provision imposes a penalty on pupils from religious minorities who utilize it by stigmatizing them as non-conformists and setting them apart from their fellow students who are members of the dominant religion" (p. 23).

Although most of this chapter has considered religion and education from the perspective of the legal protection of Catholic and Protestant rights, it would be misleading to assume that the debate over religion and education stops there. Over the past few years, another religious issues have gained prominence – to name two, the accommodation of the religious beliefs of school staff other than Catholics and Protestants, and the wearing of the Islamic veil in school.

Teachers' Religious Beliefs

A recent Québec case (*Chambly, Commission scolaire régionale* v. *Bergevin*, 1994), involved three teachers of the Jewish faith who were given a day off without pay to observe the religious holiday of Yom Kippour. The teachers grieved the salary deduction, claiming religious discrimination. The arbitration board concluded that the school board action was discriminatory and upheld the grievance. The school board appealed. A majority of the Québec Court of Appeal found that the award was unreasonable and should be set aside. Their decision was based on the following reasoning:

- the school calendar does not reflect the Catholic nature of the school board - as asserted by the arbitration board - and does not give any advantage in terms of holidays to Catholic teachers; it has no arbitrary aspects and merely reflects social realities;
- the award creates reverse discrimination in allowing the grievers the same annual salary as other teachers, while working one day less;
- if the award were affirmed, the school board could be forced to grant Muslim teachers religious holidays on the same basis;
- the financial burden on the teachers (loss of one day's pay) is not an obstacle to the free exercise of their religion; as there is no breach of this fundamental freedom, there is no duty to accommodate.

The Supreme Court of Canada held that the school calendar was discriminatory in its effect and that the loss of one day's pay was not insignificant. It was held that the school board had a duty to accommodate short of "undue hardship" and that, in this case, the payment of one day's pay did not constitute undue hardship. If, on the other hand, a teacher's religious beliefs required him or her to be absent every Friday, then that might be a different matter.

The Islamic Veil & the Public School

As noted above, the wearing of the Islamic veil or hijab, in public and private schools has been an issue of contention. One article in *The Gazette* began a story on this issue thus (Block, 1994, p. B1):

> In a society in which Muslims are often portrayed as fundamentalists and terrorists, the issue has touched a raw nerve, going well beyond the simple wearing of a head scarf. It raises questions of freedom, tolerance and the equality of women in our multicultural society.

Public attention to this issue began when a secondary school of the Commission des Écoles Catholiques de Montréal [CÉCM] refused to allow one of its students, a convert to Islam, to wear the hijab, ostensibly because it violated the school's dress code. The conflict never resulted in a court case because the student withdrew and enrolled in another school. However, the issue has arisen in other schools and has sparked considerable debate. People espousing contrary points of view relied on the Québec *Charter* to support their arguments. Consequently, the Québec Human Rights Commission decided to further the debate by means of a discussion paper.

Advice from the Human Rights Commission

The Human Rights Commission paper (1995), entitled *Religious Pluralism in Québec: A Social and Ethical Challenge*, notes that the debate on the wearing of the Islamic veil has been heated because of its association with gender inequality (p. 17):

> It must be acknowledged that the veil is sometimes an instrumental part of a set of practices aimed at maintaining the subjugation of women and that, in some more extremist societies, women are actually forced to wear the veil.
>
> A major part of the public debate of recent months has been concerned with the interpretation of the Koran itself, especially as regards the obligation to wear the veil. We do not feel it is up to us to take a position on this particular question, which we believe should be considered first and foremost within the Muslim community itself.
>
> However, many young people have expressed concern about the right to equality of young Muslim women who, consciously or not, might not wear the veil entirely of their own free will.
>
> Beyond differences in Koran interpretation and out of respect for the people who choose to wear the veil, we must assume that this choice is a way of expressing their religious affiliations and convictions. In our view, it would be insulting to the girls and women who wear the veil to suppose that their choice is not an enlightened one, or that they do so to protest against the right to equality. It would also be offensive to classify the veil as something to be banished, like the swastika for example, or to rob it of its originality by comparing it to a hat.
>
> In general terms, therefore, the veil should be seen as licit, to be prohibited or regulated only if it can be proved that public order or the equality of the sexes is threatened.

The Human Rights Commission goes on to state the following with regard to the wearing of the Islamic veil in light of the provisions of the Québec *Charter*:

- school rules which specifically forbid the wearing of the veil would constitute a form of direct discrimination;

- school rules which do not mention the veil but whose effect would prohibit it constitute a form of indirect or adverse effect discrimination;

- schools have a duty to accommodate students who choose to wear the veil and this cannot be legitimately accomplished by transferring the student to another school;

- if a student wearing the veil becomes marginalized, the school cannot remain passive, it must teach its students to respect the human rights and freedoms of that student;

- the school would be justified, however, in regulating the wearing of the veil in any of the following circumstances:

  - if it became known that certain students were being forced to wear the veil against their will;

  - where a campaign to wear the veil was organized in order to create or exacerbate tensions among students or incite discrimination based on sex;

  - for reasons of safety, such as in physical education courses and in laboratory activities where the student may be required to handle hazardous materials; "however, the risk to safety must be real and not just presumed" (p. 40).

Religious diversity is an indisputable reality of contemporary schools in Québec. While most people support the *principle* of freedom from discrimination on the basis of religion, there is still considerable disagreement on what this should mean *in practice*. As will be discussed more fully in chapter 14, coming to such a consensus is one of the "challenges of plurality."

Task Force on the Place of Religion in Schools

The Mandate

In 1997, the Minister of Education formed a Task Force on the Place of Religion in Schools in Québec, headed by Professor Jean-Pierre Proulx of the University of Montréal. The timing of this request is also noteworthy, as section 727 of the *Education Act* will lapse in 1999 unless renewed by the Government (see chap. 2).

The Task Force was mandated to define the "problem statement" concerning the place of religion in schools, including both its status and the provision of educational services, with emphasis on the evolution of Québec society since the report of the Parent Commission during the Quiet Revolution. More specifically, the Task Force has been asked to provide policy direction to the State based on an analysis of: different conceptual models which may be used to determine the place of religion in schools; the relationship between fundamental human rights and the rights of parents respecting the religious education of their children; and the rights and obligations of different stakeholders in the school system.

The Minister also enjoined the Task Force to take into account the major social values of Québec society, with explicit reference to Bill 101 and Québec immigration policy, as well as the views of various interested groups. One can therefore conclude that the Task Force was given a very broad canvas on which to sketch out a new image of this critical policy issue as a follow-up to the constitutional amendment and the creation of linguistic school boards (see chap. 6).

Contrasting Views

As the following extracts from statements quoted in chapter 6 concerning the proposed abolition of constitutionally protected denominational rights demonstrate, opinion is clearly divided on the place of religion in schools:

> As long as the parents continue to choose denominational schools, no one has a right to deprive them of it (Citizens for the Constitutional Right to Denominational Schools, 1997, p. 13/3).

> In a democratic system based on the respect of fundamental freedoms, it is unacceptable that persons who are neither Catholic nor Protestant must choose between these two privileged denominations in order to exercise their right to schooling (Centrale de l'enseignement du Québec, 1997, p. 11/9 [free translation]).

> The FCPPQ supports reform based on linguistic considerations, provided services that meet the religious and cultural need of Catholic and Protestant groups continue to [be] offered (Fédération des comités de parents de la province de Québec, 1997, p. 27/2).

The first statement typifies those who opposed the amendment and sought to preserve denominational guarantees for the school system. For this group, religion ought to remain a key defining element in the school system. The second clearly supports the amendment and, from this perspective, its logical extension - the elimination of all privilege granted to Catholics and Protestants. For this group, there is no place for religion in the school system. The third statement reflects a compromise position in support of the constitutional amendment in return for the continuation of religion in school within neutral denominational structures. For this group, the need for religion as the defining element in school board structures may have disappeared but the demand for religion in schools is as strong as ever.

The Report

The Task Force report (1999) provides a very comprehensive treatment of the subject, setting forth the major issues to be considered, the parameters of the debate and the orientations proposed by the Task Force. While recognizing that the legislative treatment of Catholic and Protestant privilege is almost identical, it notes the important differences between the approaches advocated by the Catholic and Protestant committees (p. 33):

> The Catholic Committee has sought to reconcile Catholicism and public schools by basing its educational project on a Christian humanist approach whose Catholic origins are clearly identified and named, and that is thus a denominational program. It also indicates that religious instruction should propose, but not impose, Christian faith and tradition to allow, in its words, young people to grow as human beings. The Protestant Committee proposes a vision of secular schools, Protestant in name only but inspired by a "philosophy" based on the humanist values of Protestant tradition, and religious animation services partly inspired by the Bible, but with no doctrinal references to Protestantism and open to the different world religions.

In reviewing the demographic situation of Québec schools, the Task Force notes that 90% of the French student population is Catholic, while the dominant characteristic of the English student population is pluralism - no single group forms a majority, with the Catholic students accounting for the largest group (40%). The other striking finding is that the three French school boards in Montréal account for 47% of the non-Catholic population in French boards and that together with the French school boards in Laval and the South Shore account for 69% of that population. This confirms that the image of French schools in rural Québec as all but exclusively Catholic is still accurate and that the gulf between the situation prevailing in Montréal and the rest of the province is widening.

The report poses several rhetorical questions, for example: "Should the state remain neutral, or should it base its approach on the tradition or culture of the majority to promote one or more religions?" (p. 70). However, it is clear that the authors have a difficult time reconciling the continuation of the status quo in light of the evolution of contemporary society and values (p. 71):

> Our society is also based on human rights and freedoms. We will therefore have to choose between a continuation of the system in which the rights and privileges of the Catholic and Protestant tradition take precedence in the religious instruction dispensed in schools, over freedom of conscience, freedom of religion, and the right to equality. It will be necessary to clarify, once and for all, the relationship between human rights and the right of parents to choose religious instruction for their children in keeping with their beliefs.

Without rejecting the notion that there is a place for religion in schools, the Task Force insists that any such place must be respectful of the rights of all members of the school community, not just Catholics and Protestants. In order to guide its thinking - and possibly that of others, the Task Force sets forth the following principles (p. 91):

1. Québec is a liberal democracy that must, in all areas, uphold the principle of fundamental equality of all citizens.
2. Any Québec state policy on the question of religion in schools must be subject to the requirement of egalitarian neutrality.
3. Schools fall under the shared responsibility of parents, civil society and the state. This partnership aims to provide all children with a well-rounded and high-quality education.
4. Children have fundamental interests with respect to education that must be guaranteed by the state. These fundamental interests, in addition to the development of general cognitive skills, are generally translated into the right of children to be properly prepared for their lives as citizens in a liberal democracy. This type of education must include the development of personal autonomy and critical thinking, the capacity to reason, tolerance, an openness to diversity and a sense of belonging to the community.
5. Religion may have a place in schools, as a contribution to the development of the child as a whole person, provided its teaching is organized in a way that is consistent with the principle of fundamental equality of all citizens, and provided it promotes the attainment of the goals identified as necessary for educating citizens and forging the social bond.

The Task Force survey of domestic and international law, based on three commissioned studies (Pratte, 1999; Smith & Foster, 1999; Woehrling, 1999) leaves no doubt that the status quo is discriminatory and is allowed to exist only because of the invocation of the override clause in provincial legislation. The Task Force concludes this chapter with the following summative statement (p. 114):

> The legal scholars consulted for the purposes of this study felt that a secular system respectful of the right to private education would satisfy the demands of both domestic and international law. The same would apply to courses on the study of religions from a cultural perspective. If the denominational path is chosen, the system must be egalitarian in terms of both schools and teaching, and must be respectful of both those with and those without religious affiliations. The possibility of enforcing this respect will depend on concrete circumstances.

The Task Force also took pains to examine the views of stakeholders and did not rely solely on a legal analysis to reach its conclusions. Not surprisingly it found that the written briefs it received reflected the polarized positions on the subject that we noted above in relation to the Special Joint Committee hearings on the constitutional amendment. In brief, parent associations were in favour of parental choice, while teacher and principal associations tended to favour a secular vision of schooling. However, the results of a sample of individual parents, teachers and principals reveals a greater range of differences.

Catholic parents are split, with 45% supporting some form of denominational schooling but with 53% preferring a more secular arrangement. Teacher and principal preferences are disaggregated by English and French school responses, as summarized below:

TABLE 12.1

Denominational and Secular School Types - Teacher and Principal Preferences

Viewpoint	French Catholic		English Catholic		French Protestant		English Protestant	
	Teachers	Principals	Teachers	Principals	Teachers	Principals	Teachers	Principals
Denominational	19%	18%	41%	65%	8%	18%	8%	3%
Secular	80%	81%	59%	35%	92%	82%	91%	94%

Note. Adapted from the Task Force report (1999), Tables 7 & 8, pp. 161-162; differences between column total and 100% equal residual opinions.

As can be seen from this table, only Catholic Principals show a clear preference for denominational schooling among those surveyed, with a strong minority of English Catholic teachers showing the same preference. All other groups are clearly in favour of some form of secular schooling.*

* Note. The report acknowledges (p. 140) that the number of teacher respondents from the English Catholic and French Protestant sectors, as well as the number of principal respondents from the English Catholic, English Protestant and French Protestant sectors was very low, creating a very high margin of error in these sectors.

On the basis of its analysis, the Task Force makes the following recommendations as a basis for public discussion, ones which it acknowledges "clearly represent a break with the tradition that has prevailed in Québec for more than a century" and which are "unequivocally based on respect for the right to equality and respect for freedom of conscience and religion" (p. 221).

Recommendations
1. We recommend that the Government of Québec and the National Assembly confirm the primacy of the right to equality and freedom of conscience and religion guaranteed in the Québec Charter of Human Rights and Freedoms and the Canadian Charter of Rights and Freedoms and, consequently, that they repeal or not renew the current notwithstanding clauses in education legislation which override the application of the Charters.
2. We recommend that legislation be enacted to establish a secular system of public schools dispensing preschool, elementary and secondary education.
3. We recommend that the current denominational statuses held by public schools be revoked.
4. We recommend that the Education Act be amended to stipulate that the values and beliefs of religious groups cannot be used as criteria to set up a public school for the purposes of a specific project.
5. We recommend that the basic school regulations for elementary and secondary education provide for the study of religions from a cultural perspective in place of Catholic or Protestant

religious instruction, and that the study of religions be compulsory for all students.

6. We recommend that programs for the study of religions from a cultural perspective be developed and implemented in keeping with the guide-lines and framework proposed by the Commission des programmes d'études of the Ministère de l'Éducation, and with the relevant provisions of the Education Act.

7. We recommend that the Ministère de l'Éducation encourage flexible measures for teacher in-service training for the study of religions from a cultural perspective and allocate the necessary financial resources for such measures.

8. We recommend that the Education Act authorize schools to provide common religious and spiritual support services for students of all faiths and that these services be publicly funded.

9. We recommend that the Government define the general objectives of religious and spiritual support services in the basic school regulations just as it defines those of other student services; that the local school governing boards draw up programs of activities in keeping with these general objectives; that the school boards set the criteria for hiring religious support specialists in keeping with these same objectives and without discrimination.

10. We recommend that the Education Act stipulate that the local school governing boards may, outside school hours, provide facilities to religious groups that wish to dispense religious instruction or offer services at their own expense to members of their faith attending the school; and the Act stipulate that the governing boards must exercise this power without discrimination, taking into account any priorities they may legitimately set with respect to the use of school premises.

11. We recommend that the provisions of the Act respecting the Conseil supérieur de l'éducation pertaining to the Catholic Committee and the Protestant Committee be repealed, that the provisions of the Act respecting the ministère de l'Éducation pertaining to the associate deputy ministers for the Catholic and Protestant faiths also be repealed and, consequently, that the appropriate changes be made to the organizational structure of the Ministère de l'Éducation.

12. We recommend that section 41 of the Québec Charter of Human Rights and Freedoms be amended to recognize, as stated in article 18(4) of the International Covenant on Civil and Political Rights, "the liberty of parents and, when applicable, legal guardians to ensure the religious and moral education of their children in conformity with their own convictions."

13. We recommend that any other applicable legislative and regulatory provisions be amended in keeping with these recommendations.

14. We recommend that, should these recommendations be adopted, they be implemented gradually, as follows:

General Provisions

a) Repeal of the notwithstanding clauses in education legislation which override the application of the Charters of Rights

b) Amendment of section 41 of the Québec Charter of Human Rights and Freedoms

c) Revocation, by law, of the current denominational status of public schools

d) Abolition, by law, of the Catholic Committee, the Protestant Committee and the associate deputy minister positions for the Catholic and Protestant faiths

e) Adoption of any other applicable legislative, regulatory and administrative provisions, including terms and conditions of implementation and the timetable for change.

Provisions Relating to the Study of Religions from a Cultural Perspective

f) Start of the implementation process for the appropriate programs of study

g) Assignment of a mandate to the Comité d'orientation et de formation du personnel enseignant with respect to the initial training of future teachers and the in-service training of practising teachers regarding the study of religions

h) Simultaneous implementation of plans for the initial training and professional development of teachers

Provisions Relating to Common Religious and Spiritual Support Services

    i)   Definition, in the basic school regulations, of the objectives for common religious and spiritual support services

    j)   Implementation of an initial and in-service training program for the staff concerned

    k)   Introduction of common religious and spiritual support services (pp. 221-224, footnotes omitted).

Next Steps

The Minister does not have an easy job to reconcile such profound differences. At least in the case of the first two positions exemplified above, the parties were for or against the reform in its entirety and will be pleased or displeased as the case may be with the retention of elimination of religion at the level of the school. The third group will be pleased if it retains what Boudreau describes as the "essence of Catholic education, that is religious instruction, formation of community, and service to others" (1999, p. 93). If such services are not preserved then this group may feel betrayed, as its support for the constitutional amendment and linguistics boards was predicated on this *quid pro quo*. Unfortunately for this point of view, the Minister of the time declared that the constitutional amendment and linguistics boards was one matter, the place of religion in schools quite another (see chap. 6).

In addition to the political considerations of dealing with the opposing views of different constituencies, the Minster will have to consider the possible options in light of the diverse nature of contemporary Québec society and human rights principles that now guide - or ought to guide government policy. The essence of such an approach means that the place of religion in schools must comply with human rights norms so that it neither impairs freedom of religion nor discriminates on the basis of religion. This does not necessary mean that there is no place for religion in schools - that is position defended on the basis of secularism, not human rights (see Boudreau, 1999, Sweet, 1997).

A human rights perspective would mean, however, an end to privilege to Catholics and Protestants; that whatever provision was made for religion in schools, would be made, subject to reasonable limits, available to all religions and in such a way that no individual's freedom of religion was violated, including non-adherents of any faith. Such a "rainbow approach" may be too costly or impractical to support or it may be extremely difficult to implement in a way that is respectful of all. Balancing such competing interests will not be an easy task and it will be all but impossible to satisfy everyone. At the time of writing the Minister has announced that public hearings will be held begining in June 1999 and that no changes will be implemented before September 2001. In the meantime, the Minister has also signified that the Government will renew the override clause of the *Education Act* to permit time for debate and legislative action. After that it will be up to the Government to respond and in so doing, to use the words of the Superior Council, reveal what kind of society we are and what kind we aspire to be (CSE, 1977).

CHAPTER 13
EDUCATION AND LANGUAGE

Introduction

If one had to pick one critical public policy issue that sets Québec apart from other jurisdictions, then language comes quickly to mind. As society looks to schools to perpetuate itself and defend its core values and aspirations, it is not surprising that language is equally a critical policy issue in education, as reflected by the following requirement set forth in the *Basic Regulations* (El Reg, s. 54; Sec Reg, s. 68):

Basic Regulations

The school board must take the necessary measures to make the quality of the written and spoken language, in learning and in school life, the concern of each member of the teaching staff, irrespective of the subject taught, and the concern of all other members of the school staff and the school's collaborators.

Language has gradually supplanted religion as the dominant cultural metaphor in the province. It is not surprising, therefore, that the controversy over language rights in general and the language of instruction in the schools in particular, has led to a heated debate. Québec's language policy has evolved from no policy at all, to the present regime of restricted access to English schooling (Bill 101). Bill 101 was intended to defend and promote the use of the French language and it can be argued that it has done so in a variety of domains, including education. Whether the exceptions to the general rule of instruction being given in French go far enough in protecting minority language rights or whether they go too far is a matter of opinion. One thing is certain, however, the issue of language and education will continue to be an important policy issue in the foreseeable future. In this chapter we will see how the *Canadian Charter* now sets the constitutional parameters for minority language education and the operation of current Québec legislation on language within this framework.

Background

The language of instruction had not been a major issue in Québec education before the late 1960s. This changed dramatically with a conflict between parents from the Italian community of St. Leonard and the local Catholic school board. In brief, the school board passed a resolution to replace bilingual instruction with French-only instruction, a move that was bitterly opposed by the Italian community. This purely local squabble received widespread media coverage and soon became a *cause célèbre*.

In 1969, the *Act to Promote the French Language in Québec* [Bill 63] was drafted with the hopes of appeasing opposing factions. It required school boards to offer English language instruction upon parental request (s. 2). The hope for compromise failed to materialize. The battle over the language of instruction, which had been dormant for so long, had finally been joined.

As a result of this increasing pressure, the government adopted the *Official Language Act,* [Bill 22] (1974). In a sharp reversal of the previous government's approach, this Act declared French to be the sole official language of Québec and introduced a number of measures designed to bolster the use of French. In education, parental choice of the language of instruction was abolished and for the first time admittance to English schools was restricted on the basis of language proficiency tests.

The next phase in the battle of French language rights generally, and language of instruction in particular, occurred after another change of government in 1976. One of the first pieces of legislation introduced by the new government was Bill 101. Bill 101 has been the focus of ongoing controversy, litigation and legislative amendment. The provisions regarding the language of instruction have been no less controversial and will be dealt with below. For details on the past history of this legislation, see *Historical Roots.*

Constitutional Parameters: Section 23

As alluded to above, eligibility for English language instruction is also governed by section 23 of the *Canadian Charter*:

Canadian Charter of Rights and Freedoms

23. (1) Citizens of Canada

(a) whose first language learned and still understood is that of the English or French linguistic minority population of the province in which they reside, or

(b) who have received their primary school instruction in Canada in English or French and reside in a province where the language in which they received that instruction is the language of the English or French linguistic minority population of the province,

have the right to have their children receive primary and secondary school instruction in that language in that province.

(2) Citizens of Canada of whom any child has received or is receiving primary or secondary school instruction in English or French in Canada, have the right to have all their children receive primary and secondary school instruction in the same language.

(3) The right of citizens of Canada under subsections (1) and (2) to have their children receive primary and secondary school instruction in the language of the English or French linguistic minority population of a province

(a) applies wherever in the province the number of children of citizens who have such a right is sufficient to warrant the provision to them out of public funds of minority language instruction; and

(b) includes, where the number of those children so warrants, the right to have them receive that instruction in minority language educational facilities provided out of public funds.

59. (1) Paragraph 23(1)(a) shall come into force in respect of Quebec on a day to be fixed by proclamation issued by the Queen or the Governor General under the Great Seal of Canada.

(2) A proclamation under subsection (1) shall be issued only where authorized by the legislative assembly or government of Quebec.

Overview of Section 23

Prior to 1982, there was no constitutional protection of minority language rights in Canada. As mentioned in *Historical Roots* (chap. 4), the constitutional challenge (under section 93) to Bill 22 by the Protestant school boards was rejected (*Québec (A.G.)* v. *Québec Association of Protestant School Boards*, 1984). As a result, there was heightened interest in providing for such rights in the *Canadian Charter.* Unlike other rights and freedoms included in the *Charter*, minority language rights are the expression of a political compromise, rather than the expression of inherent human rights.

Minority language rights do not contemplate all minority group languages spoken in Canada. Section 23 is limited to English and French, more specifically: English as a minority language in Québec and French as a minority language in every other province. It is also interesting to note that while these rights are constitutionally protected, the general right to education enjoys no such protection. Furthermore, minority language rights are vested in parents (not children) who are citizens of Canada.

23(1)(a): First Language Learned & Still Understood

Sub-section 23(1)(a) provides the right to English instruction in Québec or French instruction elsewhere for the child of a parent whose "first language learned and still understood" is the minority language in question. However, this right does not have any application in Québec at the present time. By virtue of section 59 (see above) this right will not come into force in Québec until the Government of Québec gives its consent. In the Québec context, the non-application of this clause means that people who do not qualify for English instruction by virtue of the "Canada clause" (described next), are denied access to English schools.

23(1)(b): Parent Educated in Minority Language

Sub-section 23(1)(b) provides the right to English instruction in Québec or French instruction elsewhere for the child of a parent who was educated at the elementary level in Canada in the minority language in question. It is this text that people commonly refer to as the "Canada clause." In the Québec context, it is this clause that extended access to English schools to those who were educated in English anywhere in Canada.* As discussed below, this right is now included in Bill 101 (s. 73(1)). However, this right does not extend to people educated in English outside of Canada.

* *Note.* Until Bill 101 was amended in 1993, the general exception for eligibility for English education was limited to students whose parents were educated in English in Québec (former s. 73(a)).

23(2): Child or Sibling Educated in Minority Language

Sub-section 23(2) provides the right to English instruction in Québec or French instruction elsewhere for a child when he or she or one of his or her siblings has been or is being educated at either the elementary or secondary level in Canada in the minority language in question. In the Québec context, this clause covers the cases of children whose parents were not educated in English in Canada but where one of the children of that family is or was educated in English in Canada. Like the preceding sub-section, this right is also now included in Bill 101 (s. 73(2)).

23(3): Instruction & Facilities Where Numbers Warrant

Sub-section 23(3) limits the rights granted above to situations "where numbers warrant." In other words, citizens have a right to minority language instruction for their children if they meet one of the criteria spelled out above (mother tongue of parent, language of instruction of parent in Canada, or language of instruction of child or sibling in Canada) *and* where there is a sufficient number of children who so qualify to warrant the actual provision of minority language instruction.

Sub-section 23(3) is divided into two parts. The first sub-section - 23(3)(a) - refers to the provision of minority language instruction *per se*. In other words, are there enough children in a given locality to justify opening classes in the minority language for them? The second sub-section - 23(3)(b) - refers to the provision of minority language facilities. In other words, are there enough children in a given locality to justify distinct facilities for minority language classes?

This division into two parts indicates that the drafters of the *Canadian Charter* foresaw that there might be situations where the number of qualified students justified the provision of minority language instruction but not the provision of distinct facilities, which presumably would require a higher number of qualified students. If section 23 were part of an ordinary statute, such as the *Education Act*, one might expect guidelines about the numbers that would justify respectively instruction and facilities. However, section 23 is part of the Constitution and not a statute and therefore there are no such regulations. Consequently, it is up the courts to decide what numbers warrant instruction or facilities and under what conditions. As we see in the discussion that follows, the courts have done just that.

The Supreme Court of Canada Interprets Section 23(3)

The Supreme Court of Canada has had two occasions to interpret section 23(3). The first case (*Mahé* v. *Alberta*, 1990) was launched by Francophone parents in Alberta who were seeking minority language instruction and facilities in Edmonton. Unsuccessful in the lower courts, they appealed to the Supreme Court of Canada which reversed the lower court rulings. The second case (*Reference Re Public Schools Act (Man.)*, 1993), arose when the Government of Manitoba decided to refer several constitutional questions to the Manitoba Court of Appeal concerning the validity of provisions of the Manitoba *Public Schools Act* respecting minority language of instruction. The Court of Appeal ruling (which was handed down before the Supreme Court decision in *Mahé*) was appealed, in part, to the Supreme Court of Canada.

Mahé v. Alberta

The Supreme Court grounded its analysis of section 23 of the *Canadian Charter* in the following general comments (pp. 82, 83):

> The general purpose of s. 23 is clear: it is to preserve and promote the two officials languages of Canada, and their respective cultures, by ensuring that each language flourishes, as far as possible, in provinces where it is not spoken by the majority of the population. The section aims at achieving this goal by granting minority language educational rights to minority language parents throughout Canada
> ....
> In addition, it is worth noting that minority schools themselves provide community centres where the promotion and preservation of minority language culture can occur; they provide needed locations where the minority community can meet and facilities which they can use to express their culture.
> A further important aspect of the purpose of s. 23 is the role of the section as a *remedial* provision. It was designed to remedy an existing problem in Canada, and hence to alter the status quo.

The principal issue addressed by the Court was the degree of "management and control" over minority language instruction which is protected by section 23. The need for clarification arose not just from the facts of the case in question but from the very language of section 23 itself, namely the ambiguous caveat "where numbers warrant," in section 23(3) to determine entitlement to minority language instruction and to minority language facilities.

The Court observed that, in determining whether the numbers warrant, regard must be had not only to those requesting minority language instruction but also to those who could potentially take advantage of such instruction if it were offered (p. 98). It interpreted section 23(3) in terms of a sliding scale of entitlement. At one extreme, where there are very few minority language children requesting instruction, there might be no entitlement at all. At the other end of the continuum, there might be enough children to justify the establishment of a separate Francophone school board. In between these two end-points, there could be a variety of situations justifying increasing degrees of management and control. While recognizing that historically, separate or denominational boards have been the preferred means to grant the minority the fullest measure of representation and control, the Court made the following statement (pp. 92-93):

> Perhaps the most important point to stress is that completely separate school boards are not necessarily the best means of fulfilling the purpose of s. 23. What is essential, however, is that the minority language group have control over those aspects of education which pertain to or have an effect upon their language and culture. This degree of control can be achieved to a substantial extent by guaranteeing representation of the minority on a shared school board and by giving these representatives exclusive control over all of the aspects of minority education which pertain to linguistic and cultural concerns.

The Court then suggested certain aspects of education over which the minority should have control; these aspects included (p. 94):

(a) expenditures of funds provided for minority language instruction and facilities; (b) appointment and direction of those responsible for the administration of such instruction and facilities; (c) establishment of programs of instruction; (d) recruitment and assignment of teachers and other personnel; and (e) making of agreements for education and services for minority language pupils.

However, the Court did not attempt to define the specific modalities that would apply in any province nor how the Government of Alberta should comply with the ruling, namely to provide the parents in question with an appropriate degree of management and control. As it stated, for courts to impose "a specific form of educational system in the multitude of different circumstances which exist across Canada would be unrealistic and self-defeating" (p. 93).

Reference re Manitoba Public Schools Act

In this case, the Supreme Court was concerned with clarifying some aspects of the *Mahé* decision and in reversing those aspects of the Manitoba Court of Appeal judgment that were inconsistent with *Mahé*. The first specific question addressed by the Court was whether section 23 required the provision of minority instruction in "distinct physical settings." The Court answered the question in the affirmative but because the case was not based on a factual situation (as in *Mahé*), it could only set forth general principles of application (pp. 734-735):

> Therefore, while I [Lamer C.J. who delivered the Court's judgement] endorse a general right to distinct physical settings as an integral aspect of the provision of educational services, it is not necessary to elaborate at this point what might satisfy this requirement in a given situation. Pedagogical and financial considerations would both play a role in determining what is required. Obviously the financial impact of the provision of specific facilities will vary from region to region. It follows that the assessment of what will constitute appropriate facilities should only be undertaken on the basis of a distinct geographic unit within the province.

The Court, after determining that the Manitoba *Public Schools Act* did not respect section 23 rights, ordered the Government of Manitoba to "put into place a regime and a system which permit the Francophone minority to exercise its rights effectively, taking into account the general requirements spelled out ... in the *Mahé* case" (p. 741). It further held that at a minimum there were at least some areas of the province where the number of students would warrant a separate French-language school board. However, the details of the legislative scheme to be adopted were another matter.

The Court repeated what it had stated in *Mahé*: that it was up to government, not the courts, to determine how to discharge the obligations under section 23, and that it must do so without delay. (The Court also noted that to date the Government of Alberta had failed to so and that it must cease to procrastinate). It added this further *guideline* respecting any legislative scheme adopted (p. 739):

> Arrangements and structures which are prejudicial, hamper, or simply not responsive to the needs of the minority, are to be avoided and measures which encourage the development and use of minority language facilities should be considered and implemented.

As the Court observed in this case and in others, language rights are the result of political compromise, by contrast to "legal rights," which are based on the legal recognition of *inherent* fundamental rights. As a result, "the courts should pause before they decide to act as instruments of change with respect to language rights .... the courts should approach them with more restraint than they would in construing legal rights" (pp. 851-852). Accordingly, although section 23 provides for important rights to the official linguistic minorities in Canada, it appears that provincial governments will be granted a large amount of discretion in putting these rights into practice.

Language Rights in Québec

As mentioned briefly above, Bill 101 was the third attempt in eight years (1969-1977) of a provincial government to provide a legislative framework for, among others issues, the language of instruction.

Bill 101 has now been in force for more than 20 years and although several amendments have been made during this time, the legislation seems to be a permanent cornerstone of public policy in Québec, as reflected in the agencies created by the Act.

Official Language Agencies

Bill 101 provides for three public agencies: the Office de la langue française [OLF], the Commission de protection de la langue française and the Conseil de la langue française.

Office de la langue française

The OLF is a five-member agency, created "to define and conduct Québec policy on linguistics research and terminology and to see that the French language becomes, as soon as possible, the language of communication, work, commerce and business in the civil administration and business firms" (Bill 101, s. 100).

Commission de protection de la langue française

The Commission de protection de la langue française is a three-member agency; abolished in 1993, it was reestablished in 1997. "Charged with ensuring compliance" with Bill 101 (s. 157), it plays a key role as the Government "watchdog" over language.

Conseil de la langue française

The Conseil is an advisory body composed of 12 members from various designated groups. It advises the Government on language policy and the application of Bill 101 (s. 186).

The Fundamental Right to French Language Instruction

In any discussion about language and education in Québec, it is important to remember that Québec's Francophone population constitutes both a majority - inside Québec - and a minority - in Canada and, more generally, in North America. Studies done for the Gendron Commission in 1972 reported that by the late 1960's more than 90% of allophone students were attending English schools (Magnet, 1995). Given the experience of Francophones outside Québec in attempting to preserve their language and culture, it is understandable that Québec Francophones felt that they had to do something to prevent the decline of the French language here in Québec.

The basic education provisions of Bill 101 are:

Charter of the French Language

6. Every person eligible for instruction in Québec has a right to receive that instruction in French.

72. Instruction in the kindergarten classes and in the elementary and secondary schools shall be in French, except where this chapter allows otherwise.

This rule obtains in school bodies within the meaning of the Schedule and in private educational institutions accredited for purposes of subsidies under the Act respecting private education (chapter E-9.1) with respect to the educational services covered by an accreditation.

Nothing in this section shall preclude instruction in English to foster the learning thereof, in accordance with the formalities and on the conditions prescribed in the basic school regulations established by the Government under section 447 of the Education Act (R.S.Q., chapter I-13.3).

Second Language Instruction

The regulatory framework for curriculum and school organization provides second language instruction for both language groups (French and English) but treats each differently, as follows.

At the elementary level, French second language instruction is provided for both cycles of instruction, while English second language instruction is not permitted until second cycle unless authorized by the Minister; provision is made for French immersion but not for English immersion (El Reg, ss. 44, 46).* At the secondary level, the same number of credits is provided for each second language course (4 per grade level); once again, provision is made for French immersion but not for English immersion. In terms of graduation requirements, 4 credits of English second language instruction at the secondary IV level is required, while 4 credits of French second language instruction at the secondary V level is required to graduate (Sec Reg, ss. 35, 69; Youth Dir, s. 2.2). The French second language requirement is reinforced by a provision of Bill 101 (s. 84) that states that no secondary school leaving certificate may be issued to a student who does not have the speaking and writing knowledge of French required by the curriculum of the MEQ.

* *Note*. In practice, French second language begins in most if not all English schools in kindergarten and is a high priority in curriculum planning in the English language school system (Advisory Board on English Education, 1995). By contrast, given that the new policy on curriculum reform (MEQ, 1997c) suggests that English second language should begin in grade 3 indicates that it many schools this is not presently the case.

Entitlement to Minority Language Instruction

Given the constitutional division of powers described above, each province determines the entitlement to minority language instruction. Although such entitlement may not be less than that guaranteed by section 23 of the *Canadian Charter*, it may provide for enhanced accessibility. In Québec this entitlement is governed by Bill 101. Given the above general statement of language policy and rights, it should not be surprising that admissibility to English schools is considered as an exception to the general rule, and one that should be interpreted restrictively.

The Right to English Language Instruction

The key provisions of Bill 101 regarding the right to English language instruction are:

Charter of the French Language

73. The following children, at the request of one of their parents, may receive instruction in English:

(1) a child whose father or mother is a Canadian citizen and received elementary instruction in English in Canada, provided that that instruction constitutes the major part of the elementary instruction he or she received in Canada;

(2) a child whose father or mother is a Canadian citizen and who has received or is receiving elementary or secondary instruction in English in Canada, and the brothers and sisters of that child, provided that that instruction constitutes the major part of the elementary or secondary instruction received by the child in Canada;

(3) a child whose father and mother are not Canadian citizens, but whose father or mother received elementary instruction in English in Québec, provided that that instruction constitutes the major part of the elementary instruction he or she received in Québec;

(4) a child who, in his last year of school in Québec before 26 August 1977, was receiving instruction in English in a public kindergarten class or in an elementary or secondary school, and the brothers and sisters of that child;

(5) a child whose father or mother was residing in Québec on 26 August 1977 and had received elementary instruction in English outside Québec, provided that that instruction constitutes the major part of the elementary instruction he or she received outside Québec.

General Rules for Access to English Schools

As can be seen from the above extracts from the Act, the general rule is that the language of instruction shall be French, unless a specific exception applies (Bill 101, s. 72). Contrary to the language proficiency tests of Bill 22 (1974), exceptions in this Act are based on parental language or upon some particular circumstance (dealt with below). The most important exceptions are contained in section 73 of Bill 101, which was amended in 1993 to remedy some problems with the former text, including conflict with section 23 of the *Canadian Charter*. It identifies five situations where children are eligible for English language instruction:

- one parent who is a Canadian citizen and who received the majority of his or her elementary instruction in English in Canada (this clause covers the vast majority of exceptions and is now consistent with the provisions of the "Canada clause" in the *Canadian Charter* - see discussion below);

- one parent who is a Canadian citizen (regardless of his or her elementary language of instruction) and the child himself or herself received the majority of his or her elementary or secondary instruction in English in Canada - brothers and sisters of that child are also eligible;

- parents are not Canadian citizens, but one parent received the majority of his or her elementary instruction in English in Québec;

- the child was receiving English instruction before Bill 101 was adopted in 1977 - brothers and sisters of that child are also eligible (this was intended to make the transition to Bill 101 rules by ensuring that students who were attending English schools, whether or not they were eligible under Bill 22, and who would not be eligible under Bill 101, could continue in an English school);

- one parent who resided in Québec in 1977 and who received the majority of his or her elementary instruction in English outside Québec (another transitional clause to cover children not in an English school in 1977, but whose parents were educated in English in the United States or abroad).

Other Exceptions Permitting Access

There are several other exemptions provided for in Bill 101.

Children with Serious Learning Disabilities

Children with serious learning disabilities may be exempted from the requirement to attend French schools and, if they are, then their brothers and sisters may also be exempted (s. 81). There is a regulation (*Regulation Respecting the Exemption from the Application of the First Paragraph of Section 72 of the Charter of the French Language Which May be Granted to Children Having Serious Learning Disabilities* [*Learning Disabilities Exemption Regulation*]) defining which disabilities qualify for exemption under this clause that also mandates detailed identification procedures.

Temporary Residents

Temporary residents - up to three years - may be exempt from the requirement to attend French schools (ss. 85, 85.1). There is a regulation (*Regulation Respecting the Exemption From the Application of the First Paragraph of Section 72 of the Charter of the French Language That May be Granted to Children Staying in Québec Temporarily* [*Temporary Exemption Regulation*]) that defines the conditions and the procedures to be followed.

Reciprocity Agreements

The Act states (ss. 86, 86.1) that Québec may make reciprocity agreements with another province that provides instructional services in French which, in Québec's opinion, are comparable to the English instructional services offered in Québec. To date Québec recognizes New Brunswick as such a jurisdiction.*

* *Note.* This exemption is of less importance now because of the "Canada clause" in the *Canadian Charter* (see discussion above).

First Nations

The foregoing restrictions and exceptions governing eligibility for English instruction do not apply to students in the Cree School Board, the Katavik School Board or to the Naskapi of Schefferville (ss. 87-88).

Other Provisions

Among the other miscellaneous provisions of the Act, two in particular should be noted. First, the Act states that "no person may permit or tolerate a child's receiving instruction in English if he is ineligible therefor" (s. 78.1). Moreover, any person who is found guilty of committing such an offence is disqualified to serve as a school commissioner for a period of five years; if the person is an employee of a school body, he will be suspended for a period of six months without pay (ss. 208.1-208.2).* Second, the Act stipulates that a school body which does not presently offer instruction in English is not required to introduce it and in fact, may not introduce it unless the Minister gives his or her approval (s. 79).

* *Note.* For many years, there were a number of *illegal* students receiving instruction in English schools, that is students, who were not formally registered because they were not eligible for English instruction. A general amnesty was eventually granted to these students as a *quid pro quo* for a cessation of this practice (see *Act Respecting the Eligibility of Certain Children for Instruction in English,* 1986). The above described provision of the Act regarding penalties was introduced to provide a powerful disincentive to this practice ever being resumed.

Certificate of Eligibility

In order to benefit from the right to English instruction a parent must obtain a certificate of eligibility in accordance with a regulation (*Regulation Respecting Requests to Receive Instruction in English*). In brief, the applicant must provide proof that the child qualifies under one of the above "exceptions" for admissibility to English schooling. The process is sometimes straightforward but not when proof of a parent's elementary schooling in English is difficult to provide.

There is one other detail about these provisions that warrants a brief comment. Section 76.1 of Bill 101 stipulates that children declared eligible for English instruction are "deemed to have received their instruction in English" even if they were educated in French.* This means that in the future, children of these children will be eligible to receive instruction in English. In other words, the eligibility of the next generation is based on the parent's eligibility rather than on the language of instruction actually taken.

* *Note.* For purposes of interpreting this provision, it should be noted that French immersion programs are considered part of English language schooling by the Québec government.

Appeals Committee

The Act provides for a three-member Appeals Committee to adjudicate appeals regarding admissibility to English schools. The decision of the Committee is final and binding; however, the Act contains the following proviso (s. 85.1):

Charter of the French Language

85.1 Where the appeals committee cannot allow an appeal ... but deems that proof of the existence of a serious situation has been made on family or humanitarian grounds, it shall make a report to the Minister of Education and transmit the file to him.

The Minister may certify eligible for instruction in English a child whose file is transmitted to him by an appeals committee under the first paragraph.

Eligibility for English Instruction in Light of Section 23

Québec meets its constitutional obligations regarding entitlement to minority language instruction, with the obvious caveat that section 23(1)(a) of the *Canadian Charter* - entitlement on the basis of "first language learned and still understood" - does not apply in Québec. However, as stated by Foster and Smith (1997a, p. 17):

> The remedy lies with the Québec Government, as only its approval can remove the exclusion. But one must not forget that the exclusion originated not with the Québec Government and not even from a compromise reached between Ottawa and Québec, but from the Federal Government which put forth the Constitution with such exclusion.

Despite this serious "gap" in minority language rights in Québec, in other ways, Québec provides broader access to minority language education in comparison to a number of other provinces. First, in most jurisdictions in Canada, eligibility for minority language instruction is limited to those who have entitlement under section 23, while Québec admits children with severe learning disabilities and children of temporary residents. Second, entitlement in Québec is not limited to cases where "numbers warrant" as provided for in section 23(3)(a), whereas most provinces include a "numbers warrant" limitation in their legislation. However, Québec compares unfavourably with at least four provinces which leave the matter of admission of the children of non-section 23 parents to minority language instruction to local school board discretion (Smith & Foster, 1997b).

Management & Control of Minority Language Institutions

As recognized by section 23, the "second tier" of minority language education rights is concerned with the establishment, management and control of minority language facilities.

Language-Based School Boards

As discussed in chapter 6, the restructuring of education in Québec was based on the creation of two language-based networks of school boards. For the first time in the history of education in Québec, the English language minority has its own public school boards. The importance of this policy for English education cannot be overestimated.

While it is true that the Protestant school system traditionally served as a proxy structure for English education in many parts of the province, the original nexus between Protestant education and English education has decreased markedly over the years. First, in recent years Francophones had become a significant percentage of the student population in several Protestant boards. Second, the English Catholic population never had their own school boards, and with few exceptions, did not even have "minority language structures" within the Catholic school boards.

The creation of this new system did not come, however, without certain "birthing pains," notably with respect to the definition of electors.

School Board Electors

It will be recalled from chapter 6 that school boards are governed by school commissioners, most of whom are elected in accordance with the *School Elections Act*. The original version of the *Linguistic School Boards Act* (1997) amended the *School Elections Act* by restricting electors in the Anglophone boards to persons who qualified for admission to English schooling under Bill 101 or whose children so qualified. After considerable opposition from the Anglophone community, the final version of the *Linguistic School Boards Act* removed the Bill 101 criterion but the law still did not leave the two school systems on an equal footing (see chap. 6). Furthermore, the need to assure Francophone nationalists that Bill 101 was not affected led to the inclusion of the following statement in the *School Elections Act* (s. 1.1):

School Elections Act

1.1 The integration of immigrants into the French-speaking community being a priority for Québec society, this Act shall not operate
    (1) to amend, directly or indirectly, the provisions of the Charter of the French Language ...
        relating to the language of instruction;
    (2) to modify or confer any minority language educational rights.
    More particularly, the fact that a person who does not have a child admitted to the educational services provided in schools of a school board chooses to vote at the election of the commissioners of an English language school board and pays school taxes to that school board, or runs for office within an English language school board, does not make the person, or the person's children, eligible to receive preschool, elementary or secondary instruction in English.

Arguably, this interpretative provision does not alter the substantive provisions of the Act, as it is better characterized as a political declaration rather than a juridical provision. However, its inclusion serves to demonstrate the centrality of Bill 101 in the determination of public policy, as much in relation to the Anglophone community, as the so-called Allophone community (see chap. 14).

Powers & Duties of School Boards

Educational structures can be thought of as an "organizational shell" in which those delegated authority can govern the unit in question (e.g. a school board). Unless those placed in charge are given some reasonable level of authority, then the structure becomes an "empty shell." Furthermore, the autonomy of such structures means little if they are, as one author puts it, "enmeshed in a regulatory swamp of rules and regulations" (Murphy, 1991, p. 41). Details about the duties and powers of school boards and schools have been dealt with earlier (see chaps. 6 & 7). Suffice it to say, for purposes of this discussion, that minority language school boards and schools have the same general powers and duties as the majority language Francophone school boards and schools.

Use of French in English Educational Institutions

In addition to specifying eligibility for English language instruction and the general scope of management and control which the English speaking community may exercise over its schools, Bill 101 also prescribes a number of areas in which French must be used in English language school boards, its schools and centres, notably with respect to administration and labour relations (see also chap. 6 & 7).

The Civil Administration

According to the Schedule of Bill 101, the *civil administration* consists of the Government and its departments, government agencies, municipal and school bodies, and health and social service institutions. School bodies are defined as school boards and the Conseil scolaire de l'Île de Montréal. It would appear that schools and centres are treated as "departments" of school boards (s. 29.1) and would be bound by any provisions governing school boards. As will be seen below, there are some provisions that appear to apply to all bodies falling under the civil administration, while school boards, their schools and centres may be exempt from certain ones. According to section 29.1, such exceptions are granted by the OLF upon the request of the school board for itself and those schools and centres of the board providing instruction in English. It is further assumed that all obligations that apply to schools and centres apply to their governing boards.

General Obligations: The following provisions apply, without exception to English language school boards or schools as part of the civil administration:

- The civil administration shall draw up and publish its texts and documents in French; this does not apply to relations outside Québec, publications in a non-French language news media, or communications with natural persons when the latter address it in a language other than French (s. 15).

- The civil administration shall use French in its written communications with other governments and artificial persons (s. 16).

- The notices of meeting, agendas and minutes of all deliberative assemblies in the civil administration shall be drawn up in French (s. 19).

- Contracts entered into by the civil administration shall be in French; however they may be in another language if contracted with a party outside Québec (s. 21).

Obligations and Exemptions: The following provisions apply as exceptions to English language school boards or schools.

- English language school boards and schools are exempt from the obligation to make knowledge of French a condition of appointment, transfer or promotion, provided that they have obtained OLF approval of their obligations to the public as per section 23 (s. 20).

- English language school boards and schools must ensure that any services not connected with teaching that it offers to the public are available in French, as must be their notices, communications and printed matter intended for the public. These measures, as well as criteria and procedures for verifying compliance, are subject to the approval of the OLF (s. 23).

- English language school boards and schools may erect signs and posters in English (or another language) and French provided that the French text predominates (s. 24).

- English language school boards and schools may use both French and English (or another language) in their names, internal communications and communications with each other; however, an individual employee may request a French version of a communication required in the exercise of his or her duties (s. 26).

- English language school boards and schools may use English in communications connected with teaching without having to use French at the same time (s. 28).

Labour Relations

Bill 101 states that the communications of all employers to staff and offers of employment must be made in French (s. 41). Positions which are advertised in a daily non-French newspaper must also be published in a daily French newspaper (s. 42). Collective agreements must be drafted in French (s. 43) but arbitration awards, either respecting a dispute or a grievance, must, at the request of one party, be translated into French or English at the parties' expense (s. 44). It is prohibited to dismiss, layoff, demote or transfer someone for the sole reason that he or she is "exclusively French speaking" or has "insufficient knowledge of a particular language other than French" (s. 45). Furthermore, an employer is prohibited from making a job dependent upon the knowledge of a language other than French, "unless the nature of the duties requires the knowledge of that other language." The burden of proof is on the employer and the OLF has the authority to settle any dispute (s. 46). Other provisions deal with related procedural matters (ss. 47-50), including the stipulation that "juridical acts, decisions and other documents not in conformity with this chapter are null" and not merely a technical defect (s. 48).

Management & Control in Light of Section 23

In terms of section 23 and the management and control of minority language facilities, the typical issue elsewhere in Canada is whether the minority language group will be granted its own school board versus control of minority language schools within a majority language school board. With the new restructuring in Québec, the issue does not even arise as the English language boards cover the entire territory of the province. Given the sparse Anglophone population in some parts of the province, this policy decision clearly goes beyond the "numbers warrant" platform as provided for in section 23(3)(b). However, as alluded to in the preceding paragraph, minority language structures only gain substance, and constitutional validity, if the minority linguistic group is given significant authority and control over minority language instruction. In fact, it is this substantial authority that flows from section 23, rather than any particular structure such as school boards.* On the basis of the still emerging case law on section 23, one can assume that the delegation of powers to school boards and schools in Québec would meet any challenge mounted on the basis of section 23.

* *Note.* Thus, for example, although Francophones in New Brunswick did not contest the abolition of school boards, they are claiming that the powers of the new provincial boards of education which are to be exercised jointly with the Minister, deprive them of effective management and control of their own schools.

Rights in Conflict

Although the use of parental language of instruction is arguably less complicated than the language proficiency tests of Bill 22, there are many cases reported where parents encounter serious problems in producing sufficient evidence of their elementary education. Moreover, there are cases which raise questions about the way that the language of instruction provisions of Bill 101 are administered.

It is difficult to assess the scope of such problems as the decisions of the appeal commission are not published. However, one can gain some insight into the nature of the process of those decisions which are appealed to the Superior Court, whose decisions are of course public, as illustrated by the following case: *Smith* v. *Québec (Minister of Education)* (1998).

Smith v. Québec

The applicant was an American citizen, who was the father of a child living in Québec with his Québecoise Francophone mother. At the time of the divorce, the parents had agreed to give their son education in English in order to enable him to communicate with his unilingual father. The MEQ ruled that the child was inadmissible to education in the English language and that decision was appealed.

The appeal committee did not find that the child was admissible by any of the criteria stipulated in Bill 101; however, it determined that in light of the facts, there was a serious familial and humanitarian problem. Accordingly, the committee referred the matter to the Minister who has discretionary authority to declare the child admissible (s. 85.1, see above).

The Minister refused the appeal, indicating in her decision that the son of the applicant was not subject to any prejudice because he attended a French school but because he could not communicate with his father in English. The father then sought judicial review of this decision.

The Court found that the Minister's decision was manifestly unreasonable and declared the child eligible for English instruction. Noting that the discretionary power of the Minister is not absolute, the Court held that the Minister's refusal to recognize the relation between the prejudice done to the child and forcing the child to attend a French school were illogical and unfounded. The Minister was found not to have adequately considered the applicable criteria, including the rights of the child and his "best interests." It was further held that the Minister should not dismiss the committee's findings of fact without good and compelling reason.

CHAPTER 14
MULTICULTURALISM, INTERCULTURALISM AND EDUCATION

Introduction

This final chapter of our study is devoted to multiculturalism, interculturalism and education policy in Québec. Many of the issues we will discuss in this brief overview are linked to issues discussed in previous chapters. For example, Chapter 4 on students with special needs deals with another "dilemma of difference," to use Minow's (1990) phrase. Issues of religion and language cannot be disassociated from a consideration of culture Responding to diversity is a major issue in social policy generally and in educational policy in particular. Public schools have a unique opportunity to impact on the way our society will develop. They can promote the culture of the dominant majority while devaluing the culture of other groups, or they can promote the development of a society where all cultures are valued. The extent to which schools move in one direction or the other will profoundly affect the future of our society.

Many jurisdictions, especially those in North America and Western Europe must develop social policies to deal with increasing diversity in their populations. In Canada, multiculturalism has evolved to respond to the increasing ethnic and cultural diversity of the country. In contrast to Canada's policy of multiculturalism, Québec has developed its own policy of interculturalism where cultural diversity is accepted in a context where the French language becomes the medium of "cultural convergence." Important as language is, cultural diversity cannot be adequately dealt with on this basis. Montréal, as well as other urban centres in Québec, is made up of an increasingly diverse population. How well we respond to this new cultural diversity in schools will determine not only the success of the education system but of Québec society itself.

Background

Multiculturalism in the Canadian context is often discussed in relation to three major groups: aboriginal or First Nations peoples, the founding or *charter* groups - English and French - and ethnic or cultural minorities. The history of multiculturalism in Canada can be seen as attempts to reconcile the different perspectives on nationhood and culture of these three major groups.

In the early 1960's, there was growing dissatisfaction with the essentially Anglo-centric character of Canada's political, economic and social institutions. Although much of the discontent came from Québec, First Nations and various ethnic groups were also demanding change. In 1963, the Federal Government appointed the Royal Commission on Bilingualism and Biculturalism [B & B Commission] which led eventually to the federal policy of "multiculturalism within a bilingual framework." Regardless of its other attributes, the policy was clearly an attempt to reconcile two competing visions of Canada. In 1988, Canada became the first country in the world to adopt a national multiculturalism law (the *Canadian Multiculturalism Act*) and federal policy in this domain that has continued to this day. As will be discussed below, Québec policy in this domain has developed in part as a reaction to federal multiculturalism.

In 1981, the ministère des Communautés culturelles et de l'Immigration [MCCI] published a plan of action respecting cultural communities entitled, *Autant de façons d'être Québécois*. This plan of action speaks of the close connection between language and culture and coined a new phrase to describe the vision of the Government - *cultural convergence* (*la culture de convergence*) (p. 12):

> The development of various Québec cultural groups shall occur through the collective vitality of the French society which constitutes Québec .... We will no longer be confronted with the juxtaposition of cultural traditions but rather with the convergence of efforts toward the realization of a collective cultural project.

In 1984, the MEQ struck a committee to examine education and cultural communities. The committee report (Comité sur l'école québécoise et les communautés culturelles, 1985a, 1985b), usually referred to as the Chancy report after its chairperson, contains several recommendations which the MEQ accepted as the basis for further policy development. In this report the above mentioned government policy on cultural development, is summarized as follows (p. 1, free translation):

> [The government] vigorously affirms the primacy of the French language in Québec and defines its orientations of a social contract as one where Anglophones and other cultural communities are invited to accept their responsibilities in the development of Québec culture and in the establishment of the French language. At the same time, the Government promises to respect minorities, contribute to their development and foster their contribution to French culture. In the same light, the Québec policy on cultural development affirms that it is not assimilative but welcoming of the contributions of these minority groups.

This policy orientation has remained unchanged to the present.

Multiculturalism, Pluralism & Diversity

The division of humankind into races* is a relatively new phenomenon. Anthropologists in the eighteenth and nineteenth centuries began to study supposed differences among peoples of the world, differences which they understood as inherent and immutable. Today, the study of genetics has led to a repudiation of these ideas and a shift from a preoccupation with racial differences to a new interest in the biological affinities among human populations (Kallen, 1982). Unfortunately, the older ideas about race, which were created from an ethnocentric European-Christian perspective, are still with us. As Kallen (1982) puts it: "Such ideas became embodied in political ideologies of White Supremacy and thus gave rise to what we refer to as modern, *pseudoscientific* racism" (p. 4).

Note: Race is a socially defined category that classifies groups of people into a typology on the basis of ancestry or descent, in addition to certain physical or biological characteristics such as skin colour or facial features.

Overview

Multiculturalism is an eclectic term based on a belief in pluralism, that is the coexistence of various cultural groups, values and perspectives, as opposed to ethnic or cultural hegemony, which is based solely on the values and perspectives of the dominant group. It is a concept that recognizes the existence of diversity, upholds its benefits to society, and acknowledges the contributions of minorities to the social and cultural order. Hazard and Stent (cited in McAndrew, 1991, p. 131) explain cultural pluralism thus:

> Cultural pluralism ... is a posture which maintains that there is more than one legitimate way of being human without paying the penalties of second class citizenship ... social justice, alone, means a fair share of the pie; as a goal ... it has usually meant an assimilative attitude. Cultural pluralism ... demands the same fair share plus the right not to assimilate.

Some definitions of multiculturalism have led to a rejection of the concept, just as the term "equality" has been judged inadequate as a way of dealing with a variety of equity concerns (Ghosh, 1996). Like equality, however, multiculturalism continues to be an almost universal term for dealing with cultural pluralism.

Minorities Defined by Majorities

Minorities are not natural entities; they are categories that are socially created, usually by majorities - the dominant group in a society. Majority/minority relations are typically based on disparities of political, economic and social power. Kallen (1989) captures the essence of this relationship in her definitions of minority and majority groups. The concept "minority" refers to any social category within a society:

- that is set apart and defined by the majority as incompetent/inferior or abnormal/dangerous on the basis of presumed physical, cultural, and/or behavioural differences from majority norms;

- that is categorically and systemically discriminated against by majority authorities and is thereby subject to some degree of oppression (denial of political rights), neglect (denial of economic rights), and/or diminution (denial of social rights/human dignity);

- that, as a consequence of the self-fulfilling prophecy of systemic or structural discrimination, comes to occupy a socially subordinate, disadvantaged, and stigmatized position within the society.

The concept "majority" refers to any social category within a society:

- that has the recognized power (or authority) to define itself as normal and superior and to define all minorities presumed to deviate from its physical, cultural and behavioural norms as abnormal and/or inferior;

- that has the power to rationalize violations of minority rights through the use of invalidation mythologies (e.g. handicapism, heterosexism, and ageism) that draw upon prevailing public prejudice in order to create "evidence" for the inherent inferiority and/or dangerousness of minority stigmata;

- that has the power to impose its will, norms, and laws on society at large and to deny/suppress the expression of alternate, minority ideas and life-styles;

- that exercises the greatest degree of political, economic, and social power in the society and is thereby able to control the life-destinies of minorities.

The Dilemma of Difference

Diversity is all about difference - different cultures, religions, abilities, interests, etc. - and the way we respond to these differences. Traditionally, some people or groups have been labelled as *different*. This practice has typically been carried out by majorities labelling minorities. Once again, the majority decides what is *normal* by reference to its characteristics and therefore anything different from these characteristics becomes *abnormal*. Minow (1990) argues that we should understand difference, not on the basis of the majority group but on the basis of the relationship between groups.

Referring to bilingual programs which pull minority language students out from the mainstream and special education programs which integrate students with disabilities into the American mainstream, Minow (1990, p. 20) describes these opposing practices in terms of the "dilemma of difference:"

> With both bilingual and special education, schools struggle to deal with children defined as "different" without stigmatizing them. Both programs raise the same question: when does treating people differently emphasize their differences and stigmatize and hinder them on that basis? and when does treating people the same become insensitive to their difference and likely to stigmatize and hinder them on that basis?
>
> I call this question the "dilemma of difference." The stigma of difference may be recreated both by

ignoring and by focusing on it. Decisions about education, employment, benefits and other opportunities in society should not turn an individual's ethnicity, disability, race, gender, religion, or membership in any other group about which some have deprecating or hostile attitudes. Yet refusing to acknowledge these differences may make them continue to matter in a world constructed with some groups, but not others, in mind. The problems of inequality can be exacerbated both by treating members of minority groups the same as members of the majority and by treating the two groups differently.

Multiculturalism in Canada

In contrast to the image of the United States as a cultural *melting pot*, Canada has traditionally been depicted as a cultural *mosaic*. Popularized by the Canadian sociologist John Porter, the term *vertical mosaic* was meant to convey a social hierarchy where certain groups were valued and prospered accordingly, while others were devalued and received relatively less in terms of power, wealth and resources. For some, the *mosaic* metaphor trivializes ethnic diversity and should be discarded. By contrast, Fleras and Elliott (1992) talk about the *new mosaic* which recognizes "diversity as an integral and legitimate component of Canadian society, ... [and which] acknowledges a new multicultural agenda based on social equity, antiracism, and institutional change" (p. 317). In 1984, the Canadian Council for Multicultural and Intercultural Education adopted the following statement describing multiculturalism (cited in McLeod, 1993):

MULTICULTURALISM

Multiculturalism fosters a society and a Canadian identity in which people and groups of all cultures are accepted. Multiculturalism promotes human and group relations in which ethnic, racial, religious, and linguistic similarities and differences are valued and respected.

The principle tenets that are inherent in Multiculturalism are:

- equality of status of all cultural and ethnic groups within the framework of our officially bilingual country;
- the freedom of all individuals and groups to the retention and development of their cultures as part of the Canadian identity;
- equality of access by all individuals and groups to employment and promotion, services and support;
- a commitment to sharing our cultures within the mainstream of Canadian society;
- an undertaking to participate in Canadian citizenship and the democratic process in terms of both rights and responsibilities;
- a belief that individuals have the freedom to choose the particular cultural attributes they prefer within the framework of our democratic principles;
- respect for and observance of human rights and civil liberties as exemplified in the Canadian Charter of Rights and Freedoms, the common law, and human rights codes.

Multiculturalism includes all Canadians
and is for all Canadians.

Canadian Charter

The *Canadian Charter* contains several interpretative clauses, most of which are designed to ensure that the *Charter* is not interpreted so as to abrogate other pre-existing rights, for example: the rule that the *Charter* "shall not be construed so as to abrogate or derogate from any aboriginal treaty, or other rights or freedoms that pertain to the aboriginal peoples of Canada ..." (s. 25). The *Charter* contains the following clause concerning multiculturalism:

Canadian Charter of Rights and Freedoms

27. This Charter shall be interpreted in a manner consistent with the preservation and enhancement of the multicultural heritage of Canadians.

Although this clause does not provide any substantive rights, such as the right to equal protection and benefit of the law, it does allow for an argument based on minority group culture to be made in court.

In Magnet's recent article on section 27, the author poses the rhetorical question: Should section 27 be taken seriously? (1996, p. 18-3). In contrast to an earlier dismissal of section 27 by Canada's pre-eminent constitutional authority, Peter Hogg, that section 27 "may prove to be more of a rhetorical flourish than an operative provision" (Hogg, 1982, p. 72), Magnet (1996) claims that the courts "have relied on section 27 to shape the meanings of fundamental freedoms and language rights [and] ... are seriously groping for ways to pour content into section 27" (p. 18-4). However, to date, the jurisprudence on the use of section 27 is sparse and not wholly coherent. For the moment at least, the jury is still out on whether Hogg's pessimism or Magnet's optimism will reflect the true utility of section 27.

Multiculturalism & Education

As alluded to in the introduction, schools are a critical forum for achieving the goals of multiculturalism. As stated by the B & B Commission: "The school is the basic agency for maintaining language and culture, and without its essential resource neither can remain strong" (1967/1984, p. 86). The CTF (1991-92, p. 126, section numbers and resolution dates omitted) supports this thrust as stated in this extract from its policy statement on multiculturalism:

> Multicultural education should be an integral part of the formal education program of every Canadian.
> The objectives of multicultural education should include:
> * the fostering and stimulation of an awareness and understanding of the cultural richness of Canada;
> * the promotion of respect for and observance of human and civil rights in Canada;
> * the enhancement, retention and development of a diversity of cultures.
>
> The principles which underlie the approach to multicultural education should be:
> * recognition of the right to retain one's culture;
> * recognition of the importance of multiculturalism;
> * opposition to any educational program, materials and/or teaching which promote or condone prejudice, discrimination, inter-group hatred or racism.

Québec Intercultural Policy & Education

Québec has rejected multiculturalism as official government policy and in its place, the government has developed a policy of *interculturalism*. This term, although apparently not officially defined, has come to mean the acceptance of cultural diversity in the context where the French language is the medium of "cultural convergence" between mainstream Francophone society and divers cultural communities. Thus, it claims to be neither the federal policy of multiculturalism where all cultures are equally valued or the American "melting pot" where all minority groups are expected to blend into the dominant culture and forfeit their identity. The reasons for developing this policy are briefly discussed below.

Reaction to Multiculturalism & Preoccupation with Language

If ethnic groups across Canada saw the B & B Commission report as an affront to their place in Canadian society, the Government of Québec saw federal multicultural policy as an affront to the special status of Québec and the delicate balance between the two charter groups. Multiculturalism was seen as an attempt to downgrade Québec's status from one of two cultural groups in Canada to one of many ethnic groups, in relation to the dominant Anglo-centric majority. Québec's response to the federal vision of multiculturalism was the creation of the policy of interculturalism defined above.

As seen in the earlier discussion of education and language (chap. 13), language has replaced religion in Québec as the dominant metaphor of culture. It should not be surprising, therefore, that Québec policy regarding ethnic and cultural minorities began, and continues, to be articulated in relation to the preservation and enhancement of Québecois culture by means of the French language. The interplay of Québec language and immigration/cultural communities policies creates a number of ironies, as stated by d'Anglejan and De Koninck (1991, p. 99, endnotes omitted):

> It is paradoxical that the language legislation, which was designed to bring about the integration of immigrants into the Francophone community as a means of combatting the demographic decline caused by the low birthrate, is responsible for bringing the Francophone community face to face with cultural pluralism.
>
> Historically, immigration, as well as the recognition accorded to cultural communities by the federal government's multiculturalism policies, have been viewed with suspicion by Francophones .... The demographic position of Francophones in Québec was sustained until the late 1950's by the group's unusually high birthrate. However, it is now apparent that, if Québec is to avoid a serious demographic decline in relation to the rest of Canada, it must both increase immigration and attempt to stem the out migration of Anglophones. Its cultural viability depends on the development of policies which can sustain the province's distinctive French identity while recognizing the contribution of other cultural communities.

Zinman (1991) points out the inherent ambivalence of Québec's intercultural policy, namely the desire to support minority cultural communities and their values and accord them equal status and respect, while at the same time subordinating these efforts to the promotion of the French language. As she puts it: "establishing the dominance of the French language and culture at the same time as establishing the place and position of various ethnocultural groups creates a situation that is full of difficulties and contradictions" (p. 69).

The Educational Challenges of Diversity

As in other important policy discussions, the Superior Council has reflected and provided its advice upon a broad range of issues relating to education and ethnic and cultural minorities. Their reports (CSE, 1979, 1983, 1987, 1993d) have emphasized the need to modify existing policies and create new ones, which would deal with the growing ethnic population in the school system, as set forth in one paper in this series (1987, p. 4):

> Québec culture, in the fullest and richest meaning of that word, is becoming pluralistic, as are the cultures of a growing number of societies ....
>
> There is little need to demonstrate at great length the importance of the educational challenges implied by this situation. The school can no more be considered a homogenous milieu than society itself. This is well known to those who have been calling upon schools and educators to become more sensitive to the diversity of situations, needs, and aspirations ....
>
> Religious and ethnic issues have often overshadowed other aspects of plurality which nonetheless have extremely important implications for Quebec's educative mission. The integration into the schools of disabled pupils, and of pupils experiencing adaptation or learning difficulties, represents only one element of diversity which schools must take into account. Others include the particular needs of gifted or talented students, and of those pupils who come from socio-economically disadvantaged areas. To the extent that the schools attempt to meet the needs of each pupil by individualizing the teaching and learning processes, they are increasingly confronted with the fact of diversity. Moreover, the complexity of the challenge increases with the diversity of situations. At the same time, we must continue our efforts to acknowledge and fully accept fundamental human differences - age, sexual

identity, etc. - which themselves imply a diversity of educational needs.

School & Interculturalism

Like any other educational policy, interculturalism only takes on real meaning at the level of the school, where children from various cultural communities are welcomed - or not - by their peers, teachers and other school personnel. For some, the diversity of the contemporary student population is a challenge, something positive to be embraced. Unfortunately for others, this diversity is seen as a problem. For example, Després-Poirier (1995) asserts that the integration of students from diverse cultural communities is viewed as increasingly problematic. She identifies five major problems (p. 261):

- the concentration of this clientele in Montréal schools, in some places as high as 95% of their student population;

- an increase in the seriousness of problems in French language acquisition and overall scholastic performance, the former particularly in schools of high ethnic density, the latter particularly in disadvantaged areas;

- the affective and social difficulties (*difficultés d'intégration psychosociale*) of certain students from cultural communities to integrate into Québec society;

- the use of English by some ethnic students to communicate among themselves creates tensions within the school, especially at the secondary level (reference is also made here to gang violence and inter-ethnic group rivalry);

- the slower rate of learning for all students and the deterioration in the quality of French language instruction and general scholastic performance of Francophone children in multi-ethnic classes.

Ghosh, Zinman and Talbani (1995) conducted a research project whose purpose was to inquire into the understanding and identification of issues and policies relating to the education of cultural communities in Québec by administrators. According to their analysis, although the school boards they studied had formal policies at the board level, there was very little enthusiasm for the support offered to the schools. Principals reported that support services were unevenly dispersed with too much at the top of the hierarchy, too much paper distribution and not enough practical advice or support at the school level. For the most part, they claim, schools continue to relegate intercultural education to the one day - or week, of multicultural "food and fair."

A recent initiative in intercultural education worthy of note is the Centre for Intercultural Education and International Understanding's [CEICI] global education project and peer coaching professional development model. CEICI is a partnership of people and organizations from the Québec education system organized into six regional networks throughout the province. Its objective is to promote awareness of, and commitment to, international awareness among teachers and other school personnel in order to infuse teaching practices with themes of global education. This is done primarily by training "multipliers" (all volunteers – teachers, school board personnel, etc.) in the educational milieu, who share expertise, skills and knowledge, thus creating bonds among one another. CEICI organizes professional development workshops for teachers on citizenship education from a global perspective, anti-racism, human rights, intercultural education, etc., runs workshops on specific issues relating to global education, produces teaching guides and documents and has set up a specialized documentation centre. In the CEICI's view, one of the essential functions of a school is to help students "acquire the skills that will allow them to actively fulfill their role as citizens in a world characterized by global and local interdependencies" (CEICI, 1998, p. 1). To do this they must define common values based on common goals. In this approach CEICI is in accord with the goals put forward by the CSE in their recent report, *Éduquer à la citoyenneté* (1998b).

School boards in Montréal faced with increasing diversity in their student population have adopted policies for dealing with cultural diversity. In 1994, the PSBGM, following the report of a task force (PSBGM, 1988), adopted policies on multicultural/multi-racial education. This policy recognized "ethnic and cultural diversity...as a positive feature of Québec and Canadian societies" and stated that "It is the responsibility of the school system to provide such opportunities so that students may learn the attitudes and skills that will enable them to succeed and to participate as fully as possible in the larger Québec and Canadian societies." The aim was to have students develop a sense of belonging to Québec and Canadian society while retaining an appreciation of their heritage. The polices were to the implemented throughout the board.

School Choice

School choice is a theme that we have already seen in the discussions on student rights, students with special needs and religion (see chaps. 3, 4 & 12). As an educational policy issue, school choice is concerned with the right to decide which school students will attend. Generally speaking, this is an urban school issue, as school choice in rural settings is often a moot point - there is only one school in the community. Traditionally in Canada, school choice has been a school board prerogative, typically with schools serving a particular geographic area or mission. Thus, for example, many school boards will designate one school for students with special needs or centralize vocational programs in one school.

The issue of school choice is complex, as a policy designed to benefit one group can have adverse effects on other groups, as well as on the group which the policy was designed to help. In Québec, the MEQ funds several private schools whose clientele are members of particular cultural communities. These schools are classified as "associate schools," that is, they are attached to a public school board for funding purposes (Ed Act, s. 215). In this way, they receive the equivalent of public school funding, rather than the reduced amounts usually granted to recognized private schools. Many view this policy as an example of positive action toward minority groups that should be lauded. Others, however, point out that this policy tends to segregate these children, rather than encouraging them to integrate into mainstream schools.

Another, and far more troubling phenomenon, concerns the desire of some school officials in Montréal to segregate students on the basis of race and ethnicity. In 1990, the CÉCM proposed sending a questionnaire to parents which included a question about their preference regarding the segregation of students based on race and ethnicity. There was considerable opposition to the idea of such a policy and the question was withdrawn, but the attitude it represents has not disappeared. The CEQ and its local affiliate, Alliance des professeurs de Montréal, have advocated a 30% quota on the number of immigrants in French schools (Talbani, 1993). Similarly, in the discussion of the future linguistic school boards under Bill 107 (see *Historical Roots*, chap. 4), some people saw that the new French language board in Montréal would be composed largely of immigrants, while mainstream Francophones (*Québécois de vieille souche*) would remain in the CÉCM. It can be argued that this possibility explains in part the decision of the Government to seek a constitutional amendment before implementing linguistic school boards.*

* *Note*. The constitutional amendment obviated the continuation of the CÉCM as a parallel structure in addition to the new linguistic boards.

Ongoing Education Policy Initiatives

The restriction of access to English instruction based on parental language of instruction (Bill 101; see chap. 13) has caused a dramatic shift in the enrolment of the Allophone* student population. According to MEQ data (Latif, 1990, p. 18), in 1978-79, only 27% of the Allophone student population in public schools were enrolled in French schools; by 1989-90, this figure had risen to 71%. D'Anglejan and De Koninck (1992, p. 98) point out that even this virtual reversal of enrolment patterns underestimates the change in school demography:

> In terms of absolute numbers, these figures actually underestimate considerably the extent of pluralism in the schools since they do not include students who report English or French as their first language but who are members of cultural minority groups, for example, Haitians, English-speaking West Indians, and Jews. Nearly 95 percent of children from immigrant families attend schools in the Metropolitan Montreal area. It should be stressed that only a few years ago, schools where minority group children now represent a sizeable proportion of the school population, or even outnumber

Québec Francophones, were almost exclusively French and Catholic.

In keeping with the emphasis on language discussed above, many of the initiatives of the MEQ and the MCCI focus on language policy.

Note. Allophone is a term widely used in Québec to designate persons whose home language is neither French nor English

French Language Programs
The first set of initiatives are concerned with French language acquisition and include "welcoming" classes (*classes d'accueil*) at the kindergarten, elementary and secondary levels for the children of immigrants who are not eligible for instruction in English, "Francization" classes (*classes de francisation*) for other students needing intensive French language support, as well as other special measures to assist in integrating non-Francophones into French schools.

The Chancy report (1985b) describes these programs as a first stage of integration, *mechanical integration*. While recognizing that they have dealt with linguistic adaptation, the emphasis has been clearly one-sided: "the various remedial measures that schools have implemented should be interpreted more as a response to the problems posed by students than a desire on the part of the schools to adapt themselves to the needs of these children" (p. 24).

Heritage Language Programs
The MEQ supports a heritage language program (*programme d'enseignement des langues d'origine* [PELO]) in public schools. The MCCI also supports heritage language acquisition and maintenance through subsidies to cultural community based organizations (*programme des langues ethniques* [PLE]). According to Després-Poirier (1995), in 1994-95, 16 different language courses were offered as part of the PELO program. Heritage language maintenance is also supported by the funding of ethnic "associate schools" (see discussion above on school choice).

McAndrew (cited in d'Anglejan & De Koninck, 1992) notes that because of the language debate in Québec, many Allophones have been more concerned with access to English instruction than in heritage language programs. There is, however, increasing demand for these programs among more recently arrived immigrants. She also states that PELO is often promoted more in French schools as a means to encourage better transition to using French and integrating into the school community than in fostering cultural pluralism. Similarly, d'Anglejan and De Koninck (1992, p. 101) assert that "this program has met with mixed reaction from many non-PELO teachers and some members of the mainstream public who claim it will lead to ethnic ghettos and an inadequate mastery of French on the part of students."

Other Forms of Support
Finally, the MEQ maintains a unit within the ministry (Direction des services aux communautés culturelles) which provides support to schools concerning the education of students from diverse cultural communities. Staff from this unit produce didactic material for teachers and have played a role in ministry initiatives aimed at the elimination of discriminatory stereotypes in textbooks and other teaching materials.

Current Policy Review

Estates General

The interim report of the Commission of the Estates General (1996a) reported that participants drew attention to the needs of students from cultural communities. Echoing comments made above by Després-Poirier (1995), it questioned the capacity of the system to integrate these students successfully, especially in schools where the Allophone students had little contact with Francophone students and spoke English among themselves. The final report of the Commission (1996b) reflects the duality of Québec intercultural policy - integration of Allophones into mainstream Québec society and, in return, openness toward members of cultural communities (p. 12):

> Schools must play a role in promoting recognition of Québec as a predominantly French society, fostering better understanding of and respect for democratic institutions and creating harmonious relations among communities with a view to building a society in which all citizens participate. Such relations should be based on consensus, with immigrants agreeing to join and make a commitment to the host society, and the latter agreeing to assist and display openness toward immigrants.

The report also calls for a new policy statement clarifying the responsibilities of the school system with respect to interculturalism and the integration of immigrant students.

A School for the Future

In 1997, the MEQ released a policy proposal, entitled: *A School for the Future: Educational Integration and Intercultural Education* (MEQ, 1997f) under the joint sponsorship of the Minister of Education and the Minister of Relations with Citizens and Immigration. This proposal has been followed by a policy statement (MEQ, 1998b) and a separate plan of action (MEQ, 1998a).

Policy Statement
The policy statement has two principal thrusts:

- *Integration* - is defined as "a long-term multidimensional adaptation process, which is distinct from assimilation." Integration first means that immigrants must acquire a certain proficiency in French, the language of instruction and public life, and must "assimilate the social codes in order to establish meaningful relations with their classmates and participate in the life of the community." This aspect of policy is also billed as a "two-way street" which "demands openness to diversity and the application of appropriate policies by the social and educational milieu that receives them" (p. 1).

- *Intercultural Education* - refers to "any educational measure designed to foster awareness of the diversity - notably ethnocultural diversity - that characterizes the social fabric and to develop skill in communicating with people from various backgrounds, as well as attitudes of openness, tolerance and solidarity." Its aim is "to foster a better understanding of culture in a pluralistic society" (p. 2).

In addition to a brief chapter describing the diversity of the student population today, the paper contains three main chapters: principles for action; an overview of the current scene; and, general guidelines for implementation, as summarized below.

Principles for Action
Three broad principles are enunciated: promoting equality of opportunity; a command of French; and, education for citizenship in a democratic, pluralistic society.

Overview of the Current Scene
The policy paper provides an overview of the school system's efforts to date respecting integration and intercultural education, namely: success in school; acquisition of proficiency in French; intercultural education programs; and, the training of school staff.

Policy Guidelines
The policy statement proposes guidelines for future action, organized into two sections to correspond to the two themes of the paper, namely educational integration and intercultural education. These guidelines do not propose specific actions or strategies, but leave it up to the schools to choose the practices best suited to their needs.

Educational Integration

Three guidelines are proposed for preparing students for success and full participation in Québec society:

- use the regular class as the principal context for the integration of recently arrived immigrants;

- provide fast, effective help to recently arrived immigrants;

- recognize that the integration of immigrant students is a shared responsibility that requires the active collaboration of schools, families and community and make this a key part of the school's mission.

Intercultural Education

The remaining five guidelines focus on intercultural education and the need to learn to live together. The paper notes that this concerns all students in the school. Mastering French, learning about shared values and acquiring the skills to participate in a democratic, pluralistic society are the main goals for all students no matter what their origins. The guidelines proposed for achieving this are:

- recognize the ongoing nature of learning French, the language of public life;

- require the educational community to present French, the language of public life and the vehicle of Québec's cultural and intellectual life, in a positive light;

- provide a curriculum and school life that reflects the heritage and shared values of Québec and is open to ethnocultural, linguistic and religious diversity;

- train school staff to meet the educational challenges associated with Québec's ethnocultural diversity;

- ensure that the composition of the school's various groups of employees also reflects the ethnic and cultural diversity of Québec society.

The Plan of Action

The plan of action (MEQ, 1998b) linked to the policy statement is meant to indicate actions which all partners in the educational community can undertake cooperatively to achieve the goal of "ZERO EXCLUSION" identified by the ministers in their introduction. The plan lists five objectives along with eleven measures that can be used to achieve each of them. Some of these objectives and measures reflect the overall reform movement that has been happening in the education sector or are inspired by suggestions that resulted from the consultation process that followed the draft policy statement. The five objectives are: implement the policy statement in the schools; facilitate the integration of all newly arrived students into their school; learn how to live together in a Francophone society that is democratic and pluralistic; ensure that school staffs receive appropriate initial and on-going training and set up an exchange network to facilitate this; and to follow up and evaluate the success of the plan of action.

The measures that are to be used to achieve these objectives are identified and briefly discussed below. In most cases the means to implement the measures involve action on the part of the MEQ.

Measures to Achieve Objectives

The eleven measures to be implemented, along with the means to do so, are:

- inform all members of the educational community about the principles and guidelines of the policy statement and plan of action through wide distribution of the documents themselves as well as a leaflet summarizing them;

- support school boards, colleges and schools in developing internal policies and action plans to implement the guidelines by means of financial and technical support;

- ensure that models of intervention adapted to different milieus are developed and that responsibility for integrating new immigrants is shared within the school and greater educational community by means of both financial and organizational support from the MEQ;

- promote the educational success of newly arrived students who are behind in school through improved diagnostic and learning tools; provide support for pilot projects and heritage language programs to ensure that schools meet the needs of these students and support parents in their efforts to help their children;

- facilitate the learning of French, the shared public language, as an ongoing process through improved access to language learning programs adapted to the diverse needs of the school population and ensure coordination between programs;

- promote French as the shared public language and vehicle of culture by means of activities that will promote closer relations between the Francophone and non-Francophone communities and facilitate access to French cultural resources;

- familiarize students with the cultural heritage of Québec and promote the recognition of diversity and respect for democratic values by incorporating these values into course materials and other printed matter;

- ensure that ethnocultural diversity is represented in schools by promoting the teaching profession as a career choice among immigrant students and their parents and encourage the hiring and promotion of staff from different cultures;

- support staff through proper training by ensuring that universities provide both pre-service and in-service teachers with competencies in ethnocultural education and that professional development fosters awareness and management of diversity and that these objectives are part of the school's educational project;

- support staff through the creation of an exchange network through the use of information and communication technologies; and

- follow up the plan of action and evaluate the effectiveness of the measures and means used to achieve its objectives through statistical analysis and research on the education and integration of immigrant students on an annual basis and to adopt corrective measures where necessary.

An Open Question

Although the policy statement and plan of action reflect the policy duality suggested by the Estates General - integration of Allophones into mainstream Québec society and, in return, openness toward members of cultural communities, the leitmotif of these documents remains *cultural convergence* through the unifying medium of the French language (see *Historical Roots*, chap. 4). It remains to be seen whether cultural communities in Québec will judge these proposals positively or negatively in light of their views and aspirations. Similarly, it is still an open question whether school commissioners, governors, administrators and teachers will find therein an adequate response to the "challenges of pluralism," challenges that have become even more acute with the creation of linguistic school boards.

The Past as Prelude to the Present

Although the focus of this text has been on contemporary themes, we have been constantly reminded how these themes are interwoven with various traditions from the past. In the introductory chapter to this volume, we included a very brief historical sketch - 300 years in three paragraphs! The brevity of this treatment did not reflect the lack of importance of the evolution of the education system but the fact that it is treated in *Historical Roots*, a separate volume in this series. The image of education in the early days in New France was small, unorganized and, "above all, the work of the Church" (*Historical Roots*, p. 7). The arrival of the British in the middle of the eighteenth century added a layer to this system but did not otherwise fundamentally change it. The new layer was equally decentralized and church dominated; however, the church was Anglican and the language of instruction was English.

It was during this time that the Province laid the foundation for what was to become the defining characteristic of the Québec education system until the present time: a dual education system, one Catholic and predominantly French, the other Protestant and predominantly English. However, it was also at this time that the Government experimented with centralization versus decentralization and with the notion of a public non-sectarian school system, as articulated by the commission of inquiry on education in 1787 under the presidency of Chief Justice William Smith.

One hundred and eighty years later, the Parent Commission was established to help shape the modernization of the Québec education system. The Parent Commission and its five volume report (1963-1966) will be remembered for many things, including its ethos of equality of educational opportunity for all, the structural changes it promoted, especially the creation of the ministry of education as the driving force of the reform movement, and the reform of curriculum and school organization.

As we have seen throughout this volume, these historically based themes are still very much with us, reminding us that our understanding of the present begins with an understanding of the past.

Themes & Traditions

We have organized the material in this volume into five major themes: foundations of the system; governance of elementary-secondary education; curriculum and school organization; human and financial resources; and, the recurring policy themes of religion, language and diversity. In this final chapter, we will attempt to pull the threads of this thematic treatment of Québec education together and then conclude by examining two cross-cutting and opposing themes which will serve to distinguish the system which is emerging from the current reform from that which has characterized Québec education since the Quiet Revolution.

Foundations

The foundations of the education system can be found in the overall policy and governance framework and in the rights and obligations assigned to students in general and to students with special needs in particular. The foundation for an education system begins with a set of values and beliefs that the system is meant to promote. The values are not often stated in one document but emerge over time as the ethos of the system. In reflecting on what the core values of the system were, we concluded that they could be summed up by two guiding principles: respect for human rights and more specifically equal educational opportunity for all.

As Smith and Lusthaus (1994a) have stated: "The school is a microcosm of society, where we gain knowledge and skills and learn to get along together with each other" (p. 67). The public school is meant to be a place of learning for *all*, hence the principle of "universal access" that posits that no one should be denied a right to education. Much of this book has emphasized the importance of rights based on a belief in the normative framework of law to guide both individual and organizational behaviour. The importance of law is often ignored, or at least undervalued, by those whose situation does not require any special protection. As Asch (1989) states, speaking of the role of law for students with disabilities: "What the law is doing best today is giving ... disabled students something against which to measure what they have. Before ... they were there on others' sufferance. They got crumbs and were never given any reason to think they should have more" (p. 202).

In relation to our education system, these values have been embedded in the Constitution, specifically in the *Canadian Charter*, and in Québec legislation, notably the Québec *Charter* and the *Education Act*. Constitutionalized rights are usually stated in broad terms and the provisions of such documents are rarely amended. The evolution of such rights occurs by means of judicial decisions. Legislated rights, by contrast, tend to be more specific and are amended from time to time, sometimes in response to judicial decisions. The normal tendency is for rights to increase, the general policy question being at what rate and to what extent will this change occur. The general rights of students have changed little in recent years, which may signify nothing more than the maturity of the education system. However, the rights of students with special needs may actually have declined in this same period.

In 1991 and 1993, the Human Rights Tribunal handed down two landmark decisions (*St-Jean* and *Chauveau*); the former was upheld on appeal, the latter was reversed by the Québec Court of Appeal, leaving the law on the matter in a state of some confusion, which the Supreme Court of Canada chose not to address by refusing leave to appeal. This was clearly an invitation to the Government to amend the *Education Act* to clarify the rights of students with disabilities to an education in the same environment as their age-appropriate peers, as many other provinces have done (Smith & Foster, 1997a). However, no such change followed, until the recent reform of the governance provisions by the *Education Amendment Act* (1997). While the spotlight was on new structures and a redistribution of powers, changes were made to two key sections of the Act dealing with children with special needs (ss. 96.14, 235). As discussed in chapter 4, these changes create new conditions to be met before integration can occur and appear to reverse the burden of proof from one where the onus was on the school board or the school to demonstrate that integration was not appropriate to one where the onus is on the parent to show that integration is appropriate. Both the substance of these changes and the process that was followed to introduce them should send signals to (self) advocates of students with disabilities that the rights of these students appear to be as "at-risk" as they are themselves.

Governance

The theme of governance is obviously a major one at the present time. For thirty years, successive provincial governments have been attempting to restructure the education system on linguistic rather than denominational lines. Section 93 of the *Constitution Act, 1867* has generally been viewed as the stumbling block to this reform making it impossible to create these new structures without the continuation of some form of parallel denominational structures. In 1998-99, the change in school board structures came into being but it took a constitutional amendment to do it.

Constitutional amendments are never made lightly, especially when they deal with entrenched minority rights. Québec is the second province in Canada to amend the constitutional rights of Catholic and Protestants to denominational schooling, Newfoundland being the first. The experience in Newfoundland made two opposing "truths" obvious, namely on the one hand that a government that proposed such an amendment did so at its own risk and peril, and on the other hand, the time for such an amendment had arrived. Recognizing the importance of the issue, the Government of Newfoundland held a referendum which approved the proposed amendment by a slim margin. The amendment itself was a compromise between the denominational past and a secular future. As often happens with compromise texts, it neither protected the past nor permitted the future and was successfully challenged in court, leading to a second referendum and a new amendment. The Government of Québec, perhaps mindful of this experience, proposed an unequivocal amendment that simply abrogated the denominational guarantees of section 93. However, if the constitutional text was clear, the intent and implications of the proposed amendment were riddled with ambiguity.

As discussed in chapter 6, the agreement of the Federal Government to accede to the Québec request depended on a consensus within Québec in support of the amendment. The unanimous resolution of the National Assembly was taken as a first solid sign of this consensus, as was the thrust of the majority of presentations made before the Special Joint Committee of the House of Commons and the Senate. However, in addition to those who opposed the amendment outright, there were those whose support was conditional on the maintenance of denominational rights at the school level. The Minister made no commitment to the continuation of such rights and instead appointed a task force on religion and school as a harbinger of more changes to come, notably at the school level.

The restructuring of school boards was complemented by the redistribution of powers, notably from school boards to schools. School reform has long been on the policy agenda of successive governments; however, it has generally been eclipsed by school board reform talk. Although the new legislation is clearly attempting to devolve greater authority to the school level, there remains a number of areas that are still within the ambit of the province and school board. The authority of schools to set their own policy direction appears to be constrained by both provincial and school board authority. Second, the extent to which authority regarding curriculum and related matters have been decentralized remains somewhat ambiguous. Third, schools have been delegated almost no authority in relation to personnel matters. Finally and by contrast, school boards have been given significant control over budget and fundraising. The points of ambiguity and "lines of tension" in the new legislation need to be resolved, partially through legislative amendment but also through new modes of practice at the school and school board levels.

Curriculum & School Organization

As if major changes in governance were not enough to cope with, we have also seen that major changes in curriculum are also in progress. The MEQ policy paper on curriculum change, *Québec Schools on Course* (1997c), follows directly from the Inchauspé report (1997) which in turn picked up on many of the ideas of the earlier Corbo Task Force report (1994). The curriculum reform is meant to respond to criticisms of the Superior Council, the Estates General and others. Henchey (1999) lists five specific complaints:

- excessive detail in programs;
- too much centralization;
- too little opportunity for schools to adapt to local needs;
- too little rigor especially in basic literacy and numeracy;
- low rate of school retention, especially for males;
- mismatch between schooling and the labour market.

Henchey further suggests that the Québec curriculum reform is in line with similar endeavours elsewhere in Canada and in other industrialized nations.

On the face of the policy document, considerable change will occur both with respect to the content of the curriculum and the organization of service delivery. However, it is not always easy to ascertain the scope of the actual meaning of these changes. This is especially true when one considers the differences between the *intended* curriculum - as printed in government documents - and the *actual* curriculum, as delivered by teachers in school. Thus, for example, the policy document speaks of the need for schools to encourage cross-curricular learning. Bridging the gap between policy and practice respecting such an intent will not be a straightforward matter and will require the collaboration of teachers across individual disciplines, something that is never easy to achieve. The core of the policy is based on a shift from "teaching objectives" to "learning results." Making such a rhetorical shift is one thing, making an actual shift in classroom practice is quite another. At this point, there are more questions than answers and those posed by Henchey (1999, pp. 13-14) provide a broad canvas for further debate:

- Where are the resources (money and expertise) coming from to do all these things properly?
- Do principals want to be curriculum leaders?
- Are we obsessed with mathematics?
- Are English schools being driven by French-immersion priorities?
- Should culturally sensitive subjects be taught in English?
- Is it dangerous to link too closely citizenship education and history?
- Why is there so little emphasis on school-work transition (work-study programs, work experience, guidance, vocational courses, tech-prep, applied academics, etc.)?
- Why is there so little emphasis on technology (use of technology in teaching, broad-based technology courses)?
- Will technology education be the poor cousin of science?
- Should distance education courses be integrated into the new curriculum structures?
- How will the definition of teacher workload be affected? Are teachers spending too much time on classroom instruction?
- Are the current collective negotiations and evaluation discussions considering the curriculum reforms?
- To what extent (if at all) are these reforms being based on research or best practices outside Quebec?
- Given (a) new linguistic school boards, (b) governing boards, (c) teacher and administrative turnover, (d) budget constraints, (e) contract negotiations, (f) school closings, (g) concerns about confessional schools, and a few other things, how much attention will be given to curriculum reform?

In addition to the foregoing, English schools must deal with the perennial problems of lack of appropriate materials in English, provincial examinations translated from French - and often not well translated - based on French curriculum materials, and a general lack of resources to deal with these problems. Furthermore, it remains to be seen to what extent curriculum will be driven from the top or whether it will reflect a *modus operendi* more consistent with the new school-based reform of the education system.

Human & Financial Resources

Education is a human resource intensive endeavour and despite the time and energy devoted to structures, technology and materials, human interactions prevail as the core of the education system. Peter Coleman and his colleagues at Simon Fraser University have been exploring the triadic relationships among students, teachers and parents. On the basis of their "close-up" examination of this triad, the authors conclude as follows (Coleman, Collinge & Tabin, 1995, p. 171):

> Schools are most likely to be improved from the inside out. Changing triad relationships is the first and most essential step in school improvement. Approaches to instruction which treat the triad of teacher, parent, and student as the basic learning unit, are fundamental to classroom and hence to school productivity.

Similarly, our recent study of "student engagement" in learning and school life across Canada (Smith, et al., 1998) found that regardless of the school or provincial contexts, all students recognized and responded to fair, caring, respectful and supportive environments which were talked about by students in terms of their relationships, especially with teachers: "Indeed, most of the students in our study have reported that having the care, support, and respect of teachers is fundamental to having a positive school experience" (p. 116).

In keeping with this focus on human relationships, we devoted two chapters of Part IV to the management of human resources, with a particular emphasis on teachers. Across these two chapters we have dealt with the teacher as an *employee* and as a *professional*. The two roles are not necessarily contradictory, but nor are they always compatible. The centralization of collective bargaining gave teachers a forum for both the pursuit of better salary and working conditions and for influencing policy and the direction of the education system generally. Having noted the background of high levels of conflict in the bargaining process, we reported that the current round of negotiations is still in progress and it remains to be seen what new patterns might emerge, especially in light of the changes in the role of schools in the recent reform. In any event, one thing is clear. Teachers now have an important role to play at every level of the system. In addition to their traditional role in the classroom, they now sit on school governing boards, as well as on school board and provincial advisory committees. Teachers now have every opportunity to be shapers of policy rather than merely recipients of policy.

If students, teachers and parents form the key triadic relationship within the school, then arguably curriculum and school organization, human resources, and financial resources form the key triadic relationship at the policy level. All three are reflected in the concept of a budget, which begins with the educational program to be offered, and then adds the human and other resources required to deliver it and the cost of same. We have also seen that the system is undergoing significant change with respect to school level governance, including responsibility over budget. This will radically alter the role of both schools and school boards in the financial management process, the other major theme covered in Part IV. These new roles may require further changes in the other two domains mentioned above as it is likely that tensions, perhaps severe tensions, will arise where one body has responsibility for programmatic decisions, another for human resource decisions and a third for budget.

We have also noted the continuing reduction in government grants, not only by general compression but more specifically by the elimination of base funding for school administration, general administration and maintenance. The cumulative effect of these reductions has virtually changed the funding policy brought into force in 1980-81. The Government can no longer claim that it pays for the basic cost of education; local school taxes have increased approximately three fold since then but still these revenues do not appear to be enough to sustain educational services at present levels. The détente reached with the municipalities in 1979 has broken down and their opposition to any further increase in school board taxation is likely to be strongly asserted.

If the two main revenue streams of public education are incapable of generating sufficient funds to support public education, then either other sources of funding must be found or public education must necessarily decline. This raises the possibilities of user fees, fund raising or commercial involvement in education as alternative funding sources, a sad prognosis for the future of free pubic education.

Religion, Language & Diversity

Part V of this text was devoted to three overlapping policy themes: religion, language and diversity. Taken together they symbolize the nature of the education system and how it has evolved over the years. As alluded to at the beginning of this chapter, in the early days of the Québec education system, religion permeated every aspect of the school system. As Confederation approached, both Catholic and Protestant groups sought constitutional guarantees to protect the denominational character of public education, while, at the same time, the State sought to affirm its control over education. The compromise which resulted from these tensions over the "management and control" of schools was set forth in section 93 of the *Constitution Act, 1867*, as discussed above. No other provision in the Constitution mentioned religion, which proclaimed neither a union of Church and State, nor their separation as a general constitutional precept. However, if the mark of religion was a single one in section 93, it was a deep mark.

Better described as a "grandfather clause" than a declaration of rights, section 93 rights are "frozen in time;" only those recognized by law in 1867 are protected. Contrary to section 93, society cannot be frozen in time. Even in 1867, when section 93 was drafted, Québec society was changing. The construction of a minority rights framework on the basis of a Catholic-Protestant dichotomy, that is more aptly characterized as a French Catholic - English Protestant dichotomy, made no provision for that evolution. The situation changed rapidly with successive waves of immigration. In the Catholic system, one of the most important waves was the immigration of English-speaking Catholics from Ireland. By and large, other immigrant groups, beginning with a large number of Jewish immigrants from Eastern Europe, gravitated to the Protestant system. According to Milner (1986), the ultramontane leaders of the Catholic system sought to maintain French Catholic schools "as free as possible of any and all outside influences" (p. 16). Although immigrants were more generally welcomed in the Protestant sector, all did not go smoothly, as reflected in the famous case of *Hirsch* v. *Montreal Protestant School Commissioners* in 1928. This case arose over amendments to the *Education Act* which had been adopted in 1903 following a court ruling that held that the Protestant School Board of Montreal could not be compelled to admit Jewish children to its schools (*Pinsler* v. *Protestant Board of School Commissioners*, 1903). As stated by Henchey and Burgess (1987, pp. 26-27):

> The arrival of English-speaking Catholics from Ireland and of Jewish immigrants from continental Europe indicated that Québec's educational structures were not designed to easily adjust to pluralism. This problem was to intensify with the arrival of other immigrants of various ethnic and religious backgrounds in the period following the Second World War.

It is well known that this immigration did not abate but has increased markedly; unfortunately, we did not kept pace with these demographic and social changes which have only been addressed in recent years.

It was immigration and in particular the gravitation of most immigrant groups to the English school system that fanned the flames of French Canadian nationalism in the 1960s and 70s. Since that time language has supplanted religion as the dominant cultural icon in Québec. McAndrew (1991) notes that until 1977 more than 80% of Québec's students of ethnic origin did not attend French schools creating a communication gap that has only been confronted with the reversal of this trend by Bill 101. Characterizing the educational history of ethnic groups as one of isolationalism and prejudice, she states that "inter-cultural communication and education is now emerging as one of the main issues in Québec schools and society" (p. 138).

As in other important policy discussions, the CSE (1987) has reflected and provided its advice upon a broad range of issues relating to education and ethnic and cultural minorities. A series of reports have emphasized the need to modify existing policies and create new ones, which would deal with the growing ethnic population in the school system, as set forth in one paper in this series (p. 4):

> Québec culture, in the fullest and richest meaning of that word, is becoming pluralistic, as are the cultures of a growing number of societies....
>
> There is little need to demonstrate at great length the importance of the educational challenges implied by this situation. The school can no more be considered a homogeneous milieu than society itself. This is well known to those who have been calling upon schools and educators to become more sensitive to the diversity of situations, needs, and aspirations....

In between the mainstream Francophone community and the newer so called ethic or cultural (Allophone) communities, lies the Anglophone community. Part of the North American majority, it is a minority in Québec. The above mentioned restrictions on immigrant access to the English schools has resulted in a marked decline in the size of the English network of schools - almost 60% between 1972-73 and 1993-94, with two thirds of English schools enrolling fewer than 200 students and more than one-third enrolled fewer than 100 students (Advisory Board on English Education, 1994).

The entrenchment of minority language rights in the *Canadian Charter* and the subsequent admissibility to English schools of children whose parents were educated in English in Canada (*Canadian Charter*, s. 23(1)(b); Bill 101, s. 73(1)) has lessened this trend somewhat but not significantly. Pleas for the entry into force of section 23(1)(a) of the *Canadian Charter*, which would admit children of parents whose "first language learned and still understood" was English, have fallen on deaf ears and it seems unlikely that government policy will change in this regard in the foreseeable future. By contrast, the creation of linguistic school boards does give an unprecedented boost to English schooling in Québec.

Although the advent of English language school boards will not make any significant difference to enrolment, this policy change will permit the consolidation of existing English schools inside school board structures whose only vocation is English language education. Unfortunately, this consolidation is likely to involve the closure of some schools as some new English language school boards have inherited small adjacent schools from the previous Catholic and Protestant school boards. Although such closures may be inevitable due to continuing budgetary constraints, extreme care needs to be taken that all schools in this new system feel that they are being treated fairly in the process.

If many French language schools will face challenges brought on by increased Allophone student populations, English schools must confront the dilemma of preserving an English language school system and meeting increasing parental demand for enhanced French language instruction, usually in some form of immersion program (Advisory Board on English Education, 1995). The opportunity has been created for a revitalized English school system but many obstacles remain to be faced, not the least of which is deciding on the place of religion in schools, now that the report of the Task Force on the Place Religion in Schools (1999) has been tabled. The perennial issues of religion, language and diversity are not likely to disappear; the only question for policy makers, administrators and educators, is how well we will deal with them.

Centralization & Ongoing Reform

The *policy talk* on the devolution of authority to schools has included at least three principal strands. First, it has been part of a long standing debate over *centralization* versus *decentralization*. In 1959 on the eve of the Quiet Revolution, Joseph Pagé, then Secretary of the Catholic Committee, described the role of the State in education thus: "The State administers education but plays only a supplementary part. By laws and regulations, it ratifies and sanctions the will and wishes of the parents and the Church, according to the particular faith of the parents" (cited in Sissons, 1959 p. 129). In the decade that followed, the State became the driving force behind all aspects of education, as summarized by Henchey and Burgess (1987, pp. 193-194):

> Whereas education in Quebec was once the exclusive preserve of the Church and the school boards and with a relatively cohesive sense of purpose, it is now a multidimensional activity in which several different groups compete for power.... Since the Quiet Revolution there has been a marked increase in the power of the provincial government, especially that of the Ministry of Education, in the whole field of education in Quebec. The powers of the Ministry to govern by regulation have left their mark on virtually every aspect of the Quebec educational scene and have resulted in a distinct weakening of the power of school boards as well as of other intermediary bodies such as colleges and universities.

If we consider briefly the policy triad referred to above - curriculum and school organization, human resources, and financial resources, we see clearly how centralized the system has been. The content of curriculum has been decided by the Ministry, the service delivery system of this content has in theory been delegated to school boards but in reality there are so many parameters spelled out in the *Education Act*, the *Basic Regulations* and the annual directives, that little discretion is left to local authorities. The remuneration, benefits and major working conditions of administrative personnel are determined centrally, either by regulation or by collective bargaining. Although school boards play a part in this process, there is no doubt that on the management side the Government is the only dominant player. Collective bargaining also serves to place further constraints on school organization through various "normative" provisions in the provincially negotiated *Ententes*. The funding of education also became very centralized, with 92% of all revenues for elementary and secondary education coming from provincial government grants in the 1980s.

Against this centralized backdrop, there has been a great deal of policy *talk* about decentralization over the past twenty years. In 1978, the MEQ launched a major consultation on education, with the publication of *Primary and Secondary Education in Québec* [green paper], which eventually led to a policy paper *The Schools of Québec* (MEQ 1979a). Following up on an earlier paper and its susequent revision (MEQ, 1975, 1977), the green paper's presentation on governance was framed as a question: Centralization or decentralization? However, according to the statements in the paper, the question was largely rhetorical: "It is clear that there is a greater and greater demand for decentralization of the school system. The Government, for its part, has announced unequivocally that it intends to proceed with decentralization" (p. 114). The emphasis in this quotation ought, with the benefit of hindsight, to have been on the word "intends." The policy paper which followed (MEQ, 1979a) did not include anything on governance or management, subjects which were deferred until further discussions with the school boards. As we noted in *Historical Roots* (p. 72):

> With the exception of the first two introductory chapters, each chapter of the Plan of Action concluded with a set of actions to be taken, primarily by the government and the MEQ. If there is one unifying theme in all of these actions, it is the focus on the MEQ as the agent of change.... This centralizing tendency set the tone of the policy agenda for Québec education for the next decade and was not questioned by the MEQ until the next Plan of Action (MEQ, 1992c ...).

Traditionally this debate was between the Government and school boards, with schools being subsumed under the latter. In addition to the assignment of various administrative and pedagogical roles and responsibilities, this debate also involved the major issue of fiscal responsibility. Once again, traditionally, this translated into the extent to which revenues for education were to come from State grants or local taxes. Decentralization was also inextricably linked to the wider debate on school board reform and the restructuring of the education system along linguistic, rather than denominational lines.

Second, the delegation of authority to schools followed from the policy of granting voice to school communities, especially to parents and teachers. In terms of parental participation, Québec led the way in Canada with the creation of various local and school board level committees in the 1970s and strengthened by Bill 107 in 1988. Parental and community participation was advanced in another policy paper released in 1982, *The Québec School: a Responsible Force in the Community*. It was primarily concerned with the restructuring of the educational system to provide for a greater role of parents in a revitalized school which was to have greater autonomy and responsibility. The white paper was also a precursor to new legislation on school board structures which was domed to failure (see *Historical Roots*, chap. 4).

Third, and more recently, the devolution of authority to schools has been associated with calls for school improvement and enhanced student success, together with increased autonomy and accountability at the school level. As alluded to above, this most recent strand can be seen as part of the world wide phenomenon of restructuring, with a penchant for a school based approach.

Smith and Lusthaus (1994b) assert that the first strand above is part of an ongoing battle over school structures should be seen as an "old debate," one characterized by a "we-they" perspective, where different interest groups compete for power and control in a "zero sum" game. The second strand is probably best characterized as being part of this old debate in that the devolution of power to the school is seen simply as a pincer movement, whereby power that school boards feel should be vested in them is taken from the top by the Ministry and from the bottom by schools. On the other hand, the policy orientation of supporting parental participation and parent-teacher collaboration (in the school governing board for example) is reflective of what we have described as the "new debate," one with a "together we're better" perspective, where different partners in the education system work together in the pursuit of common goals. The third strand, if taken at face value, is definitely part of the new debate. The expectations for school-based reform identified by Murphy & Beck (1995) are summarized by Momii (1998, p. 6):

> The logic of school-based management is that through the formal change in decision making structure

via school-based management, real change will occur in the educational power structure with stakeholders having more influence on decisions made in schools. With this empowerment of stakeholders, there will be more widespread participation in the activities of the school thereby developing a sense of ownership among the stakeholders. Participation reduces alienation, and nurtures commitment to the decisions made in schools; this will lead to greater responsibility for the decisions made in schools. At the same time, participation in the decision making process may enhance teachers' sense of efficacy leading to better school performance. Finally, participatory decision making will improve organizational health, which can be measured by efficiency of the use of resources, responsiveness and goal attainment. This will eventually improve school performance.

There may be some who see this third strand - like the second - as a disguised version of the first, namely an attempt by the Government to reduce school board power by dividing local authority between school boards and schools and setting schools up to compete with each other rather than with the Government. To ascribe the current school reform solely to such a motive is probably an act of cynicism in the extreme. On the other hand to imagine that government motives are wholly altruistic would probably be naive in the extreme. Policy changes are usually the result of a combination of motives and often what counts in the end is not why changes were made but what opportunities they afford.

In the current Québec context, the reform represents a window of opportunity for positive change. For the English speaking community this means breaking down the barriers which have separated us in the past and building a common vision together, where the collective resources of the educational community can be used for common purposes, rather than for cross purposes. This new perspective begins with the mission or goals of the school and looks at how these objectives are being accomplished. Rather than asking, Who's in charge?, we ask, Does this work? As stated by Smith and Lusthaus (1994b, pp. 3, 4):

> The focus on learning in the new debate is not merely a rhetorical device, another version of "my way is the best way for the kids." This approach means that education systems are reconceptualized. Rather than being thought of as hierarchical administrative systems, they are seen as support systems for teaching and learning. Teachers and students are at the centre of the system, not at the bottom. The new paradigm is not the old debate upside down, i.e. that authority should be located in the school, not the board; the new debate is about how the system can best be structured to provide appropriate learning experiences for all students. ...

> In contrast to the old strategies of competition, conflict and the zero-sum game, the new paradigm deals with issues using strategies of cooperation, problem-solving and partnerships. Once again, this "win-win" approach is not idealistic or utopian. It does, however, represent a whole new way of doing business which constitutes the third major characteristic of the new paradigm.

Such a transformation will not be easy but is essential if the Québec education system is to meet the challenges of the twenty-first century.

New Challenges

As stated in the Introduction of this text, schools are a microcosm of society and they often become a key arena for the debate of fundamental social purposes (Paquette, 1991). Schools are expected to fulfil a wide variety of purposes and respond to diverse social, political and economic needs. In Cuban's words, "if society has an itch, schools get scratched" (1990, p. 9). There are many who doubt the capacity of the school system to respond adequately to the pressures of the new global economy. As Paquette states (1994, p. 2, endnote omitted):

> The dominant three r's of the seventies, eighties, and early nineties have been recession, retrenchment, and restructuring. With increasing rapidity these economic three r's have been forcing educational policy to return to a focus on the traditional three r's of education, albeit with particular concentration

on the maths and sciences, and on new technologies seen as basic survival skills in the emerging world economy.

Here in Québec, as we have seen in several chapters in this text, there is increasing talk on the part of government policy makers to make changes in the education system which will make it more responsive to the needs of students and other stakeholders, especially at the school level (e.g., see CSE, 1993c, MEQ, 1993). The recent literature on school restructuring also emphasizes the importance of focussing on the school as the unit of analysis (e.g., see Brown, 1990; Fullan, 1992; Murphy, 1991). However, in shifting to a school-based perspective, we must not lose sight of the types of support systems which the school boards, the Ministry of Education and other bodies must provide the school. As we stated during the debate on the draft bill on school reform (Foster & Smith, 1997b, p. 10):

> It would be naive to believe that the simple granting of greater autonomy to schools will produce better education. Reitzug and Capper (1996) even suggest that decentralization has been more of a rhetorical success than a substantive one. In this regard, the decentralization of authority to schools is much like the policy of integrating children with disabilities in regular classes. Done properly, it can provide a range of benefits to these students and their non-disabled peers. However, if implemented without support, it can have the opposite effect, deserving the epithet of "dumping" children with problems, not integrating them. What then are the essential conditions needed to make the proposed reform a success?

Several authors identify flexibility as an essential characteristic of decentralization; however, flexibility does not automatically flow from such delegation if the line of authority must pass through what Murphy (1991) describes as a "regulatory swamp" of government rules and regulations. In Québec, the *Basic Regulations*, the annual *Directives*, the budgetary rules and the collective agreements have long been identified as major stumbling blocks to educational change. "The importance of reducing the scope of these regulations cannot be underestimated. The new Act may confer wide powers upon school governing boards but unless the pervasive burden created by the regulatory environment is reduced considerably, their new found powers will be largely illusory" (Foster & Smith, 1997b, p. 11). Finally, as we have already argued, such change requires sustained support from school boards and the Ministry (Foster & Smith, 1997b, p. 11):

> In keeping with the image of restructuring as "a whole new way of doing business," not only schools, but school boards and the ministry, will have to learn to take on new roles as well. This means engaging in systemic capacity building at every level of the system, beginning with schools.
>
> School governing boards will require training and other forms of support that recognize the diverse needs of individual school communities. Such support will range from the mundane - how to run a meeting - to the sublime - how to support the development of a sustainable culture of teaching and learning in the school. Governing boards will also have to learn the boundaries between governance - their purview - and management - the purview of the principal.

It is incumbent on school administrators, teachers and other school-based personnel to become involved in these discussions, if they wish to influence the future direction of policy. Arguably, the first prerequisites of an informed debate are knowledge of the issues and a willingness to listen to various points of view. We hope that this text has at least contributed to the first prerequisite by providing information about the Québec education system, as well as by pointing the reader through numerous references to a wide variety of primary and secondary sources of material. Ideally, we also hope that it has contributed to the second prerequisite of an open mind, by exposing the reader to diverse points of view on a range of significant educational issues. Whether we have achieved this dual objective is an open-ended question. Like so many issues raised in this text, the answer is up to you, the reader.

REFERENCE LIST

Statutes, Regulations and Directives

Act Respecting Access to Documents Held by Public Bodies and the Protection of Personal Information, R.S.Q. c. A-2.1.

Act Respecting the Conditions of Employment in the Public Sector and the Municipal Sector, S.Q. 1993, c. 37.

Act Respecting the Conseil supérieur de l'éducation, R.S.Q. c. C-60.

> *Regulation Respecting the Qualification of Teachers having Charge of Catholic Religious Instruction in Public and Private and Elementary and Secondary Schools not Recognized as Catholic*, O.C. 1859-87, 9 December 1987, G.O.Q. 1997.II.4308, O.C. 84-92, 29 January 1992, G.O.Q. 1992.II.865, O.C. 1151-93, 9 November 1993, G.O.Q. 1993.II.6029.

> *Regulation Respecting the Recognition of Elementary and Secondary Schools of the Public School System as Catholic and their Confessional Character*, O.C. 1857-87, 23 December 1987, G.O.Q. 1987.II.4300, O.C. 112-88, 27 January, 1988, G.O.Q. 1988.II.1179, O.C. 1579-90, 14 November 1990, G.O.Q. 1990.II.2847, O.C.85-92, 29 January 1992, G.O.Q. 1992.II.866, O.C. 1551-93, 9 November 1993, G.O.Q. 1993.II.6029.

> *Regulation Respecting the Recognition of Private Educational Institutions as Catholic and their Confessional Character*, O.C. 1858-87, 9 December 1987, G.O.Q. 1987.II.4300, O.C. 113-88, 27 January 1988, G.O.Q. 1988.II.1181, O.C. 86-92, 12 February 1992, G.O.Q. 1992.II.868, O.C. 1551-93, 9 November 1993, G.O.Q.1993.II.6029.

> *Regulation of the Protestant Committee of the Conseil supérieur de l'éducation Regarding Protestant Moral and Religious Education as well as the Recognition of Educational Institutions as Protestant*, O.C. 967-91, 31 July 1991, G.O.Q. 1991.II.2879.

> *Regulation Respecting Teaching Permits and Teaching Diplomas*, O.C. 592-66, 1966, G.O.Q. 1966.II.2255, as am. by A.C. 578-69, 26 February 1969, A.C. 2727-70, 15 July 1970, M.O., 27 August 1997, G.O.Q. 1997.II.4399.

Act Respecting the Election of the First Commissioners of the New School Boards and Amending Various Legislative Provisions. S.Q. 1997, c. 98.

Act Respecting Elementary and Secondary Education, S.Q. 1984, c. 84.

Act Respecting the Eligibility of Certain Children for Instruction in English, S.Q. 1986, c. 46.

Act Respecting Health Services and Social Services, R.S.Q. c. S-4.2.

Act Respecting Labour Standards, R.S.Q. c. N-1.1.

Act Respecting the Ministère de l'Éducation, R.S.Q. c. M-15.

Act Respecting Municipal Taxation, R.S.Q. c. F-2.1.

Act Respecting Occupational Health and Safety, R.S.Q. c. S-2.1.

Act Respecting Private Education, R.S.Q. c. E-9.1.

> *Regulation Respecting the Application of the Act Respecting Private Education*, O.C. 1490-93, 27 October 1993, G.O.Q. 1993.II.5813, as am. by O.C. 1139-97, 3 September 1997, G.O.Q. 1997.II.4590.

Act Respecting the Process of the Negotiation of the Collective Agreements in the Public and Parapublic Sectors, R.S.Q. c. R-8.2.

Act Respecting the Regrouping and Management of School Boards, S.Q., 1971, c. 67.

Act Respecting School Elections, R.S.Q. c. E-2.3.

Act to Amend the Education Act and Various Legislative Provisions, S.Q. 1997, c. 96.

Act to Amend the Education Act, the Act Respecting School Elections and Other Legislative Provisions, S.Q. 1997, c. 47.

Act to Ensure for Children the Right to Education and to Institute a New Schooling Collective Agreement Plan, S.Q. 1967, c. 63.

Act to Promote the French Language in Québec, S.Q. 1969, c. 9.

Act to Promote School Development on the Island of Montreal, S.Q., 1972, c. 60.

Act to Secure the Handicapped in the Exercise of Their Rights, R.S.Q. c. E-20.1.

Bill 40, *An Act Respecting Public Elementary and Secondary Education*, 4th sess., 32nd Leg., 1983.

Bill C-68, *An Act in Respect of Criminal Justice for Young Persons and to Amend and Repeal Other Acts*, 1st Sess., 36th Parl., 1999, (1st reading 24 March 1999).

Canadian Bill of Rights, S.C. 1960, c. 44, reprinted in R.S.C. 1985, App. III.

Canadian Charter of Rights and Freedoms, Part I of the *Constitution Act, 1982*, being Schedule B to the *Canada Act 1982* (U.K.), 1982, c. 11.

Canadian Multiculturalism Act, R.S.C. 1985, c. 24 (4th supp).

Charter of Human Rights and Freedoms, R.S.Q. c. C-12.

 Regulation Respecting Affirmative Action Programs, O.C. 1172-86, 30 July 1986, G.O.Q. 1986.II.2084.

Charter of the French Language, R.S.Q. c. C-11.

 Regulation Respecting the Exemption from the Application of the First Paragraph of Section 72 of the Charter of the French Language Which May Be Granted to Children Having Serious Learning Disabilities, O.C.1758-93, 8 December 1993, G.O.Q. 1993.II.6921.

 Regulation Respecting the Exemption from the Application of the First Paragraph of Section 72 of the Charter of the French Language to Children Staying in Québec Temporarily, O.C. 608-97, 7 May 1997, G.O.C. 1997.II.1970.

 Regulation Respecting Requests to Receive Instruction in English, O.C. 1758-93, 8 December 1993, G.O.Q. 1993.II.6921.

Civil Code of Québec

Constitution Act, 1867 (U.K.), 30 & 31 Vict., c. 3, reprinted in R.S.C. 1985, App. II, No. 5 (formerly *British North America Act, 1867*).

Constitution Act, 1982, being Schedule B to the *Canada Act 1982* (U.K.), 1982, c. 11.

Constitution Amendment, 1997 (Québec), SI/97-141.

Convention on the Rights of the Child, GA Res. 44/25, Annex, 44 UN GAOR, Supp. No. 49, UN Doc. A/44/49 (1989) 167.

Criminal Code, R.S.C. 1985, c. C-46.

Education Act, R.S.O. 1990, c. E.2.

Education Act, R.S.Q. c. I-13.3.

 Basic School Regulation for Preschool and Elementary School Education, O.C. 73-90, 24 January 1990, G.O.Q. 1990.II.435, as am. by O.C. 741-97, 4 June 1997, G.O.Q. 1997.II.2496.

 Basic School Regulation for Secondary School Education, O.C. 74-90, 24 January 1990, G.O.Q. 1990.II.440, as am. by O.C. 1636-92, 11 November 1992, G.O.Q. 1992.II.4999, O.C. 586-94, 27 April 1994, G.O.Q. 1994.II.1586, O.C. 514-96, 1 May 1996, G.O.Q. 1996.II.2217.

 Basic School Regulation Respecting Educational Services for Adults in General Education, O.C. 732-94, 18 May 1994, G.O.Q. 1994.II.2064, as am. by O.C. 958-96, 7 August 1996, G.O.Q. 1996.II.3855, O.C. 961-96, 7 August 1996, G.O.Q. 1996.II.3856.

 Basic School Regulation Respecting Education Services for Adults in Vocational Education, O.C. 733-94, 18 May 1994, G.O.Q. 1994.II.2086.

 Education in the Youth Sector: Preschool, Elementary School and Secondary School. 1998-99 Directives. (Ministère de l'Éducation du Québec).

 General Education for Adults: 1998-99 Directives. (Ministère de l'Éducation du Québec).

 Regulation Respecting the Number of Admissible Students for the Computation of the Maximum Yield of the School Tax, O.C. 840-90, 27 June 1990, G.O.Q. 1990.II.2521.

 Regulation Respecting the Computation of the Maximum Yield of the School Tax for the 1996-97 School Year, O.C. 563-96, 15 May 1996, G.O.Q. 1998.II.2994.

 Regulation Respecting the Computation of the Maximum Yield of the School Tax for the 1998-99 School Year, O.C. 696-98, 27 May 1998, G.O.Q. 1998.II.2142.

 Regulation Respecting the Conditions of Employment of Management Staff of School Boards, M.O., 23 September 1998, G.O.Q. 1998.II.4052.

 Regulation Respecting Consultation of Parents Concerning an Application for Recognition or Withdrawal of Recognition of a School as Catholic or Protestant, M.O. 1-89, 8 November 1989, G.O.Q. 1989.II.4174, as am. by M.O. 1-92, 19 February 1992, G.O.Q. 1992.II.1122.

 Regulation Respecting Exceptional Cases for Admission, M.O. 1-93, 21 January 1993, G.O.Q. 1993.II.570.

 Regulation Respecting Teaching Licences, M.O., 27 August 1997, G.O.Q. 1997.II.4399.

 Vocational Education: 1998-99 Directives. (Ministère de l'Éducation du Québec).

Education Act, S.Q. 1988, c. 84.

General and Vocational Colleges Act, R.S.Q. c. C-29.

 College Education Regulations, O.C. 1006-93, 14 July 1993, G.O.Q. 1993.II.3995, as am. by O.C. 551-95, 26 April 1995, G.O.Q. 1995.II.1351, O.C. 962-98, 21 July 1998, G.O.Q. 1998.II.3594.

Juvenile Delinquents Act, R.S.C. 1970, c. J-3.

Labour Code, R.S.Q. c. C-27.

Official Language Act, S.Q. 1974, c. 6.

Public Schools Act, R.S.M. 1987, c. P-250.

Professional Code, R.S.Q. c. C-26.

Universal Declaration of Human Rights, GA Res. 217 (III), UN GAOR, 3d Sess., Supp. No. 13, UN Doc.

A/810 (1948) 71.

University of Québec Act, R.S.Q. c. U-1.

Young Offenders Act, R.S.C. 1985, c. Y-1.

Youth Protection Act, R.S.Q. c. P-34.1.

Teacher Ententes

Entente Between the Employer Bargaining Committee for Protestant School Boards (CPNCP) and the Provincial Association of Protestant Teachers (PAPT), 22 May 1980 (including subsequent amendments) [Round 4].

Entente Between the Employer Bargaining Committee for Protestant School Boards (CPNCP) and the Provincial Association of Protestant Teachers (PAPT), 1 February 1996 (including subsequent amendments) [Round 8].

Case Law

Adler v. *Ontario*, [1996] 3 S.C.R. 609, 140 D.L.R. (4th) 385.

Brossard (Town of) v. *Québec (Commission des droits de la personne)*, [1988] 2 S.C.R. 279, 53 D.L.R. (4th) 609, 18 Q.A.C. 164.

Canadian Civil Liberties Association v. *Ontario (Minister of Education)* (1990), 71 O.R. (2d) 341, 65 D.L.R. (4th) 1 (C.A.).

Collège Notre-Dame du Sacré-Coeur v. *Québec (Commission des droits de la personne)*, [1994] R.J.Q. 1324 (Sup. Ct.).

Commission scolaire régionale de Chambly v. *Bergevin*, [1994] 2 S.C.R. 525, 115 D.L.R. (4th) 609.

Eaton v. *Brant County Board of Education*, [1997] 1 S.C.R. 241, 142 D.L.R. (4th) 385.

Gould v. *Regina (East) School Division No. 77*, [1997] S.J. No. 843 (Q.B.).

Hirsch v. *Montreal Protestant School Commissioners*, [1928] A.C. 200, [1928] 1 D.L.R. 1041 (P.C.).

Hunter v. *Southam*, [1984] 2 S.C.R. 145, 11 D.L.R. (4th) 641.

Mahé v. *Alberta*, [1990] 1 S.C.R. 342, 68 D.L.R. (4th) 69.

Myers v. *Peel County Board of Education*, [1981] 2 S.C.R. 21, 123 D.L.R. (3d) 1.

Operation Dismantle v. *Canada*, [1985] 1 S.C.R. 441, 18 D.L.R. (4th) 481.

Phelps v. *The Mayor and Burgesses of the London Borough of Hillingdon* (1997), 147 N.L.J. 1421.

Pinsler v. *Protestant Board of School Commissioners* (1903), 23 Que. C.S. 365.

Protestant School Board of Montreal v. *Minister of Education of Quebec*, [1976] C.S. 430, 83 D.L.R. (3d) 645; leave to appeal refused (1978), 83 D.L.R. (3d) 679n (Que C.A.).

Québec Association of Protestant School Boards v. *Québec (A.G.)*, [1985] C.S. 872, 21 D.L.R. (4th) 36.

Québec (A.G.) v. *Greater Hull School Board*, [1984] 2 S.C.R. 575, 15 D.L.R. (4th) 651.

Québec (A.G.) v. *Québec Association of Protestant School Boards*, [1984] 2 S.C.R. 66, 10 D.L.R. (4th) 321.

Québec (Commission des droits de la personne) v. *Commission scolaire régionale Chauveau*, [1993] R.J.Q. 929 (Que. Human Rights Trib.), rev'd [1994] R.J.Q. 1196, 64 Q.A.C. 31 (C.A.).

Québec (Commission des droits de la personne) v. *Commission scolaire de Saint-Jean-Sur-Richelieu*, [1991] R.J.Q. 3003 (Que. Human Rights Trib.), aff'd [1994] R.J.Q. 1227, 117 D.L.R. (4th) 67, 64 Q.A.C. 1 (C.A.).

R. v. *Big M Drug Mart*, [1985] 1 S.C.R. 295, 18 D.L.R. (4th) 321.

R. v. *Jones*, [1986] 2 S.C.R. 284, 31 D.L.R. (4th) 569.

R. v. *M.(M.R.)* (1999), 166 D.L.R. (4th) 261 (S.C.C.).

Reference re Education Act of Quebec, [1993] 2 S.C.R. 511, 105 D.L.R. (4th) 266.

Reference Re Public Schools Act (Man.), [1993] 1 S.C.R. 839, 100 D.L.R. (4th) 723.

Smith v. *Québec (Ministère de l'Éducation)*, [1998] R.J.Q. 566 (Sup. Ct.).

Winnipeg Teachers' Association No. 1 v. *Winnipeg School Division No. 1*, [1976] 2 S.C.R. 695, 59 D.L.R. (3d) 228.

X (Minors) v. *Bedfordshire County Council*, [1985] 2 A.C. 633 (H.L.).

Zylberberg v. *Sudbury Board of Education* (1988), 65 O.R. (2d) 641, 52 D.L.R. (4th) 577 (C.A.).

Government Documents, Periodicals, Books and Reports

Advisory Board on English Education. (1994). *The reorganization of school boards along linguistic lines: Bill 107 - an English language perspective* (Report to the Minister of Education). Montréal: Author.

Advisory Board on English Education. (1995). *Language learning in the English schools of Québec: A biliteracy imperative* (Report to the Minister of Education). Montréal: Author.

Advisory Board on English Education. (1996). *The integration of the new information and communication technologies in the English schools of Québec* (Report to the Minister of Education of Québec). Montréal: Author.

Advisory Board on English Education. (1997). *Evaluation of learning in the English schools of Québec* (Report to the Minister of Education). Montréal: Author.

Anderson, G. & Rahming, J.H. (1983). The educational project: From policy to practice. *McGill Journal of Education, 18*, 94-103.

Asch, A. (1989). Has the law made a difference?: What some disabled students have to say. In D.K. Lipsky & A. Gartner (Eds.), *Beyond separate education: Quality education for all* (pp. 181-205). Baltimore: Paul Brookes.

Atkinson, M.M. (1993). *Governing Canada: Institutions and public policy*. Toronto: Harcourt Brace.

Bala, N. (1988). The Young Offenders Act: A legal framework. In J. Hudson, J.P. Hornick, & B.A. Burrows (Eds.), *Justice and the young offender in Canada.* (pp.11-35). Toronto: Wall & Thompson.

Bezeau, L.M. (1993). Efficiency in education. In L.L. Stewin & S.J.H. McCann (Eds.), *Contemporary educational issues: The Canadian mosaic* (2nd ed., pp. 380-392). Toronto: Copp Clark.

Bezeau, L.M. (1995). *Educational administration for Canadian teachers* (2nd ed.). Toronto: Copp Clark.

Black's law dictionary (1990). (6th ed.). St. Paul, MN: West.

Block, I. (1994, December 3). Behind the hijab debate. *The Gazette*, pp. B1, B2.

Boudreau, S. (1999). *Catholic education: The Quebec experience*. Calgary: Detselig.

Brown, D.J. (1985). Financing education: The issues and alternatives. *Canadian School Executive, 5*(3), 14-15.

Brown, D.J. (1990). *Decentralization and school-based management*. London: Falmer Press.

Brown, A.F. (1991). *Legal handbook for school administrators* (2nd ed.).Toronto: Carswell.

Burrup, P.E., Brimley, V., Jr. & Garfield, R.R. (1993). *Financing education in a climate of change* (5th ed.). Boston: Allyn & Bacon.

Canadian Teachers' Federation. (1991-92). *Government, administration and policy handbook*. Ottawa: Author

Canadian Education Association. (1990). *Sentenced to school: The Young Offenders Act and Canadian school boards.*Toronto: Canadian Education Association.

Chapman, D.W. & Walberg, H.J. (1992). Cross-national perspectives on educational productivity. In D.W. Chapman & H. Walberg (Eds.), *Advances in educational productivity: Vol. 2: International perspectives on educational productivity* (pp. 3-18).Greenwich, CT: JAI Press.

Centrale de l'enseignement du Québec. (1997). L'article 93 de la Loi constitutionelle de 1867 doit être modifié: Memoire présénté au Comité mixte special au sujet de la modification de l'article 93. In *Mémoires présentés au comité mixte spécial*. (Cartable I/11). Unpublished compilation.

Centre for Intercultural Education & International Understanding. (1998). *Citizenship education with a global perspective* (pamphlet available from the association). Montreal: author.

Citizens for the Constitutional Right to Denominational Schools. (1997) Brief on the amendment to section 93 of the constitution. In *Mémoires présentés au comité mixte spécial*. (Cartable I/13). Unpublished compilation.

Coleman, P., Collinge, J. & Tabin, Y. (1995). The coproduction of learning: Improving schools from the inside out. In B. Levin, W.J. Fowler & H.L. Walberg (Eds.), *Advances in Educational Productivity: Vol. 5: Organizational Influences on Educational Productivity* (pp. 141-174). Greenwich CT: JAI Press.

Commission des droits de la personne du Québec. (1995). *Religious pluralism in Québec: A social and ethical challenge* (A document submitted for public consideration). Montréal: Author.

Commission for the Estates General on Education. (1996a). *The State of education in Québec*. Québec: Author.

Commission for the Estates General on Education. (1996b). *Renewing our education system: Ten priority actions*. (Final report of the Commission for the Estate General on Education). Québec: Author.

Commission d'étude sur la formation des adultes (1982). *Learning: A voluntary and responsible action*. Québec: Ministère de l'Education.

Comité provincial de l'enfance inadaptée. (1976). *L'éducation de l'enfance en difficulté d'adaptation et d'apprentissage au Québec*. Québec: Ministère de l'Éducation.

Comité sur l'École Québécoise et les Communautés Culturelles. (1985a). *L'école québécoise et les communautés culturelles*. Québec: Ministère de l'Education du Québec.

Comité sur l'École Québécoise et les Communautés Culturelles. (1985b). *Québec schools and cultural communities* (summary of the committee report). Québec: Ministère de l'Education du Québec.

Conseil supérieur de l'éducation du Québec. (1977). *The education of Quebec children suffering from learning or emotional disorders* (Advice to the Minister of Education). Québec: Author.

Conseil supérieur de l'éducation du Québec. (1979). *School and the children of various ethnic and religious groups* (Advice to the Minister of Education). Québec: Author.

Conseil supérieur de l'éducation du Québec. (1983). *Intercultural education* (Advice to the Minister of

Education). Québec: Author.

Conseil supérieur de l'éducation du Québec. (1985). *Réussir l'intégration scolaire des élèves en difficulté* (Advice to the Minister of Education). Québec: Author.

Conseil supérieur de l'éducation du Québec. (1987). *The educational challenges of plurality* (Advice to the Minister of Education). Québec: Author.

Conseil supérieur de l'éducation du Québec. (1993a). *Le défi d'une réussite de qualité* (Rapport 1992-1993 sur l'état et les besoins de l'éducation). Québec: Author.

Conseil supérieur de l'éducation du Québec. (1993b). Educational administration: The need for a new model (Advice to the Minister of Education). Québec: Author.

Conseil supérieur de l'éducation du Québec. (1993c). Education management: A new model is needed. *Educouncil, 11*(4).

Conseil supérieur de l'éducation du Québec. (1993d). *Pour un accueil et une intégration réussis des élèves des communautés culturelles* (Advice to the Minister of Education). Québec: Author.

Conseil supérieur de l'éducation du Québec. (1994a). *Des conditions pour faire avancer l'école* (Advice to the Minister of Education). Québec: Author.

Conseil supérieur de l'éducation du Québec. (1994b). Meeting the challenge of achieving quality. *Educouncil, 11*(4).

Conseil supérieur de l'éducation du Québec. (1994c). Prerequisites for progress in education. *Educouncil, 11*(5).

Conseil supérieur de l'éducation du Québec. (1995). *Vers la maîtrise du changement en éducation* (*Rapport annuel sur l'état et les besoins de l'éducation, 1994-1995*). Québec: Author.

Conseil supérieur de l'éducation du Québec. (1996a). *Pour un nouveau partage des pouvoirs et responsabilités en éducation* (*Rapport annuel 1995-1996 sur l'état et les besoins de l'éducation*). Québec: Author.

Conseil supérieur de l'éducation du Québec. (1996b). *L'intégration scolaire des élèves handicapés et en difficulté.* (Advice to the Minister of Education). Québec: Author.

Conseil supérieur de l'éducation du Québec. (1997a). *L'Insertion sociale et professionnelle, une responsabilité à partager* (*Rapport annuel 1996-1997 sur l'état et les besoins de l'éducation*). Québec: Author.

Conseil supérieur de l'éducation du Québec. (1997b). *L'autorisation d'enseigner: Le projet d'un règlement refondu.* (Advice to the Minister of Education). Québec: Author.

Conseil supérieur de l'éducation du Québec. (1998a). *L'école, une communauté éducative. Voies de renouvellement pour le secondaire.* (Advice to the Minister of Education). Québec: Author.

Conseil supérieur de l'éducation du Québec. (1998b). *Éduquer à la citoyenneté.* Québec: Author.

Conseil supérieur de l'éducation du Québec. (1998c). *Pour un renouvellement prometteur des programmes à l'école.* (Advice to the Minister of Education). Québec: Author

Conseil supérieur de l'éducation du Québec. (1998d). *Les services complémentaires à l'enseignement: des responsabilités à consolider.* (Advice to the Minister of Education). Québec: Author

Conseil supérieur de l'éducation du Québec. (1999). *Les enjeux majeurs des programmes d'études et des régimes pédagogiques.* (Advice to the Minister of Education). Québec: Author

Cuban, L. (1990). Reforming again, again, and again. *Educational Researcher, 19*(1), 3-13.

d'Anglejan, A. & De Koninck, Z. (1992). Educational policy for a culturally plural Quebec: An update. In B. Burnaby & A. Cumming (Eds.), *Socio-political aspects of English second language* (pp. 97-109). Toronto: OISE Press.

Department of Justice Canada. (1999, March). *Youth Criminal Justice Act* [WWW document]. URL http://www.canada.justice.gc.ca/News/Communiques/1999/yoaback_en.html.

Després-Poirier, M. (1995). *Le système d'éducation du Québec* (2nd ed.). Montréal: Gaëtan Morin.

Dickens, B. (1981). The modern function and limits of parental rights. *Law Quaterly Review, 97,* 462-485.

Donahue, H.M. & Smith, W.J. (1986). *Every child's right to a free and appropriate education: A study of the funding of special education in Québec.* Montreal: Service des relations professionnelles Talleyrand.

Fédération des comités de parents de la province de Québec. (1997). Brief to the Special Joint Committee of the Commons and Senate. In *Mémoires présentés au comité mixte spécial.* (Cartable I/27). Unpublished compilation.

Fleras, A. & Elliott, J.L. (Eds.). (1992). *Multiculturalism in Canada.* Toronto: Nelson.

Foster, W.F. (1986). Educate or litigate. *Canadian Journal of Education. 11,* 122-151.

Foster, W.F. (1993). Child abuse in schools: The statutory and common law obligations of educators. *Education and Law Journal, 4,* 1-59.

Foster, W.F. (1996). Medication of pupils and related issues. In W.F. Foster (Ed.), *Education in transition: Legal issues in a changing school setting* (pp. 176-204). Chateauguay: Imprimerie Lisbro.

Foster, W.F. & Smith, W.J. (1997a). *Restructuring education in Québec: The amendment of section 93* (Policy research paper No. 97-02). Montreal: McGill University, Office of Research on Educational Policy.

Foster, W.F. & Smith, W.J. (1997b). *Policy Talk: Restructuring education in Québec: Decentralizing authority to schools*. Montreal: McGill University, Office of Research on Educational Policy.

Foucher, P. (1997). *Constitutional guarantees and linguistic school boards in Québec*. Montréal: McGill University, Office of Research On Educational Policy.

Fullan, M.G. (1990). Rethinking policy for children: Implications for educational administration. In B. Mitchell & L. Cunningham (Eds.), *Educational leadership and changing contexts of families, communities, and schools* (Part II, pp. 69-90). Chicago: University of Chicago Press.

Fullan, M.G. (1992). *Successful school improvement*. Toronto: OISE Press.

Gagnon, A.-G. & Montcalm, M.B. (1990). Quebec: Beyond the quiet revolution. Toronto: Nelson Canada.

Gall, G.L. (1995). *The Canadian legal system* (4th ed.). Toronto: Carswell.

Gaskell, J. (1995). *Dilemmas of educational choice*. Paper presented at The National Conference on Public Education Meeting the Challenges. Ottawa: Canadian Teachers Federation.

Ghosh, R. (1996). *Redefining multicultural education*. Toronto: Harcourt, Brace, Jovanovich.

Ghosh, R., Zinman, R. & Talbani, A. (1995). Policies relating to the education of cultural communities in Quebec. *Canadian Ethnic Studies Journal*, 27, 18-31.

Giles, T.E. & Proudfoot, A.J. (1994). *Educational administration in Canada* (5th ed.). Calgary: Detselig.

Girard, J.-C. & Blanchard, A. (1999). Responsabilité civile des conseils d'établissement. In P. Chagnon (Ed.), *Développements récents en droit de l'éducation* (pp. 85-117). Cowansville, QC: Yvon Blais.

Goode, B. (1994). Major reforms bring brighter employment prospects for Quebec students. *McGill Journal of Education, 29,* 267-73.

Guthrie, J.W. (1988). Educational finance: The lower schools. In N. Boyan (Ed.), *The handbook of research in educational administration* (pp. 373-389). New York: Longman.

Handscombe, J. (1989). Mainstreaming: Who needs it? In J.H. Esling (Ed.), *Multicultural education and policy: ESL in the 1990's* (pp. 18-35). Toronto: OISE Press.

Henchey, N. (1983). The educational project: A convivial tool. *McGill Journal of Education*, 18, 149-158.

Henchey, N. (1999). *Curriculum reform in Quebec and implications for teacher education*, Unpublished manuscript.

Henchey, N. & Burgess, D.A. (1987). *Between past and future: Quebec education in transition*. Calgary: Detselig.

Hogg, P.W. (1982). A comparison of the Canadian Charter of Rights and Freedoms with the Canadian Bill of Rights. In W.S. Tarnopolsky & G.-A. Beaudouin (Eds.), *Canadian Charter of Rights and Freedoms* (pp. 2-23). Toronto: Carswell.

Hoglund, C. (1997). Parental permission forms: Minimizing liability during school excursions. *Capsle Comments*, 6:3, 1-4.

Hoy, W.K. & Miskel, C.G. (1987). *Educational administration: Theory, research, and practice* (3rd ed.). New York: Random House.

Kallen, E. (1982). *Ethnicity and human rights in Canada*. Toronto: Gage.

Kallen, E. (1989). *Label me human: Minority rights of stigmatized Canadians*. Toronto: University of Toronto Press.

Kirp, D.L. (1983). Professionalism as a policy choice: British special education in comparative perspective. In J.G. Chambers & W.T. Hartman (Eds.), *Special education policies: Their history, implementation and finance* (pp. 74-112). Philadelphia: Temple Univeristy Press.

Latif, G. (1990). L'école québécoise s'ouvre à la pluralité. *Vie pédagogique*, *67*, mai-juin, pp. 18-21.

Laverdière, A. (1999). Loi sur l'instruction publique: Révocation du brevet d'enseignement (art. 26 à 34.3). In P. Chagnon (Ed.), *Développements récents en droit de l'éducation* (pp. 119-137). Cowansville, QC: Yvon Blais.

Leduc, C. & De Massy, P.R. (1989). *Sharing a better life together through human rights*. Montréal: Modulo Éditeur.

Lessard, C. (1991). Equality and inequality in Canadian education. In R. Ghosh & D. Ray (Eds.), *Social change and education in Canada* (2nd ed., pp. 142-157). Toronto: Harcourt, Brace, Jovanovich.

Lombard, A. (1995, April). *The new negotiations in Québec: A meeting between emotion and reason*. Paper presented at the conference of the Canadian Association for the Practical Study of Law and Education, Ottawa.

Magnet, J.E. (1995). *Official languages of Canada*. Montréal: Les Éditions Yvon Blais.

Magnet, J.E. (1996). Multiculturalism in the Canadian Charter of Rights and Freedoms. G.-A. Beaudoin & E. Mendes (Eds), *The Canadian Charter of Rights and Freedoms* (3rd ed., pp.18/2-18/50). Ottawa: Carswell.

Manley-Casimir, M.E. & Pitsula, P. (1988). The Charter, culture and the public school curriculum: Emerging perspectives and guidelines. *Education and Law Journal, 1*, 37-69.

McAndrew, M. (1991). Ethnicity, multiculturalism, and multicultural education in Canada. In R. Ghosh & D. Ray (Eds.), *Social change and education in Canada* (2nd ed., pp. 130-141). Toronto: Harcourt, Brace,

Jovanovich.

McLeod, K.A. (1993). Multiculutral education: The state of the art [Special issue]. *Multiculturalism, 15*(2/3).

Michaud, P. (1989). Equity of educational finance in Eastern Ontario. In S.B. Lawton & R. Wignall (Eds.), *Scrimping or squandering?: Financing Canadian schools* (pp. 127-139). Toronto: OISE Press.

Milner, H. (1986). *The long road to reform: Restructuring public education in Quebec.* Kingston, ON: McGill-Queen's University Press.

Ministère des Communautés culturelles et de l'Immigration. (1981). *Autant de façons d'être québécois* (Plan d'action du Gouvernment du Québec à l'intention des communautés culturelles). Québec: Author.

Ministère de l'Éducation du Québec. (1970). *Règles budgétaires pour l'année scolaire 1970-1971: Commissions scolaires.* Québec: Author.

Ministère de l'Éducation du Québec. (1975). *Towards a new method of functioning for the elementary and secondary education system in Québec.* Québec: Author.

Ministère de l'Éducation du Québec. (1977). *Politique de fonctionnement générale du système d'enseignement élémentaire et secondaire au Québec.* Québec: Author.

Ministère de l'Éducation du Québec. (1978). *Primary and secondary education in Québec* (Green paper). Québec: Author.

Ministère de l'Éducation du Québec. (1979a). *The schools of Québec: Policy statement and plan of action.* Québec: Author.

Ministère de l'Éducation du Québec. (1979b). *The schools of Québec: Policy statement and plan of action: Children with difficulties in learning and adaptation.* Québec: Author.

Ministère de l'Éducation du Québec. (1980a). *Adapting schools to their milieux: Policy statement for schools in economically disadvantaged areas.* Québec: Author.

Ministère de l'Éducation du Québec. (1980b). *The school's educational project.* Québec: Author.

Ministère de l'Éducation du Québec. (1982). *The Québec school: A responsible force in the community* (Rev. ed.). Québec: Author.

Ministère de l'Éducation du Québec. (1984). *Continuing education program: Policy statement and plan of action.* Québec: Author.

Ministère de l'Éducation du Québec. (1991). *Education: Driving our future.* Québec: Author.

Ministère de l'Éducation du Québec. (1992a). *The challenge of teaching today and tomorrow.* Québec: Author.

Ministère de l'Éducation du Québec. (1992b). *Educational success for all: Special education policy update.* Québec: Author.

Ministère de l'Éducation du Québec. (1992c). *English-language education in Québec: A response to the Task Force on English Education.* Québec: Author.

Ministère de l'Éducation du Québec. (1992d). *Joining forces: Plan of action on educational success.* Québec: Author.

Ministère de l'Éducation du Québec. (1992e). *Teacher probation: The probation system: A procedural guide.* Québec: Author.

Ministère de l'Éducation du Québec. (1992f). *Teacher training: Secondary school general education: Orientations and expected competencies.* Québec: Author.

Ministère de l'Éducation du Québec. (1993). *Moving ahead: Elementary and secondary school education in Québec: Orientations, proposals and issues.* Québec: Author.

Ministère de l'Éducation du Québec. (1994a). *Teacher training: Preschool and elementary school general education: Orientations and expected competencies.* Québec: Author.

Ministère de l'Éducation du Québec. (1994b). *Teacher training: The practicum.* Québec: Author.

Ministère de l'Éducation du Québec. (1996a). *Teacher training: Special education.* Québec: Author.

Ministère de l'Éducation du Québec. (1996b). *Teacher training: The comité d'agrément des programmes de formation à l'enseignement (CAPFE).* Québec: Author.

Ministère de l'Éducation du Québec. (1997a). *A new direction for success.* Québec: Author.

Ministère de l'Éducation du Québec. (1997b). *A new direction for success. Supporting Montréal schools.* Québec: Author.

Ministère de l'Éducation du Québec. (1997c). *Québec schools on course: Educational policy statement.* Québec: Author.

Ministère de l'Éducation du Québec. (1997d). *Teacher training: The arts, physical education and second language education. Orientations and expected competencies.* Québec: Author.

Ministère de l'Éducation du Québec. (1997e). *L'autorisation d'enseigner et la période probatoire des enseignants et des enseignantes (Version préliminaire).* Québec: Author.

Ministère de l'Éducation du Québec. (1997f). *A school for the future: Educational integration and intercultural education.* Québec: Author.

Ministère de l'Éducation du Québec. (1998a). *Plan of action for educational integration and intercultural education.* Québec: Author.

Ministère de l'Éducation du Québec. (1998b). *A school for the future: Policy statement on educational integration and intercultural education.* Québec: Author.

Ministère de l'Éducation du Québec. (1998c). *Toward a policy of lifelong learning* (Consultation paper). Québec: Author.

Ministère de l'Éducation du Québec. (1999). *Adapting our schools to the needs of all students* (Draft policy on special education). Québec: Author.

Ministère de l'Éducation du Québec. Direction de la coordination des réseux. (1992). *Interpretation of the definitions used to classify students with handicaps or learning or adjustment difficulties.* Québec: Author.

Ministère de l'Éducation du Québec, Direction générale du financement. (1990a). *Règles budgétaires pour l'année scolaire 1990-1991: Commissions scolaires.* Québec: Author.

Ministère de l'Éducation du Québec, Direction générale du financement. (1990b). *Règles budgétaires pour l'année scolaire 1990-1991: Commissions scolaires: Document complémentaire sur la méthode de calcul des paramètres d'allocation.* Québec: Author.

Ministère de l'Éducation du Québec, Direction générale du financement et des équipements. (1996a). *Règles budgétaires pour l'année scolaire 1996-97: Commissions scolaires.* Québec: Author.

Ministère de l'Éducation du Québec, Direction générale du financement et des équipements. (1996b). *Règles budgétaires pour l'année scolaire 1996-1997: Commissions scolaires: Document complémentaire sur la méthode de calcul des paramètres d'allocation.* Québec: Author.

Ministère de l'Éducation du Québec, Direction générale du financement et des équipements. (1997a). *Règles budgétaires pour l'année scolaire 1997-98: Commissions scolaires.* Québec: Author.

Ministère de l'Éducation du Québec, Direction générale du financement et des équipements. (1997b). *Règles budgétaires pour l'année scolaire 1997-1998: Commissions scolaires: Document complémentaire sur la méthode de calcul des paramètres d'allocation.* Québec: Author.

Ministère de l'Éducation du Québec, Direction générale du financement et des équipements. (1998a). *Règles budgétaires pour l'année scolaire 1998-99: Commissions scolaires.* Québec: Author.

Ministère de l'Éducation du Québec, Direction générale du financement et des équipements. (1998b). *Règles budgétaires pour l'année scolaire 1998-1999: Commissions scolaires: Document complémentaire sur la méthode de calcul des paramètres d'allocation.* Québec: Author.

Ministère de l'Éducation du Québec, Direction générale des ressources matérielles et financières. (1985). *Règles budgétaires pour l'année scolaire 1985-86: Commissions scolaires.* Québec: Author.

Minow, M. (1990). *Making all the difference: Inclusion, exclusion and American law.* Ithaca NY: Cornell University Press.

Momii, K. (1998). School-based management theory and the decentralization of educational governance in Québec (Policy Research paper No. 98-01). Montréal: McGill University, Office of Research on Educational Policy.

Murphy, J. (1991). *Restructuring schools: Capturing and assessing the phenomena.* New York: Teachers College Press.

Murphy, J., & Beck, L. G. (1995). *School-based management as school reform: Taking stock.* Thousand Oaks, CA: Corwin Press.

National Research Council of Canada. (1990). *National building code of Canada, 1990* (Including errata and revisions as of January 1994). Ottawa: Author.

Newell, R. (1978). Teacher malpractice. *Case Comment, 83*:4, 3-4.

Paquette, J. (1989). The quality conumdrum: Assessing what we cannot agree on. In S. B. Lawton & R. Wignall (Eds.), *Scrimping or squandering: Financing Canadian schools* (pp. 11-28). Toronto: OISE Press.

Paquette, J. (1994). *Publicly supported education in post-modern Canada: An imploding universe?* Toronto: Our Schools/Our Selves Education Foundation.

Paquette, J.E. (1991). *Social purpose and schooling: Alternatives, agendas and issues.* London: Falmer Press.

Posno, T.R. (1986). *A resource cost model as a decision support system for planning special edcuation.* Unpublished doctoral disssertation, University of Toronto.

Protestant School Board of Greater Montreal. (1988). *A Multicultural/multiracial approach to education in the schools of The Protestant School Board of Greater Montreal* (a report of the Task Force on Multicultural/Multiracial Education). Montreal: Author.

Protestant School Board of Greater Montreal. (1994). *Multicultural multiracial education policies.* Montreal: Author.

Quebec Federation of Home & School Associations. (n.d.). *It's about us* (pamphlet available from the association). Montreal: Author.

Rebore, W.T. & Rebore, R.W. (1993). *Introduction to financial and business administration in public education.* Boston: Allyn & Bacon.

Reitzug, U.C. & Capper, C.A. (1996). Deconstructing site-based management: Possibilities for emancipation and alternative means of control. *International Journal of Educational Reform, 5*, 56-69.

Report of the Royal Commission of Inquiry on Education in the Province of Quebec (Vols. 1-5). (1963-1966). Québec: Government of Québec.

Report of the Special Joint Committee to Amend Section 93 of the Constitution Act, 1867, Concerning the Quebec School system. (1997). Ottawa: Senate of Canada/House of Commons.

Richards, D.M. & Ratsoy, E.W. (1987). *Introduction to the economics of Canadian education.* Calgary: Detselig Enterprises.

Roher, E.M. (1997). An educator's guide to violence in schools. Toronto: Canada Law Book Inc.

Royal Commission on Aboriginal Peoples. (1996). *Gathering strength.* (Report of the Royal Commission on Aboriginal Peoples, Vol. III). Ottawa: Canada Communication Group.

Royal Commission on Bilingualism and Biculturalism. (1984). The official languages and education. In J.R. Mallea & J.C. Young (Eds.), *Cultural diversity and Canadian education* (pp. 85-95). Ottawa: Carleton University Press. (Reprinted from the *Report of the Royal Commission on Bilingualism and Biculturalism*, Book 1, chap. VI, pp. 121-131, 1967, Ottawa: Minister of Supply and Services Canada)

Saskatchewan Teachers' Federation. (1989). *The administration of medication and the provision of health support services in schools.* Saskaton: Saskatchewan Teachers' Federation.

Sissons, C.B. (1959). *Church and state in Canadian education: An historical study.* Toronto: Ryerson.

Smith, W.J. (1989). *The education of exceptional children in Québec: A study of government policy goals and legislative action.* Montréal: Service des relations professionnelles Talleyrand.

Smith, W.J. (1992). Special education policy in Québec: Evolution or status quo? *Education Canada, 32*(1), 40-48.

Smith, W.J. (1997). *Policy Talk. Restructuring school boards in Québec: Can the window of opportunity be opened?* Montréal: McGill University, Office of Research on Educational Policy.

Smith, W.J., Butler-Kisber, L., LaRocque, L.J., Portelli, J., Shields, C.M., Sturge Sparkes, C. & Vibert, A. (1998). *Student engagement in learning and school life: National project report.* Montréal: McGill University, Office of Research on Educational Policy.

Smith, W.J. & Foster, W.F. (1997a). Equal educational opportunity for students with disabilities in Canada: How far have we progressed? *Education and Law Journal, 8*, 183-226.

Smith, W.J. & Foster, W.F. (1997b). *Policy talk. Restructuring school boards in Québec: First steps toward school-based renewal.* Montréal: McGill University, Office of Research on Educational Policy.

Smith, W. J. & Foster, W. F. (1998). *School governance in Québec: Delegation of authority or responsibility?* Paper presented at the annual conference of the Canadian Association for the Practical Study of Law and Education [CAPSLE], Kananaskis, Alberta.

Smith, W.J. & Lusthaus, C. (1994a). Equal educational opportunity for students with disabilities in Canada: The right to free and appropriate education. *Exceptionality Education Canada, 4*, 37- 73.

Smith, W.J. & Lusthaus, C. (1994b). *Policy talk: Linguistic school boards: A window of opportunity for e-quality schools.* Montréal: McGill University, Office of Research on Educational Policy.

Sturge Sparks, C. & Smith, W.J. (1998). Student engagement in Québec. In W.J. Smith, H. Donahue & A. Vibert (Eds), *Student engagement in learning and school life: Case reports from project schools, Vol. II* (pp. 93-185). Montréal: McGill University, Office of Research on Educational Policy.

Sweet, L. (1997). *God in the classroom. The controversial issue of religion in Canada's schools.* Toronto: McClelland & Stewart.

Talbani, A. (1993). Intercultural education and minorities: Policy initiatives in Quebec. *McGill Journal of Education, 28*, 407-419.

Task Force on Curriculum Reform (1997). *Reaffirming the mission of our schools* (Report to the Minister of Éducation). Québec: Ministère de l'Education.

Task Force on Elementary and Secondary School Learning Profiles. (1994). *Preparing our youth for the 21st century* (Report to the Minister of Education). Montréal: Author.

Task Force on the Place of Religion in Schools in Québec (1999). *Religion in secular schools: A new perspective for Québec* (Report to the Minister of Éducation). Québec: Ministère de l'Education.

Thomas, M.A. (1973). Finance: Without which there is no special education. *Exceptional Children, 39*, 475-480.

Ward, J.G. (1987). An inquiry into the normative foundations of American public school finance. *Journal of Education Finance, 12*, 463-477.

Zinman, R. (1991). Developments and directions in multicultural/intercultural education, 1980-1990, the Province of Quebec. *Canadian Ethnic Studies, 33*(2), 65-80.